A HISTORY OF THE RUSSIAN
SECRET SERVICE

By the same author:

THE PRIVATE LIFE OF MR GLADSTONE
MADOC AND THE DISCOVERY OF AMERICA
JOHN DEE
A HISTORY OF THE BRITISH SECRET SERVICE

A History of The Russian Secret Service

RICHARD DEACON

NEW ENGLISH LIBRARY
TIMES MIRROR

First published in Great Britain 1972 by Frederick Muller Ltd,
110 Fleet Street, London, EC4.
© 1972 Richard Deacon

*

FIRST NEL PAPERBACK EDITION JULY 1975

*

NEL Books are published by
New English Library Limited from Barnard's Inn, Holborn, London, E.C.1.
Made and printed in Great Britain by Hunt Barnard Printing Ltd, Aylesbury, Bucks.

45002337 0

Contents

I

Introduction

THE PROBLEM about the Russian Secret Service is not so much the obtaining of facts as the assessment of them. It is nearly always clear what other Secret Services are aiming at. But the Russian Secret Service, whether in its medieval form, under the Czars or under the Supreme Soviet, is characterised by its innate deviousness, its obsession with the tactics of the *agent provocateur* and an almost tortuous concern to mask its objectives. Its strength in modern times is perhaps best emphasised by pointing out how the Russian revolution of 1917 succeeded. Only a ruthlessly efficient counter-espionage organisation, indulging in *agent provocateur* tactics, made that success possible. Its weakness is exemplified in the fact that the deviousness of Russian foreign policy – a strange mixture of diplomacy and espionage – and the phobic suspicions of the late thirties very nearly led to the defeat of Russia by Nazi Germany.

It is the national habit of suspicion allied to that innate cruelty which Maxim Gorky called 'the most prominent feature of the Russian character' that have moulded the Russian Secret Service over the ages and made its counter-espionage agencies the most dreaded of all. And it is the love of secrecy bred of these characteristics which has made it almost impossible for the worst features of that Secret Service to be eliminated over the centuries.

The only difference today is that the false picture of a belief in democratic rights, which the Soviet built up so hypocritically at a time when it was practising the reverse within its own borders, has created an external public opinion which needs occasionally to be appeased or reassured in its illusions. It is now necessary for internal despotism to seem no longer to exist. For this reason alone the purges and executions which typified the first quarter-century of communism are no longer so visible to the outside world.

One other change away from secrecy should be noted. In recent years Soviet Russia has decided that as a matter of deliberate policy she should lift slightly the curtain which masks her Secret

Service. The object has been blatantly and unashamedly to glorify her own successful spies, to name several of them and to tell something of their achievements. This is an unusual step for any great power to take, especially when relating to contemporary spies. For Russia, with her obsession with secrecy, to indulge in an espionage striptease is even more remarkable.

To understand the modern workings of Russian espionage one must try to grasp the effects of history on this vast land mass extending from Europe to the most eastern parts of Asia. For centuries Russia was a huge, underpopulated, indeterminate area, with ill-defined borders, never an effective nation, but rather a loose collection of tribes who were in the main ignorant, barbarous, suspicious of all authority and anxious only to retain their individual identities. These tribes were devoted to their homeland, but had little confidence that they could defend it of their own accord. Thus somewhere around A.D. 850 the Russian community in Novgorod sent a message to the chief of the Varangians stating 'Our land is great and beautiful, but there is no order in it. Come and rule over us!'

It was this request that resulted in Rurik, the Varangian leader, imposing his authority over several tribes and creating a single nation. The next man to inflict his will on Russia, or at least over a great part of it, was the dreaded Genghis Khan and it was he who gave the country its first taste of that mixture of barbarous ruthlessness and diabolically clever espionage which became so imbued in the Russian character. The Mongols' long-term aim was to invade Western Europe and to achieve this they employed and trained a large number of Russians as agents. By 1221 the Mongols had advanced into South Russia as far as the Donetz basin. It was an unprecedented military victory. At the beginning of the century Genghis Khan was an obscure Mongol chieftain living with his tribesmen among his flocks and herds. First he sought supremacy in his own tribe, then over the neighbouring tribes. Everyone who opposed him was slain while all who obeyed were welded into a disciplined and terrifying army. They were, wrote Jeremiah Curtin, 'formidable in battle, tireless in campaign and on the march utterly indifferent to fatigue and hardship, of extraordinary prowess with bow and sword. . . . They conquered China . . . India also. . . . Persia in the same way fell into their hands. . . . They struck down the Russians at a blow and trampled the land into bloody mire beneath their horses' feet.'

Yet despite their barbarian origins, they were efficient in administration and organised a system of intelligence to discover the weak points of their next opponents. The Russians who succumbed to them were used as a network of agents to find out the weaknesses of those peoples they next wished to conquer, the European nations. To achieve their next objective the Mongols needed and developed a Secret Service. It was from their Mongol conquerors that the Russians first learned the arts of infiltration. The methods adopted were to send out scouts to tribes not yet conquered and to pose as deserters from the ranks of Genghis Khan, laying false trails of information. These scouts would return in due course, having obtained detailed intelligence about the terrain they had visited and the state of its defences. A successful invasion usually followed.

Subutai, the most formidable and restless of all Genghis Khan's generals, is not popularly regarded as one of the most famous of military leaders, yet his exploits compare with those of Napoleon or Alexander the Great. From easternmost China to the banks of the Danube he conquered thirty-two nations and tribes and won sixty-five battles. He was one of the first to claim that wars were won on the strength of espionage. In this he was fully supported by Genghis Khan, who insisted on knowing every detail about a potential enemy's resources before he would venture his armies against them. These intelligence probes would be carried out at a distance of ten days' travelling time from Mongol advanced head-quarters, yet, by using a system of relays of fast riders, Khan would insist on having news back within twenty-four to thirty-six hours.

For two and a half centuries the Mongols and the Tartars dominated Russia. Throughout this period the people were con-ditioned to accept rule through an efficient but ruthless internal police, aided by informers. It was not until 1492 that Ivan the Great expelled the intruders and formed something approaching a Muscovite empire. Yet the pattern of terror and informers, of counter-espionage and police rule, imposed by the Mongols was not to be changed. Indeed, the Russian people and especially the Soviet thinkers of today put most of the blame for Russian back-wardness on the Mongols. The pre-Revolution Russian scholar, B. J. Vladimirtsoff, is at one with the Marxists in accepting this thesis.

The task of compiling this history is made all the greater because the Russian espionage network is world-wide to an extent matched only by the United States among the other great powers. And, in contrast to the Secret Services of most other nations, its separate counter-espionage organisation operates as extensively abroad as it does at home. Thus it has been necessary to seek on-the-spot reports of the workings of the Soviet Intelligence not only through-out Europe, but all over Asia, Africa, the Americas and even Australia and New Zealand. The true picture emerges by checking one report against another. Thus the story given by a defector from

9

Georgia about activities in Istanbul and Cyprus was corroborated by an informant in Switzerland, while that of a defector from the Ukraine about spying in Italy was proved false by an inquiry in Berlin.

In modern times by far the greatest amount of inside information on Russian espionage activities comes from defectors from the Soviet Union. Russia has always employed far more secret agents than any other power and depended on numbers rather than on the quality of the information obtained. Similarly she has generally spent much more on intelligence than any other nation. In the employment of large numbers lies her greatest weakness.

But defectors' stories, as I have found to my cost, always require very careful checking whenever this is possible. The percentage of reliable information thus obtained is small, perhaps on average as low as fifteen per cent. It is known that a fair percentage of these defectors are *agents provocateurs*, allowed out of the Soviet Union to pose as deserters just as they did in Genghis Khan's time, and actually feeding false information or trying to infiltrate the Secret Services of the West. Other genuine defectors are so inflamed against the régime, so obsessed with besmirching the name of the Soviet that they tend to invent stories which they foolishly believe will assist their cause.

This book is not intended to be in any way ideological or propagandist, but an objective assessment of the Russian Secret Service throughout history, giving credit for brilliant work where it is due but pointing out weaknesses and failures. It is not always easy to take a dispassionate view of the fact that no other country has for so many centuries been subjected to the tyranny of a Secret Service as has Russia. It is estimated that the Soviet Intelligence system employs in all more than 100,000 professional agents. This gives it something like parity with the U.S.A., and a tremendous lead over any other power.

Any nation operating a Secret Service of this size must be regarded as turning it into a weapon of war rather than using it as a form of defence. To dwell on the Russian characteristic of obsessive suspicion may explain its concentration on espionage, but it would be folly to believe that the mere removal of the causes of this suspicion alone would end the problem.

2

Ivan the Terrible and His Oprichniki

THE FORERUNNERS of the *Ochrana* and the *Cheka* were the *Oprichniki*, or Secret Police, instituted by the Czar Ivan IV, nick-named 'The Terrible'.

Ivan was as cruel, ruthless and tyrannical as his soubriquet suggests, yet for the times in which he lived he was an extremely efficient and far-seeing ruler. In Russia, alas, these traits so frequently go together. It has been one of the tragedies and ironies of Russian history that the liberal, idealistic rulers have been gentle and weak, inefficient and disastrous, whereas the tyrants have been competent and successful.

Indeed, not to put too fine a point on it, Ivan had something in common with the early Communists, whose historians have always treated him with a degree of respect. While he developed the thesis of the autocratic, omnipotent monarch, he opposed the very class closest to him, the privileged, land-owning aristocracy of the *boyars*. First and foremost his enemies were the princes and he made it his task systematically to destroy their influence and acquire their estates. To bring this about he created *Oprichnina*, an innocent-sounding name taken from the title previously given to the estates which in former times had been allotted to widowed princesses for life. Yet the very name was to strike terror into the hearts of the Russian people.

Ivan's clash with the boyars developed out of the misfortunes of the Livonian War. At first the Muscovites had triumphed by sheer superiority of numbers over the Livonians, a people who had deserted the orthodox Christian faith of Russia for a fanatical form of Protestant evangelism. Then, when the Polish-Lithuanian troops aided the Livonians, the Muscovites suffered a series of setbacks. Ivan blamed the boyar commanders for these failures and even accused them of treachery. When Prince Andrew Kurb-sky, the Muscovite commander-in-chief in Livonia, fled to Lithu-ania in 1564, Ivan finally had proof of what he called 'boyar treason'.

Ivan's suspicions were not altogether without justification, for the boyars took the view that while the Czar was a symbol of unity and sovereignty, they should be the real rulers. Ivan determined to create an all-powerful absolute Russian autocracy vested in his name. The means of establishing this was to be the creation of Oprichnina, the weapon for carrying it out the Oprichniki, or Czar's Secret Police.

Curiously little is known of how the Czar formed the Oprichniki who carried out his doctrine of Oprichnina. But when Ivan left for Alexandrovsk at Christmas, 1564, he had secured his rear with a faithful retinue who formed the hard core of what were to be the Oprichniki. They were instructed to lie low, but to negotiate with the Moscow townsmen whom they sought to win as allies away from the boyars. At this stage the Oprichniki were merely nameless agents of the Czar, cloaking the fist of ruthlessness under the glove of promises of commercial aid. Their first aim was to win over the merchants and to promise them posts as official agents of the Muscovite Government at places like Constantinople, Antwerp and even London.

The Oprichnina operation was in the first place mainly concerned with land and securing it for the Czar; its second aim was a bloodless revolution aimed at winning over the commercial classes and controlling the nation's trade. Ivan felt surrounded by enemies and was irked by the knowledge that he depended on the boyars to lead his troops.

The plan he conceived was arrived at only after weeks of agonising reappraisal of his problem. Contemporary writers stated that during the weeks in which Ivan was trying to come to a decision he aged visibly. He made up his mind alone in absolute isolation from any of his advisers and decided to put it to the test by going away from the capital. He wanted his people to feel something of his dilemma, to sense he was in isolation and to remain in doubt as to his motives. First he allowed it to be made known he was going away. Then in January, 1565, he went to Alexandrovsk, taking with him a large retinue of trusted attendants, soldiers and courtiers and the whole of his personal treasury. In Moscow those he had left behind waited uneasily; they suspected something was afoot, but failed to divine his intentions.

In Alexandrovsk Ivan spoke. His message was clear, but his intentions remained masked: 'Not wishing to endure your treachery,' he stated, 'we with great pity in our heart have quitted the Czardom and have gone wherever God may lead us.'

His next move was to assure the merchants and the people of his goodwill. Then he put forward his demands. The first and most important of these was that all his foes must surrender to him unconditionally. Only when that happened would he return to Moscow. To ensure the safety of his realm and of the Czardom itself he proposed to create a personal guard and provide a special establishment for himself. The latter was to be known as the Oprichnina and would be an independent state within the Czardom, ruled by him alone, not as Czar, but as 'proprietor'.

Ivan decreed that from his realm, now swollen by the acquisitions from the boyars, there should be 'set apart an extension of Oprichnina'. This was to cover the financing and rewarding of the new special guard and secret police, to be known as the Oprichniki. In this manner the Czar created a powerful instrument for extending his influence over the former territories of the treacherous boyars, in effect a land-owning security force. The territories not administered by the Oprichniki were to be known as the *Zemschina*, these to be entrusted to the rule of the faithful boyars, such as Prince Ivan Belsky.

Immediately the Oprichniki rounded up those boyars listed as 'traitors' to be surrendered to the Czar. Many of them were executed summarily within a few days, others were banished for life to Kazan with their wives and children and their property was confiscated.

Professor Pokrovsky in his own *History of Russia* took a Marxist view in his interpretation of the aims of Ivan and the functions of the Oprichniki. He criticised the 'modern historians' who saw in the Oprichnina 'the establishment of a corps of gendarmes charged with the detection of domestic sedition, the protection of the Czar and the defence of the realm. The Oprichniki, he argued, represented something quite different – 'the establishment of a new class régime'. Certainly a new class of the community was created, a class leavened by the traders and commercial envoys, even a privileged class, but it was one nevertheless built on terror and using terror as a weapon.

The Marxist view of Russian history tends to play down the rôle of the Oprichniki, to excuse the terrorism of Ivan IV and to approve the defeat of the boyars' power structure because their downfall led to the creation of a new social class. Undoubtedly Ivan achieved worthwhile results by his assault on feudalism and privilege, but far from freeing the people, or uniting them, he succeeded only in terrorising them into flight. The truth was that Ivan used the Oprichniki as a nation-wide organisation of spies, informers, torturers and executioners to smell out and put down his enemies wherever they were to be found and to condemn to death or flight a large number of innocent people as well. When the Czar decided to punish a city he believed to be of doubtful loyalty to his cause he instructed the Oprichniki to kill every Russian encountered on the way in order to keep secret the punitive expedition he had launched.

Panic and terror seized vast areas of the country as the Oprichniki spread their influence and invaded new territories. Not only whole families but entire communities ran from their homes and did not stop until they were far out of reach of the dreaded secret police. Some cities, such as Moscow, and indeed the whole province of Moscow, were depopulated by a third as a result of the activities of the Oprichniki. The peasants scattered far and wide, moving as far as they could from the centre of government, some to the north where grain was scarce and a miserable existence barely possible, others to the steppes where they were at the mercy of the Tatars.

It is, of course, easy to assert that the true rôle of the Oprichniki was obscure. It was meant to be obscure just as the true rôle of every form of secret police in Russia since then has remained largely obscure. The Russian love of secrecy lends a tortuousness and circumlocution to every form of espionage and counter-espionage. In other countries of the Western World there have always been certain inhibitions about the rôle of the secret police and counter-espionage and there has rarely been any pretence that this has been other than a somewhat disreputable but necessary part of national security. But not in Russia. The secret police both now and then have tended to become a status symbol within the community.

For example, the Oprichniki had to swear absolute obédience to the Czar, to report all traitors and to make no friends outside the sphere of the Oprichniki. Parents, wives, children and all relatives were of less consequence than the Czar; thus there was no loyalty to anyone other than the Czar. But the rewards for such obedience were considerable – status as members of a privileged community, handsome pay and estates confiscated from the boyars. In Moscow whole streets and suburbs were taken over and given exclusively to the Oprichniki and a palace was built for their headquarters.

Ivan's biographers have been equally baffled by the Czar's motives for setting up the Oprichniki. Some even suggest that he himself was not entirely clear what their ultimate rôle should be. But much of this history is wishful thinking, based on a romantic theory of absolute monarchy, or in modern times on a communist conception of Russian grandeur. It is abundantly clear that the prime purpose was to set up a nation-wide security system, even to the extent of creating a nation within a nation which would protect the Czar totally. The original plan was for the Oprichniki to total one thousand picked men. But the Russian fondness for numerical strength carried the day and the force eventually grew to six thousand. They wore a black uniform and rode black horses, and on the saddle of each horse was the insignia of a dog's head and a broom. The symbolism of this insignia was clear to all: the dog's head indicated the traitors they were sworn to find, the broom was the symbol of the sweeping up of these traitors.

The Oprichniki abused their privileges. They plundered the estates of the boyars, they looted and raped and took full advantage of their immunity from the law, spending extravagantly and making little effort to develop or improve the estates they had acquired. Though they frequently exceeded their duties and maltreated innocent subjects, Ivan made no effort to check their excesses. There was an occasion when the Oprichniki raided the homes of some merchants known to have especially beautiful wives. They abducted the wives by force, brought them to the Czar, who, making his own selection of the women first, gave permission for the remainder to be kept by the Oprichniki for the night. His only concession was that when the night of rape and plunder was over he ordered that the women should be returned to their homes.

Three hundred specially selected members of the Oprichniki became Ivan's personal guard, or his 'brotherhood', as he called them. They dined and wined with the Czar and after dinner Ivan would often visit the torture chambers to listen to the interrogation of the latest batch of suspects arrested by the Oprichniki. On State occasions the secret police wore special gold uniforms, no doubt to appear less sinister in front of the ambassadors.

One brave man spoke out against the oppression of the secret police. The Metropolitan, Philip, refusing to give Ivan the blessing he sought in Uspensky Cathedral, condemned the Czar in forthright terms: 'In the most heathen and barbaric realms justice exists and there is compassion for the people. But in Russia there is neither. The goods and lives of our citizens go unprotected. Everywhere there is robbery and murder and these dastardly actions are carried out in the name of the Czar.'

Momentarily Ivan was defeated. Even so absolute an autocrat as he did not dare to take matters further against the Metropolitan of the Orthodox Church in his own cathedral without any legal pretext. His eyes blazed with hatred as he left the cathedral, vowing to wreak vengeance on the prelate. Orders were given to the Oprichniki to build up a case against Philip and what evidence was lacking was swiftly invented. On 8 November 1568, while Philip was conducting a service in Uspensky Cathedral, the Oprichniki entered and tore off the Metropolitan's vestments. He was arrested on several charges, one of which (in an effort to discredit him with the populace) was an allegation of witchcraft practices.

Perhaps the Metropolitan was luckier than most; he suffered only life imprisonment.

Novgorod was one city which bore the full brunt of Ivan's wrath and the Oprichniki's reign of terror. Abbots and monks were seized without trial and beaten to death and all treasures removed from the cathedral. A special court of interrogation was set up and the tortures 'resembled those of the Spanish Inquisition . . . Special fires and heated pans were used to scorch flesh, laid bare by cruel flogging with whips which flayed the victims to the bone. Pincers, sometimes red-hot and sometimes cold, pulled the ribs from men's chests. Nails were driven into bones and needles levered the nails from feet and hands.'

For five weeks the interrogations, the tortures and executions continued. Women and children were tied to sleighs, dragged through the streets to the river and thrown into the icy water. In all some 60,000 men, women and children were massacred and the rivers were choked with corpses. Ivan, still unsatiated, still suspicious of traitors, turned his attention back to Moscow. More arrests and executions followed here and in the wake of the mass killings and as a result of the putrefying corpses littering the streets, plague struck down the remaining inhabitants and decimated the survivors as had already happened at Novgorod.

Yet despite Ivan's rule of oppression and terror, of torture and mass arrests, the vast majority of the people remaining in the cities stood not merely in awe of him but actually held him in reverence, as though he was an avenging god come down from the heavens to punish them for their sins. To them he was still a divine figure and the symbol of the nation. But neither the incredible loyalty of the long-suffering people, nor the strength of the Oprichniki made Ivan feel sure of himself. So great was his personal feeling of insecurity that he vacillated between periods of insensate rage and moments when he even considered finding a sanctuary overseas to which he could retreat if worse treachery befell him. The land to which he turned was the England of Queen Elizabeth I. He had always shown great interest in England and befriended the English merchants who came to Moscow, assuring them alone of his protection from the Oprichniki. He gave Anthony Jenkinson, the envoy sent to Moscow by Elizabeth, a secret message for the Queen, asking her to 'license masters to come unto him which can make ships and sail them' and requesting that, if misfortune came to him, Elizabeth would grant him asylum, offering an alliance of the two nations as part of any such bargain.

Ivan's mistake was, perhaps, to offer the Queen an equal asylum in Russia should she ever desire it. This suggestion made

Elizabeth suspicious, though she agreed to promise him a refuge should he ever need it. But, added the Queen with a tart spiritedness, she had herself no need of asylum for 'we have no manner of doubt of the continuance of our peaceable government without danger either from our subjects or from other foreign enemies.'

The significance of this appeal for asylum in England is that Ivan was beginning to have doubts about the instrument of Oprichnina and belatedly he was realising what a monstrous force he had created. In his will his instructions expressed a certain disillusionment with the Oprichniki and gave his successor the right to choose whether he disbanded or retained them. By 1572 Ivan had begun to find serious faults with the Oprichniki. In particular he blamed them for failing to protect the Czarina from witchcraft from which he believed she had died. He suspected that some of the Oprichniki had been guilty of treachery at Novgorod and finally he accused them of failing effectively to defend Moscow against the Tatars even though in the end the Tatars had been routed. Superstition and a tortured conscience played some part in Ivan's thinking at this period; certainly the former was one reason why he wanted to lure Queen Elizabeth's astrologer and soothsayer, John Dee, to the court of Russia. 'With such a man on my side I would need no further intelligence,' he declared, but Dee was not to be tempted.

To be charitable to this tyrant it is possible that a stricken conscience was one reason for his re-thinking on the Oprichniki. He realised just how much they were hated and dreaded by the people. As long as the guards were one hundred per cent loyal to him he was prepared to accept the people's hatred as a necessary evil. Even more he must have appreciated that the reputation of the Oprichniki had done him great harm overseas and possibly ruined the chances of negotiations with such countries as England, Poland and Lithuania.

Eventually the Oprichnina was disbanded and the Oprichniki were dispossessed of their estates. Chaos followed their disappearance, though some historians – Karamzin, Klyuchevsky and Solovyev – claim that though the title of Oprichnina was abolished the actual establishment secretly continued. This view is refuted by S. V. Veselovsky but there is little doubt that in some form or other the secret police remained as a permanent factor in Russian life.

Externally, Russia's espionage was extremely limited in this era and did not effectively extend beyond the ineffectual attempts at intelligence of envoys overseas. It is certain that Elizabeth knew far more of what was going on in Russia than Ivan learned of events in England. The turbulence inside Russia, the task of trying to unite or coerce disparate communities and to ward off threats from the Tatars and Livonians so fully engaged the authorities that spying was mainly concentrated in the domains of the Czar.

Ivan IV was succeeded by his feeble-minded son, Feodor, who married Irene, the sister of a powerful boyar, Boris Godunoff. Boris became the real power in the country and when Feodor died the boyars elected him as Czar. Boris almost immediately repaid their support by weakening their powers. He also employed spies whose sole job it was to search the land for any real or pretended descendants of Ivan IV or Feodor with a view to having them eliminated. It was not altogether a successful campaign for it did not prevent one of the pretenders – he claimed to be Dimitri, a son of Ivan IV – from actually invading Russia from Poland.

The death of Boris plunged Russia into disorder once more. His son Feodor became Czar, but was murdered by the mob. Other false claimants to the throne came forward and the search for an acceptable ruler became so desperate that a group of boyars was even anxious to have James I of England as ruler of Russia. They petitioned an Englishman, Thomas Chamberlain, to make the approach to James. Chamberlain, who was somewhat of an adventurer, fell in with the plan and suggested that James should send envoys to Russia 'to treat with the people', adding that the project offered 'much glorie to His Magestie, much charitie towards these oppressed people . . . much policie in regard of the increase of our shipping and trade.'

But this little plot was ended before it got off the ground by the election of Mikhail Romanoff as Czar. The Romanoffs learned a lesson from this episode, however, and decided that if the throne of Russia was to be bartered overseas, it was essential to keep a close independent check on their courtiers and ambassadors in their contacts with foreigners.

So with the coming of the Romanoff dynasty the nation began to take on a more bureaucratic structure. The *dyaks*, or minor officials, took a hand in running the country; they acquired an authority which previously had been vested almost solely in the boyars, or, under Ivan IV, in the Oprichniki. Even the nobles deigned to accept dyakships and in 1610 several Moscow members of the nobility actually petitioned to be appointed dyaks. It was at this time that the Czar decided to surround himself with a few carefully chosen foreigners to advise him on any plots between the boyars and foreign potentates. One such was Arthur Dee, the son of Queen Elizabeth's astrologer and one of Walsingham's secret agents. He was nominally appointed physician to the Czar, but for some years he advised Mikhail and cast horoscopes for him. Unofficially he was an intelligence officer to the court.

Mikhail died in 1645 and was succeeded by his son, Alexis, an abler monarch who made the still somewhat incoherent and ill-defined Secret Service of the nation into a bureaucracy. This was his creation of the Bureau of Secret Affairs, an establishment known as *tainiy prikaz*. Here again the penchant for secrecy led to an obscurity in organisation and purpose which have baffled many historians in trying to unravel the workings of this Bureau. The title 'Secret' seems to have applied to the fact that the Bureau was so highly confidential that the 'boyars and men of the Duma [the Prince's Council] did not enter and did not handle affairs'. This in itself gives some idea of the secret nature of the Bureau, but only a part of its true purpose. The Bureau actually kept watch over the men of the Duma and could to some extent manipulate them and the officials who carried out their work. When ambassadorial appointments were made, or military commanders given commissions, the *podyaks* of the Bureau accompanied the ambassadors and commanders and were responsible for keeping the Czar informed about their activities.

Here again it was more counter-espionage than espionage which was the main purpose of the Secret Bureau, though by its scope for infiltrating Russian embassies it was able to develop some espionage of its own. *Tainiy prikaz* was really an organisation for maintaining the autocratic rule of the Czar. Alexis borrowed the idea partly from the Oprichniki and, when he travelled, the Secret Bureau kept him informed of all that was going on. Its size was extremely modest, nothing like as large as the Oprichniki, comprising a chief clerk and five assistant clerks, surely the smallest espionage staff in existence at that time. The Czar Alexis himself invented the codes for its use.

It will be noted that in some respects the Secret Bureau was similar to the K.G.B. today, but the plan to put men of the Duma under control of men who were outside the Duma was something quite new at that time. Members of the Bureau and their podyaks were treated with great respect and even flattery in the hope that they would give the Czar some satisfactory reports of his men of government, his ambassadors and military commanders.

In 1663 the Muscovite state set up its own foreign postal service and immediate use was made of this to provide intelligence. Letters coming from abroad were all delivered first to the Russian Foreign Office, but curiously no attempt was made to hide the fact that these letters were opened and read by Foreign Office intelligence agents. All worthwhile information gleaned in this way was passed on to the government.

Nevertheless, foreigners were equally adept at this time in

penetrating Russian secrets and, despite the Secret Bureau, in finding for themselves posts of influence with the Czars. J. P. Kilburger, the seventeenth-century historian, wrote that all trade in Archangel was in the hands of the Dutch and the Germans and that foreigners had actually gained membership of the College of Gosts, comprising merchants to whom special privileges were extended, and had become unofficial agents of the Czar. The English were at this time particularly well informed about what was going on inside Russia.

Tainiy prikaz was abolished after Alexis' death but the Secret Bureau was re-created under Peter the Great in 1704. It was known as the 'Special Office of the Czar' and the secret police actually came under the Chancellor, Biron. Those responsible for gathering and co-ordinating information for the Special Office were directed by a competent and industrious bureaucrat named Makaroff, specially chosen by the Czar. He was above all else a loyal subject of Peter, never making a move without consulting his monarch.

Peter the Great was the first Czar to Europeanise Russia and he introduced a number of reforms. But Russia was still governed by a tyrant, albeit a progressive tyrant, and he was forever ordering the Special Office to investigate the loyalty of officers and to probe the affairs of anyone suspected of treachery. The records show that the Office investigated 280 such cases up to the time of Peter's death. That many of these cases were trivial in the extreme is confirmed by Count P. A. Tolstoy, who was brought into the Special Office to make decisions on them. He found that he was wasting his time on 'exceedingly frivolous matters' and asked to be relieved of some of his work. His views may well have led to the cutting down of the Special Office and Private Chancery, which for several years was operated like a yo-yo by the Czars who closed it down and opened it up again in confusing fashion.

Drastically reduced towards the end of Peter the Great's reign, it was combined with another office in 1726 and abolished completely three years later. Then, until 1731, the Supreme Privy Council handled cases of treachery. But in 1731 the Secret Office was revived as the Secret Chancery, but abolished again in 1762 by Peter III. As an institution it had become extremely unpopular with the boyars and the ruling classes who were increasingly clamouring for more freedom.

Throughout history the rulers of Russia vacillated between a policy of extremities in their use of a secret police. Either they employed them as a weapon of terrorism and absolute power, or in a fit of fear at what they had created they disbanded them altogether. It was this lack of consistency which makes it so

20

difficult for an historian to follow the early development of a Secret Service in Russia. Even when these forces were disbanded, as with the Oprichniki and the Political Police, everything points to the fact that some kind of underground secret police was maintained, though to whom they reported, whether to Czar or government, is not always clear.

3

Comic Opera Espionage

IN THE eighteenth century espionage was almost blatantly the task of diplomats. It was also practised personally by a number of European monarchs.

Russia was then almost a prime centre of espionage. Sir Robert Murray Keith, the English Minister in Russia, admitted that he was provided by his Government with £100,000 for spying and bribery and for 'such gratifications as I may judge it necessary to make from time to time to particular persons'. Another English Ambassador to Russia, Lord Hyndford, paid out £1,500 in bribes within a period of two years. The French spent such vast sums on spying in Russia and in bribing Russian officials that France almost bankrupted herself.

The fear of assassination and the fact that it frequently happened made it of paramount importance for the Czars to protect themselves with a secret-police force, one which would also ascertain all plots made against them. Yet despite the existence of a secret police Moscow and St Petersburg were ripe for espionage in the eighteenth century and bribes still achieved more than the threat of secret-police vengeance could ever do. Russia was still a semi-civilised, semi-Asiatic nation, cut off from Europe and the reforms of Peter the Great had touched only a relatively small part of the nation.

Even so, Peter the Great had made Russia a power to be reckoned with. He had given to the Russian empire through the Treaty of Nystad in 1717 the territories of Livonia, Esthonia, part of Finland, Karelia and the districts of Wiborg and Kexholm in Swedish territory. But the end of Peter's reign had, as so often before, meant the end of orderly progress and the return of disunity and internal chaos. It was not until Elizabeth, the daughter of Peter the Great, came to the throne that something approaching order was restored. Elizabeth became Sovereign in a sudden upsurge of revolt against the Germans whose influence inside Russia had made them thoroughly detested.

Czarina Elizabeth, a handsome woman, was an easy prey to the sycophants who surrounded her. Intrigues at the Russian court were numerous. Espionage presented almost a comic opera picture. Everyone in the court was playing some game of his or her own with a foreign power, gleaning a certain amount of intelligence for his own country no doubt, but also giving away a great deal. Espionage by barter was the order of the day. Bestuchev, the Imperial Chancellor, was passing information to the English Minister, Sir Charles Hanbury-Williams, who was also a close friend of the Grand Duchess Catherine. To counteract this the tutor of the Grand Duke Peter, Brummer, and Catherine's mother were actually in the pay of the French Ambassador, the Marquis de la Chétardie. The Czarina was neutral.

The Czarina had been on the throne for fourteen years by this time and was mindful of the fact that it was French influence which had in part brought about the palace revolution resulting in her succeeding the Empress Anne. There was in the court at St Petersburg a strong pro-French faction and consequently a marked antagonism to the King of Prussia. King George II of England had two years earlier sounded out the Russian court on whether he could expect assistance from Russia in the event of an attack on Hanover and if the Czarina would supply some 40,000 troops to invade Prussia. Nothing came of this proposal for a few years, but when Sir Charles left for Russia he was instructed to pay the Russians a subsidy of £40,000 per annum when the troops actually marched to the Prussian frontiers.

Sir Charles knew well that in Russia at this time nothing could be achieved without bribery and that even for the drawing up of an agreement between the two countries there was a recognised scale of fees. So he promptly offered Alexei Bestuchev £10,000 if he could bring about an agreement between England and Russia. But more than this was needed to produce results so both the Vice-Chancellor, Vorontzoff, and the Chancellor's secretary, Volkoff, were promised £1,000 and £500 respectively.

Bestuchev was an energetic Minister and an impressive personality despite a somewhat unprepossessing appearance. He had a blotchy face and a livid colouring and when he laughed it was said to be 'the laugh of Satan'. Charming as he could be to the English Ambassador, he had a habit of making enemies easily and of quickly taking offence. He was a skilled operator in the sphere of intelligence and he took full advantage of the fact that the Czarina was not greatly interested in foreign policy. He had his spies everywhere and through his 'Black Cabinet' organised the interception of diplomatic dispatches, especially those of the French Ambassador, Chétardie. No pretence was made of hiding the fact that diplomatic dispatches were intercepted. Chétardie himself wrote that 'it is without any shame or precaution that they unseal letters here'. Nevertheless he believed that his dispatches were relatively safe from prying eyes because they were in cipher. The Russians, he was sure, did not possess the key to this cipher.

In this he was originally correct. But the Russians soon found a method of deciphering them. They learned that the Germans had become skilled in tackling ciphers and codes and under Bestuchev's orders three Germans were employed in the Muscovite Post Office. Soon the cipher was broken and Bestuchev was the happiest man in Russia. He may have been angered by Chétardie's comments on his character, but he was delighted that the Ambassador had been rash enough to make the most scandalous references to the Czarina, who, declared Chétardie, was 'given entirely to her pleasures and, having a more and more decided aversion for business, will no longer have faithful Ministers to whom she can entrust the care of government . . . a princess so frivolous and dissipated.'

Bestuchev passed on the contents of these dispatches to the Czarina and urged her to send Chétardie packing. The next day the chief of Bestuchev's personal Secret Service stopped Chétardie as he was entering his house and handed him a note from the Czarina, accusing him of bribery and corruption and demanding that he should leave the country within twenty-four hours. When Chétardie protested that the charges were untrue the Russians read to him some of his own dispatches. Without further ado the Ambassador returned to France.

It was against this background that Russia came to ally herself with England and Austria against Prussia. The head of the Russian Imperial Secret Service at this time was Alexander Schuvaloff, a cousin of Count Ivan Schuvaloff who was a favourite of the Czarina. His official title was Head of the Inquisitional Tribunal. He was as pro-French as Bestuchev was pro-English and there was a constant silent battle of intrigue between the Secret Service chief and the Chancellor who had his own espionage network. Schuvaloff, together with his relatives and the Vice-Chancellor Vorontzoff, formed an alliance aimed at defeating Bestuchev and removing him from power. Sir Charles Hanbury-Williams was well aware of the nature of these intrigues and how they threatened his own negotiations. He feared most the trinity of the Schuvaloffs, Ivan,

Alexander and Peter, the Master-General of Artillery.

The French provided their own answer to the gambits of the English Ambassador. Louis XV sent one of the strangest spies in history to Russia to fulfil a rôle that resembled something out of fiction rather than living history. The young man chosen for this mission was the Chevalier Charles Geneviève Louis Auguste André Timothée d'Eon de Beaumont, who went to St Petersburg disguised as Mademoiselle Lia de Beaumont and by his good looks and charm dazzled the court of the Czarina. The young Chevalier was no mincing quean; he had proved himself an accomplished swordsman and been elected *grand prevôt* of the *Salle d'Armes* as a result. Academically, d'Eon had not only succeeded in being admitted to the French bar but by his intellectual talents had drawn himself to the attention of Louis XV. His ability to pose as a woman was largely due to a quirk of his mother's. For some undisclosed reason she had dressed him in a girl's clothes at the age of four and these he had worn constantly until he was approaching puberty. D'Eon was slight in build, with delicate features and a pretty face, making him an admirable choice for the rôle he was selected to fill.

His mission was to detach the Russians from adopting a pro-English policy and to win them as allies. He took with him to Russia a copy of Montesquieu's *L'Esprit des Lois*, in the binding of which were hidden a letter from Louis XV to the Czarina and a special cipher. The French knew that the Czarina was surrounded by spies, those of Bestuchev and those of the Secret Service under Alexander Schuvaloff. The only hope of getting one of their spies close to the Czarina was by infiltrating a female spy, or a male disguised as a female.

It was essential for the success of the mission for 'Lia' to appear to be shy and of a retiring nature rather than coquettish. Any attempt at flirtation might have been disastrous, especially as the Russian courtiers needed only the slightest encouragement to make the boldest advances. Notwithstanding this the attractiveness of 'Mlle Lia' swiftly became something of a legend at the Court and a number of painters asked permission to paint 'her' and record her 'pink and white complexion' or 'capture the gentle expression'.

The reason for the multifarious intrigues and rival espionage groups at the Court and within the Russian Secret Service at this time lay not least in the character of the Czarina Elizabeth herself. She was by temperament nervous and timid, she disliked politics and was oblivious to intrigue. Indeed the officer of the Preobrazhensky Guard, the French Ambassador Chétardie and her favourite, Lestocq, had the greatest difficulty in persuading her to agree to their plot to place her on the throne. However, in one sphere she was not timid – that of the bedroom. From her youth she had indulged in a variety of amorous adventures, not of a type normally associated with a royal personage. Lackeys, choirboys, coachmen, all these were to be numbered among her many lovers. Thus it is not surprising that those in the Government decided that for Russia's sake it was essential for the Secret Service to know what the Czarina was doing and who she was sleeping with. If she would not intrigue, or provide a lead, then her courtiers made up for this by playing politics and espionage against one another and keeping a watch on the Czarina at the same time.

For a long time Chétardie had had most influence with her, notwithstanding that she gave loyal support to Bestuchev. The French Ambassador had even become the Czarina's lover in an effort to make her an ally of Louis XV. But, as we have seen, Bestuchev successfully scotched that plan. But despite the watchfulness of Bestuchev's agents, the impersonating Chevalier was presented to the Czarina by Vice-Chancellor Vorontzoff and shortly afterwards 'Mlle Lia' became a maid of honour to Elizabeth.

Some little time after this Sir Charles Hanbury-Williams was reporting back to London that Bestuchev was 'finding it impossible to induce Her Majesty to sign the Treaty we so earnestly desire'. He does not seem to have guessed the reason for this and apparently was never aware of the extent of the Chevalier's deception.

Bestuchev made full use of Hanbury-Williams as an informant and it was usually through the good offices of the English Ambassador that he was able to keep a few steps ahead of Schuvaloff. The French had cunningly arranged for 'Mlle Lia' to have a Scotsman as chaperon, believing that he would arouse less suspicion than a Frenchwoman. So the Scotsman, a Mr Mackenzie Douglas, posed as the 'uncle' of 'Liá' and was instructed to contact the English Ambassador in an effort to disabuse any who might think he was other than a loyal British subject. Sir Charles, however, had his own network of spies and quickly learned that the Scotsman had Jacobite connections which made him automatically suspect. A few more inquiries revealed that he was almost certainly acting under French orders so Sir Charles tipped off the Russian police and Bestuchev. Douglas was arrested and put into prison where he remained until 1757 when the French Ambassador intervened successfully on his behalf.

Surprisingly Sir Charles does not seem to have suspected 'Lia'. The Chevalier was luckier than his confederate. Not only did he win the Czarina's confidence, but he became more or less immune from any outside interference. Eventually he told the Russian monarch who he really was. She not only forgave him the subterfuge, but is said to have offered him a post at Court and in her government. One must assume that this was done with the probable knowledge and agreement of Schuvaloff who seems to have made great efforts to win the services of the Chevalier as a double-agent, that is serving Russia as well as France. But d'Eon graciously declined the offer and eventually returned to France. By that time the Czarina was once again much more inclined to support the French cause.

Sir Charles Hanbury-Williams soon found a new and unexpected ally at the Russian court. This was the Grand Duchess Catherine, a sparkling twenty-six-year-old who was as gay and gifted as her husband, the Grand Duke Peter, was sullen and stupid. While Catherine, determined that one day she would be Czarina, spent her time acquiring knowledge and influence, he idled his time playing with toy soldiers and dolls. The English Ambassador was charmed by Catherine: 'she has by every method in her power,' he wrote in a dispatch to London, 'endeavoured to gain the affection of the nation. . . . Her person is very advantageous, and her manner very captivating. She has a great knowledge of this Empire and makes it her only study.'

The Chancellor, Bestuchev, aided by Sir Charles, did his utmost to insinuate into Catherine's circle spies intended to report back to him her every move and, if necessary, to become her lovers. With diplomatic cynicism, Sir Charles, though professing his personal devotion to the Grand Duchess, thoroughly approved of this duplicity. He felt that if he had Catherine and Bestuchev on his side he could ensure his plan for an alliance between England and Russia. Soon the acquaintanceship between the Grand Duchess and the English Ambassador ripened into a close and secret friendship and Catherine was passing on information to Sir Charles and even sitting up all night to translate a dispatch from Constantinople for him.

But in the end, through no fault of his own, the English Ambassador failed. Just when he was on the point of achieving an alliance between England and Russia news came from the Russian Ambassador in London to Bestuchev that England and Prussia had signed an alliance. As the Czarina hated the King of Prussia her anger against England and Hanbury-Williams ruined all hope of further negotiations. The latter was blamed for something that was beyond his power to prevent and he was equally angry about what had been done in London behind his back. Bestuchev's power was now on the wane and it was Alexander Schuvaloff, the head of the Secret Service, and his relatives who gained most from the catastrophe of the Anglo-Prussian arrangement. The Czarina demanded the recall of Hanbury-Williams to London, dubbing him 'a comedian, a deceiver, a traitor and an intrigue-maker'.

The correspondence of the Grand Duchess Catherine and Sir Charles Hanbury-Williams during this era reveals how the future Czarina felt the need for her own secret intelligence. It is clear that not only was she pro-English, but that she honestly believed that the information she passed on to him would be used ultimately for the benefit of Russia as well as England. Their secret arrangement was conducted most discreetly. The authors of *The Life of Sir Charles Hanbury-Williams* – the Earl of Ilchester and Mrs Langford-Brooke – stated: 'So well was the exchange carried on, that the correspondence remained unknown outside their own tiny circle. To all intents and purposes it eluded the spies of the Great Chancellor, who were ever on the watch for signs of secret relations between them. For though Bestuchev at last got wind of some hidden channel of communication, he was never able to find out the real source.'

As Bestuchev was so close to the English Ambassador and they had worked together to influence Catherine this ignorance on his part is perhaps surprising. On the other hand probably Sir Charles feared Bestuchev's secret agents more than he did the Chancellor. After all the ramifications of intrigues at the Court were both varied and complex. While Catherine was pro-English, her husband was committed to the King of Prussia, while the Schuvaloffs were dedicated to an understanding with France.

It is clear that there was an implicit understanding between Sir Charles and Catherine that when she came to the throne there would be something like a firm and comprehensive alliance with England. Perhaps the trust that existed between them and the true nature of the problems that faced the Grand Duchess are best illustrated by this letter which Catherine wrote to Sir Charles regarding how she would safeguard herself and her interests when the Czarina died:

'You have allowed me to call you my friend. Your title awes me, but as my designs are in no way criminal, I make so bold as to communicate to you and to ask your advice upon the thoughts forced upon my mind by the increased indisposition of certain persons during the last twenty-four hours. This is my dream. After being informed of her death [the Czarina's], and being certain that there is no mistake, I shall go straight to my son's room. If I meet, or can quickly get hold of, the Grand Master of the Hunt, I shall leave him with him and the men under his command. If not, I shall carry him off to my room. I shall also send a man that I can trust to warn five officers of the Guards, of whom I am sure, who will each bring me fifty soldiers (this is understood at the first signal),

27

and though I may perhaps not use them, they will serve as a reserve in case of any difficulty. (N.B. They will take no orders, except from the Grand Duke or me.) I shall send orders to the Chancellor, Apraksin and Lieven to come to me, and meanwhile I shall enter the death-chamber, where I shall summon the captain of the guard, and shall make him take the oath and retain him at my side. It appears to me that it would be better and safer if the two Grand Dukes were together than if only one went with me; also that the rendezvous for my followers should be my ante-chamber. If I see the slightest signs of commotion, I shall secure, either with my own people or with those of the captain of the guard, the Schuvaloffs, and the adjutant-general of the day. Besides, the lower-grade officers of the bodyguard are trustworthy; and though I have had no communication with all of them, I can count sufficiently on two or three, and on having enough means at my disposal to make myself obeyed by everyone who is not bought.'

In Russia there was then no single omnipotent security or intelligence service, but several splinter groups, all serving different policies and different persons. It was Catherine's intention when she became Czarina to end all this, and to achieve that she needed to destroy Alexander Schuvaloff and his secret police.

As to Sir Charles, there are conflicting reports as to whether he was ever the lover of Catherine. That he regarded her through romantic eyes cannot be doubted. 'When you are settled on this throne,' he wrote to Catherine on 3 September 1756, 'if I am not there, I shall come at once. I should like the right to come and go and to profit by your leisure hours: for I shall always love Catherine better than the Empress.'

Alas, the dream never came true. Three years later Sir Charles was dead and Catherine's conception of an Anglo-Russian alliance was in ruins.

4

Catherine's 'Secret Expedition' and the 'Yellow Box'

DAUGHTER OF a Prussian field-marshal, the Grand Duchess Catherine had been selected by the Czarina Elizabeth as the wife of the heir to the Russian throne as long ago as 1745. Catherine's contempt for her boorish and inept husband and her realisation of his incapacity to rule convinced her at an early age that she must prepare to seize the reins of power when Elizabeth died. She had had a long time to prepare for such an eventuality. Hanbury-Williams had aided and abetted her in this plan, given her encouragement and confidence in herself. By his death she lost a great friend and when the Czarina Elizabeth died in 1761 things did not exactly work out as Catherine had planned.

While her mother was on the throne Catherine and her husband had never been allowed to make themselves the centre of an independent court. Bestuchev saw that the Grand Duke was utterly unfitted for succeeding his mother and he knew, too, that Peter was pro-Prussian. Thus it was not unnatural that at first he had been somewhat suspicious of Catherine, fearing that, as the daughter of a Prussian field-marshal and the wife of a pro-Prussian, her sympathies might lie in that direction, too. Catherine herself had at first taken great pains to appear to be neutral, but when Bestuchev forced his own spies into her entourage he gradually learned that the Grand Duchess might be won over to a pro-English viewpoint.

The Grand Duke Peter succeeded to the throne and almost immediately provided evidence of his unfitness to rule. What had previously been eccentricities of conduct were now magnified into acts of madness. At Mass he put his tongue out at the officiating priest; he behaved like a fool and burst into maniacal laughter at ministerial conferences. He indicated that he would try to divorce Catherine. When Peter made peace with the King of Prussia and indulged in pro-German activities he soon made many enemies at Court.

Catherine took great pains to win the support of the clergy and the Army so she was able to mount a conspiracy against her husband. With great energy, moral courage and industry she set about establishing her own secret service, gathering information on her husband's pro-Prussian proclivities. She was determined not to leave anything to chance, or to rely too much on any one person. This organisation was small, probably not numbering more than twenty trusted men at that time, but it was efficient and diligent. It was indirectly to her advantage that her husband had abolished the Secret Chancery and that many exiles had returned from Siberia. Peter III had, however, abolished only the Secret Chancery to start up his own pro-Prussian spy service.

Despite her German origins Catherine's popularity with the people grew when it was realised that she did not share her husband's views. Peter III was warned by his spies that his wife was plotting against him and let it be known that he was not only proposing to divorce her but to have her imprisoned as well. But he talked and postponed action, and that was a fatal error. Catherine's fellow conspirators decided to act while the Czar dithered. Most prominent among these conspirators were the Princess Dashkova, Potemkin and the Orloffs. The wretched Czar was forced to abdicate, stripped of his decorations and put under arrest. Later his death was announced, the official proclamation stating that he had succumbed to an intestinal haemorrhage, but there is little doubt that he was assassinated, probably by one of the Orloffs and certainly with Catherine's connivance. She promptly forgave and even rewarded the Orloffs when she came to the throne.

No one blamed Catherine, for Peter had been disliked in Russia and mistrusted abroad. Even Voltaire commented cynically, 'I know that Catherine is reproached with some trifles on account of her husband, but these are family affairs in which I do not mix.'

Catherine proved to be as able a ruler as Peter the Great and she mixed enlightened and even liberal policies with that personal ruthlessness which in Russia has always seemed necessary in any successful ruler. The next legitimate heir to the Russian throne was, of course, Catherine's son, Paul, but she regarded her son as unfit to rule like his father and, allowing it to be bruited around that he was mad, set aside his right to occupy the throne which she claimed for herself. While creating a strong central government and keeping a much closer watch on the organisation of intelligence than her immediate predecessors, she also provided provincial government for no fewer than fifty provinces. She reorganised the Army, gave the traders and the middle classes a status in the community and, above all, gave to the nobility freedom and privileges they had never before known. By eighteenth-century – indeed even by sixteenth-century – standards this freedom and these privileges may seem insignificant, but to Russia they marked a tremendous advance. The boyars were exempted from compulsory state service, though encouraged to take it up voluntarily; they were given civil rights, the right to be tried by their peers and, more important, the chance to travel abroad freely, thus enlarging their minds and enriching their experience.

These were considerable achievements, but the great blemish on Catherine's reign was her extravagance, especially in the financing of military adventures. The occupation of eastern Poland, the defeat of the Turks and the annexation of the northern coast of the Black Sea left the Russian treasury almost insolvent. And though these victories were won by her generals, it was as often as not Catherine herself who gave the day-to-day orders to them. She worked at the actual job of governing for as long sometimes as fourteen hours a day, insisting that all intelligence reports came directly to her and being her own Minister for Foreign Affairs, Finance and War.

It was Catherine again who reorganised the Secret Service. She abolished Peter III's spy service and almost immediately after her proclamation created a new Secret Office which she designated the 'Secret Expedition'.

Few of her closest supporters were men of much talent; in fact she generally preferred them to be loyal rather than intelligent. The Orloffs, and particularly Gregori Orloff, her lover, were exceptionally stupid men even for that age. There were no great master-minds of intelligence during her reign until the advent of Prince Gregori Alexandrovitch Potemkin. He had taken part in the conspiracy which ended in the assassination of the Czar Peter III, but it was not until later in Catherine's reign that his influence became paramount. Unlike Catherine's other male supporters and lovers Potemkin was not just content to be a boudoir playmate or hanger-on. By 1776 he was not only the acknowledged favourite of the Czarina but her chief adviser on foreign affairs and her chief intelligence officer. Whether they were ever secretly married remains a mystery, but some assert that they were betrothed at the Church of Saint Samson in Petersburg in 1774.

The love affair of Catherine and Potemkin was tempestuous and romantic in the Russian tradition, a mixture of passion, mysticism and masochism on Potemkin's part. He was of a jealous nature and never ceased to taunt Catherine with having had so many lovers. In the end Potemkin's ardour cooled somewhat and his jealousy waned, but he was still fascinated by his royal mistress and wished to retain power and influence to continue as her adviser. Potemkin knew that if the security of the realm were to be preserved and he was to remain privy to Catherine's secrets he must somehow be in a position to control her lovers. For with increasing age Catherine's sexual appetite in no way abated and her passions demanded a series of younger lovers to gratify her promiscuous nature. Potemkin suddenly ceased to accuse her of unfaithfulness and instead made himself her pimp-in-chief. He began to select for her one after the other a series of handsome young men. Catherine accepted his judgement without demur and from each lover Potemkin demanded personal loyalty to him and any secrets or intelligence they could bring him.

Potemkin retained Catherine's affection until his death. When that occurred in 1791 she refused to see anybody for weeks. She wrote to Grimm, the author of the fairy tales, saying of Potemkin that he was 'my pupil, my friend, my idol. . . . Whom can I rely on now?'

The curse of Russia for centuries was that too often a strong and efficient ruler was followed by one who was little better than a moron, thus setting back imperial progress for many years. It always seemed that for every two steps Russia took forward in one reign she took three backwards in the next. So it was after the death of Catherine the Great in 1796. Her son Paul was clearly inadequate and had been kept in relative obscurity from childhood. When he succeeded his mother he showed his resentment of her by reversing her policies. She had formed an Anglo-Russian-Austrian alliance, which he proceeded to discard. Goading and provoking the English and Austrian ambassadors, he had their dispatches intercepted by his Black Cabinet.

Not surprisingly he learned some unpleasant truths about himself. 'The Czar,' wrote Ambassador Whitworth of England, 'is literally not in his senses. This truth has been for many years known to those nearest to him and I have myself had frequent opportunities of observing it. But since he has come to the throne his disorder has gradually increased.'

The dispatch was in cipher, but it was read nevertheless, for the Russians had acquired great skill in mastering codes and ciphers and now required no outside aid in this kind of work. As a result Whitworth was ordered to return to London.

Czar Paul not only retained the Secret Expedition but conceived a novel idea for boosting its sources of information. It was a typically Russian inspiration and perhaps it was one of the sanest he had. The tragedy was that Paul was not the man to take advantage of it. His idea was that anyone in the realm, boyar, merchant, police informant, peasant or returned exile, should have the opportunity of providing him with secret intelligence, anonymously if necessary. So outside the Winter Palace he had placed the Yellow Box into which any of his subjects could place a communication whether of straightforward intelligence, complaints or allegations of treachery.

A Czar who wanted to know what his people thought and felt and to learn what they observed might have gleaned much from the Yellow Box. But Paul merely allowed these reports to develop into phobias in his own mind so that on the strength of hearing that an officer wore his hat at the wrong angle he had him sent to Siberia. Though Paul had discarded his mother's policies, he had no clear idea of what he wanted to put in their place. So government dissolved in chaos. Ministers quarrelled among themselves and while Rostopchin, the Chancellor, was pro-French, Panin, the Vice-Chancellor, was pro-Austrian. Paul disastrously attempted to make a secret agreement with France, but two Army officers, General Benningsen and Platon Zuboff, a former lover of Catherine's, decided the time had come to intervene. The boyars had tasted real freedom under Catherine: they were not going to throw it away under Paul. First acquiring the tacit consent of Paul's son, Alexander, these two officers with eight others plotted the assassination of the Czar. Paul was killed in his bed, strangled with a sash, and the palace revolution brought Alexander to the throne.

As was the case with Catherine in her benign attitude to the killers of Peter III, so Alexander rewarded his father's murderers. Benningsen was made Governor of Lithuania and Zuboff became the Czar's favourite and organiser of his personal intelligence service.

The new Czar had decidedly original ideas on developing the Russian Secret Service, almost as novel as his dream of giving his country a form of representative government. But for the war with Napoleon Alexander might indeed have taken some cautious steps towards the latter aim, but war and age made him lose much of his liberal ardour and seek harsher means of ruling his diverse empire.

But if he merely day-dreamed about representative government, he took swift and positive action on the Secret Service. First, on 1 April 1801, he abolished the Secret Expedition, declaring that 'in a well-ordered state all crimes must be judged and punished on the basis of existing laws, and not merely at the discretion of persons at the head of the "Secret Expedition". . . . Not only is this institution abolished, but its name also forever and eternally removed, all current business to be turned over to the State archives and there committed to oblivion.'

That seemed categorical enough, but if anyone thought that the idea of a secret police had been dropped for all time they were swiftly to be disillusioned. Alexander's main purpose was to curtail the rôle of a Secret Bureau or Secret Service which was both prosecutor and judge and its own jury into the bargain. But he still wished enemies of the state to be caught and prosecuted.

A year later he asked his Minister of Internal Affairs, V. P. Kochubey, to look into the question of a new intelligence service. Kochubey spoke to the Governor-General of St Petersburg who quite blandly replied that there was a Secret Police Office in that city and that it concerned itself with 'all objects, actions and speeches that tend towards the dissolution of the autocratic power and . . . in short, all that relates to the Czar personally, or his administration.'

Alexander pondered until 1805 before deciding on the exact shape of his Secret Service. He believed in extending this service by making use of foreigners so that he would not be so dependent on the formalised intelligence from abroad normally supplied by his envoys, or the bureaucrats of the secret police. At that time the

French police-spy system was the most efficient in Europe and Alexander, learning of Napoleon's close attention to his own intelligence service, sought to emulate the French colossus.

'I am told,' said Alexander to Zuboff, 'that Napoleon not only spends every day reading intelligence reports, but that he actually tells his agents where to go and what to do. I intend to follow his example.'

Two of the first foreign agents employed by the Russian Secret Service in this era were the Comte d'Antraigues and another Frenchman named Michel. The Comte d'Antraigues, who lived in London, obtained all manner of diplomatic secrets and sold them to Russia, Austria and England. His chief source of supply were two brothers named Simon who worked in the French Foreign Ministry and the War Office respectively. Michel somehow managed to gain access to Napoleon's private archives, containing information of great value on military and financial matters. Almost the entire contents of these archives were passed to Russia over a period of ten years.

This was, if not the heyday of the Russian Secret Service, at least the period in which at last St Petersburg began to compete on equal terms with the rival espionage organisations in Europe. No one appreciated this more than Maurice Talleyrand de Périgord, that subtle ex-priest who became Napoleon's Foreign Minister. When in 1807 Talleyrand began to realise that Napoleon's ambitions were threatening his chances of survival, he left the Foreign Office and promptly betrayed the French leader's secrets to Alexander. No wonder that Napoleon when in exile at St Helena reproached himself with the question, 'Why did I not have Talleyrand shot?'

Alexander also instituted reforms in intelligence in the domestic sphere. In order to be less dependent on the orthodox sources of information such as the secret police he ordered military intelligence to be properly organised and pursued a somewhat devious policy of dividing and ruling, encouraging the creation of rival intelligence agencies so that he could check one against another. He also set up a supreme advisory body, the Special Committee for the Dispatch of Crimes Threatening the Public Safety, which included among its members the Ministers of Justice, Internal Affairs and War as well as two Senators. Finally, on the advice of Speransky, a commoner, the Czar approved the formation of a separate Ministry of Police, at the head of which was set A. D. Balashoff, the Governor-General of St Petersburg. The ministry was largely based on the French secret police organisation under Fouché.

Napoleon had ordered changes to be made in the cipher system to be used by the French. But in aiming at speed and simplification he had sacrificed security. The Napoleonic Grand Cipher comprised less than 200 signs whereas the Grand Cipher used by Louis XIV had 587. The latter was used by skilled cryptographers who took great pains to avoid composing repetitive messages which could more easily be detected. Napoleon's Grand Cipher was entrusted to his marshals alone, admirable soldiers, no doubt, but clumsy and unsubtle cryptographers.

When the Czar Alexander commiserated with Marshal Macdonald on the French defeats by the Russians on the occasion of their meeting after the wars, he said: 'We were always greatly assisted by knowing exactly what your Emperor planned from his own dispatches. We captured a number of them.'

Marshal Macdonald replied that he supposed somebody had given the Russians the key to the French ciphers.

The Czar denied this. 'I give you my word of honour that nobody betrayed you. The answer is quite simple. We were able to decipher all your dispatches.'

One of the mysteries of this era was the dismissal of the Comte d'Antraigues from the Russian Secret Service without compensation a few weeks after the signing of the secret Treaty of Tilsit by the Czar and Napoleon aboard a raft moored in the River Niemen on 25 June 1807. The object of this meeting on a raft was to preserve the utmost secrecy in negotiations and to keep away spies and other intruders. The secrets of the Treaty of Tilsit were officially well guarded and the actual text of what was arranged there was not published until 1891. Only the King of Prussia, besides the Czar and Napoleon, knew the terms agreed. All diplomats, including even the Russian Ambassadors in London and Paris, were kept in ignorance of events. The terms of the Treaty were that France and Russia should support each other 'in every war' in which they might be engaged against a European power. As the King of Prussia was in the secret this was obviously directed against Britain. A further clause made it even more apparent that the Treaty was, if not a directly hostile act, at least a threatening warning to Britain by France and Russia. This was that the Baltic was to be closed to Britain, and Denmark and Spain and Sweden were to exclude British ships from their ports.

It is now apparent that somehow the full details of the Tilsit meeting were made available to Britain within days of the Treaty being signed. But was this more a triumph for patriotic Russians inside their Secret Service who opposed Alexander's new policy rather than a successful coup by British agents? How exactly the news was leaked is still to some extent a puzzle, but that Britain was warned in time to stop the Russians and the French from dominating the Baltic is clear enough. The British, having learned about Tilsit, sent an ultimatum to Denmark demanding the handing over of the Danish fleet, in exchange for which the Danes were promised a subsidy and an alliance. The ultimatum was rejected and the British fleet immediately bombarded Copenhagen. Denmark then capitulated and her fleet was captured.

Was d'Antraigues dismissed from the Russian Secret Service because he was a double-agent and had warned the British about the terms of Tilsit? Or was he permitted and indeed encouraged by that Secret Service to leak the information to Britain, and was his dismissal a mere covering up of a coup which the Russian Secret Service wished to hide from the Czar? It is said that Canning, the British Foreign Secretary, granted d'Antraigues an annual pension of £400. On the other hand there is evidence that the British obtained some of the information about Tilsit from other sources.

Napoleon undoubtedly set out to charm Alexander and to press for an agreement in the first place. He played on the Czar's vanity by treating him as an equal. But the advantages to Russia were few. True, she had France as an ally instead of an enemy, but the Russian generals must have known that this was an agreement of temporary convenience to Napoleon at the very best. The chief advantage was that Russia gained time to build up her defences at a moment when Napoleon had immensely more powerful forces at his disposal. But the Tilsit Treaty could make France more powerful and dominant in the Baltic as, while Alexander was given a theoretical freedom of action in Turkey, Napoleon had in effect nullified this by expressly forbidding him to capture Constantinople.

D'Antraigues may have received information about Tilsit from the Russian Ambassador to England, Count Vorontzoff, who, though kept officially in ignorance of the terms of Tilsit, had his own channels of communication. It is even possible that Vorontzoff, who was strongly pro-British, deliberately gave d'Antraigues the intelligence to pass on to Canning. As under the two Czarinas, Elizabeth and Catherine, and under Czar Paul, there had always been warring pro-British and pro-French factions at St Petersburg, each considering themselves as patriotic Russians as their adversaries.

Vorontzoff was devoted to Britain, he preferred life in London to St Petersburg, loathed Napoleon and was a close friend of Canning. Also he was in constant touch with those of the Czar's intimates who were opposed to Alexander's alliance with Napoleon, especially Prince Czartoryski. The latter had his personal intelligence service and indulged in a good deal of espionage on his own account.

But no ruler of Russia since Ivan the Terrible, except possibly Catherine the Great, had succeeded for long in maintaining an absolute, comprehensive Secret Service that imposed total security. Rival factions at the Court had invariably played their own espionage games and used them to thwart official policy as well as to put their own policies into being.

Whoever passed the information to the British it is certain that this was done with the connivance of one branch of Russian intelligence. Vorontzoff learned about the Treaty within two weeks of its being signed. He wrote to his son Michael on 14 July: 'My spirit is disquieted by the news which arrives from all sides, stating that the Czar is going to make peace with Bonaparte and that he had an interview with that monster. I hope to God that this is false.'

Two days later Canning knew all about Tilsit. Vorontzoff's rôle in all this is illuminating. He knew that something was afoot that threatened the survival of the Russian Empire and was determined to find out what was planned. He had been in touch with Prince Czartoryski and also with a Captain Hervey, who appears to have brought him a message from Memel. Another interesting and significant detail is that Vorontzoff's son, Michael, an officer in the Russian Army, was aboard the raft in the River Niemen during the talks. Had he been planted there by the Russian Secret Service?

There seems also to have been an arrangement at this time between the Russian and the British Secret Services, prompted by Canning and d'Antraigues in London and by Prince Czartoryski in St Petersburg. The chief intermediary between the two Secret Services appears to have been Sir Robert Wilson, an English adventurer who was privy to the passing on of the secrets of Tilsit. It was he who took a letter from Czartoryski to Vorontzoff in London and this missive gave the impression that Vorontzoff had already been told about the Treaty. It is dated 2 September 1807 and, after mentioning that 'the Chevalier Wilson' was the courier, added 'Knowing your attachment to the glory and prosperity of your country, I imagine all that you must have suffered at learning of the fatal events which have terminated the Prussian campaign . . . the disastrous transactions of Tilsit . . . and before things reached such an extremity, in not having ceased to warn and enlighten the Emperor by . . . representations – which he never heeded – on the abyss which he prepared for himself.'

Gradually there was a reversal of policy inside Russia and, while Alexander and Napoleon remained on friendly terms, from this moment onward the real power in shaping events was in the hands of the Russian Secret Service. They were determined to open the Czar's eyes to the extent of Napoleon's ambitions, his duplicity and his ultimate plans to dominate Europe. No longer was it a question of a branch of the Secret Service directed by Czartoryski playing a double game: the entire espionage services of Russia were concentrated against France. If the Czar still had faith in Napoleon, this was no longer a view shared by his advisers and, under a young colonel, Tchernichev, a team of spies planned for the war with France which they now felt to be inevitable.

Four years after the signing of the Treaty of Tilsit Tchernichev arrived in Paris and set himself up in luxurious apartments. His task of organising a spy service in the French capital was made all the more difficult because the Russian Ambassador in Paris at that time was Prince Alexander Borissovitch Kurakin, who had been one of the signatories of the Treaty of Tilsit. He had been Vice-Chancellor and had been sent to Paris on account of his marked pro-French sentiments.

Tchernichev had acted with great circumspection during his stay in Paris, taking care to have no French servants in his house and employing only a German domestic and an eccentric Russian *moujik*. In the early months of his sojourn in Paris no effort had been made by Napoleon to challenge his authority because he knew that Tchernichev was an aide-de-camp to the Czar and had considerable influence with him. Apart from this, Napoleon still wished to play for time. He wanted to keep up the pretence of friendship with the Czar while amassing as much information as possible to enable him to launch a successful invasion of Russia. For a long time Bonaparte held his hand against premature action on Tchernichev, despite the fact that his Minister of Police, Savary, warned him that the Russian was probably a spy. Bonaparte, though suspicious of the colonel, too, felt that to call Tchernichev's bluff too soon might invite reprisals against his own agents and diplomats in Russia. He ordered Savary to allow the Russian colonel complete freedom. It was a fatal error and by the time he was fully convinced of Tchernichev's true rôle the damage had been done. Not only had Tchernichev established contact with Michel, the spy in the French War Office who had long been aiding the British, but he had entered into secret communications with Talleyrand who was no longer in office and was sympathetic to the Russian cause. Sympathy was turned by Tchernichev's persistence and cajolery into active aid to the Russian Secret Service. Talleyrand introduced Tchernichev to important French military leaders such as General Jomini and Marshal Bernadotte, an avowed enemy of Napoleon. The Russian colonel's plans were well laid and he proved himself to be the ablest spy

Russia had produced for many years. From Paris he even organised a German resistance movement which was to start a revolt immediately diplomatic relations were broken off between France and Russia.

Talleyrand's rôle was of the utmost importance and he and Tchernichev seem to have arrived at a complete understanding. The cynicism of the former French Foreign Minister was perhaps his saving virtue: it prevented him from succumbing to the prevailing weakness of the age, the deadening touch of flattery. Napoleon was well aware of his talents; he described Talleyrand as one who had 'much that is necessary for conducting negotiations: the experience of a man of the world, knowledge of European courts, finesse, or something more, immobility of countenance, which nothing can alter, and finally a great name.' Napoleon made Talleyrand a duke in 1807, but this did not blind Talleyrand to Napoleon's failings. By the following year he felt sure that Napoleon was aiming too high, that his territorial ambitions would be his downfall. He left the Foreign Office and from that time pursued a pro-Russian policy in secret.

At last Napoleon made a formal complaint to Kurakin about Tchernichev. Following this the French secret police maintained a close watch on the colonel and, when he was away, searched his rooms. They discovered there a letter from Michel who had been conducting a correspondence with Tchernichev through the intermediary of the *concierge* at the Russian Embassy. What Michel had passed on to Tchernichev was something of tremendous importance: it revealed the treachery of the French and was nothing less than the French Army's plans for invading Russia.

It was soon clear to the French that Michel had been spying for the Russians continuously since 1804 and that it was his intelligence reports which had brought Tchernichev to Paris. The young colonel had swiftly made many feminine conquests while in the French capital and from these had greatly supplemented the information he received from Michel.

By the time Michel's treason was discovered the Russians knew that the French armies were ill-prepared to invade their country, that they would inevitably come to grief. For Michel had reported that the French gun carriages had not been designed to travel on the rough Russian roads. Napoleon belatedly ordered the arrest of Tchernichev, but the colonel, warned of what was coming, escaped from the country. Michel, however, was arrested and shot. Napoleon ordered the French press to publish an attack on the Czar. It was, of course, blatant hypocrisy, for Napoleon had been organising in Russia spying activities which matched those of Tchernichev in Paris. His ambassador in St Petersburg had been asked to provide details about the strength of the Russian forces and to obtain maps of the Russian Empire, including the engraved copperplates from which these had been printed. It was obvious that Napoleon was planning to betray his ally.

When the French invasion of Russia began the Russians were ready for them. They planned to infiltrate the French ranks with Secret Service agents. Of these the most outstanding spy was one Colonel Figner, specially chosen for the task because he was a master of disguises and multi-lingual. He slipped across the French lines close to Moscow, sometimes as a wandering vagrant, sometimes as a salesman, occasionally posing as a French officer. Altogether he made as many as fifteen sallies into the enemy camp, returning each time with a wealth of information on French dispositions, the morale of their troops and their supplies. Later, after the retreat from Moscow, Figner again disguised himself as a senior French officer and entered the city of Danzig, then held by the French. He was even welcomed by the commandant of the French troops, General Rapp, and from him learned all about the garrison, the numbers and calibre of the French guns. Rapp wined and dined Figner, toasted him and expressed his complete trust in the spy by giving him dispatches to take to Napoleon. Needless to say they never reached Paris, but found their way to St Petersburg.

In the period after Waterloo and Napoleon's downfall the Russians became concerned at Austria's post-war motives, and the intrigues of Prince Metternich whose secret service was perhaps the best organised in Europe at that time.

The Czar Alexander himself was the target for the machinations of foreign spies, of those who wished to seduce him into making secret alliances and those who merely wished to keep themselves informed. He had earlier in his reign shown a particular vulnerability to women spies. The Russian Secret Service had first detected this in the days before Tilsit when French female spies had been introduced into his entourage. Then they became perturbed at the friendship he had formed with the Baroness Barbara Juliana von Krudener, who was suspected of mixing political intrigue with religious mysticism. Alexander had been an atheist; his conversion to Christianity had taken an individualist turn which agitated the Orthodox Church. For once Church and State combined in concerted Secret Service action, first to track down Alexander's suspected links with foreign religious sects, secondly to combat the growing popularity of such sects inside Russia. Alexander's unconventional views on religion had encouraged such sects to be more openly active.

Agents of the Secret Service found that when the Czar was staying in Paris the baroness was lodging in an hotel close to his headquarters. There was consternation when they learned that a private passage connected the two buildings and that this was used by the Czar to attend secret prayer meetings conducted by the baroness in her hotel suite. It soon became evident that the baroness's plan was not merely to win the Czar as a convert to her religious rites, but to urge him to make a 'Holy Alliance' by which he would advance to the south-west, declare war against the Moslems and free the Christians of the Middle East from Turkish and other Moslem oppression. A constant watch was kept on the baroness afterwards and eventually the Czar was warned that her aims were political rather than spiritual. Though Alexander invited the baroness back to St Petersburg he seems to have been persuaded not to take her grandiose schemes seriously. His interest in the baroness appears to have been relatively platonic, but most of his relations with women were of a distinctly amorous character. The dangers of such relations were noted by the Secret Service who decided that the safest plan was to ensure that at least some of his mistresses were in their employ.

This ruse worked well, especially after Tilsit, though some of these women turned out to be double agents. One such was the Princess Catherine Bagration who spied for the Czar and then informed the Secret Service of his activities. Another courtesan named Wolters, employed by the Russians, used to smuggle herself into the palace disguised as a boy and became the mistress of the Czar's adjutant, Volkonsky.

In reforming the Secret Service and aiming originally to make it his own instrument by creating competitive agencies within that organisation, Alexander had in the end built something bigger than himself: a Secret Service independent enough and comprehensive enough to keep even the Czar himself in check. Each spy chief went his own way. Balashoff, for example, made the Ministry of Police into a ministry of espionage and established many contacts abroad, in Sweden and Germany as well as in France. There were many talented spy chiefs in Russia in this era, perhaps the one singled out most by the contemporary historian, I. M. Dolgorukoff, was Alexander Dmitrievich, one-time Minister of Police, who 'possessed a talent for espionage in the finest measure, and accordingly was bound to this low craft. At this time, when cunning was called wisdom, and the ability to deceive a human achievement, he seemed an indispensable man.'

But few of these Secret Service heads of departments trusted one another and the Czar in turn was suspicious of each of them. It was a fandango of mutual suspicion that was performed in St Petersburg and Moscow with Balashoff spying on his master, Speransky, and the agent De St Glin spying on Balashoff on behalf of the Czar, while even the court doctor, Dr Ellisen, spied on both Speransky and Balashoff. The last-named retaliated by getting a young man named von Vock, a friend of De St Glin's mother, to spy on De St Glin and to seek evidence that he was in league with French spies. Such ridiculous cavortings in the secret police gave an excuse for Alexander to create a new form of military intelligence in the guise of a secret political police force in the Army. The organisation of this body was given to General Vasilchikoff and a sum of forty thousand roubles a year was allotted to it. This plan was eventually approved and put into action in 1821.

The older Alexander became the more he womanised. He reached the pinnacle of his philandering at the Congress of Vienna where he spent his whole time dancing and entertaining beautiful women, all at the expense of the Austrian Emperor who was footing the bill for this most brilliant and extravagant of festive conferences. 'It is as well that St Petersburg is so far distant from Vienna,' he told the Austrian Emperor. 'If it were nearer, I should come here every other week.'

The Emperor must have thanked God that this was not the case for the cost of entertaining the Czar had made huge inroads into the Hapsburg treasury. The Russian Secret Service must have echoed that prayer, for the cost of watching Alexander must have been quite considerable, too.

5

Nicholas I Creates the Third Section

ALEXANDER, so the orthodox historians tell us, died in 1825 at Taganrog and once more Russia was plunged into internal dissensions. But there is still a good deal of unresolved mystery about his death and it was a subject which occupied a lengthy and growing dossier in the files of the Secret Service.

Alexander himself largely gave rise to the persistent rumours that he might still be alive. He had become somewhat of a schizophrenic figure in his latter years, delighting in the company of women and wining and dancing, yet on other occasions expressing a fondness for the contemplative life, being absorbed in the examination of strange religious sects. Often he had spoken of abdicating and becoming a monk or living anonymously in Switzerland. Then at the age of forty-eight he went to Taganrog and gave a message to his counsellors that he was sick with malaria. A doctor recorded that the Czar had 'refused all medical assistance'. Four days later Alexander was stated to have died.

Perhaps no questions would have been asked if the succession had not been the subject of controversy and even constitutional irregularity. Constantine, the next son of the previous Czar, Paul, had renounced his claim to the throne. Thus Alexander was succeeded by Nicholas, the next brother, and this led to some political discontent. Men of ultra-liberal tendencies, deeply influenced by the French Revolution and by the increasing liberalising tendencies in Europe, planned to have a proper constitution drawn up for Russia.

The story went around St Petersburg that the Czar had staged his own death by disappearing and having the body of another man substituted for his own. One rumour was that he had gone to Siberia and shut himself up in a monastery, another was that he had gone to Palestine, a theory advanced by his biographer, Maurice Paléologue.

The growing liberalism inside Russia manifested itself in the campaign of the Decembrists, so called because they launched their plans in December 1825. In fact the Decembrists, or Dekabrists, as they were more generally known, had been making plans for some time before 1825. The military intelligence later claimed to have discovered a Dekabrist plot inside the Russian Army, but the importance of this seems to have been underestimated.

It was primarily the French Revolution which stirred the intellectuals and especially the writers of Russia into political action and many of these were prominent among the Dekabrists. There was a bloody confrontation with the Government and the rising was quelled. Five of the plotters were executed and many more were sent to Siberia.

Despite this the revolutionary underground in Russia was at last firmly established even though it existed as a precarious minority. Some of its members were students and writers, thinkers who had positive thoughts on what Russia should become, others were members of secret societies of a type which had grown up in Europe in the post-Napoleonic era. One of their leaders, P. I. Pestel, defined their aims when he founded the 'Southern Society', stating that 'by decisive revolutionary means' they should overthrow the throne and in extreme necessity kill any persons who might represent invincible obstacles.

When the Czar Nicholas I put down the Dekabrist revolt he was anxious to learn the reasons for this new revolutionary spirit so that he could anticipate any further outbreaks. He appointed an investigating committee for this very purpose and ordered all ringleaders and many of the rank and file revolutionaries to be interviewed. Though there were some intellectuals who had given serious thought to the creation of a freer and happier Russia, it was soon apparent that much of the questioning and plotting behind the scenes was the direct result of the returning Russian armies coming back from Europe after the Napoleonic wars contrasting conditions there with those they found at home. Officers and men alike had tasted the sweets of victory in a foreign land and their appetite for similar freedom at home was whetted.

This alarmed the Czar who decided that from now onwards 'foreign influences' must be ruthlessly discouraged, but perhaps he was even more alarmed that this latest attempt at revolution was not just a power struggle in the palace but the first occasion on which some of the governing class had concerned themselves with setting the people free.

Nicholas I, in an effort to prevent any similar outbreaks before they could take root and to stabilise his own position, took it upon himself to reorganise the Secret Service. The creation of the investigating committee was followed by Nicholas setting up a Special Corps of Gendarmerie, at the head of which he appointed Count Constantin Benckendorff.

Thus Nicholas did not create the modern version of the political police, as has sometimes been suggested. What he developed was a Third Section of His Majesty's Private Imperial Chancery, bringing the Gendarmerie closer to the throne and making them responsible directly to him. Curiously enough, in achieving this, he gave them the semblance not merely of respectability, but even of nobility and grace, designing for his Gendarmerie elegant blue uniforms with white straps and white gloves so that Henri Merimée described them as 'the Inquisition in a pink peignoir'. With the firm hand in a velvet glove, Nicholas controlled the state through the Third Section.

One of the first problems the Third Section examined was that of Alexander's death. There was some doubt as to whether the royal physician, Dr Tarassov, had actually signed the report or whether his signature had been forged. Tarassov under pressure insisted he had not signed it, and he repeated this statement in his memoirs. The vital point was that the report of the doctors did not coincide with the condition of a man suffering from malaria. Those who saw the Czar's body said it had changed beyond all recognition. The Secret Service believed that Alexander had substituted another body for his own and had 'disappeared' to become a monk in Siberia. Nicholas suppressed these reports, but in 1864 when a monk named Fedor Kusmich died in Siberia it was believed by the Third Section that he was Alexander.

Slowly Russia slipped back into a state of far more rigorous autocracy than she had known in the two previous reigns. Nicholas made exile in Siberia not merely a frequent form of punishment but used it as a deliberate policy for isolating trouble-makers. Count Alexander Benckendorff came from the Baltic provinces and his family had a long tradition of faithful service to the Czars. He ruled the Special Corps with an efficient military discipline, but he was himself an untypical Secret Service chief in that age, being absent-minded, courteous and gentle. Nevertheless he carried out the wishes of his ruthless royal master so faithfully that the Third Section held people in a permanent state of fear and terrorised the whole Russian bureaucratic machine into absolute subservience. Nicholas never said *'Le Troisième Bureau, c'est moi,'* but he must have always thought it was and certainly behaved as though this were true. His creation of the Third Section was the nearest thing that Russia had known in modern times to Ivan IV's Oprichniki. The total police state had returned and the foundations of the modern espionage and counter-espionage system in Russia had been truly laid. Nicholas turned the whole function of government into instructing the entire nation as to how they should think and behave. His police agents were active in schools and universities, snuffing out any originality of thought, however innocent, and were instructed to report not only university professors with suspected liberal views but even a teacher in the most junior school, if his methods of discipline were considered too soft. The punishment was at the best immediate expulsion, without appeal, sometimes even banishment to Siberia as well. By such methods Nicholas retained his grip on the empire, but he created such silent resentment against himself and the office of the Czar that the ultimate fate of Czardom was sealed long before 1850.

Benckendorff at least believed that the true purpose of the new force was simply to protect the Russian people from internal and external oppressors. He communicated this belief to some, if not all, of his subordinates and managed to curtail the worst excesses of a secret police. Strangely enough there was no permanent address for the Third Section before 1831. Nicholas's first idea was that the Bureau should not advertise its presence in any way whatsoever. In that year headquarters were established in a house at the corner of the Moika and Gorokhovaia Streets in St Petersburg. By 1838, when the Section had grown considerably, it moved to the home of Count Kochubey, near the Chain Bridge, and came to be known somewhat melodramatically as 'The House on Chain Bridge', a place which was honeycombed with secret passages through which people came to be interrogated.

Alexander Herzen, who with Prince Kropotkin was one of the most energetic of the underground revolutionaries of the era, had this to say about Count Benckendorff and his secret police: 'I am disposed to believe, whenever I remember the insignificant expression of his face, that Benckendorff did not do as much harm as he might have done. He had neither the energy, nor the will, nor the heart for that.'

Benckendorff was, however, much more efficient than Herzen suggested, though it is true that he was not a tyrant and had no stomach for butchery. A. T. Vasilyev, a former head of the Russian secret police under the last of the Czars, took a more lenient view of the secret police under Czar Nicholas. He expressed the belief that banishment to Siberia was 'the kindliest form of self-protection that could be adopted by the State'. He also told the story of Czar Nicholas giving Count Benckendorff a white handkerchief, sardonically bidding him to use it 'to dry the tears of the widows and children' of the oppressed. The truth is that Nicholas was never completely satisfied with the way Benckendorff did his work and when the latter died in 1844 he appointed a much more ruthless man in his place, Count A. F. Orloff. Benckendorff was certainly no sentimentalist, but he never acquired the reputation for stark inhumanity that Orloff gave to the Third Section.

The spies of the Third Section operated all over the Russian empire. But, as is often the case with espionage organisations given unlimited powers, corruption affected efficiency and quite often they failed to find the real revolutionaries because individual agents were so busily occupied in working off private grudges and having people arrested or sent to Siberia because of some personal vendetta unconnected with reasons of security. The result was that the Third Section of the Gendarmerie failed completely to catch the Petrachevsky group, the largest of the underground movements, and it was the ordinary police under the Ministry of the Interior who eventually unmasked this party.

The Third Section also occupied itself a good deal with propaganda as well as espionage. This was largely apologist propaganda designed to create a favourable public opinion to Russia both at home and abroad and especially to explain away the Dekabrist revolt. In 1832 the Third Section started to send agents abroad to 'organise a system of correct observation at the most crucial points' and to infiltrate the ranks of Russian exiles.

The rule of terror continued unabated throughout the reign of Nicholas I. In the grim Trubefskoy State Prison ringleaders of revolutionary movements were held for years without trial and in Siberia the practice of *katorga* was introduced. This was hard labour meted out to exiles whose hands and feet were shackled, a brutal form of punishment maintained until the present century, the prisoners' hands being shackled to the carts which bore ore from the mines.

Yet the underground was never absolutely silenced. Some idea of how the secret police were used to combat sedition, alleged or otherwise, is gleaned from two facts. In 1834 full-time 'inspectors' were created to watch the extra-curricular activities of students and to report on these, and, in an effort to curtail the breeding of liberal tendencies, the numbers in the universities were reduced to a maximum of three hundred. Students and teachers were not allowed to study overseas or in any foreign land and even the university curriculum was drastically censored so that the teaching of constitutional law and philosophy was abolished. The result of this was a steady stream of exiles who managed to escape to Western Europe.

The difference between Benckendorff and Orloff was that Benckendorff was cautious where Orloff acted precipitately and that the former had a conscience while the latter suffered from no such inhibitions. When asked to form a special police force in 1826 Benckendorff has written with certain reservations about this policy: 'A secret police force is unthinkable; honourable people would be afraid of it and scoundrels would adapt themselves to it easily.' But the Dekabrist revolt caused him to revise his opinion so that he could declare: 'A network of secret agents could be employed only under pretext of the emergency, and with the greatest economy of means.' He added that the interception of correspondence was one of the most effective and cheapest ways of achieving their objects: 'all that is necessary for this purpose is to have postmasters, known for their honesty and zeal, in a few cities'.

Benckendorff continued to insist on the need for 'moral strength' in his force; it was after he left that corruption set in to a high degree. He divided the Third Section into four offices, one for 'political matters' and espionage referring to this, the second on religious sects and criminals, the third to watch over foreigners in the country and the fourth to deal with complaints and appeals. Later a fifth office, that of censorship, was added. The Third Section grew from sixteen persons in 1826 to more than forty within twenty years. These figures cover the bureaucrats, of course, and not the agents and other personnel.

The director of the Third Section's Chancery was M. I. von Vock, who had previously had Secret Service experience in the

Ministry of Internal Affairs' special section. He was a particularly skilled and lucid writer, even a friend of Pushkin, and he prepared the annual 'Surveys of Public Opinion' for the department. A shrewd and competent observer of people and trends, he frequently warned the Third Section that in official circles there was a dangerous tendency to ignore the causes of revolt in Russia. He warned particularly of the growth of secret societies in the country.

Benckendorff had been a Guards officer since his youth and brought a soldier's mind to bear on the Third Section and the Gendarmerie. His gendarmes were paid according to military rank and expenses were allowed them accordingly on the same scale. But they were not popular and even Benckendorff was regarded in St Petersburg society as 'a spy' and somewhat of a traitor to his caste. Even the man called by Herzen 'the most intelligent man in the Third Section', Leonty Vasilevich Dubelt, felt deeply the stigma attached to his profession. When he was offered a post in the Section his wife wrote to him objecting to such employment. He was stung to the quick and replied ' "Don't be a gendarme", you say. But do you understand . . . the essence of the case? If, entering the Corps of Gendarmes, I became an informer, an eavesdropper, then certainly my good name would be sullied. But if, on the other hand, not mixing in cases that relate to the internal police, I became a bulwark for the poor, a shield for the unfortunate . . . if I came to insist that justice be done for the oppressed . . . then would you reproach me?'

Dubelt eventually became Chief of Staff of the Corps of Gendarmes and Director of the Third Section Chancery. He continued to dislike that part of his work which concerned informers, but he directed the whole network of secret agents with great efficiency, if disdain. The Czar, always quick to sense a man whose stomach was not strong enough for such work, wanted to sack him, but was deterred by Benckendorff's threat of resignation if this happened. And when Orloff succeeded Benckendorff Dubelt still remained at his post.

Some of the agents employed by the Third Section in these days were remarkably diverse personalities. There was Boshniak, who was a botanist, Viskovatoff, a poet, Madame Sobanskaia, a courtesan, Platonoff, a Jew converted to the Orthodox faith and, most remarkable of all, John Sherwood, a Briton whose family had emigrated to Russia. Sherwood enlisted as an ordinary soldier in the Russian Army and eventually became an officer. While in the Army he had shown a desire to enter Intelligence and was secretly assigned to the Third Section for special work. He must have impressed his masters for in 1827 he was sent by Benckendorff on a mission to Kiev and Odessa to recruit agents for the Third Section, which shows an almost unparalleled trust in a foreigner. After that he seems to have moved on to Moscow and the Caucasus whence he reported regularly to Benckendorff. In 1828 he returned to St Petersburg and began to boast about his relations with the Third Section. News of this was passed back to the Third Section by another of its agents, Elizabeth Khotiantsova, who claimed that he had bragged that he 'saw the Czar every day' and that Russia was 'administered by consultation with Sherwood'.

But Benckendorff continued to employ Sherwood, sending him off to the Ukraine. Here again unfavourable reports on the man trickled through to his superiors. In 1830 he was dismissed from the Third Section and he volunteered for service in the Polish campaign. No doubt Benckendorff thought he had rid himself of a braggart who was unsuited to intelligence work, but Sherwood started a campaign against the Third Section. This was no mere bravado, foolish though it might be. Sherwood allied himself with the Grand Duke Michael and gave him a dossier exposing the failures of the Third Section in dealing with the remnants of the Polish and Dekabrist secret societies.

Complaints and unfavourable reports about Sherwood continued to come in to the Third Section's Chancery bureau, yet when in 1842 Sherwood, now in need of money, wrote asking to be re-instated in the service, Benckendorff actually recommended that he should be re-employed and sent to the Caucasus. This suggests that there may have been some private arrangement between Benckendorff and Sherwood and that the latter may have been used as an *agent provocateur*. But there is no proof of this. Before Sherwood received Benckendorff's instructions he was arrested and exiled to his own estate in Smolensk. He still refused to be silenced and sent the Grand Duke further indictments of the Third Section. Dubelt was asked to comment on these charges of mal-administration and muddle. This he did in a singularly terse and laconic manner, stating that all was well in the Section and that they expected 'even greater improvements in the future; the only ones who are dissatisfied are those who would be so, no matter how things stood. . . . This report of Sherwood's is based entirely on rumour.'

The Czar, who took an interest in the case, was convinced that Sherwood had discovered some corruption and inefficiency in the service and, though Sherwood was sentenced to imprisonment, he was allowed special privileges denied to any other prisoners and eventually released.

The one revolutionary the Third Section found it most difficult to contain for some years was Alexander Herzen. The illegitimate son of a wealthy Muscovite, Herzen had been active for many years in underground movements, but he was a highly respected writer who had friends in high places, even inside the Third Section. Herzen was regarded not so much as a dangerous revolutionary as one who stimulated revolutionary ideas. He was watched by the Third Section, but they tended at first to handle him gently, sending for young students and others who associated with him and warning them against Herzen rather than approaching him directly. His memoirs throw much light on the methods of the Third Section.

He was eventually arrested on a trifling matter and there seems little doubt the evidence against him was manufactured by the secret police. Some Third Section agents had encouraged some students to sing seditious songs at a banquet and the students were alleged quite wrongly to be known to Herzen. On another occasion Dubelt sent him a warning in the middle of the night, warning him that he might be exiled. 'Our government is paternal,' said Dubelt; 'everything is done as privately as possible.' Dubelt had enormous powers of self-deception.

When Herzen left Russia in 1847 he went to London where he started an underground newspaper which was smuggled into Russia. The Third Section sent agents to London to keep watch on him there, but they still did not prevent copies of the paper from reaching Russia.

Some of the Third Section's time was wasted by whims of the Czar himself. On one occasion Nicholas wanted to revenge himself on a married woman who had once refused his advances. In 1851 she ran away with a nobleman named Trubetskoy which enraged the Czar. He ordered the Third Section to drop all other work and to track down the runaway couple. At that very moment Dubelt was engaged in tracking down revolutionaries in conjunction with the Austrian and Prussian governments. His mission was called off, the revolutionaries got away, but the pair of lovers were traced to Tiflis and arrested.

For much of the time the Third Section concerned themselves more with examining the works of Russian writers and philosophers than with catching revolutionaries. They sniffed sedition in almost every manifestation of literature and their files read like a hotch-potch of hostile literary reviews written by philistines. Ideas were regarded as almost more dangerous than bomb-throwers. A typical report in the Third Section files was this received on 27 December 1832, by Benckendorff of the philosopher Chaadaev, a friend of Pushkin's:

'He leads a strange life and is writing something of which it is impossible to find out. But it is well known that these works are quietly read and it is said that they are predicated on the reform of Russia and the introduction of the Catholic religion.'

Benckendorff ordered an immediate investigation, only to find that Chaadaev lived a devout and uneventful life, belonged to the Orthodox Church and spent much of his time in prayer. Yet Chaadaev continued to be hounded by the secret police. At the same time Boshniak, the botanist, was sent out with his net and notebook into Pskov province to spy on the poet, Pushkin, because he was suspected of inciting the peasants to revolt. Boshniak was at least honest: he reported to his masters that Pushkin was staying at a monastery, writing an historical play.

The secret police maintained their watch on Pushkin, but the poet managed to retrieve his position quite fortuitously. Late in life he married a beautiful young woman named Natalia Goncharova who immediately caught the eye of the Czar with whom she indulged in a mild flirtation. The Czar, oddly enough, was not jealous of Pushkin, but suddenly became solicitous on his behalf and commissioned the poet to write a history of Peter the Great. The irony of this was that the annuity which the Czar awarded Pushkin was paid by the Third Section! They seem to have got their own back by making irregular payments and by ensuring that he stayed in St Petersburg where they could more easily keep a watch on him. And they still opened all his letters.

When Alexander II became Czar in 1855 there were immediate and dramatic changes in government. Once again a liberal Czar had succeeded a tyrant, but in this instance not even the most humane and liberal of all the Czars could stem the tide of discontent. The evils of Nicholas's reign had burned deeply into the Russian soul: the revolutionaries just could not bring themselves to believe they had a Czar who was anxious to improve their lot. True, Alexander II moved cautiously and perhaps too slowly for the more impatient of the liberal thinkers. Yet he quickly showed his detestation of the police state.

The Third Section had lost much of its original purposefulness by the time Alexander II came to the throne. Its attempt to be the 'educator' of the people and the guardian of their thoughts had long since been frustrated by the ineptness of its handling of the intellectuals and the time wasted in persecuting innocent writers who posed no real threat to anyone. But above all the Third Section had failed to come to grips with the most serious problem it faced – that of the growing menace of Russian revolutionaries in exile. Herzen still managed to have what he called 'the first independent Russian newspaper' printed in a back street off the Caledonian Road in London and smuggled into Russia, yet in 1852

Turgenev was sent to prison for a month because of an obituary he wrote on Gogol.

In the last years of Nicholas's reign increasing attention had been paid by the Third Section to religious sects. This was chiefly at the behest of the Czar himself who regarded the Old Believers, the Chlysty, Skoptsky and Molokani sects as 'dangerous'. A census of the sects was taken by Third Section agents and a detailed report on them given to the Czar. The cult of unorthodox religions had begun simultaneously and without any link between them in France, Germany, the United States and, to a lesser extent, in Britain in the early part of the nineteenth century. By the fifties this cult, which often showed a tendency towards religion with erotic overtones, had reached social circles close to the court of St Petersburg. The Princess Engalychev was put under surveillance because she had been discovered actually creating an heretical sect, while Prince Ivan Sviatopuk-Mirsky was declared insane and incarcerated in a mental home. His 'crime' was that he bought some land in Algeria where he planned to emigrate together with thousands of members of various dissenting sects to found a colony.

Alexander II wanted to move in the direction of liberalisation and dissolved the Special Corps of Gendarmerie, asking for a report to be prepared on the Third Section. At the same time he released a large number of prisoners. It was a major gesture of conciliation, even a risky one, but at the same time the new Czar sought to mitigate the evils of serfdom. But these actions merely ended the worst features of the previous reign, they did not in themselves set right the inequalities and injustices of centuries, nor introduce reforms to which even Catherine the Great had pledged herself.

When Alexander became Czar, Herzen returned to Russia and for a brief period actually co-operated with the authorities. But he was swiftly disillusioned.

The mood of revolutionary thought changed as quickly as the new Czar made modest reforms. The moderate Liberals such as Chicherin were regarded with contempt by men like Herzen. Herzen in his turn was mistrusted by the younger Radicals because he had tried to co-operate with the régime. And so the revolutionary movement swung further to extremes, culminating in the rise of the Anarchists, the Nihilists, Russian Jacobinism and a whole variety of secret societies

The Third Section was no longer the power it had been; its functions had been drastically clipped and the rights of the secret police were considerably reduced. On the other hand Alexander's attempts at moderation had failed, but it would be unfair to attach blame to him alone. He had to contend with the backlash of agitation and resentment against Czardom as a legacy from his predecessor's reign. He was not helped by those Liberals among his bureaucracy who were too timid to progress fast enough and the error was made of failing to accept the proffered co-operation of the moderate Liberals among the revolutionaries. In dissolving the Special Corps of Gendarmerie, Alexander had weakened authority's hold on subversive movements and robbed himself of the one weapon which could have controlled or destroyed the extremists before they had time to gather strength.

In ultimately abolishing the Third Section all the Czar achieved was to merge its members with the civil police under the Ministry of the Interior. What looked on the surface like the ending of the secret political police only meant their perpetuation in a different form, a less dignified and less disciplined form and ultimately a more brutalised force.

This statement may seem a contradiction in the light of the hatred which the Third Section engendered under Nicholas, but harsh and ridiculous as their officers may have been they at least showed some semblance of civilised behaviour. For as the threat of revolution grew so the Czar had to depend more and more on an extensive secret-police network for his own protection. Dolgorukoff became the Czar's new police chief and he took the easy path by advocating drastic censorship of newspapers and keeping watch on such well-known and relatively harmless revolutionaries like Chernyshevsky. As the latter had tried to achieve reforms by the peaceful enough procedure of petitioning the Czar the secret police found it difficult to pin any serious charges against him. In 1861 Chernyshevsky had petitioned the Czar to 'summon delegates elected by the entire Russian nation', stating that this was now the only way of solving satisfactorily the problems which had been raised. Chernyshevsky was by temperament a gentle, reasonable man who had even warned Alexander II of the dangers of a peasant revolt if reforms were not undertaken. The secret police's chance came when they intercepted a letter from Alexander Herzen which had been sent to Chernyshevsky inviting him to co-operate with revolutionaries in exile in London. This gave them the excuse for arresting Chernyshevsky in July 1862. Even then it was two years before he was brought to trial, due to the fact that there was so little real evidence against him that it had to be manufactured. In 1864 he was condemned to fourteen years' hard labour in Siberia.

As the influence of the Liberal leaders waned and as the moderates were arrested so the more fanatical of the revolutionaries extended their activities, not merely inside Russia but to France, Germany and Britain. One of the latter was Pisarev, the son of a noble who had fallen on hard times. He had originally been engaged in running a women's magazine intended as uplifting reading for young ladies of gentle birth, but this most unrevolutionary venture was soon succeeded by the production of a journal called *The Russian Word*, which had a strong radical flavour.

As a politician Pisarèv was a nonentity; he lacked gifts of leadership, quarrelled with other Radicals and his health and mental stability were never strong enough for the cut and thrust of political adventure. He was a sad failure right up until his mysterious death by drowning in July 1868. Yet, one of the founders of nihilism, his inspiration led to the adoption of this creed by many young students whose dress and behaviour were curiously like those of the Hippies of today. And indeed nihilism was in many respects like student anarchism of the nineteen-sixties. It meant the rejection of tradition, history and all ancient wisdom, or, in Pisarev's words, 'What can be smashed, must be smashed. What stands the blow is good, what flies into smithereens is rubbish. In any case hit out right and left; no harm will come of it.'

The secret police concentrated on the young Nihilists. Their agents were sent out to make lengthy reports on them and it is interesting to note how these reports paid more attention to criticising the Nihilists' dress and appearance than to their plots or meetings. Thus, this report on a young female Nihilist: 'She had cropped hair, wears blue glasses, is slovenly in her dress, rejects the use of comb and soap and lives in civil matrimony with an equally repellent individual of the male sex or with several such.'

One name which struck terror into the hearts of many revolutionaries throughout Europe in this era was that of Wilhelm Stieber, the notorious Prussian who revolutionised the whole system of espionage. Stieber started in the legal profession and specialised in criminal cases and, through his close associations with the police, turned to espionage. When in 1848 Europe was in the thralls of political agitation with foment in France and Karl Marx's brand of socialism in Germany, Stieber came into his own. He introduced to Prussia the technique of *agent provocateur*, using it to uncover and trap Radicals and working-class supporters of socialism. The story is told how he influenced Friederich Wilhelm of Prussia by posing as a rabble-rouser in a mob that confronted the King and then managing to get near enough to the monarch to whisper to him that all was well and that he, Stieber, was protecting the King by infiltrating the mob. Whatever the truth of this story Stieber was soon the chief spy-master of Prussia. But this rôle lasted only as long as Friederich remained on the throne. When the latter was pronounced insane and succeeded by Wilhelm I Stieber was given short shrift. His enemies spoke up against him and he was removed from office.

In 1851 Stieber, in his capacity as head of the Prussian espionage service, had gone to London to investigate the activities of Prussian Radicals living in the British capital, including Karl Marx himself. He had not been welcomed by British officialdom and had been given to understand that his investigations in London were disliked. What Stieber had noted then was that a number of Russian revolutionaries were active in London and left unwatched by the authorities.

Seven years later Stieber recalled this discovery and looked up the dossiers he had compiled on the subject. He also remembered that on one occasion he had done the Russians a good turn by hushing up a scandal involving the wife of a Russian attaché in Berlin. So off he went to St Petersburg, to remind the authorities there of his past assistance to a Russian envoy and to give them his dossiers on the Russian revolutionaries in London.

The tactics of the *agent provocateur* were second nature to the Russian Secret Service, but Stieber was able to prove that they could be even more usefully employed outside Russia than inside the country. Despite their suspicion of foreigners, the Russians were impressed by Stieber's dossiers and, guardedly, they asked for his help in reorganising their Secret Service. Stieber could hardly have arrived in St Petersburg at a more opportune moment. The Special Corps of the Gendarmerie had been dissolved and the Third Section was in the process of being absorbed into the control of the Ministry of the Interior, while the Czar was anxious to re-cast the whole Secret Service.

It was an astonishing change of mood and of policy on the part of Alexander II. When he came to the throne he dismissed with ignominy the favourite of Nicholas, the efficient spy-master, General Dubelt, and he had discouraged enthusiastic informers who sought an audience with him. One such brought the Czar some tittle-tattle about a chess player's indiscreet remarks about royalty when his king was in danger of checkmate. Alexander calmly handed the informer twenty-five roubles and told him he was dismissed from the Intelligence Service. Much of the information obtained at a ridiculously high price was fatuous and futile, but Alexander would have been wiser to have called for an overhaul of his Secret Service earlier rather than simply to pooh-pooh such reports as he received. By the time Stieber arrived in St Petersburg the writing was on the wall for Alexander and it was clear that he could no longer afford to neglect even the meanest intelligence report. The price he had paid for his lenience, tolerance and disdain for the secret police and their informers was that his life was permanently in danger. The more fanatical of the revolutionaries were constantly plotting to assassinate him.

Russian historians have differed as to whether Nicholas or Loris Melikoff instituted the Ochrana. Archives prove nothing conclusively and some dispute the exact rôle played by Stieber in its creation. Suffice to say that under Alexander the Third Section was restored and the Secret Police were merged into a Department of State Protection which ultimately became the *Okhrannoye Otdyelyenye*, or the Ochrana.

Wilhelm Stieber was certainly not trusted sufficiently to allow him to play a part in the formation of the Department of State Protection as far as its internal work was concerned. Nor did he stay long in Russia. But he was undoubtedly well paid for the work he did there. His assignment was to advise on and to help organise an external spy system for Russia which would enable them to track down revolutionaries, Radicals, criminals, blackmailers and forgers who had left their homeland. Unquestionably Prussia remained his first concern and he passed on to the Russians information concerning only their own nationals abroad and never gave away any Prussian secrets. Ultimately he became the supreme spy-master in Europe under Bismarck.

Stieber suggested to the Russians that if they set out to locate Russian criminals, forgers and blackmailers in Paris, London and elsewhere, they might be able to 'persuade' them to spy on suspected Russian anarchists and revolutionaries in the areas where they lived. The idea was that the criminals in exile could be offered immunity from arrest if they agreed to assist the Russian Secret Service and would be paid to spy on their fellow-countrymen and, more important, to play the part of *agents provocateurs*.

The new head of the secret police was Count P. A. Schuvaloff, an able Europeanised Russian, conservative in outlook, but full of energy and with a grasp of foreign policy that made him invaluable to the Czar. He had his doubts about the wisdom of the Stieber policy all the time he held this post from 1866 until 1874. Then he reverted to the Diplomatic Service and became Ambassador in London. His experiences in London convinced him that, as he mentioned in a dispatch to St Petersburg: 'There is no end to this game of spies. From what I see here in London you set the criminal exiles to spy on the Radicals and then, to be quite sure, you need to find spies to watch the criminals, and it has even happened that a criminal is spying on the very Radical who has been selected by one of my attachés to spy on the criminal. I do not say this is but an exception, but the fact that it happens at all is surely an indication of how such madness can spread.'

6

The Ochrana

AN ECHO of Russian espionage in the seventies of the last century was heard in a celebrated High Court case in February 1927, when Captain Peter Wright brought an action for libel against Lord Gladstone, the son of the great Liberal Prime Minister of Britain.

The case for the prosecution was based on a letter Lord Gladstone had sent to the secretary of the Bath Club, of which Wright had been a member, calling Wright 'a foul fellow'. These proceedings arose out of a book written by Wright in which he stated that Gladstone the Prime Minister had the habit 'in public to speak the language of the highest and strictest principle, and in private to pursue and possess every sort of woman.'

As the trial developed Wright sought to justify these allegations. He maintained that Gladstone had constantly made the acquaintance of London street women, and argued that his attitude towards the Turkish-Russian troubles at the time of the Bulgarian atrocities had changed completely as a result of his consorting with Olga Novikoff, a 'beautiful spy' sent to England by the Czarist Government, who were well aware of Gladstone's weakness, for the express purpose of seducing him.

This assertion produced much argument and counter-argument. An extract was quoted from a book entitled *The Fall of Czardom*, by Carl Joubert, which referred to the '*Corps d'élite*' of ladies' who, on behalf of the Czarist régime, were despatched to the various capitals of the world as emissaries. Nevertheless, Peter Wright was unable to establish his allegations about Gladstone and lost his case.

There was, however, more than wild tittle-tattle and malicious innuendo behind these charges. Had Captain Wright made deeper research into the subject he could have found much more evidence that was damaging to Gladstone's political judgement and ill-chosen associations with women even if he could not support charges of moral turpitude.

Carl Joubert's allegation of a '*Corps d'élite*' of ladies acting on behalf of the Czarist régime as emissaries and spies was not without foundation, though in his book he so sensationalised his account of them and their activities that some of it ceased to be credible. But these women were not employed by the Ochrana: their activities were usually either confined to direct reports to the Czar or to the Russian Foreign Office. A number of them were to be found in Paris, some in London and, surprisingly enough, as many as ten in Washington.

One of the reasons for their presence in Washington was to stir up trouble between the United States and Britain. Relations between Russia and Britain were strained between 1876 and 1880 and war between the two nations seemed imminent on more than one occasion. Scope for trouble-making, reported one of the Russian ladies in Washington, Anna Popova, lay in 'aiming to make common cause between the Government of the United States and the American-Irish rebels, or the Fenians, as they call themselves.'

This report back to St Petersburg was pondered on in the Foreign Office and regarded with grave suspicion by the diplomats. They were horrified at the idea of having any truck with the American-Irish rebels, assuming them to be the same as any other revolutionaries, dynamiters and assassins. Possibly because of this the report was shown to General Loris Melikoff, who had helped to abolish the old Political Police and was now building them up again with the object of using spies to infiltrate revolutionary organisations. Melikoff immediately saw possibilities in Madame Popova's suggestion. True, these revolutionaries were not Russians, but they were nevertheless a secret society dedicated to revolution and, by infiltrating them, something might be learned of their methods. At the worst, new light might be shed on revolutionary tactics; at best, the Fenians could be used as allies against Britain in time of need.

So Madame Popova was instructed to make contact with the Fenians and to send detailed reports to St Petersburg.

Madame Popova knew some of the Fenian leaders such as O'Donovan Rossa and Colonel Clingen. She was able to report back to Russia that the Fenian membership totalled more than 11,000, that they had a complete secret society organisation, with passwords, codes, solemn oaths and penalties for giving away information which included the death sentence. They were pledged, as part of their constitution, to 'prepare unceasingly for an armed insurrection [against Britain] in Ireland'.

This wily spy suddenly announced that for health reasons she was leaving Washington and going to spend the winter in Florida. Here she set herself up in a villa and entertained various Americans of influence in both Congress and the Senate. One of these was Senator Jones of Florida and Anna used her wiles to persuade him to put Dr Carroll, one of the Fenian leaders, in touch with the Russian Ambassador in Washington. Soon Carroll and the Ambassador were discussing the feasibility of Irish intervention on the side of Russia should war break out in Europe involving Britain.

Thomas Beach, a British spy who had infiltrated the Fenian Society, learned of these talks between the American-Irish revolutionaries and the Russians and reported back to London on the matter. 'Wild and absurd as the idea at first appears,' he wrote, 'these negotiations were in the end completed and developed to the stage of regular diplomatic contact at headquarters in Russia.'

Nothing much came of the overtures, but that was largely because of doubts on the wisdom of the project in St Petersburg. But Anna Popova attempted a little further mischief on her own account and for her own financial benefit. She had at one time been the mistress of a senior Russian naval officer who had been keenly interested in the development of the submarine. A German, Wilhelm Bauer, had been responsible for designing the first German submarine in 1850. This project had been taken up by the German Army, but hastily dropped when the diving trials ended disastrously. Bauer next tried to interest the Austrians in his plan for a submarine and then, having failed with them, went to England and found an ally first in Prince Albert and then in Lord Palmerston. But Bauer's new craft sank during trials and all his crew with her. So Bauer took himself off to Russia where he made a surprise and spectacular entrance into port to show off his submarine. When Alexander II was crowned Bauer shipped over a band to Russia to celebrate the occasion by playing the Russian national anthem under water.

Bauer had no luck with the Russians, but Anna Popova's lover somehow acquired the plans of his craft and, when he died, they came into Anna's possession. She sold the plants to the Fenians for a reputed sum of 500 dollars. Whether or not they actually worked on these plans is not clear, but they managed to build at a cost of 37,000 dollars a submarine torpedo boat on the Jersey side of the North River. But, according to the report of the British agent, Beach, nothing came of the plan and the craft lay at New Haven until it rotted.

Gladstone's attempts at diplomatic ventures with the Russians were carried out single-handed, in great secrecy, and with the co-operation of at least two women. It should be explained that one of the reasons, political prejudice apart, why Gladstone in his lifetime and after his death was alleged to be a notorious womaniser was because of his extraordinary spare-time activity of rescuing prostitutes. Gladstone walked the streets of London in quest of fallen women, whom he befriended and tried to rescue.

Sometimes he took them back to his own home to meet his wife. He spent more than £80,000 of his own money in this rescue work, helping to found a number of 'homes of mercy' for them.

One of the girls Gladstone rescued was listed in the records as 'K.F.' She became a young lady's maid, then a nurse to a Russian family and finally English governess to two young Georgian princesses in Tiflis, daughters of the ex-King of Georgia. In 1878 'K.F.' returned to London and sought an interview with Gladstone, after which she wrote to a friend, a Mrs Baglay: 'What was most gratifying was that Mr G. told me that three years ago my report on what was happening not only in Bulgaria, but in Bosnia and at Salonica . . . had convinced him that he must write a pamphlet on this subject as this was the first report he had had from someone on the spot.'

'K.F.' may have been reformed in the sense that she was no longer a prostitute, but she had utilised the talents she had acquired in the oldest profession in the pursuit of espionage for the Russians. 'K.F.' had become the mistress of an agent of the secret police who was quick to realise the importance of her past links with Gladstone. He soon enrolled her as a Russian spy, taking care to insinuate that Russia desired only the friendship of England and to win Gladstone's support. Soon 'K.F.', who was known by the code-name of 'Katerina', was supplying regular intelligence to St Petersburg, especially on events in Georgia. It was from 'K.F.' in Tiflis that Olga Novikoff, one of the most assiduous Russian spies of the day, learned of Gladstone's passion for reforming whores and of how much 'K.F.' owed to the great statesman.

The background to all this was that in the spring of 1878 the Balkans were ablaze when a revolt against misrule sprang up in Bosnia and Herzegovina and the Turks put down a rising in Bulgaria with great brutality. Russia, Austria and Germany agreed upon a plan for imposing on the Turks a number of reforms to be carried out under the supervision of certain European countries. France and Italy indicated they would join in, but England, as represented by Disraeli, refused point-blank to have anything to do with the proposals. Gladstone took the view that Britain was in honour bound to take some action. In resounding speeches up and down the country he demanded that the Turks 'one and all, bag and baggage, shall I hope clear out from the province they have desolated and profaned.'

It was this Balkan problem which brought Gladstone into direct contact with Madame Novikoff. She was then thirty-eight years old, strikingly handsome and irresistibly fascinating to men. She came from an old Muscovite family, the Kireieffs and had been brought up in an atmosphere of keen intellectual pursuits. Olga

Kireieff's older brothers were leaders of what was known as the Slavophil movement. With the Aksakoffs and the Homiakoffs they proclaimed against the westernised Liberals that the Russian people, with its devotion to authority and its deep religious faith, had a special mission in the world since Western civilisation, having become materialistic and rationalistic, was nearing its fall. They had a vision of Russia as a land of free Christian communes under a fatherly autocracy preserving their faith and bringing new life and light into the world.

In due course some of those closest to the Czar felt that, despite Olga Novikoff's Slavophil ideas, certain of her sympathies could be enlisted in the services of the Czarist régime. She was sent on various missions to London, which she had already visited on many occasions in the early seventies. Superficially they were innocent enough. At that time her interests were chiefly ecclesiastical and she was regarded with much respect in London as an authority on such affairs as the Ecumenical Conference.

Originally it was Madame Novikoff's ecumenical ideas which most appealed to Gladstone. As her spy-masters in St Petersburg had told her, this was the way to Gladstone's heart. Then, playing on the theme of her brother's death in action against the Turks, she sought to stir his imagination on Turkish atrocities. At various dates throughout 1876 Gladstone and Olga Novikoff were meeting and writing to one another, mainly on political topics. In her book, *Russian Memories*, Madame Novikoff described how she attended a conference at St James's Hall, London, on the Eastern question and that, as she left the hall, Gladstone 'gave me his arm' and escorted her on foot to Claridge's Hotel.

The rôle Olga played during the long crisis which led up to the Russo-Turk War of 1877–78 after nearly provoking a rupture between Britain and Russia was a subtle one and Olga was worth at least two battalions, if not more, to the Russian cause. The intelligence she obtained in London was certainly of great value to the Russians for she uncovered much of the deviousness of British foreign policy at the time and, with a woman's intuition, interpreted it accurately.

Olga Novikoff was not a spy in the conventional sense of the word: she was far too outspoken an idealist and too much of an individualist for that. But she served the purposes of the Secret Service and the more devious minds of the Russian military. They both wanted to press ahead in the Balkans and against Turkey. As the Russian general Skobelev said when Russia declared war against Turkey in 1877, 'The stronger Russia is in Central Asia, the weaker England is in India and the more conciliatory she will be in Europe.'

*　　　*　　　*

During the sixties and seventies of the last century a number of Russian Radicals formed an exiles' colony in Switzerland where they set out to propagate their ideas for revolution. On the advice of the Third Section the Czar ordered them to return to the fatherland, in default of which they would lose their passports.

The threat largely succeeded and a number of the Radicals returned to Russia where they set up the innocently named Truth and Freedom Society, the aims of which were the abolition of the Czarist Government and a socialist state. Some of the leaders were arrested and sent to Siberia and the society became very much an impoverished underground movement which existed in cellars in the large cities. But widespread disaffection and dismay at the manner in which Russia threw away the advantages gained at the end of the Russo-Turkish War helped to swell their membership and the society linked up with the much more formidable Nihilist organisation. Matters reached a climax when a Nihilist girl, Vera Zassulich, shot the chief of police, General Trepoff, in St Petersburg.

The General had been a hated figure for many years on account of his record of brutality. Vera Zassulich was determined if necessary to be a martyr for her cause. She shot down Trepoff openly in his office and made no attempt to escape afterwards. The Government was convinced that she would easily be convicted, but this belief was swiftly shaken. The attractive and youthful Vera won the sympathy of the masses and, more important, of the jury, and she was acquitted. The police tried to re-arrest her as she left the court, but she managed to escape and went abroad.

The success of Vera Zassulich caused the extremer Radicals and the Nihilists to believe that a systematic campaign of assassination would succeed where other measures failed. The plotters made a list of notable men who were to be killed. This had the effect of losing the revolutionaries the support of the Liberals, but it greatly strengthened the underground movement. In August 1878, two revolutionaries, Kravchinsky and Mikhailoff, killed Mezentsev, then head of the Third Section, by stabbing him at midday in a crowded street in St Petersburg, escaping afterwards in a carriage. A pamphlet, entitled *A Death for a Death*, distributed surreptitiously in the streets, explained the purpose of the killing. It was clear that the revolutionaries' first aim was to destroy the key figures in the Secret Police, then to find and burn their archives and, finally, to disrupt the Secret Service. Soon afterwards the Governor of Kharkov, the chiefs of police in Kiev and St Petersburg and other high officials were assassinated.

The next step taken by the revolutionaries was to sentence the

Czar to death at a secret meeting of the Truth and Freedom Society. A few months later the plotters struck again: a young man approached the Czar as the latter took his usual unaccompanied stroll in the streets and fired a shot at him. But he was so nervous and inexperienced that he missed completely. Two further attempts were made on the Czar's life, but he continued to have a charmed existence. A train in which he was thought to be travelling was dynamited; twenty people were killed, but the Czar was elsewhere. Then a Nihilist named Stepanoff made his way into the Winter Palace, placed a bomb near the dining-room, which was completely destroyed, but again the Czar escaped injury.

By this time it was clear even to the Czar that the reorganisation of the Secret Police was far from effective and it was he who sent for General Loris Melikoff and asked him to take charge of all counter-espionage activities, including the building up of the *agents provocateurs*.

Melikoff's direction of the new organisation made an immediate impact. He was a shrewd judge of character and, moreover, knew how to pick infiltrators. His orders were that Mikhailoff, the killer of the former head of the Third Section, was to be caught at all costs. Very soon his infiltrators succeeded in trapping not only Mikhailoff, but Goldenberg, another member of the Truth and Freedom Society. Under cross-examination Goldenberg cracked and revealed that the society was in such a desperate plight that only a speeding up of their terror killings could save them from extinction: the truth was that their terror tactics had frightened away many would-be supporters. It then transpired that in order to speed up the killings the society had secured the services of an engineer named Kibaltchich, who had invented a new type of bomb. Goldenberg revealed much more than this: he gave Melikoff the names and addresses of other key figures in the society as well as information about the secret presses on which the underground newspapers were printed.

'Who controls these presses?' Melikoff asked Goldenberg.

'The master-mind is Mikhailoff,' replied Goldenberg.

Melikoff then gave orders that the prison guards who kept watch on Mikhailoff were to be replaced by his own spies. The latter were given instructions to pretend to be mildly sympathetic to the cause of the Truth and Freedom Society and to pretend to smuggle out of prison any letters Mikhailoff might try to give them. Mikhailoff was suspicious at first, but eventually asked one of the guards to take a message to his fellow revolutionaries.

This message was delivered to General Melikoff. It was a lengthy document and in cipher. Fortunately Melikoff had not only organised a new cryptographical department but had sent members of his force to study cryptography in Germany, then regarded as supreme in this field. His cipher team did not take long to break down the codes used and they found that the document was a long article on the misfortunes of the working classes which was evidently intended to be published in one of the underground newspapers. Melikoff then knew that if he allowed the message to be dispatched it would inevitably lead to at least one secret press, and possibly others as well.

His deduction proved right. One of the presses was discovered and other arrests were made. But Melikoff did not make these arrests at once. He took a note of the addresses of all the new suspects and infiltrated his spies into their lodgings with the result that instead of arresting just a few revolutionaries a round-up was made of several others. It was as well for Melikoff that he took this precaution for he learned to his consternation that one of the revolutionary leaders was actually a man holding a prominent position inside his own department. As a result of this he also learned of another plan for the assassination of the Czar.

The plan was vague and lacking in detail, but it was clear that it had been much more carefully thought out than any previous attempt and that the plotters aimed to remove the elements of failure which had previously marred their efforts.

Melikoff was in a quandary that might have caused a lesser man to panic. He had been charged by the Czar to reorganise the Secret Police and to wipe out those who were inefficient or of doubtful loyalty inside his service. To reveal what he had discovered might give the Czar cause to dismiss him from office. And, if he prematurely revealed the fact that another coup was being planned, he also ran the risk of not finding out its full details. Arrests would only drive the men chosen to carry out the assassination into cover.

Some have suggested that Melikoff was less anxious about the Czar's life than he was to round up the Nihilists and revolutionaries. Others have even hinted that he believed that with the Czar out of the way he felt he could achieve more positive results in defeating the Nihilists. Such allegations, however, ignore the fact that Loris Melikoff and the Czar were both liberal in their outlook. Melikoff had, in fact, acquired wide powers because of his liberal reputation. All the police forces, the Third Section and the Ministry of the Interior had come under his control and his task was to co-ordinate them. He had not only relaxed press censorship to some extent, feeling that this might curtail the underground newspapers, but he had urged Alexander to sign a constitution which would have made some slight concessions to the Liberals.

Melikoff took a bold risk in allowing Mikhailoff to be released from prison and then having him shadowed. To make sure Mikhailoff did not try to escape, or in case he suspected he was being watched, Melikoff assigned thirty men to take it in turns to follow him in threes. Mikhailoff led the spies who were shadowing him to the headquarters of the Nihilist Executive Committee, which, most incongruously, was situated in a cheese factory.

Melikoff was puzzled at first as to why a cheese factory had been chosen for the secret headquarters and why some of the Nihilists appeared to be carrying on business selling cheese. It then dawned on him that the clue to this probably lay in the choice of the street – Malaya Sadova Street. It was along this street that once or twice a week the Czar passed regularly either on foot or in his carriage to visit his former mistress, the Princess Catherine. It must be here, argued Melikoff, that the assassins were planning their new coup.

And so it proved to be. Kibaltchich had designed a new bomb which, at whatever angle it was thrown, or at whatever angle it hit its target, would explode. This time the plotters had decided to leave nothing to chance. From the cheese factory they had dug a tunnel under the street and mined it at regular intervals; they had also nominated four bomb throwers to complete their work if the mining failed. And if Melikoff had fooled Mikhailoff, the latter had also deceived Melikoff, for it was learned that all the time he had been in prison he had passed out detailed instructions to all the Nihilists taking part in the coup. Not even Melikoff's cipher team had realised that Mikhailoff had concealed a second cipher in the enciphered document he had sent to the underground press. He had passed on a series of messages concealed in the text of the article by employing a Russian variant of the celebrated Bilateral Cipher of Francis Bacon.

The result was that Melikoff's efforts to destroy the plotters failed. He did not dare to tell the Czar what he had discovered about the cheese factory, but merely begged him to remain in his palace while he carried out certain secret investigations. Had the Czar agreed to this plan, Melikoff believed he would have had time to round up the killers. But the Czar insisted on making his usual trips outside the palace and was irritated by Melikoff's evasiveness about why such precautions were necessary. There had been so many abortive attempts on his life that Alexander was now almost indifferent to them. Melikoff, in a desperate attempt to save the situation, arrested Zhelyaboff, the second-in-command of the conspiracy under Mikhailoff. He was certain that this would delay the activities of the plotters and cause them to postpone the attempt on the Czar's life. But Melikoff reckoned without those precise ciphered instructions which Mikhailoff had smuggled out of prison. Zhelyaboff's place was automatically taken over by his mistress, Sophya Perovskaya, who took over the leading rôle. It was she who, on Sunday, 1 March 1881, gave the signal with a white handkerchief that the Czar's sledge was about to pass along Malaya Sadova Street.

The first bomb killed two of the Czar's Cossack guards; then, as Alexander dismounted to go to their aid, a second bomb killed him.

Thus Mikhailoff's careful planning, his patience and allowance for all possible risks had paid off. He had anticipated that the prison guards who posed as sympathisers of the revolutionaries might show the correspondence he was smuggling out to his comrades to the Secret Police. Again he feared that the Secret Police would be able to decipher his article, but he knew they would let it go through to his confederates if only to find out where his secret press was situated. The cipher within a cipher was Mikhailoff's own idea. Most men would have been content to risk that alone. But not Mikhailoff, who knew that Melikoff had an expert team of cipher-crackers. In writing in his second message into the article Mikhailoff had to indicate the hidden dispatch by breaks between the letters. But he anticipated that if he made obvious breaks, the cipher-crackers would become suspicious, so he put the text in five-letter groups and, when wishing to indicate that the count was to end on a given letter, he lifted his pen between that letter and the next, and, when he wished it to continue, ran the letters together.

Zhelyaboff, Sophya Perovskaya and Kibaltchich, who invented the bombs, were all executed. Yet Melikoff's biggest blunder was in paying so little attention to Kibaltchich when he busily scribbled away in prison. His scribblings and diagrams were immediately suspected of containing secret messages and were handed over to the cipher-cracking team. The latter could make no sense of any of them and, instead of questioning Kibaltchich, they decided to destroy the papers in case they contained a cipher they could not crack.

Kibaltchich had insisted that his writings and his sketches were merely plans for an aeroplane. One military expert who saw them insisted they were genuine and contained technically accurate plans for the construction of a flying machine with detailed instructions of how it was to be used. But Melikoff was adamant: the papers were to be burnt.

And burnt they were, so the Russians lost a chance of putting themselves far ahead of any nation in the world in aerial development.

The Ochrana developed slowly at first out of the Secret Police system of Alexander's reign. It was responsible not merely for watching revolutionaries inside Russia, or for keeping under surveillance conspirators abroad, but for the organisation of a great deal of foreign espionage and for controlling the issue of passports.

It was, in fact, a comprehensive, co-ordinated espionage and counter-espionage organisation, the most total form of espionage devised in the latter part of the nineteenth century and still forming the basis of Soviet espionage and counter-espionage organisations today. It developed from many influences, from the ancient tradition of a Russian police state, from the ideas of individual reformers of the secret police system and, not least, from foreign experiments, especially the ideas of Stieber and Bismarck.

Officialdom in Russia had a great admiration for the German system of espionage and counter-espionage and, as we have seen, a determined attempt was made as far back as the middle of the eighteenth century to learn from the Germans the arts of cryptography and deciphering. By the latter part of the nineteenth century Russia had much benefited from this. It was, however, an extremely difficult business in St Petersburg to be sure of the secrecy of any cipher, because every embassy was inevitably obliged to employ Russian servants and subordinates in the domestic affairs of the house, and it was an easy matter for the secret police to obtain agents among their number.

The main fault of the Ochrana organisation lay in its extravagance, the vast sums of money spent on carrying out its work and the large number of agents it employed. True, it obtained results, but often at a disproportionate cost and in a lowering of its own standards through employing so many mediocrities both in the field and in its own bureaucratic ranks. Its motto, briefly, was to turn Russia into a nation of spies, imbuing everyone with the belief that it was a patriotic duty to spy on one's fellow citizens. Thus espionage became an essay in mass observation.

So much mass information merely multiplied the number of bureaucrats called upon to handle and sift it. Much of the information through which they laboriously had to pore was ineffectual, inaccurate, irrelevant or even false. Innocent people were condemned as spies by malevolent persons seeking revenge for personal reasons. Many dangerous revolutionaries went unsuspected.

No doubt some of the allegations made against the Ochrana were grossly exaggerated, but it was nevertheless a terrifying organisation and employed methods of torture and interrogation quite as barbarous as anything practised in earlier ages. When a secret police organisation is as unwieldy, as all-powerful and as clumsy as the Ochrana was, it must inevitably be prone to abuses.

The Ochrana also suffered from the practice that when a new

Minister of the Interior was appointed he retired his Chief of Police and brought a new man to this post. This seriously interfered with the efficiency of the Ochrana by destroying continuity of experience and knowledge. A retiring Police Chief would often take his secrets with him and not pass them on to his successor. Quite often he would take his files with him, too.

The Minister of the Interior was still empowered to open private correspondence as a measure of protection to the State. Similarly the Police Department maintained regular contact with the heads of the Post and Telegraph Office on the subject of whose correspondence was to be examined. Almost all post coming from foreign countries was intercepted. The censorship posts, set up at all large centres, were known as 'Black Cabinets'. That such censorship went on was well known to the Russian people and equally to Russian exiles overseas, so that not a great deal of worthwhile information was obtained in this way from straightforward correspondence. It was the hidden message which the censors were always on the look out for and gradually methods were introduced to defeat the censorship. Invisible inks began to be employed and at first these were found to be more effective than new ciphers which the Ochrana bureaucracy were adept at cracking.

The Ochrana agents had their own secret codes for communications and sending of reports, usually depending not so much on codes or ciphers as on translating material into what sounded like ordinary commercial transactions. This was a humourless, somewhat obvious technique that owed more to a study of the rigid Teutonic methods of espionage than to Slav imagination. Thus when an agent was sent to track down a suspect he would send out terse daily telegrams to indicate his progress and to let his superiors know what he was doing. If he lost contact, a telegram might simply say 'Parcel lost in transit'; if he had located where his man was he would signal 'consignment arrived safely'; if the man had escaped from Russia, he would probably telegraph 'consignment re-routed to Zurich'. The Ochrana headquarters in St Petersburg would then hand over the quest for the suspect to their Foreign Agency. These businesslike communications were effective in that they were simple and terse, but the agents, not being trusted with ciphers, could not go into details when making reports in this way. Consequently the lack of information often left headquarters guessing at the real state of affairs.

The revolutionary societies were quick to detect any lack of diligence by the Ochrana and equally swift in combating the watchfulness of the Ochrana by ruses of their own. The leaders of these secret societies kept their true identities hidden far better than did the Ochrana agents more often than not. Their true names were hidden not only from the Ochrana but from their own rank and file, using nicknames or code-names. Rarely could any revolutionary be sure who his leader was and all communications between them were carried on by using false addresses. In addition most of the leaders fixed themselves up with false passports on which they often travelled to and from Russia. Whenever possible these secret societies set up headquarters outside Russia; Switzerland was a favourite place and many revolutionary activities were directed from cells in Berne and Zurich.

Even in the seventies the revolutionaries had been successful in infiltrating the Secret Police. A. D. Mikhailoff had succeeded in getting one of his henchmen, Kletochnikoff, into a key post in police headquarters and while there Kletochnikoff had provided the revolutionaries with lists of names of police spies and details of movements and arrests. Even after the executions that followed Czar Alexander II's assassination the revolutionaries went underground and re-formed into new groups.

The new monarch, Alexander III, was a strong ruler, but inflexible. He was inclined to back Sergei Yulyevich Witte, who eventually became Minister of Finance, in his effort to create a new, industrialised Russia, but it was an experiment doomed to failure in the long-term because in effect it impoverished the peasants in order to provide capital for industrial development. This made the peasants turn more towards the revolutionaries, but Russia owed a great debt to Witte, who was far-sighted, vigorous and efficient and encouraged foreign capital to come into Russia. Witte was one of the first to realise the value of commercial espionage and funds devoted to this did not endear him to the Ochrana who were always suspicious of any independent espionage organisation.

A. T. Vassilyev, the historian of the Ochrana, declared that the Ochrana had 'a very much more difficult task to perform than the police of any country in Western Europe'. This was not, he said, because the Russian people were more troublesome to rule, but 'while in England, France and America the intelligent classes of the people in earlier times were always genuine patriots and fought to uphold national institutions, that was in Russia unfortunately not the case, and had not been so from the first years of the nineteenth century.'

The agents of the Ochrana were organised into detachments responsible for specific duties. For example one detachment would be told to watch theatres and hotels and to report on people seen there; others would be detailed to keep watch at railway stations and on trains. Their hours were long and the demands made upon them exorbitant. They were expected to make lengthy reports whether there was anything worthwhile reporting or not. The result was frequently a mass of dreary, unconnected, incoherent observations which made a farce of the profession of espionage. Agents were frequently called upon to disguise themselves as cab-drivers, porters, door-keepers, newspaper-vendors, soldiers, sailors or railway officials. The Ochrana kept a vast store of uniforms and clothes, wigs, medals and even of horses and cabs in a central store in St Petersburg that was open day and night to provide suitable disguises.

Lyov Tolstoy provides a perfect record of the absurdities of much of the Ochrana information-gathering. Describing how in 1897 he was shadowed while visiting St Petersburg, Tolstoy said that he was never left alone by the Ochrana the whole time he was in the city. This is borne out by the Ochrana records of the period in which he was listed not as the celebrated writer but as 'Lieutenant Lyov Nikolaievitch Tolstoy, retired'. Thus he was described on his file card which recorded in great detail the colour of his hair, his clothes, what type of tobacco he purchased when he entered a shop, the menu he had for his lunch, how long he stayed at his table, how much his meal cost, where he walked, to whom he raised his hat. And Tolstoy in this period was one of the best known figures in Russia and certainly not indulging in subversive activities.

The training of agents was thorough, but hardly imaginative. The new recruit was appointed to a town or district. First he had to learn the topography of the area, to know all the streets and lanes in it. Then he had to visit and become thoroughly acquainted with every tavern, café and bar and to memorise the railway time-tables for the area and the times at which local factories started and ceased work each day. He was compelled to put in a daily detailed report of where he had been and what he had seen, even including such minutiae as the comings and goings of students and what they did in their spare time. It was on these reports that he was judged, not so much on the quality of his observations as on the quantity of details he recorded.

Once he had proved himself he was given tasks which took him further afield and which often thrust him into real danger. He was then informed that any sentimental attachment to his wife, parents or children would be regarded with disfavour and as a mark of 'unreliability'. Those agents who progressed in their work had to show great initiative and to prove themselves competent in a variety of jobs. For example, the really first-rate agent was expected to drive a horse and cab like a professional, for all such agents were frequently required to pose as cab-drivers and to keep watch on suspects this way.

There was a certain snobbery in their spying. The important suspect was often graded according to his rank or birth. The nobler he was the more agents were assigned to watch him; the humblest would be assigned to a single agent.

The main body of the Ochrana were dedicated policemen and bureaucrats who lived for their work and retired only through old age. But the vast army of recruits to the service included members of the nobility, members of the Duma, professors, students, former criminals (usually employed as professional assassins) and prostitutes. The Foreign Agency in particular had to cast its net very wide to find a type of agent who would not easily be recognised as an Ochrana member, or be suspected of being one. It was this branch of the service that employed prostitutes and courtesans and they often proved invaluable in watching revolutionaries in exile abroad, sometimes themselves posing as revolutionaries and aiming to get employment as couriers for the revolutionary and socialist secret societies.

Though total expenditure on this form of espionage was great, the pay to individual agents was not high. A first-rate agent might hope to earn as much as fifty to eighty roubles a month, but more often pay was not much more than forty roubles on average and the vast majority received as little as twenty a month. Many Jews found themselves attracted to the Ochrana, more out of fear and in the hope of personal security than for the actual money obtained. Usually Jews were volunteers who came into the service by offering information, or by betraying colleagues; very rarely were they actually recruited by the Ochrana itself. They had the reputation of being prepared to betray people for trifling sums and this may have induced outbreaks of that anti-semitism which have so often been prevalent in Russian history. In fact the Jews got a bad name not only for aiding the Ochrana but for being revolutionaries as well. They were well represented in both camps.

Yet if this was the case, it was at least understandable. From the beginning of the century the Jews had been forced to live in the fifteen provinces of the Pale in south-west Russia. They were discriminated against and often persecuted, not merely individually but sometimes in particularly barbaric pogroms. Therefore it was not surprising that in order to survive some sought the safety of officialdom, especially in a service such as the Ochrana and occasionally in the foreign branch of the Secret Service.

The Jews were particularly useful in providing intelligence during the Russo-Turkish war of 1877–78 and it was largely through their aid that a new code prepared for Osman Pasha, the Turkish leader, by experts from Germany was laboriously broken down. This coup was to some extent aided by the fact that Osman

Pasha did not himself have a copy of the special limited edition of the new Turkish army code-book. The only officer who possessed this had gone on a scouting expedition while Osman fumed impatiently for his return before he could read an important dispatch. But three days passed before his return and by that time the Russians had cut Osman's communications with Constantinople and surrounded him at Plevna. The Russians had discovered that it was exceedingly difficult to obtain dependable spies among the population in Turkish-held lands and at first they had to rely mainly on the Jews. However, the successes against the Turks, as the Russians advanced, eventually convinced the Slavs in territories adjacent to Turkey that the Czar was their liberator. From then on the foreign branch of the Russian Secret Service depended heavily on Bulgarians.

One pro-Russian of somewhat hybrid origins – part Slav, part Turk and part Greek – offered his services to the Russians during the war of 1877–78 and joined the Greek Legion of the Czar. It wasn't long before his linguistic abilities and knowledge of the Turkish terrain were brought to the attention of the military intelligence of the Czar. This agent, listed in the records as 'Zec', was asked to pose as a Turkish soldier. He packed a Turkish uniform in a waterproof cape, swam across a river into Turkey and made his way to Plevna. There he more than justified the confidence the Russians had placed in him. He linked up with a battalion of Turkish troops, and by a secret messenger service which he arranged himself sent regular reports of Turkish movements, supplies, details and sketches of batteries and gun emplacements and full accounts of what was going on in the garrison. Finally he slipped out of the Turkish lines and brought to the Russians the news that Osman had decided to move out of his fortress.

Under Alexander III the Ochrana underwent important organisational changes when Ratchkovsky was appointed head of the Foreign Branch of the Secret Service. Ratchkovsky turned to the French for ideas and borrowed many of their techniques in espionage. He was as pro-French as he was anti-German; he had an obsessional mistrust of the Germans and suspected that they were well aware of Russian methods and had learned too much from Stieber about how the Russian Secret Service worked.

Ratchkovsky rose to power from humble beginnings. He had scant education, but by diligence and cunning had been promoted from the rank of a minor clerk in Government offices in Kiev and Odessa to become a secret agent of the Third Section in 1879. Yet evidence suggests that he had started to revolutionise Ochrana tactics as far back as the sixties.

For a while he won the favour of Alexander III, but he overstepped the mark when he started to pry into the private life of the Princess Iurievskaya, the widow of Alexander II, who had gone to live in France. He compiled a dossier containing some disgraceful allegations of immorality and intrigue about the Princess and her children. When news of this report reached the Czar he sent for Ratchkovsky and ordered him to cease meddling in such matters or else he would be instantly dismissed.

Curiously, Ratchkóvsky did not learn his lesson from this incident. Under Czar Nicholas II he became alarmed at the number of charlatans and fortune-tellers who insinuated their way into the Court, mostly at the behest of the superstitious Czarina. He made an adverse report on one of them, a dubious schemer and crystal-gazer named Philippe. Plehve, the Minister of the Interior, learned of the report, feared repercussions from the Czar and asked the then chief of police, Lopuchin, to investigate Ratchkovsky. Lopuchin put in a devastatingly unfavourable report on Ratchkovsky who was dismissed after the Czar had been consulted. But this was far from being the end of Ratchkovsky's career.

The real power of the Internal Agency of the Ochrana under Nicholas II, who succeeded Alexander III, was, however, Zubatoff, head of the Moscow Ochrana. Encouraged by the Czar to build up an expensive but efficient counter-espionage service, he re-modelled the Ochrana in the latter part of the last century. He saw clearly that the revolutionary movements were in most cases as cunningly and competently organised as the Ochrana itself and that, because there were so many of them, they presented a bigger threat than a single revolutionary organisation would have done. His aim was to win adherents from the revolutionaries themselves. Whenever the Ochrana arrested any suspects Zubatoff would insist on interviewing each separately in a private room. After the tough methods of the professional interrogators the interviews with Zubatoff were comparatively civilised. He would at once put a prisoner at his ease, ask him to sit down, sometimes offer him a drink of vodka, and then deliver a mild homily on the hopelessness of revolutionary methods and the nobility and justice of the Government's aims in trying to stamp them out. Zubatoff's personality was such that he made a tremendously favourable impression on the arrested men and won them over to his way of thinking. They would be released and put on parole, and a condition of parole was that they became sub-agents of the Ochrana.

Zubatoff was a highly imaginative and intelligent operator who studied the methods of crime detection of other European nations, and he not only introduced a new records system for the Ochrana but set up branches of the service in the smaller towns of Russia. Of all Russia's chiefs of Intelligence he was perhaps the one who held power longest and was certainly the best administrator in recent times. He insisted on the keeping of the most minute anthropometric records of prisoners and suspects, an attention to detail that was to prove of immense value to the Ochrana. He also insisted that as soon as any agent's nickname or code-word became too well known in the Ochrana hierarchy it was to be changed immediately; he also made it a rule that when an agent was given a code name it had no connection with any member of his family, his place of birth or residence, or provided any clue to his profession.

7

Ievno Azeff and 'Provocation' Tactics

THE RETARDING influence on Russian progress, both economically and politically, in the latter part of the century was Konstantin Petrovich Pobedonostsev, leader of the conservative forces. He was in a unique position in his relationship to the Czardom for Alexander II had asked him to tutor his sons and it followed naturally that he had great influence both with the short-reigned Alexander III and Nicholas II, the last of the Czars.

Pobedonostsev had been a professor of law. Then in 1880 he had been made Chief Procurator of the Holy Synod, a post which enabled him to acquire secular control of the Orthodox Church. The job also brought him in close assocation with the Czar and thus he was able to influence decisions on appointments of Ministers. He believed in autocratic rule and the divine right of kings; he was also suspicious and critical of Western influences and to some extent the enemy of industrial progress.

Not surprisingly Pobedonostsev had some influence on the Secret Service and especially on the Ochrana. It was he who persuaded Alexander III to dismiss Loris Melikoff and Ignatiev because he regarded both of them as too liberal and favouring a form of constitutional monarchy. As a result it was Pobedonostsev's choice, Dmitri Tolstoy, who became Minister of the Interior in 1882. Again it was Pobedonostsev who wanted to restrict university entrance to the sons of 'politically reliable classes', stressing that among those who should be excluded were the sons of 'Jews, coachmen, servants, cooks, washerwomen and small shopkeepers'.

Pobedonostsev was markedly anti-semitic and falsely attributed the assassination of Alexander II to the Jews, thus paving the way to the pogroms that occurred in Odessa and Kiev in the early eighties. There sprang up the organisation known as the Black Hundred which openly baited Jews and even plotted ritual murders of them, as well as publishing a work known as *The Protocols of the Elders of Zion*, which told of an international Jewish plot to promote Jewish control of the world. As a result more and more Jews were driven into the underground revolutionary movements. They also founded their own Social Democratic (Marxist) association, the Bund.

By the mid-eighties the Russian revolutionaries were as well organised overseas as they were inside Russia, but there were only two countries where they flourished with any degree of freedom, or where the laws permitted them to remain for any length of time – Switzerland and Britain. It was to these two countries, therefore, that the Foreign Agency of the Ochrana paid special attention. They also introduced the most stringent passport control regulations of any nation in the world, which enabled them to keep track on Russians travelling abroad almost as easily, if not more so, as on those who stayed in Russia.

The brain behind the External Agency and the man specially responsible for training agents for overseas work was Eustraty Myednikoff. He founded the first permanent school for secret agents in Moscow and the marked improvement in the quality of the External Agency operators was largely due to his emphasis on training and skill not only in picking men but in handling them. Whereas Zubatoff was the complete bureaucrat and perfect administrator, Myednikoff was the individualist and unorthodox practitioner. It is said that he made a point not merely of getting to know each of his agents personally but of learning about and memorising all their idiosyncrasies, their likes and dislikes, their virtues and vices, their talents and recreations. He demanded a stern sense of discipline among his men and for this reason preferred to recruit from non-commissioned Army officers. He made a habit of calling together all his agents who happened to be in Moscow each night for conferences in the Ochrana headquarters. There he talked to each man separately, discussed his reports with him and gave personal instructions. In this way he assessed the value of each agent and marked down those he thought deserved promotion. His aim was to turn conventional, disciplined agents into resourceful, imaginative and unorthodox operators.

'To travel,' declared Myednikoff, 'you need imagination, otherwise you will never observe the things you should observe. To make use of that observation you must be original, you must always be able to do the unexpected thing, to leave everyone guessing at your purpose. Never allow the act of any man you are following divert you from following that man.'

His instructions paid off on many occasions, especially after he created his Special Section of the External Agency which comprised crack agents. There was the occasion when an Ochrana operator saw a man he was watching throw away some scraps of paper. Remembering Myednikoff's advice, the agent called a street urchin, gave him some money to recover the scraps of paper and bring them to him at a certain address, but meanwhile continued to follow the man. Thus he tracked down his man to the latter's address and later was given the scraps of paper which, when pieced together, revealed the organisation of a secret society. By this means he knew where to arrest the man and obtained full details of the ramifications of the society. This may seem a trite example of espionage, but it is an apt illustration of the thoroughness of Ochrana methods. The weakness of the organisation may have lain in extravagance, unwieldiness and duplication of work, but its strength – and indeed the strength of Soviet espionage today – was in its pertinacity, its thoroughness, its refusal to be diverted from one objective to another. The Russian spy will always seek to kill two birds with one stone as the agent mentioned did.

A. T. Vassilyev excused the tactics of 'provocation' by saying that the 'only one efficient means of becoming informed as to the intentions of the enemy' was for the Political Police to 'get in touch with various individuals in the camp of the revolutionaries'.

Vassilyev cites as an example a female student named Zhutshenko, who assisted the Ochrana for many years in tracking down revolutionaries. She was at the same time a member of the Revolutionary Socialists who once entrusted her with carrying out a plot against the life of General Kurloff, at that time Governor of Minsk. With the connivance of the Ochrana, Zhutshenko actually threw a bomb at General Kurloff, though the bomb had previously been rendered harmless so that it did not explode.

The hierarchy of the Ochrana, especially under the direction of Zubatoff and Myednikoff, fully realised that with such a huge amount of information pouring into their offices it was essential for reports to be checked and double-checked. Hitherto the Ochrana had suffered from the acceptance by its bureaucrats of far too much unproven and even palpably false reports. From the nineties onwards several agents were detailed to watch each known revolutionary society, making sure as far as was possible that none of these knew the others. Another system of checking was by using the External Agency as a check on the Internal Agency when this was appropriate, as each body operated independently of the other. In the hierarchy itself were bureaucrats who specialised in the activities of subversive organisations. For example, there was a specialist on Anarchists, another on Democratic Socialists and yet another on Revolutionary Socialists and so on. Sometimes suspicion of revolutionary tendencies went to such ridiculous lengths that innocent organisations were watched.

The section of the Ochrana mainly concerned with *agent provocateur* tactics was the Central Agency. Despite its successes it was always opposed by a small minority of Ochrana chiefs. This opposition became extremely vocal after what was known as *L'affaire Azeff*.

Ievno Azeff, the son of a poor Jewish tailor, Fischel Azeff, was born in 1869 in Lyskovo in the Grodnensky province. His father was anxious to break away from the ghetto to which they were confined by Russian law and to branch out on his own elsewhere. So the family moved to Rostov, a rapidly developing city where opportunities were plentiful for those with resource. Here Azeff senior opened up a draper's shop, but he seems to have made little progress financially for twenty years later when the secret police were checking on young Azeff's records they reported that his family were 'in very poor circumstances'.

Nonetheless the father had given his children a fair education and young Ievno was quick to take advantage of this. He was in turn a tutor of sorts, a clerk, commercial traveller and reporter on a local paper, *Donskaya Ptchela*. At the same time he made the acquaintance of a number of young revolutionaries, eventually marrying a young woman dedicated to the cause. In 1892 he was suspected of having distributed revolutionary propaganda and his arrest seemed imminent. Azeff, in his capacity as a commercial traveller, had just received a large consignment of butter. He promptly sold it and absconded with the money, escaping to Karlsruhe in Germany where he entered the Polytechnic Institute.

Here he linked up with a number of Russian students with revolutionary sympathies and joined the Russian Social Democratic Group. It then dawned on him that the way to money and safety was for him to betray this Group to the police. On 4 April 1893, he wrote his first letter to the Police Department, stating that 'two months ago a circle of revolutionaries was formed here whose aim is . . . ', followed by an account of the group's activities and plans and a list of the names of members. He asked that a registered letter should be sent to him at a certain address if the Ochrana felt that his information was valuable. He omitted his true name when writing this letter.

The following month Azeff received a cautious reply: 'We know of the Karlsruhe Group and we are not very interested in it [in fact, they knew hardly anything about it and were indeed extremely interested]; therefore you are not of such a great value to us; nevertheless we are prepared to pay you – on condition, however, that you reveal your name, for we have strict principles and will have no dealings with certain people.'

Azeff replied immediately and asked for only fifty roubles a month pay, but still did not reveal his true name. But the Ochrana tracked down his identity by his handwriting and by ascertaining that he must have gone to Karlsruhe from Rostov. They received a report from the Rostov police which said that 'Ievno Azeff is intelligent and a clever intriguer. He is in close touch with young Jewish students living abroad and he could be of real use as an agent.'

This clinched the matter and Azeff was taken on as an Ochrana agent from June 1893. Up to this time he had, in his relations with the revolutionaries, appeared to be a moderate. Now he veered to the left and started to urge terrorist tactics. He travelled around not only in Germany but in Switzerland as well and in 1893 at Zurich attended the International Socialist Congress and various meetings of Russian exiles. The following year he visited Berne where he met the Zhitlovskys, the founders of the Union of Russian Social Revolutionaries Abroad, which he promptly joined.

It is surprising that any intelligent revolutionary should ever have been taken in by Azeff, for his faults and weaknesses were always evident. He was intelligent and industrious, but he was unlikeable and revengeful and rarely missed an opportunity of jeering or sneering at other people's faults. It is perhaps even more surprising that the police should have trusted him. He was known to be capable of petty crime and untrustworthy with money; heavily built, with a puffy, yellow face, thick lips and a flattened nose, he was altogether a somewhat repulsive personality. But by the time he completed his course of studies Azeff was generally accepted in Russian student circles abroad as a confirmed and dedicated revolutionary and was actually elected chairman of the student meetings. But he seems to have shied away from becoming a public speaker, preferring to remain an agitator in the background.

And the Ochrana, after preliminary doubts as to his character and capability, began to be pleased with him. He sent in regular reports in great detail and covering a wide range of revolutionary activities abroad. In 1899 his salary was raised to a hundred roubles a month and he was paid bonuses in addition. In 1899, after obtaining the diploma of an electrical engineer at Darmstadt, he returned to Russia at the suggestion of the Ochrana who promised not merely to increase his salary but to find him a post as an engineer. By this time his name had come to the attention of Zubatoff.

Once in Moscow Azeff got in touch with the local leaders of the Union of Social Revolutionaries Abroad, armed with a letter of recommendation from the Zhitlovskys. In the meantime he met Zubatoff. Perhaps no one but Zubatoff would have trusted Azeff in the first place, or certainly not have marked him down for more important work. But Zubatoff was not merely a disciple of Ratchkovsky but that most remarkable of all Ochrana chiefs – a man who was an intellectual and a former member of students' groups on the fringe of the revolutionaries. Zubatoff was never a committed revolutionary himself, but he had been of liberal outlook in his youth and it was perhaps because of how he had seen young and promising liberals wooed into the revolutionary ranks that had afterwards become so anxious to win back their adherence to the régime. The truth was that Zubatoff had joined the Ochrana in much the same way as Azeff originally: he had volunteered information about revolutionary students and as a result of this a number of them had been arrested.

Thus Zubatoff had a fellow-feeling for Azeff in the beginning. He saw the young Jew as he had been himself years ago. But Zubatoff had not continued as a mere informer: his ambition had propelled him towards greater distinction. He had the air of an intellectual with his small, neat beard, his hair brushed back, his precise manner and his tinted glasses that he always wore, the latter being a mannerism he carefully cultivated to impress his agents. Zubatoff had risen within ten years from the rank of mere police informer to the head of the Moscow Ochrana and had never forgotten how betrayal paid dividends. Early on he had learned how important it was to trim his sails, to make a virtue of deviousness. His policy was to 'divide and rule' and so obsessed was he with these tactics that he extended them far beyond mere Secret Service work. Zubatoff felt that the Ochrana should also mould policy outside the Service, that it should studiously make amends for the omissions of the politicians. His idea was to support, even to cosset, some of the working classes, if by doing so he could switch their allegiance away from the extremist revolutionaries. Who but Zubatoff would have gone out of his way to support labour legislation and to sponsor the cause of workers in their disputes with employers? It was he who created legal workers' organisations on the understanding that they came under police control. As far as he was concerned they could battle for their rights against employers as long as he knew what they were doing and that their demands were confined to purely economic reasons. Win the workers over to the régime but push the intellectuals into further acts of violence until they defeated themselves was his motto. It was a cynical, dual policy, fraught with risks, but to Zubatoff's devious mind it was pragmatic and bore results.

It was, of course, a policy of playing with fire and it was not long before Zubatoff's over-confidence resulted in his burning his fingers. Azeff himself was to prove that. It was through Zubatoff's influence that Azeff became an engineer in the Moscow office of the General Electrical Company. At the same time he became a member of the 'Intellectual Aid Society', an organisation which included in its membership many of the leading intellectuals of Moscow. Azeff reported to his master on a wide range of revolutionary societies, but particularly on the Union of Social Revolutionaries and of the printing presses they possessed. He told Zubatoff about the establishment of a printing press that had been set up in Finland on the estate of a woman landowner who sympathised secretly with the party. Soon Zubatoff received from Azeff a complete list of the leaders of the society. As a member of that society Azeff was foremost in urging terrorist tactics and while he was in receipt of funds from the Ochrana he was embarking on plans for violence and terrorism.

It is still somewhat of a mystery as to how much Azeff was dedicated to the revolutionaries and how much he faithfully served the Ochrana. Years later Zubatoff was to say of him that 'Azeff's was a purely mercenary nature . . . looking at everything from the point of view of profit, working for the Revolution for the sake of personal gain, and for the Government out of no conviction but also for the sake of personal profit.' But this was hindsight. In the meantime Zubatoff encouraged Azeff to pursue his rôle of *agent provocateur*. But Azeff was cunning enough to keep the truth from both his revolutionary comrades and from the Ochrana so nobody could be sure how much he intended his terrorist tactics to succeed. It was through Azeff's information that the Ochrana raided a printing press in Tomsk and rounded up a number of terrorist leaders. But so well did Zubatoff conceal the source of this information that Azeff was never suspected by his comrades. Indeed after the arrests and the disaster of Tomsk they made Azeff their leader.

Azeff had already informed Argunoff, the man he was succeeding as leader, that he would have to go abroad on personal business. In consequence Argunoff told him everything – the code names of all leaders abroad, the names and addresses of associates and the places where cells existed. The Ochrana knew from that moment the full extent of the revolutionaries' ramifications. Zubatoff urged

Azeff to penetrate the cells outside Russia.

By this date, early in 1900, Azeff was receiving one hundred and fifty roubles a month from the Ochrana. Soon this was increased to five hundred roubles, an incredible sum for a secret agent. As soon as Azeff left Russia the Ochrana arrested Argunoff and deported him to Siberia.

From Berne, Berlin and Paris Azeff reported back to Moscow on the extent of the Social Revolutionaries' movement on the continent. 'In Berlin and in Paris I have penetrated into the very heart of things,' he wrote. He advised the Ochrana about G. A. Gershuni, one of the chief organisers of Russian revolutionaries in Europe and creator of the 'Battle Organisation' of the party which aimed at the assassination of a number of Russian politicians. Yet even when he gave the Ochrana the date of his departure from Berlin and his proposed itinerary in Russia, Azeff urged that Gershuni 'must not be arrested yet'. Here the hierarchy of the Ochrana blundered badly. They could easily have arrested the man, but they took Azeff's advice. And Gershuni, who appears to have been tipped off that he was being watched by the police, was able to escape from the attentions of the Ochrana. Worse than this he was able to go ahead with the plan for the assassination of Sipyagin, the Minister of the Interior. Preparations for this were made in Finland and it was from this country that Balmasheff, the chosen killer, set out on 15 April 1902. Disguised as an officer in the uniform of an aide-de-camp, he announced himself as an emissary of the Grand Duke Sergei and when confronted by Sipyagin killed him outright with revolver fire.

This was the first coup of the 'Battle Organisation' campaign of assassination. It was a coup that could have been prevented if Azeff had not insisted that the Ochrana should not arrest Gershuni, but it still did not dawn on the Ochrana that their ace agent was playing a dangerous game, if not a downright treacherous one. Azeff was as vigilant as ever on the Ochrana's behalf, sending in a stream of reports from Berlin, but about this time he started to keep back a good deal of information from his Secret Service masters. He even went to great pains to inform the Ochrana that Gershuni was in no way concerned in the assassination of Sipyagin. Only after Gershuni had once again left Russia did Azeff reveal that he had discovered that Gershuni was involved in the 'Battle Organisation'.

The Ochrana believed – and here they may well have been right – that Azeff's position in the party was dependent on his friendship with Gershuni and that if Gershuni were arrested suspicion might fall on Azeff. It would seem that Azeff was more than once on the point of betraying Gershuni, but that at the last moment he hesi-

6

tated. Perhaps reports on Gershuni were more lucrative than the satisfaction of having him arrested, but Ratayeff, one of Azeff's associates, believed that Gershuni had a hypnotic influence over his fellow conspirator. Azeff reported on a dynamite factory the revolutionaries had set up in Switzerland, but added in a message to the Police Department: 'We must have a personal conversation about my further work. My position has become somewhat dangerous. I am now playing a very active part among revolutionaries. It would be unprofitable to retreat now, but any action calls for the greatest care.'

Now it is certain that at this time Azeff must have known all the revolutionaries' plans under what they continued to call the 'Battle Organisation'. But though he revealed to the Ochrana Gershuni's plans for attempts to kill W. K. Plehve, the new Minister of the Interior, and Zubatoff himself, he made no reference to the next killing listed on their plan – that of Obolensky, the Governor of Kharkov.

'His reports about Gershuni are particularly characteristic,' wrote Boris Nicolaievsky, Azeff's biographer. 'It had now become impossible to conceal the latter's connection with the "Battle Organisation"; far too many people were aware of this. Azeff no longer attempted to deny the fact, but he strove to convince the Department that Gershuni played but a secondary part, such as collecting money and recruiting young terrorists. According to his assertions the "Battle Organisation" was directed by a group of outlaw revolutionaries unknown to him. The reasons for his attitude are obvious. While safeguarding Gershuni as his chief support within the party, Azeff wished to betray the less important members of the "Battle Organisation", making them out to be its leaders in the eyes of the Department.'

It was agreed to give Azeff a personal hearing and he was this time called to St Petersburg. Changes had been made in the personnel of the Ochrana. Plehve had appointed A. A. Lopuchin as director and the task of dealing with the purely political aspect of the Ochrana's work had been handed over to Zubatoff. This change around of personnel had by no means helped the smooth running of the Department and disconcerting differences of opinion occurred within the Ochrana hierarchy. Lopuchin wanted to create a special Secret Service section to combat the 'Battle Organisation' and he asked Plehve, the Minister of the Interior, to order Azeff to penetrate the top planning committee of the 'Battle Organisation'.

In October 1902 Azeff attended such a committee meeting in Kiev, where Gershuni, Kraft and Melnikoff, the principal plotters of assassination, were present. The Ochrana had taken the precaution of having Azeff shadowed all the way to Kiev and they insisted that he should point out to their agents on the spot the principal members of the revolutionaries present. Azeff was now treading a perilous path; all the key revolutionaries were watched for months afterwards, but no arrests were made. But later when Azeff went to Moscow, Kharkov and Saratov a number of arrests were carried out as a result of his tips.

Azeff then made St Petersburg his base and the Petersburg Social Revolutionary Committee was at that time entirely under his direction. He started to form several new revolutionary groups, concentrating on recruiting students, but quite often such groups were largely manned by Ochrana agents. The instructions to these agents were simplicity itself: they were to take part normally in all meetings, and when such meetings were addressed by propagandists who handed out leaflets and pamphlets they were to hand these over to the police.

But if the revolutionaries were satisfied about Azeff, Zubatoff began to have grave doubts about his ace agent. He now suspected that Gershuni was a far more important member of the 'Battle Organisation' than Azeff had hinted. Orders were given for Gershuni's arrest and a nation-wide hunt for him to be made.

It would seem at this stage that Azeff was prepared to betray Gershuni, but only at his own price and on condition the reward was paid to him alone. It had been rumoured that the Czar had offered a reward of 15,000 roubles for Gershuni's detection. Azeff wanted 50,000 roubles and an assurance that whoever arrested Gershuni he would get the money. Azeff was sent for by Lopuchin and accused of concealing information, but he counter-attacked by asserting that the Ochrana had not paid sufficient attention to his reports.

Shortly afterwards Azeff met Gershuni secretly in Moscow and during the meeting it is almost certain they discussed plans for killing Bodganovitch, the Governor of Ufa. At any rate, immediately after the meeting Gershuni went to Ufa and on 19 May 1903 Bodganovitch was shot down by two terrorists.

The hunt for Gershuni was then intensified, though he had escaped from Ufa without difficulty. But he made the error of sending a telegram to a colleague, warning him of the time of his arrival in Kiev. The telegram fell into the hands of an *agent provocateur*. Gershuni was met at the railway station by a posse of detectives, arrested and after a trial by court martial sentenced to death. The penalty was afterwards commuted to penal servitude for life.

Now Azeff was in supreme command of the revolutionary group and the director of terrorist tactics. The following month he appeared in Geneva to consult with party members. He immediately applied himself with zeal and increasing venom to the task of organising further killings.

The reason for this, perhaps, is not too difficult to find. Azeff was still deep in his subconscious mind a Jew. His father might have escaped from the ghetto, he himself may have disavowed the Jewish faith and insisted that he was a Russian above all else. But the memory of his Jewish childhood and of the people with whom he was brought up was strong. When news came of the anti-Jewish pogrom in Kishenev, when dozens were killed and hundreds injured, when homes were wrecked and shops looted, the sense of belonging to these persecuted people welled up in Azeff.

So Azeff had a personal motive for killing Plehve, but the profit motive also influenced him to retain his links with the Ochrana. As the chief of the 'Battle Organisation' he now had large sums of money under his control. There is abundant documentary evidence in the files of the Ochrana that he obtained sums of money for himself, both from police and revolutionary funds.

The plan to assassinate Plehve was organised by Azeff with great attention to detail. He knew that the Minister of the Interior regularly visited the Czar each week and that he always used the same route. For this reason Azeff decided to keep careful watch on the exact times of these visits and where at various points on the route he would be at a given moment. Revolutionaries disguised as paper-sellers, hawkers and even road sweepers were used to keep watch on the route, while experts prepared the explosives. It is curious to note that one of the revolutionaries on the planning committee was afterwards to become not only a distinguished Russian citizen but one respected and trusted by Winston Churchill – Savinkoff, who later led the White Russian anti-Bolshevik crusade.

Meanwhile Azeff's immediate chief in the Ochrana was now Ratayeff rather than Zubatoff, for the former was the Chief of the Russian Political Police abroad. He was ill-fitted for such a rôle, because he lacked Zubatoff's imagination and drive and was apt to neglect his work for philandering and social life. In Ochrana headquarters his lack of zeal had been freely commented on and Plehve, who had a poor opinion of him, had given him the new post chiefly to get him out of the Special Branch of the Political Police. Ratayeff travelled a great deal and often went to Paris as an excuse for a weekend of wenching and wining. His idleness was cleverly exploited by Azeff who manipulated him for his own ends. When Ratayeff asked for information, Azeff fobbed him off with excuses that he had not completed his inquiries. Indeed, Azeff had some problems of his own at this time for news filtered through the underground grapevine that S. Klitchoglu, a woman terrorist, had founded her own group of assassins and was planning her own attempt on Plehve's life. There was some dissatisfaction with Azeff as leader among his group and he knew too well that success by a rival group, led by a woman at that, could redound against him.

Here, then, was Azeff's chance to break his silence to Ratayeff and to give the Ochrana some worthwhile news, while at the same time destroying the power of Klitchoglu. He seized the chance eagerly and informed Ratayeff of the plot. The Ochrana, however, were still doubtful about Azeff's reliability and insisted that Azeff should meet Klitchoglu, allowing the police to follow him to their rendezvous. Somewhat reluctantly Azeff agreed, but on condition that no arrest was made immediately, but only some days later. Ratayeff agreed to this proposition, but his superiors considered that unless prompt action was taken Klitchoglu could give them the slip as Gershuni had done so many times before his capture. So Klitchoglu was arrested the moment Azeff left her, an action that angered both Ratayeff and Azeff. This had the unfortunate effect of bringing Ratayeff and Azeff into closer collusion and to Ratayeff holding back some of Azeff's information from the Ochrana.

There was mistrust inside the ranks of the Ochrana and an equal measure of mistrust and suspicion inside the revolutionary group dedicated to killing Plehve. More than once an attack on the Minister was planned, each time it was called off. Sometimes suspicious plotters failed to turn up on time either because they feared a traitor in their own ranks or because they believed they were being followed by the police. But hatred of Plehve prevailed over fear and caution: on 18 July 1904, Savinkoff was detailed to hurl a bomb at Plehve's carriage. His aim was true and the Minister of the Interior was killed instantly.

Plehve's assassination shocked the Ochrana. They had long been aware that Plehve was a principal target for the revolutionaries, but they had had no tip about this final attempt on his life. Ratayeff was recalled from Paris to explain what had gone wrong and why Azeff had not reported the plot, for it became obvious that this must have been carried out by the 'Battle Organisation', of which Azeff was the head. Savinkoff had fled to Warsaw and Azeff was in Vienna from whence he had the impertinence to inform Ratayeff that 'Plehve's assassination was a complete surprise to me'.

Ratayeff still supported Azeff, so the Ochrana directorate remained nonplussed at events. One can only conclude that Plehve was as much hated by some of the heads of the Ochrana as he was by the rest of his fellow-countrymen. Yet if the investigation into

Plehve's assassination had been properly carried out and the findings assessed correctly, Azeff's complicity must have been proved. Azeff had been in Vilna with Sazonoff just before the killing, Sazonoff had been heard to mention Azeff's code-name among the 'Battle Organisation' group – 'Valentine'.

Then the killer group struck again. The Grand Duke Sergei Alexandrovitch was murdered. There seems to be no doubt that the Czar was the next target for the assassins. Even the Liberal press alleged that Azeff had acted as an *agent provocateur* and arranged these crimes. It was freely whispered that a police spy had plotted the murder of the Czar's uncle, the Grand Duke. Later in his memoirs the then Prime Minister, Count Witte, subscribed to the belief that the Grand Duke had been killed on 'the direct orders of Azeff, the police agent'.

There was, of course, a strong case for reversing the *agent provocateur* tactics of the Ochrana on the grounds that these had got out of hand. But Witte at the time took no steps to put matters right. Indeed, in appointing P. N. Durnovo as the new Minister of the Interior he ensured that the same methods were carried on.

8

Ratchkovsky the Manipulator

THE AZEFF affair continues to baffle historians even today when more documents and information have come to light than in Vassilyev's time. Even so recent a historian as Graham Stephenson, writing in 1969, says of Ievno Azeff that 'so skilfully did he conceal his tracks that it is still impossible to say which side he mainly betrayed'. But he adds that Azeff's party, the Socialist Revolutionaries, 'were not an important force. In spite of their numbers and fanaticism, their doctrine was too archaic and their organisation too undisciplined to constitute a serious threat to the State in 1905.'

Azeff had played his rôle as terrorist leader to perfection. When necessary, that is to say when he actually gave out orders, he did so in his naturally brusque, even brutal manner, hinting at death to those who failed. But with new recruits to the terrorist ranks he was solicitude itself. Zenzinoff, one of the terrorists, recalled afterwards that 'Azeff appeared to us to be extraordinarily attentive, tactful and even kind-hearted. All his fellow-terrorists not only respected him very highly, but loved him warmly.'

On the organisational side he arranged for the setting up in Paris of a laboratory to turn out dynamite and made the plans for its being brought into Russia. If he found among his fellow-terrorists any who opposed his policies, or who seemed faint-hearted or untrustworthy, he immediately liquidated them by reporting them to Ratayeff. He would inform the spy chief that they were the most dangerous terrorists in the group.

Russia's defeat in the Far East by Japan and rising unemployment contributed to a tense situation inside the country. Resentment against the Czarist régime was welling up and the masses had been impressed by the acts of the 'Battle Organisation'. When five workers were dismissed from a factory in St Petersburg it was the signal for action. All workers at the factory went on strike and soon workers at other factories were stopping their machines and putting down their tools. The whole city was at a standstill. A crowd of many thousands, carrying icons and even portraits of the Czar, made its way peacefully but determinedly to the Winter Palace to present a petition to the Czar in person, setting out their complaints and their requests. But the vast crowd was never able to get near enough to carry out this petition: it was met by crossfire from the lines of soldiers guarding the Palace and hundreds were killed.

This was 'Bloody Sunday', 22 January 1905, the day on which authority triumphed with a hollow victory, but one which marked the ultimate end of Czardom. A gesture by the Czar, the calling off of his armed troops, might have given liberalism a chance, albeit a slender one. But the brutal action of the military ended all hopes of compromise. The revolutionaries were able to say to the Liberals, 'We told you so. The Czarists do not understand liberalism, they merely crush it. The only path to success is by terrorism.' From then onwards the Czar survived only with the sullen acquiescence of the masses: behind their inertia was a bitter hatred.

The 'Battle Organisation' was ready to go into action again and probably the Czar himself would have been their next victim. But one of their plotters made a mistake in charging his bombs and blew himself to pieces. The Ochrana closed in on the remaining plotters, only Azeff and Savinkoff escaping their net. This time, however, the information which led to the arrests did not come from Azeff, but from another *agent provocateur* in the Ochrana service, N. Tataroff. This man had been mixed up with revolutionary movements since 1892 and had been sent to East Siberia in 1901. He had joined the revolutionaries originally because he wanted to be in the forefront of the more dashing of the students;

he desired to show off. Tataroff was not a revolutionary by conviction and exile swiftly killed any enthusiasm he may have had for the movement. He had influential connections in high places and had been at school with the son of Count Kutaisoff, the Governor-General of Eastern Siberia. The latter took a liking to him, was soon convinced that he was only a lukewarm revolutionary and tried to win him over.

Count Kutaisoff suggested he might be able to obtain freedom for Tataroff if the latter would agree to become an *agent provocateur* for the Ochrana. Tataroff accepted the suggestion with alacrity and Kutaisoff got in touch with the Ochrana. He could hardly have chosen a more propitious moment. The Ochrana were dissatisfied with Azeff and if Tataroff had close associations with the Social Revolutionaries, he seemed worth taking on. So they telegraphed permission for him to be released and to return to St Petersburg, the official reason given being the illness of his father.

Tataroff became a travelling agent of the Central Committee of the Social Revolutionaries while in the pay of the police. Though he never succeeded in getting into the inner councils of the 'Battle Organisation' as did Azeff, he nevertheless provided a great deal more information than Azeff was sending in at that time. He also paved the way for more arrests.

Despite these successes the Ochrana were still faced by the fact that the present leaders of the 'Battle Organisation' remained undetected. There was widespread criticism of the Ochrana and this began to be voiced by the Czar himself. There was a demand for a scapegoat and the authorities did not have far to look. Trepoff, the Governor-General of St Petersburg, angered by the killing of the Grand Duke Sergei, openly accused Lopuchin, the Director of the Police Department, of being a murderer. 'Your criminal folly in neglecting to find out about this plan for assassination makes you a murderer,' stormed Trepoff at Lopuchin. The latter defended himself by alleging that the Moscow Department of the Ochrana knew about the attempt to kill Sergei in advance of the deed, but that they withheld this vital information from him. This allegation was partly correct, but no one would speak up on Lopuchin's behalf.

Trepoff had a talk with the Czar and reminded him that it was Lopuchin who had been instrumental in dismissing Ratchkovsky. Might not Lopuchin have been wrong? he hinted. The Czar, who prior to the affair of Philippe had been favourably disposed to Ratchkovsky, agreed that something ought to be done about Lopuchin and more or less demanded his resignation. Thus was Ratchkovsky able to gain his revenge for he was now given the post of the very man who had precipitated his previous downfall.

The return of Ratchkovsky to a key appointment like this was putting the clock back for the best part of half a century. Ratchkovsky was steeped in the intrigues of earlier days and his methods were more reactionary than those of either Zubatoff or Ratayeff. He had weathered the Ochrana intrigues and political storms of a great many years and was still a ruthless operator. But the man who had revolutionised Secret Service techniques in the sixties and seventies was hardly the man for the current situation: his appointment was like dropping a match in a barrel of petrol.

Ratchkovsky, the man who had developed the *agent provocateur* techniques to extreme lengths, was appointed at a time when those very techniques were being openly criticised and unmasked not only in the Duma but in the press. In another country in a similar situation the new police chief would probably have played down these tactics, even reversed them. But this was yet another example of how the bureaucrats of the Russian Secret Service throughout the ages, when discredited by some blunder, instead of back-pedalling and acting cautiously discard discretion and adopt even more reactionary tactics.

Ratchkovsky was a dabbler in politics as well as being a Secret Service chief. He was much more in the tradition of Alexander I than Nicholas II. He had manoeuvred himself into a strong bargaining position that outweighed the disadvantage of his age. He was on close terms with General Hesse, the Commander of the Palace Guard, who, being an intimate of the Czar, was able to use his influence with the latter in Ratchkovsky's favour. His relations with leading Russian and French politicians were particularly influential. He used his close ties with Paris to amass a fortune on the French stock exchange and his financial deals were frequently of a doubtful, even illegal character. One debt Russia undoubtedly owed him was that he had shown great energy and resourcefulness in influencing the French to agree to the Franco-Russian alliance. No Secret Service chief of his time was so subtle a politician and used espionage so adroitly to bring about changes in foreign policy. He loathed the Germans and through his systematic spy service built up a lengthy dossier on the extent of German armaments and shipbuilding. This information he manipulated in a variety of ways. He gave some of it direct to the French Intelligence in return for information about Russian revolutionaries in France, proving that he was France's ally against her most dangerous enemy. He passed other tit-bits on to the international press and quite often utilised his knowledge to foment armament scares and to indulge in shady stock market manoeuvres.

Ratchkovsky's use of *agent provocateur* tactics was quite different from the wiles employed by either Zubatoff or Ratayeff. It was much more subtly political because Ratchkovsky was above all else a political animal in the sense that he had his nose to the ground; he knew how to manipulate and even to mould public opinion. He encouraged bomb-throwing and even put up the money for the making of revolutionary bombs through his agents. But he took good care that the bombs were not exploded in his own territory, or where they could bring criticism directly upon his own head. For example, he directed and controlled the *agents provocateurs* who planted the 'Russian revolutionary bombs' found in Paris in 1890. And it was Ratchkovsky who tipped off a grateful French Intelligence where the bombs could be found. Thus he created a public opinion in Paris against revolutionaries in general and Russian ones in particular. He did the same thing in Belgium, for it was his agent, Jagolkovsky, who launched a series of Anarchist bombings in that country, including a plan to blow up Liège Cathedral.

Even when he was chosen to succeed Lopuchin, Ratchkovsky indulged in political intrigues to safeguard his position and consolidate power in his hands. The wily old agent of the sixties had lost none of his cunning. He insisted on having the title of Special Commissioner to the Ministry of the Interior as well as controlling the St Petersburg branch of the Ochrana, thus giving himself personal access at all times to the Minister. He also asked that his ally, Trepoff, should be promoted to be assistant to the Minister of the Interior. Trepoff returned this compliment by getting Ratchkovsky made Vice-Director of the Police Department with control over the Department's political section.

Thus Trepoff and Ratchkovsky held the reins of power between them and jointly axed all leading personnel who had been appointed by Zubatoff and Lopuchin. One of the first to go was Ratayeff. From that moment Azeff came under direct control by Ratchkovsky and one of the latter's first acts was to order Tataroff to keep Azeff under observation.

Ratchkovsky had Azeff like a rat in a cleft stick. Azeff knew that unless he came forward with some really worthwhile and dramatic information it would be only a matter of time before his double-dealing was discovered. Perhaps Ratchkovsky wanted to lull him into a state of carelessness, because curiously he increased Azeff's salary to six hundred roubles and even allowed him to draw the sum of 1,300 roubles for expenses. In return for this generosity Azeff promised to give the Ochrana evidence which would result in the arrest of Savinkoff and other leading terrorists. He said that he would go to Saratov where he could locate both Sakinkoff and Breshkovskaya.

If he thought the Ochrana were going to let him off the hook completely, he was soon disillusioned. Ratchkovsky instructed Myednikoff, chief of the Investigation Department, to accompany him and to be followed by a posse of detectives and agents. Yet even in this predicament Azeff only gave away information leading to the capture of a dynamite factory in Saratov and one in Moscow and the arrest of a handful of terrorists. Neither Savinkoff nor Breshkovskaya were at the address he gave the Ochrana. The 'Battle Organisation' was still intact.

Infiltration was not all one way in this period. The revolutionaries had managed in a very modest way to infiltrate the ranks of the Ochrana and one of them, L. P. Menstchikoff, an experienced revolutionary, had acquired a considerable reputation for himself by the clarity and lucidity of his reports. He found out that Azeff was a member of the Ochrana and sent a message to the Social Revolutionary Committee to warn them that 'the engineer Azeff is betraying the party'. He also added that an ex-convict from Siberia was also in the pay of the Ochrana and that he had betrayed the party. This pointed clearly in the direction of Tataroff.

Surprisingly, considering that Azeff had been under suspicion previously, the report against him was not believed. Amazingly, it was not even investigated. But the case of Tataroff, which was much vaguer, was the subject of detailed inquiries. He was suspended from the party, but no further action was taken. Azeff was furious: he insisted that Tataroff should have been summarily executed by the revolutionaries. Nor did he cease to press for drastic action until in April 1906 the terrorists of 'Battle Organisation' finally stabbed Tataroff to death in his own home.

It was risky work that the *agent provocateur* undertook in these times. But it was also well paid. Tataroff received for his work for the Ochrana over a total period of well under a year the sum of 16,100 roubles.

Then came a political bombshell from the Czar himself. In October 1905 he decided on liberal action: he issued a manifesto which granted 'fundamental personal liberties' to the people, gave more enfranchisement and the Duma legislative powers. It was a gesture that two years earlier might have made a great difference. Now it was too late. At best it merely halted terrorism and slowed down the inevitable process of revolution.

From the eighties onwards the Russian Secret Service had greatly stepped up its espionage overseas. The key areas were first in the Balkans and Vienna, secondly in those territories adjacent to India and China and, thirdly, in London. Efforts to carry on spying activities in Japan had been singularly unsuccessful and here the

Russians often had to rely on double-agents, or at best on free-lance spies who sold their secrets to the highest bidder.

One particular organisation which proved of help to the Russian Foreign Secret Service was the I.M.R.O., or International Macedonian Revolutionary Organisation, aimed at making Macedonia an independent state. The director of the I.M.R.O. was a former Bulgarian army officer named Boris Saraffoff. As leader of a band of guerrillas in 1897 he had captured Melnik from the Turks and held the town for a whole day. This was not in itself a particularly effective feat, but it was excellent propaganda and it caused Saraffoff to become a legendary hero. From that day he was the key figure in the Macedonians' campaign for liberation. He travelled around Europe, seeking funds for his crusade, using his reputation as a lady-killer to persuade rich widows, heiresses and the wives of wealthy men to part with their money. He was astute enough to seek out the less favoured in looks as they were more susceptible to flattery.

In the nineties a great deal of Russia's information on Balkan intrigues came directly or indirectly through Saraffoff. Finally, the Macedonian revolutionaries began to suspect that their leader was subsidising himself as well as them from the exploits of his espionage. Because they discovered his links with the Russian Secret Service and suspected that he was also in league with King Ferdinand of Bulgaria, the Macedonians, prompted by their other leader, Zandansky, ordered him to be shot. Saraffoff was assassinated as he was leaving the royal palace at Sofia.

While Russia had, if not exactly neglected Japan, at least made only desultory efforts at espionage in this territory, at the turn of the century she was forced to take more aggressive action by the discovery that the Japs had themselves organised a spy network inside Russia. They had utilised the ancient system of getting their agents to marry Russian nationals.

In September 1904, two Japanese clerks employed in a business firm in St Petersburg were arrested by the Ochrana. They had lived in Russia for many years and had never previously been suspected. Yet it transpired that they had been spying over a long period, that they were in fact Japanese naval officers and had devoted their time to naval espionage. One of them had married a Russian woman and even joined the Orthodox Church.

This was a triumph for the Ochrana, for the woman to whom the other Japanese was engaged to be married was one of their agents. Colonel Gerassimoff, chief of the St Petersburg Secret Police, had for some time been disturbed by the revelation that a number of Japanese were marrying Russian women. He selected one of his most brilliant woman agents to ensnare the Japanese clerk. She not only succeeded in her mission but discovered incriminating documents in the possession of her lover and found that the two clerks were naval officers.

This coup revealed the extent to which the Japanese had established a network inside Russia and there is no doubt that the organisation played a valuable part in the ultimate defeat of Russia by Japan in the war of 1904–5. Orders were given – alas, too late – to launch a counter-attack against the Japanese both in the fields of espionage and counter-espionage. Only a few weeks before the war started a foreign agent of the Ochrana succeeded in capturing a cipher-book used by the Japanese Embassy at The Hague and at the same time learned that Japanese espionage was master-minded from this embassy. The Russians, now able to read certain diplomatic dispatches of the Japanese, to which they managed to gain access, learned altogether too late of the war plans of their enemy. Even this success did not last long, for the Japanese soon discovered the theft and changed their ciphers.

The agent who brought off this coup was Manassyevitsh-Manuiloff, who received rapid promotion and later became private secretary to Stürmer, the President of the Council of Ministers. Manassyevitsh-Manuiloff was a skilled operator for many years. His ultimate mistake, which led to his arrest in 1916, was his capacity for intrigue and serving too many masters. He had been a journalist while acting as an Ochrana agent, he had taken grave risks in becoming too friendly with personnel in foreign embassies, risks which paid off as regards information but made him suspect as well. He was, however, a faithful servant of Russia and was highly regarded by Count Witte, for whom he also worked as a kind of one-man secret service. According to Boris Nikolaievsky, it was Manassyevitsh-Manuiloff who recruited into the Secret Service the priest Gapon, who, crucifix in hand, had led the crowds to the Winter Palace on 'Bloody Sunday', 1905. Gapon, who escaped the bullets of the soldiers that day, became a popular hero for a while and was fêted everywhere he went. Adulation went to his head and, after joining the Social Democratic Party, he broke with it because they would not make him leader. Meanwhile, the man who had been revered as a priest on the side of the people descended to the depths of debauchery, spending his time travelling to such places as Monte Carlo and Paris on the proceeds of the sale of his autobiography, whiling away his nights in low night clubs and drinking with prostitutes.

Manassyevitsh-Manuiloff quickly realised that Gapon might be won over as a spy and that he could easily be blackmailed. He put him in touch with Ratchkovsky. It was easy for the spy chief to play on Gapon's vanity: he was flattered and told that 'Bloody

Sunday' had been a great mistake, that it should never have happened, and that he, with his great gifts and influence with the masses, should use these in forming a labour movement in Russia on peaceful and non-revolutionary lines.

Once Gapon's interest had been aroused it was a simple matter to persuade him to work for the Ochrana. Ratchkovsky, an astute psychologist, not only flattered Gapon's ego, he even encouraged his ambition. 'I am old now,' said Ratchkovsky. 'I cannot carry on my work much longer and there is nobody fit to take my place. Russia has need of men like you. Why shouldn't you succeed me? But first of all you must help us. You must tell us what the revolutionary organisations are doing.'

Gapon not only succumbed to Ratchkovsky's blandishments; he agreed to help and volunteered the useful information that 'my good friend, Rutenberg, an engineer, is a member of the "Battle Organisation" and will give me the terrorists' latest plans'.

Whereas Ratchkovsky was optimistic about the outcome of his plans for Gapon, Colonel Gerassimoff, chief of the Petersburg Ochrana, doubted very much whether Rutenberg, known as a dedicated terrorist with no vices or weaknesses, could be won over. He feared that Gapon would fall into a trap, and warned strongly against employing him.

It all turned out much as Gerassimoff had feared. When Gapon met Rutenberg and made somewhat injudicious overtures, his evasiveness to questions and shifty manner caused Rutenberg to suspect he had entered the employ of the police. But he pretended to fall in with Gapon's plans and, as a result, swiftly learned that Gapon was trying to buy information from him with Ratchkovsky's money.

Gapon's ideas about money now that he hankered after a life of luxury and debauchery were such as to leave the Ochrana chiefs aghast. He demanded 100,000 roubles from Ratchkovsky, who retorted that the Ochrana never paid such sums. However, Gapon stuck out for this amount and the matter was referred to Durnovo, then Minister of the Interior. Durnovo replied that he could be paid 25,000 roubles, but not any more. Gapon still insisted on a hundred thousand, so both Ratchkovsky and Durnovo referred the matter to Witte, the President of the Council. Witte did not give a direct answer. In his memoirs he stated that he had urged caution but at the same time told the Ochrana not to waste time with bargaining. It is not clear how much Gapon actually received in the end, but it was probably nearer 100,000 roubles than 25,000.

Azeff learned from Rutenberg of Gapon's treachery and immediately urged that he should be liquidated. But the inner committee of the 'Battle Organisation' decided that it was not enough to kill

Gapon alone, but that he and Ratchkovsky should be slain together.

At the Commission of Inquiry into the Ochrana's activities in 1917 it was stated in evidence by Gerassimoff that Azeff had warned Ratchkovsky about Gapon. Thus it is clear that Azeff, always putting his own survival first, decided to ingratiate himself once again with Ratchkovsky by warning him against both Gapon and Rutenberg and telling him of the latter's plot to kill the spy chief. By doing this he prevented the plan for the killing of Ratchkovsky and Gapon together, but allowed an alternative plan to go forward – that of killing Gapon alone.

One winter's day Gapon was lured to a lonely villa outside St Petersburg. Here he was met by Rutenberg while, hidden in an adjacent room, other revolutionaries listened to the tale of treachery that the priest put forward. They burst into the room in which Rutenberg and Gapon were talking, seized the priest and hanged him with a clothes' rope on a rafter.

Ever since the fifties and sixties of the nineteenth century, London, and its East End in particular, had become a hide-out for refugees and revolutionary exiles from Russia. They turned to Britain because of all countries at that time life was more tolerant, the laws more liberal and personal freedom more highly valued and respected.

Elsewhere in Europe they were subjected to surveillance by the local police, or thrown out as undesirables. Also they found that in France, Germany and Switzerland they were much more closely watched by the Ochrana. In London, however, they were free to come and go as they pleased. They were allowed to form political clubs in Whitechapel, Houndsditch, Stepney and Limehouse, where Anarchism and other extremist creeds flourished as political theory was expounded in committee rooms.

At first Anarchism as a political philosophy gained more ground in London among the Russian exiles than it had inside Russia. It had all started with Proudhon's theory that any form of government was bad, but soon this was moulded into something more activist by such Russian thinkers as Bakunin and Kropotkin. Theoretical Anarchism had been superseded by the doctrine of 'propaganda by deed', on the principle that the more dastardly the deed the more effective the propaganda. From about 1883 onwards most European nations had passed severely repressive measures against Anarchists, but Britain had taken no action with the result that the East End of the capital became the safest refuge they could find. In the eighties there were at least seven revolutionary clubs run by Russians in London's East End. One, named the

Jubilee, and founded under this innocuous title in 1887, was the centre of the Anarchists, and there was also a West End headquarters known more romantically as the Bohemian Club.

Margaret Prothero, in her *History of the C.I.D. at Scotland Yard*, wrote that 'In 1894, Anarchists and Nihilists from Russia were at work in England', while Sir Basil Thomson, the first head of Britain's Special Branch of the police, declared that 'the East End of London ever since the Jack the Ripper murders had become a city of refuge for aliens whose countries had become too hot to hold them'.

Meanwhile a new complication arose. By the middle of the eighties at least the Czarist Government had financed a counter-revolutionary force which they set in action in the East End of London with the aim of discrediting and unmasking the Anarchists. This was a new type of *agent provocateur* which the Russian Secret Service put in the field and the processes of thinking behind this move were often so obscure that it is difficult even now to understand them. Frequently the projects envisaged for these agents, who were told to infiltrate the various revolutionary movements, were so bizarre, so complicated and even absurd that in carrying out their orders those concerned seemed to be behaving more like characters in *Alice in Wonderland* than police agents.

Carefully selected 'secret assistants' of the External Agency of the Ochrana would be sent to London to make contact with revolutionaries and then to join their organisations. They would remain in London until they were sufficiently trusted by the revolutionaries to be sent back to Russia ostensibly as couriers to their confederates in Russia. But a few of these 'secret assistants' were ordered not merely to provoke the revolutionaries into committing crimes but to commit crimes themselves and see that the blame for these was attributed to the revolutionaries. One such counter-revolutionary agent was Serge Makharoff, alias Ivan Nikoliaieff, who, years later, according to Soviet sources, was the original 'Peter the Painter' of the Sidney Street siege. Makharoff, who belonged to an aristocratic but impoverished family, first entered the Russian Army, and then, following a duel with a brother officer, resigned his commission and served with the Secret Police. He was then assigned the task of spying on revolutionaries in Paris, London and elsewhere.

The methods adopted by Makharoff show clearly to what lengths the technique of the *agent provocateur* was taken in this period. His instructions were to locate the revolutionaries, who were then mainly in London, to compromise them and find some means of involving them in trouble with the British police. The object of this would seem to be to create a public demand among the British people for the expulsion of the revolutionaries from Britain.

Commonsense would suggest that it would have been far simpler and much less costly for the Czarist Government to make representations to the British Government for the deportation of the revolutionaries. But the Czarist Government was just as secretive as Soviet governments have been and just as reluctant to discuss internal problems with foreigners. Apart from this even unofficial representations to Britain on this very subject had been unsuccessful.

Makharoff, together with other agents, played a subtle game of inducing certain Anarchists to commit crime. He was so successful that some of the latter had to leave London to avoid arrest on criminal charges. The revolutionaries, who were not usually engaged in criminal activities, were tricked by Makharoff into lending their names to criminal enterprises in the belief that they were really waging war against the Romanoffs, and, in doing so, were providing the sinews of war for the revolutionary cause at the expense of the Czarist régime. The object was to encourage them to plunder some jeweller's shop on the understanding that the spoils would be sold to raise funds for the revolutionaries.

Sir Basil Thomson's reference to the 'Jack the Ripper' murders in London's East End in 1888 in connection with the Russian revolutionaries is not as far-fetched as it may seem. The British Secret Service, of course, discouraged police action against the Anarchists on the grounds that this would play into the hands of the Russian Government agents and make fools of the police. One of the criminals who almost certainly escaped arrest was the man responsible for the 'Jack the Ripper' murders. He was named as a suspect in the Metropolitan Police archives as Mikhail Ostrog, a Russian medical student or doctor, who had a whole string of aliases and was said to have been used as an *agent provocateur* by the Ochrana.

The theory that 'Jack the Ripper' was an Ochrana *agent provocateur*, deliberately sent to London to commit a series of murders to discredit the revolutionaries, is so fanciful that at first sight it hardly seems worth further investigation. Yet William Le Queux, who claimed to have been given access to a great quantity of documents found in a safe in the cellar in Rasputin's house after the death of the strange *moujik* monk, alleged that in these was evidence of the identity of 'Jack the Ripper'.

Le Queux asserted that the information came from a Russian in London named Nideroest, who was told the story by an old Anarchist, Nicholas Zverieff. Quoting from Rasputin's manuscript, Le Queux stated: 'The report of Nideroest's discovery amused our Secret Police [i.e. the Russians] greatly, for, as a matter of fact, they knew the whole details at the time and had themselves actively aided and encouraged the crimes in order to exhibit to the world certain defects of the English police system. . . . It was indeed, for that reason that Pedachenko [one of Ostrog's aliases], the greatest and boldest of all Russian criminal lunatics, was encouraged to go to London and commit that series of atrocious crimes, in which our agents of police aided him.

'Eventually, at the orders of the Ministry of the Interior, the Secret Police smuggled the assassin out of London and, as Count Luiskovo, he landed at Ostend and was conducted by a secret agent to Moscow.'

This extraordinary story does reveal something of the complex and obscure relationships between Russian Secret Police, the External Agency, British police, the British Secret Service and Anarchists and revolutionaries in London in this period. Nideroest did, in fact, exist, though he was not a Russian, as Le Queux suggested, but a Swiss, and a member of the Russian and Lettish Socialist Club in the East End. It is more than likely that he was a double-agent, or an agent of the Ochrana as well as being a revolutionary. In 1909 the British police discovered that he had been selling information to the newspapers about bombs made in Whitechapel. The police found his reports were totally untrue. Six years later he was deported as an undesirable alien.

Each year the Ochrana published a volume of information about revolutionaries with details of their programmes and lists of their members. This book was circulated among senior officials. At some date between 1902 and 1905 at fortnightly intervals they produced a lithographed paper called the *Ochrana Gazette*, which was distributed solely to the heads of each Ochrana section. This paper was a summary of various intelligence reports sent in both by the Internal and External Agencies, code names being used for agents mentioned in the reports.

The *Gazette* contained one specially illuminating item that throws a little more light on the 'Jack the Ripper' murders. This was an official announcement, declaring as 'officially dead' a man known under the names of Pedachenko, Luiskovo, Konovalov and Ostrog, 'who was wanted for the murder of a woman in Paris in 1886, for the murder of five women in the East Quarter of London in 1888, and again for the murder of a woman in Petrograd in 1891.'

Now the description of this man certainly tallied with the official Scotland Yard description of the man wanted for the 'Ripper' murders. Even more significant is the fact that Sir Melville Macnaghten, a former head of the Criminal Investigation Department at Scotland Yard, declared that a Russian surgeon was on the list of suspects, not to mention the evidence that Scotland Yard received a communication from the Russian police on the subject.

The extent of Russian espionage in the Far East in the last century has been somewhat overdrawn by fiction writers. It never compared in scope with the net which the Ochrana cast over Europe and the story of the Russian use of spies to stir up trouble against the British empire in India is little more than a myth, manufactured in the twentieth century by film-makers and others for the purpose of cashing in on the anti-communist vogue of the Western world.

Certainly in the latter part of the last century Russia was easily leading all the great powers in spending on espionage. In 1886 it was calculated that the British and the Germans were spending about £65,000 a year each on their Secret Services, far less than were the Russians. Some estimates show that Russia was spending more than a million pounds a year on spying in the seventies and eighties and certainly the figure was approaching £1,700,000 a year at the turn of the century.

Russia's main interest in India *vis-à-vis* Britain was similar to her interest in the Middle East today, not so much a desire to acquire territory as to increase her influence and, incidentally, to provoke any trouble which would weaken her potential or imagined enemies. To understand this policy one must understand the fundamental differences between Russia and the other great powers in the last century. Like the other European powers Russia was anxious to extend her influence in the Far East and the Middle East, where her conquests in Central Asia had been achieved between 1864 and 1878. But Russia's empire was unlike those of the other great powers: their empires were scattered, Russia's was one great land mass.

Persia was a centre of rather more spying activity between Russia and Britain because this was a territory where the two powers were frequently clashing. Even during the Boer War Russia sought to take advantage of Britain's preoccupation in South Africa by fomenting trouble in Persia and spies were ordered to spread rumours that there were large reinforcements of Russian troops in Trans-Caspia, when in fact there were probably no more than two thousand. Perhaps the most conspicuous Russian espionage success was their infiltration of Shapsal Khan, a Karaite Jew from the Crimea, educated in St Petersburg and a skilled agent, into the ruling circles of Persia. Shapsal Khan first became tutor to the Shah's son, Mohammed Ali, and then when he succeeded to the throne his most trusted adviser and head of the Persian secret police. This post gave him every opportunity of using the Persian espionage system for the Russians.

Hardly less successful was Colonel Kosagovsky, the head and organiser of the Persian Cossack Brigade on behalf of the Shah. The colonel received his orders direct from St Petersburg and was given full powers to direct espionage inside Persia. In his papers Colonel Kosagovsky described how he prevented the Shah from having this Brigade officered by Germans and how he made Martiros Khan, a Moscow-educated Armenian refugee and an Ochrana agent, his chief of staff.

With the advent of the Russo-Japanese War in 1904 great efforts were made to improve Russian Intelligence on the Japanese front. General Harting, a key figure in the overseas section of the Ochrana, was sent to Manchuria to develop counter-espionage against the Japanese. He was provided with carefully chosen agents and large sums of money, but even then it was a long time before he produced any worthwhile results. The Japanese had proved themselves more skilled in their spying, far more orderly in their planning of espionage and, above all, better placed in their use of foreigners as agents. They had shown a Teutonic thoroughness in preparing for this war and their espionage machine went smoothly into action from the start. For example, the Japanese used the Chinese as spies and helped them to infiltrate behind the enemy lines so that they could glean information.

Early on the Russians had tended to employ individualist adventurers as agents in the Far East much as the British had done with such men as Sir Richard Burton. There was Peter Alexandrovitsh Badmayeff, a Mongolian herbalist who rose to become a court intriguer. As a result of his reputation as an amateur medico who had acquired the secret herbal recipes of the Tibetans he was made an Army doctor in the Russo-Turkish war. Badmayeff has sometimes been portrayed as an evil genius similar to his associate Rasputin. It has been suggested that Rasputin paid him to administer small doses of poison to the Czarevitch and then to stop these as soon as Rasputin was called in to pray for the child's life. A. T. Vassilyev says that Badmayeff was 'the subject of the foulest calumnies', but that these were the inventions of 'shameless journalists' and that he personally held him in the highest esteem. That he was a remarkable doctor with a deep insight into Tibetan medicines and native cures is not questioned by those who knew him intimately. Though a skilled intriguer and adept at manipulating affairs in his country's interests, he was never the charlatan described by some writers. In his peculiar way Badmayeff was a do-gooder. He devoted much of his time and money to charities and to advocating the cause of those less fortunate than himself.

He genuinely wished to improve the lot of the people in Eastern Siberia, a mission hardly guaranteed to make him popular in high places. But this remarkable man had his own way. He was given permission to take a delegation to Eastern Siberia. Beneath that mask of charitable intentions and academic pretensions lay a shrewd mind, politically astute and imbued with an encyclopaedic knowledge of the remote parts of Russia, Mongolia and Tibet. In the Russian Secret Service he was the foremost authority on Mongolian and Tibetan affairs and the first agent to provide a detailed dossier on the Forbidden City of Lhasa. If he possessed a fault it was a fondness for using his influence with the Czar to find posts for his patients.

Under cover of promoting the building of railways across Siberia and Manchuria Badmayeff acquired a considerable amount of intelligence on the Far East generally. During the war with Japan he was entirely responsible for bringing in the Mongolian chiefs on Russia's side. He was a great patriot and intensely loyal to the Czar.

Both the Russians and the Japanese began to employ Chinese as spies against each other. It was, of course, economical for both powers to do so as such spies were obtained at very low rates of pay – for a few roubles a Chinese would be prepared to carry out the work of an Ochrana agent earning ten times as much. For a long time the Japanese were much more successful in their use of the Chinese as agents than were the Russians. As a result the Japanese were able to locate the areas where the Russians had laid mines, where they had set up their hidden searchlights and even the locations of their electric power stations.

Thus General Harting's problem was to find an answer to Japanese superiority in this field. In the beginning he relied heavily on his own nationals. One of these was a Russian soldier who disguised himself as a Chinese and found his way into a Japanese camp where he was promptly arrested. The Japanese tried him, sentenced him to death and then, having killed him, showed such a high regard for his bravery, dignified bearing and devotion to duty that they sent a report to the Russian C.-in-C., General Kuropatkin, praising his 'noble bearing and honesty'. It was perhaps the last example of chivalrous generosity in modern warfare.

General Harting found it easier to make contacts with the Chinese espionage bureau than did the Japanese. Here he gained an advantage. The Chinese were well aware of the infiltration of Japanese spies among their coolies and, being concerned about the long-term effects of this and about Japanese intentions towards China, they tended to favour the Russians slightly. Harting played on this fear and established relations with Yuan Shi K'ai, head of the Chinese secret police. The latter informed Harting that in his estimate twelve out of every hundred coolies around Port Arthur were Japanese and from that moment there was a high degree of co-operation between the Chinese and the Russians.

The ignominious defeat of the Russians in 1904–5 by Japan resulted in a complete reversal of Russian policy and in consequence there was an overhaul of the Secret Service. The pro-German elements in that Service had been routed on many previous occasions, but always a few of them had crept back into power. Now there was a demand for their total removal.

Imperialism in the Far East had been a disastrous adventure and there was no desire to revive it. So Russia turned towards Europe once more, with an eye to possible long-term advantages in the Middle East, regarding the latter as a vital flank against the intrigues of European powers and as a gateway to the Mediterranean. This flank, the Russians knew, must be protected at all costs, with concessions where necessary. Curiously, in her hour of defeat Russia kept her head and became markedly realistic in her appreciation of the position in Europe and the Middle East. Notwithstanding that Britain had sided with 'little Japan' against Russia and that the Kaiser had sympathetically encouraged the military adventure against Japan, Russia began to seek areas for agreement with Britain and cooled off in her relations with Germany.

An interesting sidelight on the extremely long arm of the Russian counter-espionage was provided by an incident during the Russo-Japanese War. The Russian fleet had been ordered to sail east to destroy the Japanese fleet and as the Russian ships were stationed in the western ports they had to sail from the North Sea to the Mediterranean and then on to the Far East. A heavy fog descended when the Russian ships were bearing down on the Dogger Bank and, in a moment of panic, due no doubt to the low state of morale and incompetent leadership, the Russians opened fire on a British fishing fleet in the belief that it was the Japanese Navy. The incident strained almost to breaking point relations between Britain and Russia and the London *Daily Mail* sent Edgar Wallace, then one of their correspondents, to Vigo, the next port of call for the Russians, to ascertain what had happened. In Vigo Wallace found two petty officers from the Russian fleet and they explained how the fog had created the utmost confusion, that the fishing vessels had made no response to signals and that the Russian officers had been convinced that a small detachment of the Japanese fleet had deliberately tried to trap them in the shallows. Wallace's report of all this was wired to the *Daily Mail*, who, not unnaturally, felt that the story was somewhat thin. They ordered Wallace to proceed to Tangier, the next port of call of the Russian fleet, to obtain more facts. When he got there he learned that the petty officers had been executed and buried at sea. The Russian counter-espionage in Vigo had obviously acted swiftly.

In the political changes that followed the Japanese War Witte returned to power. It was on his advice that the Czar had agreed to his manifesto of October 1905 in which he granted freedom of speech, conscience and meetings, and parliamentary elections. True, Witte, who became Prime Minister, did not last long before he was dismissed by the Czar, but this brief period of the old man's final ascendancy to power was sufficient to bring about an upheaval in the Secret Service. British agents who had been enemies suddenly became friends, Germans who had helped the Russian cause and backed her against Japan were immediately suspect. Friendly contacts were reopened with the Japanese, largely through Witte's own private espionage service in the commercial field. Russian spies were actually withdrawn from Japan and sent to Shanghai and Peking.

There was the seemingly insignificant, but totally symbolic case of Sidney Reilly, who was for the next twenty years to be sometimes the hero of the Russians, sometimes their most wanted villain with a price on his head. Born in South Russia, not far from Odessa, on 24 March 1874, Sidney Reilly was, as far as records tell us, originally Sigmund Georgievich Rosenblum, the son of Pauline and Grigory Jakovlevich Rosenblum, a Polish-Jewish landowner who came from Warsaw. That much seems certain. But the story that Reilly told to a few of his intimates in the latter part of his life was that as a child he was brought up to believe that he was the son of a Russian mother of Polish descent and that his father was a colonel in the Russian Army with connections at the court of the Czar. Then, so Reilly alleged, he discovered at the age of nineteen that he was not his father's son at all, but the product of an illicit union between his mother and a Jewish doctor from Vienna and that his real name was Rosenblum. Whatever the truth may have been, the youth's one desire seemed to be to put the furthest distance between himself and his home, to cut himself off from his family and seek a new life in anonymity. So he ran away to South America and, quite by chance, met an agent of the British Secret Service whose life he was supposed to have saved. The reward for this was a passage to Britain for the young Russian and an introduction to a key figure in the British S.I.S.

Reilly became an agent of the British and, doubtless on the strength of his own stories about his past, was a highly successful spy inside Russia well before the turn of the century. Then, shortly before the Russo-Japanese War, he turned up in the Far East, a double-agent serving both the British and the Japanese. Reilly – for this was the name he had adopted when he took a British passport – had a keen sense of politics and was something of a prophet. He warned of the imminence of the Russo-Japanese War and, when informing his Secret Service chief in London of this, asked for a year's leave of absence on the grounds that he did not want to become embroiled in the forthcoming conflict. No doubt at heart he still had a great affection for Russia, but few agents, even in those days when the individual spy was given far greater latitude, would have made such terms with their masters. Reilly's case was that Britain's future lay with Russia and that he did not wish to do anything which might spoil his relations with the Russians. His plea was granted and he went underground for a period in China where he lived in a lamasery in the province of Shen-Si and became a Buddhist.

Curiously Reilly still retained the respect and trust of his British masters and at the same time made secret approaches to Witte, principally, it would seem, on commercial espionage and Chinese intelligence. Before he returned to London he made a secret trip to Russia and saw Badmayeff, giving him extensive information about China. By this time Reilly had ceased to have any contact with the Japanese, but he was certainly used by the Russians. The latter encouraged him to spy on the Germans and, in view of the *Entente*, he was as happy to do this for them as for the British. In those vital years in the early part of the twentieth century he was keeping Russia fully informed on German rearmament plans.

Reilly became a member of the most exclusive gambling club in St Petersburg, the Koupetchesky, where his luck at the tables and his conquest of the ladies were a legend of society. He was a charmer, gregarious, an excellent mixer at all levels, with a reputation as a man who could arrange complex cosmopolitan business deals and a gay Lothario who loved parties. All who knew him spoke of his magnetic personality and his supreme gift of coaxing people to do things for him. He disarmed suspicion by behaving in a roisteringly extrovert manner, even deliberately courting attention. The truth was that he made far more money out of spying for the Russians, but probably gave better value for much less money to the British.

It was about 1906 that Reilly began to work for the Russian Intelligence. The Czarist régime was markedly anti-semitic, especially under that last Czar, Nicholas II. Thus Reilly would be anxious to cover all traces of his Jewish ancestry while in Russia and the story of a father who was a Russian colonel might well have served him well in pursuing his relations with the Ochrana.

Years afterwards Reilly's last wife – he was married at least three times and at least once bigamously – drew aside the curtain on some of his activities in Russia in these years prior to World War I. 'In Petrograd he held an important post with a firm of Russian naval contractors. . . . He had a sumptuous flat, part of which was quite a museum of objects of Renaissance art, and his library of the finest editions extended to more than three thousand volumes. He drove the smartest equipages and had as fine horses as were to be found anywhere in Russia.'

One of the tasks which the Russian Secret Service set for Sidney Reilly was to build up a dossier on the notorious international arms salesman, Basil Zaharoff. This sinister figure, who moved in the shadows of the seats of power all over the world, had already become something of a legend by the early nineteen-hundreds. He had not only benefited from the international arms race, he had almost created it. No one quite knew what his origins were and Zaharoff, like Reilly, gave different people contradictory versions about his parentage and nationality. In his youth he had been a brothel tout in Constantinople, graduating to the rôle of small-time moneylender and then salesman for Maxim-Nordenfelt's arms firm. But by 1905 he was the chief continental salesman for the then amalgamated company of Vickers of England and Maxim-Nordenfelt, earning £86,000 a year in commissions and a free company house in Paris. He sold arms to both sides in any war.

In Russia the need to rearm coincided with a new surge of nationalism, but the nationalists were insisting that orders should be given to Russian firms. Zaharoff was equally determined to sell his own arms to Russia and, to achieve this, he played on Russian suspicion and spy-fever. He informed the Ochrana that the Russian arms firm of Putiloff was the secret centre of sabotage-practising revolutionary workers and that in an emergency they could not be relied upon. It was true enough, as the Ochrana soon established, that the Putiloff works contained a number of Bolshevik cells, but they had an uneasy feeling that Zaharoff himself might have planted them there.

They had some reason to be suspicious because the rumour was in Russian Secret Service circles that Zaharoff was not, as he had suggested, a Greek born in Asia Minor, but the son of a Jew named Sahar, who had lived in Odessa. At this time Sidney Reilly was telling the Russians that he had been born near Odessa. What better man, thought the Ochrana, to make some inquiries into Zaharoff's past.

Zaharoff and Reilly became secret foes of one another from about 1907–8 and it is hard to say who won their long duel of wits, a duel made more difficult and hazardous for each because while Reilly served in both the British and Russian Secret Services, Zaharoff had influence in high places in Britain, Russia and France. What Reilly discovered is a matter of some conjecture, but the *Ochrana Gazette* identified Zaharoff as 'Basilius Zacharias, formerly of Odessa, Russian subject, born in Constantinople, wanted for desertion, theft and revolutionary activities', and in 1924 the Soviet authorities furnished the Turkish Government with a dossier on Zaharoff's origins.

Myednikoff, head of the Moscow Ochrana, was convinced that Zaharoff was a deserter from the Russian Army and that it was because of his Army service that he had acquired a knowledge of the purely technical and mechanical side of armaments. What worried the Ochrana was neither his desertion, nor his theft, but his links with the revolutionaries. For before he had become one of the chief salesmen of armaments throughout the world, Zaharoff had been an active revolutionary.

The Russians remained wary of Zaharoff – at least their Secret Service did – for in one report that Myednikoff made during this period he stated: 'Reports from independent sources suggest that M. Zaharoff is firmly on the side of the *Entente*. No doubt he is, in his own interests. But we must remember two things: first, that M. Zaharoff is interested in oil and that is our long-term interest which may conflict with his. Secondly, M. Zaharoff has been selling arms to Russia since 1888. He has a very strange method of doing this: he believes that arms can best be sold through the good offices of the mistresses of influential people. This is how he sold guns to Russia when he made friends with the ballerina who was the mistress of the Grand Duke in charge of our artillery. Zaharoff prospers on bribes and bribes can spell treachery.'

As a double-agent Sidney Reilly combined his job of spying with that of giving political advice. However rascally he may have been in his private life Reilly was not at this time a double-agent in the worst sense of the word: he was not a traitor to either side. Whatever spying he did for Russia did not harm Britain and his efforts on behalf of Britain were designed to improve relations with Russia. As far back as 1907 Reilly warned the Ochrana that a Caucasian named Josef Vissarionvich Dzhugashvili, who was one of their agents, was betraying their secrets to the revolutionaries. The Czarist police either ignored or disbelieved Reilly's allegations and so the man who was later to be known as Josef Stalin escaped the wrath of the Ochrana to become the bloodiest tyrant the Russian people have known since the days of Ivan the Terrible.

Born in 1879, the early career of Josef Stalin bore close resemblance to those of Gapon the priest and Azeff himself. He first studied for the priesthood in a theological seminary at Tiflis, his sole aim being to gain some education. Then at the age of seventeen he became a secret revolutionary. When he was twenty-five he joined the Ochrana as an informer, offering to act as an *agent provocateur* on account of his close associations with the revolutionaries.

The Ochrana pointed out to Reilly that Stalin gave them valuable information about other revolutionaries. 'Of course he does,' replied Reilly, 'but if you examine that information closely you will find that the information concerns not his friends, the Bolsheviks, but his enemies, the Mensheviks.'

9

The Fall of Azeff

BY THE year 1907 the Russian Secret Service was concentrating its espionage activities against Germany, spending vast sums of money in this sphere and obtaining good results. That was the credit side of the picture. On the debit side the Ochrana had been effectively infiltrated by a number of revolutionaries and the Bolsheviks in particular had, as a result, built up not only a counter-espionage organisation of their own, but a kind of shadow secret service which was being groomed to take over the Ochrana in the event of a successful revolution.

Stalin, Azeff and Felix Dzerzhinski, the son of a Polish aristocrat who had joined the revolutionaries, were only a few from the underground movements who had penetrated the heart of the Ochrana. The tactics of the *agent provocateur* eventually boomeranged against the Ochrana, yet only one or two of its chiefs could see this. Vassilyev stated: 'During the whole of my service in the Police Department I strenuously opposed the so-called Central Agency – that is, the practice followed by the Ochrana of associating with itself, as co-workers, people who were themselves at the head of revolutionary societies. . . . Experience has shown that . . . useful results could hardly ever be attained.'

Vassilyev also criticised the 'endless red tape' in the affairs of the Secret Agency. 'It might, and did, happen that in some districts, though the Secret Police were quite well informed by their assistants of the abominable practices of the revolutionary societies, the people in charge of the Sections in question would calmly go on piling up papers, and never make up their minds to intervene in any energetic fashion. Such bureaucratic methods were, in the Ochrana, even more out of place than in any other branch of the State Service, and the situations to which they gave rise were sometimes quite grotesque.'

By the beginning of 1906 it was clear that the revolutionaries were becoming so well organised that the Ochrana needed to make internal changes to meet this situation. M. I. Trusyevitsh, the new Chief of Police, devised a system of allotting specially trained agents, who underwent a crash course in counter-revolutionary measures, to cover specified areas in which the revolutionaries operated. But the mistake he made was to put young Army officers at the head of these Sections and it was their lack of experience in this kind of work which militated against the success of the plan.

Often there was an unbelievable naïvety in the manner in which highly placed Ochrana chiefs put their trust in revolutionaries who offered them information. A typical example was the sad case of Colonel S. G. Karpoff, the chief of the St Petersburg section of the Ochrana. Early in 1909 confidential reports leaked out of another plot to assassinate the Czar and the Prime Minister, Stolypin. At the same time news was sent to the Ochrana by the governor of the prison at Saratov that a revolutionary named Petroff, who was held there, was prepared to give full details of the plot in exchange for his freedom. The man was allowed to escape from prison, the Ochrana were tipped off and they first shadowed him and then made contact. Petroff provided some information which was not of much importance and some of which was actually inaccurate. This should have been a warning to the Ochrana that they were dealing with a dangerous man, but they persisted in allowing him his freedom. Somehow Petroff won the confidence of Colonel Karpoff and then made an extraordinary proposition to him.

'You have given me your trust,' said Petroff, 'and because of the freedom of movement you have allowed me I have been able to meet important members of the revolutionary movement. I now know the broad details of the plot to kill the Czar. All that we need now are the final, last-minute details so that all the plotters can be rounded up.

'But from now on my life will be in danger if I am seen visiting you. There is only one way in which we can remain in the closest contact and yet keep our association a secret. We must live together in the same apartment for the next week or two, or until I get the final details. You will remain hidden there and not show yourself to anyone.'

It was an astonishing request, yet Colonel Karpoff accepted the proposal. An apartment was hired at a secret address in Archangel Street and, incredibly, Petroff was allowed to make all the arrangements for furnishing the place. No Ochrana agent kept watch on what Petroff was doing; presumably Petroff's request for absolute secrecy had been too literally interpreted. The result was that he installed electric bells in the apartment; there was a wire from the street door and one from the door of the flat. The wire to the door bell was controlled by a switch which could put the bell out of action. Petroff then placed a charge of dynamite under a table in the apartment and linked this by a set of concealed wires to the bell system.

Thus when Colonel Karpoff arrived at the flat the street door bell had been disconnected and the bell did not work. So he climbed the stairs to the apartment and was shown in by Petroff. The latter talked for a few minutes, made an excuse that he had to go out, went down the stairs, and put on the switch to make the downstairs bell ring. Then, when he was outside the front door, he pressed the bell which caused the charge to detonate. Karpoff was killed instantly.

Extension of the Russian spy system abroad led to increasing use being made of attachés in Russian embassies. Their very amateurishness, however, led to their being quickly detected by the counter-espionage services of foreign powers. But it was not easy in those days, when protocol counted for so much, to get rid of them. Expulsion of a diplomat or attaché was almost tantamount to a declaration of war: at the best it meant an international incident which threatened to escalate the war fever. A further complication was the fact that, generally speaking, Russian attachés were usually extremely popular in the social life of a capital. One such was Colonel Zantiewitsch, a Russian military attaché in Vienna. The colonel was the toast of the ladies of the Viennese court and much liked by the men. He was discovered to have been paying bribes for information over a long period.

Nobody dared to expel him, so the Emperor Franz Josef hit on the device of ostentatiously ignoring him at a court ball. Colonel Zantiewitsch quickly interpreted this as a signal that his spying activities had been detected and he quietly asked St Petersburg to recall him.

The Russians' greatest successes were achieved in Germany where they not only had a highly skilled team of spies, including the double-agent Sidney Reilly, but succeeded by bribery and corruption in infiltrating the German and Austrian Intelligence systems. They were among the first to discover the lesson that homosexuals in the intelligence game are singularly vulnerable. One such man they swiftly spotted was Colonel Alfred Redl, head of the Austrian espionage and counter-espionage organisation, the *Kundschafts Stelle*, which came directly under the orders of the head of the Austrian Secret Service, General Baron von Giesl. Redl had worked his way up the military ladder the hard way; what he lacked in birth, influence and wealth he compensated for in military virtues, an astute mind and first-class qualities for organisation. He was a gifted linguist, had travelled widely and built up a remarkably competent intelligence system which had been of great benefit to Austro-Hungary and indirectly to Germany.

Russian spies of the External Agency had been warned to ascertain the weaknesses of key figures in foreign intelligence services. One of these reported back to St Petersburg that the Achilles' heel of Colonel Redl was his secret passion for boys. Armed with this knowledge, the Russians set out ruthlessly to blackmail him.

The Colonel's appointment as head of the *Kundschafts Stelle* had been made in 1900. Within five years the Russians had contacted him, warned him that they had abundant evidence of his homosexual activities, and threatened to expose him unless he agreed to work for them. Thus Redl became one of the most valuable spies the Russians possessed in Europe.

St Petersburg's prime interest was in obtaining a full list of every Austrian spy in Russia and in obtaining complete details of the Austro-Hungarian military code. Redl not only provided the answers, but for good measure gave the Russians details of Austria's war plans in the event of an attack on Russia. For the last seven years of his service Redl spent half his time spying on behalf of the Russians and the other half for Austria.

Redl made a point of having every visitor to his office, as far as was possible, photographed and fingerprinted, and many of these records were passed on directly to the Russians. Hidden cameras photographed each visitor both full-face and side-face and fingerprints were obtained by a variety of ruses, the most usual being to ask the person to help himself to cigarettes from a box which was treated in a manner that enabled the prints to be retained.

The Russians had their failures, of course, but these were mainly due to excess of zeal. There was the energetic Colonel Bazaroff, their military attaché in Berlin, who made the fatal mistake of assuming the gathering of information was all too easy and who failed to bear in mind that his predecessor, Colonel Michelsen, had been detected by the Germans and asked to leave the country. A cautious man would have bided his time, but Bazaroff immediately set out to bribe officials in the Cartographical Section of the

German War Office. A close watch had been kept on Bazaroff by a sergeant-major in the military intelligence and he reported the attempts to obtain copies of secret maps. Bazaroff was immediately asked to leave Germany. Relying on the inhibiting influence of the magic word protocol, Bazaroff decided that attack was the best mode of defence and he declared that to be accused by a non-commissioned officer was a breach of military etiquette and an insult to his country. The Germans were unimpressed: they ordered him to go.

Meanwhile inside Russia Ievno Azeff was as active as ever. He maintained his links with the 'Battle Organisation' and continued to work under A. V. Gerassimoff, head of the St Petersburg section of the Ochrana. At regular intervals Azeff and Savinkoff went abroad to learn the latest techniques in dynamiting and the use of explosive mines. In 1906 Azeff established a new headquarters for the 'Battle Organisation' in Finland. In league with Gerassimoff he had decided to recommend that the organisation should be dissolved on the grounds that their methods were now out of date and that the Ochrana had learned how to combat them. They must, urged Azeff, cease all activity for a period and then re-form in an entirely new unit.

Savinkoff opposed Azeff's plan and wanted to go ahead with even more ambitious schemes of terror and assassination. Though Azeff eventually won over Savinkoff to his own way of thinking, he was unable to carry the day with some of the other revolutionaries. The 'rebels' in the organisation then started a unit of their own. Azeff in disgust went temporarily to live in Alassio on the Italian Riviera.

But if Azeff was disgusted at his failure to keep full control of revolutionary activities, Gerassimoff was quick to realise that without Azeff's aid he was working completely in the dark. 'Gerassimoff,' wrote Boris Nicolaievsky, 'saw clearly that he could not cope with the terror without Azeff, and that Azeff must, at all costs, be put back in his former position.'

So Azeff was recalled from his retirement on the Italian Riviera and given full authority and ample cash to ascertain the up-to-date position of the revolutionaries. He reported to Gerassimoff that the terrorists had found a new ally in a retired Russian Navy lieutenant named Nikitenko, who moved in social circles in St Petersburg, was an acquaintance of the Grand Duke Nicholas and belonged to the exclusive English Club. In consequence the Ochrana kept watch on Nikitenko and discovered that he had suborned a young Cossack in the Czar's entourage. Within a short time no less than twenty-eight terrorists were arrested, including Nikitenko.

Gerassimoff was rewarded for his part in all this by being promoted to the rank of General by the Czar. Azeff disappeared to the Crimea and it is a tribute to his skill in covering his tracks to note that Savinkoff said of him at this time: 'My confidence in Azeff was so great that I should not have believed in his guilt even if I had seen it stated in his own handwriting. I should have considered it a forgery.'

Vassilyev in his history of the Ochrana said that his predecessor as Chief of Police, A. A. Lopuchin, 'some time after his retirement . . . committed the grave indiscretion of communicating to Burtsev [a revolutionary sympathiser] . . . that Azeff had been a secret agent of the Ochrana.' He added that Burtsev had lost no time in publishing his conversation with Lopuchin in the Opposition press. This is somewhat unfair to Lopuchin, as the facts are somewhat different. V. L. Burtsev, the editor of an historical review entitled *Byloye*, was an academic revolutionary, one who was more concerned with the history of the whole revolutionary movement than in the actual job of making revolution. Knowing full well that none of his friends in the active revolutionary ranks would pay any attention to his theories that Azeff was a police spy, he decided to play the rôle of a lone detective. He had made various overtures to Lopuchin after the latter's retirement, begging him to write his memoirs for *Byloye*. But his reason in seeking these was that he felt Lopuchin could help to provide the background to a history of the revolutionary movement. Lopuchin had always declined these offers.

Burtsev's obsession about Azeff's treachery was such that he was determined to expose the double-agent and he regarded Lopuchin as a valuable ally in realising this ambition. For by 1907 Azeff had acquired even greater authority in the regrouping of the revolutionary ranks. A new plot to assassinate the Czar was being devised, involving the creation of a modified type of 'Battle Organisation' allied to a unit known as 'Karl's Flying Detachment'. This was a dedicated, highly disciplined revolutionary *corps d'élite* whose members lived frugally and ascetically without in any way depending on party funds. Indeed, they not only lived independently but actually *contributed* money to the Party. The organisation had its headquarters in Finland and the principal targets for its attacks were key figures in the police, prison governors and military prosecutors. 'Karl's Flying Detachment' was responsible for a number of assassinations.

Burtsev had discovered Azeff's links with Karl and he warned a member of the 'Flying Detachment' about the traitor in their midst. Azeff, whose spies were everywhere, soon heard about Burtsev's warning and decided the time had come to destroy the organisation. So he told Gerassimoff that Karl's headquarters were in Finland and gave him some vague details of a plot to infiltrate the State Council and kill all its members by bomb attack.

Azeff's tip-off was lacking in detail (once again he took care not to give away too much information in case suspicion might fall on him), but it was enough for the Ochrana to launch a large-scale search for 'Karl' and to obtain permission from Stolypin, the Prime Minister, to violate Finnish territory, in the process. In December 1907 a band of Ochrana agents crossed into Finland and raided apartments where they discovered the archives of the 'Flying Detachment'. Thinking they were safe in neutral territory, the revolutionaries had taken no special precautions. Several arrests followed and the Ochrana were shortly able to announce that a plot to assassinate members of the State Council had been thwarted.

Burtsev was determined to confront Lopuchin with the evidence he had gathered against Azeff. He arranged to be on the train that Lopuchin was taking from Cologne to St Petersburg after a visit to Germany, but, to make it appear that this was a chance encounter, Burtsev talked first of all about his literary work and then mentioned that he was shortly going to expose the activities of a police agent who was at the head of the Social Revolutionary Battle Organisation.

Not until Burtsev mentioned the code name of 'Raskin', by which Azeff was known in Ochrana circles did Lopuchin evince much interest in Burtsev's story. Then, as the tale of treachery was unravelled, Lopuchin was first puzzled, then astonished at the extent of Burtsev's knowledge of Azeff. As he listened Lopuchin began to realise for the first time that it must have been Azeff who had planned the assassinations of the Grand Duke and of Plehve. If that were so, then much else that had previously perplexed Lopuchin became much clearer. It dawned on him that the man behind Azeff must have been Ratchkovsky who must not only have known all about the assassinations, but even encouraged them so that Ratchkovsky's chief enemy, Plehve, could be removed. This surmise made even more sense when Lopuchin recalled that Ratchkovsky was the man who had organised the anarchist explosion in Liège Cathedral through one of his agents, Yagolovsky. Ratchkovsky must have used Azeff as a deliberate instrument to ensure his comeback to power.

In the light of Burtsev's formidable evidence there was little point in Lopuchin denying what he knew to be true and indeed he had no desire to do so. But Lopuchin was still cautious: 'I know

113

nobody of the name of Raskin,' he said, 'but I have seen the engineer, Ievno Azeff, several times.'

This was enough for Burtsev. He set to work to publicise the treachery of Azeff both through his writings and in correspondence with revolutionaries. The latter continued to regard Burtsev as the victim of gossip and ignored his warnings. Then Burtsev learned in 1908 that Azeff was attending a conference of revolutionary delegates in London. Burtsev sent a letter to Teploff, who was attending the conference and was also a member of the Central Committee, who then decided that Burtsev ought to be 'tried' for libelling Azeff.

Fortunately, Savinkoff, that dedicated and incorruptible revolutionary, was convinced that Burtsev was sincere in making his allegations and that his motives were beyond reproach. To try to convince Burtsev that he was wrong, Savinkoff told him many things about Azeff that were new to Burtsev, but which only confirmed his suspicions. The result of these talks was an open letter to members of the Social Revolutionary Party which was duly published.

The 'trial' of Burtsev was carried out by revolutionaries in their so-called Court of Honour in Paris, curiously enough in Savinkoff's apartment in that city. For a long time, under rigorous cross-examination, Burtsev loyally kept Lopuchin's name out of the discussions, but the prosecution against him was relentless: one witness after another testified to Azeff's invaluable services over many years to the revolutionary cause.

'As a historian of the Russian revolutionary movement,' said Savinkoff, who was one of the prosecutors, 'now that we have told you of Azeff's achievements, can you tell us whether there exists in the history of the Russian revolutionary movement a more brilliant name than that of Azeff?'

Then came the final thrust from Figner, who was one of the judges: 'Do you know what you will have to do if your accusations are proved groundless?' he asked Burtsev. 'You will have nothing left but to shoot yourself for all the harm you have done to the Revolution.'

It was only under this pressure that Burtsev broke his promise to Lopuchin, describing his meeting with the former police chief. This revelation caused some of the judges to revise their opinions. After heated debate it was agreed that Burtsev's trial should be ended, but that a further investigation into Azeff's conduct should be carried out.

Possibly Azeff had begun to believe that his position as a double-agent was impregnable. In Ochrana circles his part in destroying 'Karl's Flying Detachment' had safeguarded him from any suspicions in that sphere, while in the revolutionary ranks he had had evidence enough that rumours against him were dismissed as malicious gossip. To the revolutionaries he had criticised 'Karl's Detachment' as being badly organised, totally lacking in security precautions and therefore deserving of destruction and they had accepted his strictures as valid. At the same time Azeff was tipping off the Ochrana that the funds of the Central Committee of the revolutionaries were being boosted to the extent of 300,000 roubles through a raid on the Charjui Government treasury. Gerassimoff, who received this information, did not ask Azeff to arrange for this money to be captured by the Ochrana, despite the fact that Stolypin had given orders that the raiders should be arrested and the money restored to the authorities. As far as Gerassimoff was concerned, he was content to allow Azeff to obtain for himself a major share of this money on the tacit understanding that he did not ask for a rise in his police salary. So Azeff arranged for the money to be transferred to Turkestan and collected his share there.

Gerassimoff also was living something of a double life at this time. While working for the Ochrana in an executive capacity, he had cut himself off from them by living under an assumed name at a secret address known only to Azeff. All the time he was working closely with the double-agent and passing on information to him.

Azeff's wife was a whole-hearted, idealistic revolutionary who knew nothing of her husband's rôle with the Ochrana. Had she done so, it is almost certain that she would have denounced and discarded him. Their married life was thus to a large extent a strain upon Azeff who could never be completely relaxed in his home and needed to be away from it as often as possible. Partly because of this he formed a liaison with a woman who was known under the code name of 'Bella Heddy'. She was German by birth and after leaving school had sought her fortune as a cabaret singer in St Petersburg.

'Bella Heddy' had made herself the toast of young Guards officers in St Petersburg and had supplemented her income so effectively as a courtesan that in 1906 she had actually been able to invest some 50,000 roubles of her money in a Siberian gold mine. But the gold mine turned out to be a mirage and at the time 'Bella Heddy' met Azeff she was looking for some means of retrieving her fortune. Azeff began to lavish expensive presents on her and to pay her bills, but he explained this away to inquisitive revolutionaries on the grounds that she was able to keep him posted on news of Czarist society.

While Burtsev's campaign was being waged against him Azeff

was living in luxury with 'Bella Heddy' in Paris. He fully realised that events were moving inexorably to a show-down and that he could not long continue his double rôle, but he believed he still had a trump card to play. For yet another plot had been hatched to kill the Czar and Azeff was its principal organiser. If this plot succeeded, no evidence against him would be accepted by the revolutionaries. It would surely be unthinkable to them that a man who would arrange the successful assassination of the Czar could be an Ochrana agent.

A new Russian cruiser, the *Rurik*, was being built at Glasgow. It was to sail to Russia where it was to be inspected by the Czar. Azeff went to Glasgow to make arrangements for the assassination attempt. Two projects were considered: one was to hide a revolutionary aboard the cruiser, the other was to persuade a member of the crew to shoot the Czar. Azeff had gone to Glasgow, obtained permission from a naval engineer named Kostenko to look over the ship and decided that the killer must be a member of the crew. This task was assigned to a sailor named Gerassim Avdeyeff, who was given a revolver and detailed instructions. The sailor was a dedicated revolutionary who had been persuaded to give Azeff a letter explaining his motives for his action, on the understanding that this would be published after the attempt on the Czar's life had been made.

So Azeff was able to sit back in his Paris apartment, awaiting a telegram which would tell him that the Czar had been killed and then, with Avdeyeff's letter in his possession, he could finally silence all his hostile critics. The ship sailed to Russia and the Czar boarded the cruiser, but the attempt on his life was never made. Kostenko, the naval engineer, afterwards revealed that the rest of the crew had been planning a mutiny, that they discovered what Avdeyeff was proposing to do and ordered him to desist on the grounds that an attempt on the Czar's life would ruin the mutiny plan and the crew's project for seizing Kronstadt.

The failure of the attempt on the Czar's life sealed Azeff's last hope of escaping detection. In a desperate effort to stave off disaster he hurried to St Petersburg to see Gerassimoff whom he begged to persuade Lopuchin to repudiate Burtsev's statements. But Lopuchin not only declined to do this, but went to London to repeat his story to members of the revolutionary tribunal. From then on the revolutionaries were convinced of Azeff's complicity in the affairs of the Ochrana. They sent a delegation to see him in France and a further cross-examination took place. Azeff persisted in indignantly denying his guilt and the delegates seem to have lost their nerve for they ended the meeting by getting Azeff to promise to see them again the following day.

Of course this error on their part gave Azeff his chance to escape, He left his apartment in the middle of the night, but took care to leave the sailor Avdeyeff's letter on his desk. On 6 January 1909, Azeff left for Germany and rejoined 'Bella Heddy' there. It was the end of his career as an Ochrana agent and both Gerassimoff and Stolypin were furious with Lopuchin for the part he had played in Azeff's downfall.

The Czar ordered Lopuchin to be tried for the betrayal of official secrets, but it was in fact a mockery of a trial. Lopuchin was prevented from making a statement which would have shown that both Stolypin and Gerassimoff had acquiesced in Azeff's double rôle. Lopuchin was exiled to Siberia.

Lopuchin's statement about Stolypin's part in this affair was not revealed until the inquiry into the Azeff affair set up by the Provisional Government in 1917. As this statement is an illuminating commentary on the intrigues that went on in the Ochrana in those days it is worth quoting: 'Once in the spring of 1906 my former associate in the Police Department, Makaroff, told me, on my questioning him about Azeff, that he was still working for Ratchkovsky and Gerassimoff, and that his informative rôle was greater than ever. Soon after, my old school friend, Stolypin, with whom I had renewed acquaintance only two years previously, became Minister of the Interior. I immediately told him about Azeff, and gave him details of the Police printing press which had been used for printing pogrom manifestoes discovered by me in January 1906. Stolypin, it seemed to me, was equally indignant at Azeff's rôle as an *agent provocateur* and at the Department's pogrom policy, and he expressed his determination to put an end to both of them. I went abroad a few days later and there read the report of the Duma session at which Stolypin replied to questions about the activities of this printing press. His explanation was such a perversion of the facts that I was forced to conclude either that Stolypin was lying to the Duma, or that he had been deceived by his subordinates. As I had no grounds for suspecting him of the first, I wrote an official letter to him in which I warned him of the deception and set before him the evidence which I had told him orally.

'The explanations which took place between us when I returned from abroad left no doubt that Stolypin was deliberately perverting the truth in his statements to the Duma. . . . In September 1906 Stolypin angrily accused me of being a manifest revolutionary, and, as Minister of the Interior, warned me to regulate my conduct accordingly. I replied that after his false statements in the Duma I no longer trusted him in anything, and . . . I also warned him that, if it came to my knowledge that Azeff was acting as a police agent, I would make every effort to expose him and end the matter.'

The finale of the Azeff affair created widespread mutual mistrust inside the ranks of the Ochrana. Stolypin sent Gerassimoff on leave, but indicated that on his return he would be promoted and given overall direction of the Secret Police. By the time he came back to St Petersburg Gerassimoff found that he himself was under a shadow and that the Ochrana directorate was being ruthlessly re-deployed. As for the revolutionaries, the revelation of Azeff's guilt demoralised their ranks. Treachery increased and even those innocent of any double-dealing were suspected of being *provocateurs* by their comrades.

Azeff set off on a long holiday with 'Bella Heddy', visiting Italy, Greece and Egypt, but all the time he was expecting an attempt to be made on his life. If he heard of any Russians staying at an hotel into which he had booked, he left immediately. He was constantly changing his name and his passport. Not only were the revolutionaries seeking revenge, but agents of the Ochrana were searching for him.

Eventually he arrived in Germany, settling down as a stockbroker under the name of Alexander Neumayer. Burtsev tracked him down and had a long interview with him, solely for the purpose of obtaining information for his history of the revolutionary movement. Azeff boasted that he would have killed the Czar, if Burtsev had not launched his campaign against him. He argued that he had done more for the revolutionaries than ever he did for the Secret Police, suggesting that the assassination of Plehve and the Grand Duke Sergei far outweighed in importance his betraying of Sletoff, Lomoff and Vedenyapin to the Ochrana.

World War I ruined Azeff's comfortable life in exile. He lost his fortune and was finally discovered by the German secret police who arrested him not because he had been an agent of the Ochrana, but because he was regarded as a dangerous revolutionary. He was released from prison in 1917 and went with his 'Bella Heddy' to live in Berlin where on the 24th April 1918, he died.

10

Stalin's Rôle as an Ochrana Agent

LONDON CONTINUED to be a focal point for the activities both of the Ochrana and the revolutionaries until the outset of World War I. An example of the confusion caused in British police circles as to which Russian was on which side is provided by Detective-Sergeant B. Leeson, whose work took him among Anarchists in London's East End. Leeson told how in 1908 occurred 'the great strike of Jewish dockers in the Whitechapel district, organised by one Perkoff, perhaps Russia's first *agent provocateur* to operate in London. It was a strike organised on Chicago racketeer lines, a method to which the Anarchists were very partial.'

This statement is full of inaccuracies. Perkoff was not, of course, the first Anarchist leader to operate in London, nor was he the first *agent provocateur* to be sent there by the Russians. He was not really an Anarchist, not, at least, in 1908, but a Bolshevik and he belonged to the same revolutionary group as Stalin.

It is not generally known that Stalin himself was involved in Bolshevik activities in London and that he paid surreptitious visits to that city under the name of Josef Georgi. Indeed, Stalin, as much as anyone, was a leading figure behind the scenes in the affair of the Siege of Sidney Street in 1910.

This incident which resulted in a five-hour rifle battle between Anarchists and Scots Guards provided an excellent example of Russian counter-espionage techniques as used abroad. A police sergeant, investigating a report of 'strange noises' coming from a house in Sidney Street, Houndsditch, called there and was shot dead. When other police surrounded the house and demanded that the occupants surrendered they were met by a barrage of fire from automatic pistols. Two more police were shot dead and Winston Churchill, then the Home Secretary, ordered out the Scots Guards to assist the police. One thousand police, supported by the Guards, kept up a fire on the house, which was eventually burnt down.

It was established afterwards that the 'Sidney Street Gang', as they became known, were recruited from a small colony of about twenty Letts from Baltic Russia, but the identity of their leader was never officially confirmed. The mysterious character was known as 'Peter the Painter' and long afterwards the Soviet Government alleged that he was Serge Makharoff, the Czarist *agent provocateur* mentioned in a previous chapter.

But was he? There are varying points of view. Mr James Burley, of Woodhouse, near Sheffield, recalls that in 1910 he was living in Soho, the Latin quarter of London, and that he spent a lot of time at the Continental Café in Little Newport Street, which was a centre of the Nihilist movement. 'The café was popular,' states Mr Burley, 'because it was only a short walk from the Communist Club in Charlotte Street. Josef Stalin used the Continental Café a lot. Josef Georgi he called himself. He was a bombastic little man, not very big. But there was always an air of mystery about him.'

Mr Burley claimed that Stalin knew all about the events which led up to the Sidney Street affair several days before it happened. 'He was looked up to as one of the leaders and I'm sure he had a hand in planning the burglary which was the cause of the police investigations in the first place. Stalin was the leader of the group and it was he who was keeping a close watch on the mystery figure known as "Peter the Painter".'

Stalin returned to Russia shortly afterwards and it may be that he was keeping 'Peter the Painter' under surveillance, or that he actually aided and abetted his escape. Gerald Bullett, who investigated the Sidney Street affair in some detail, stated that there was a 'certain amount of corroborative evidence that Peter the Painter so far from being the leader of the gang was in fact an agent of the Russian Government, entrusted with the delicate and dangerous task of posing as a comrade of the anti-Tsarist conspirators, and of persuading them to engage in criminal activities such as house-breaking, which would attract to them the attention of the London police and ensure their ultimate deportation to Russia.

'In all probability it was Peter the Painter, *agent provocateur*, employed by the police of Tsarist Russia, who by elaborate trickery encompassed the defeat and dispersal of the Houndsditch murderers. It was at his instigation, I suggest, that the jewel robbery was planned,' stated Bullett.

The reference to the 'jewel robbery' is explained by the fact that the immediate cause of the Sidney Street siege was the planning of the burglary of a jeweller's shop in Houndsditch. An ex-officer of the Ochrana had stated that the jeweller in question had been entrusted with the safe custody of treasure belonging to the Romanoffs. That this statement was a distortion of the facts is more than likely. This is the kind of story a Czarist agent would be likely to invent to incite the revolutionaries to burgle the jeweller's premises.

'Peter the Painter' has been variously identified as Serge Makharoff, Jacob Peters, Fritz Svaar, Jacob Vogel and Peter Straume. In 1918 it was reported that Peter the Painter was still alive and that he was Jacob Peters, the man responsible for the execution of hundreds of men and women in Moscow under the Bolshevik terror. Peters was born in 1886 in Courland and came to England in 1909 when he secured employment as a presser with a firm of wholesale second-hand clothes dealers in North London. Then, on 22 December 1910, Peters was arrested on suspicion of being concerned with other men in the wilful murder of the three police officers. When tried at the Central Criminal Court the defence counsel suggested that Peters had been mistaken for his cousin, Fritz Svaar, who had lost his life in resisting arrest at Sidney Street. Peters was accordingly acquitted.

Peters remained in his job in London until April 1917. Then the London Russian Delegate Committee sent him to Russia. Soon after his arrival in Moscow he became an open and active Bolshevik and after the October Revolution occupied a post in the Russian Foreign Office. Later he became President of the Committee for Combating Counter-Revolution and Sabotage, an organisation with unlimited powers for dealing summarily with all those presumed to oppose Soviet authority.

Two years after the Sidney Street siege Peters married an English girl to whom he still wrote after he returned to Russia. His wife worked at a munitions factory during World War I.

On the other hand Vassilyev, a former Ochrana chief, stated that when Rasputin's house was searched for documents after his death they found information showing that a man named Nideroest, a member of the Russian Socialist Club in London, had helped 'Peter Straume, a Latvian in Whitechapel, to escape to Australia . . . later I was able to confirm from independent sources that this was indisputably correct.' The only British police chief to mention Straume was Sir Basil Thomson, who in *The Story of Scotland Yard* states that Peter the Painter was 'Peter Straume, a Latvian living in Whitechapel, who, it is believed, escaped to Australia, and died in U.S.A. in 1914.'

Detective-Sergeant Leeson, who was badly wounded in the Sidney Street affair, wrote afterwards that Peter the Painter 'fled to Australia'. Some time later Leeson went on a convalescent trip to Australia and encountered Peter the Painter in the booking-hall of Sydney's Central Station. Leeson had by that time left the police force, though doubtless Peter thought he had come to arrest him. 'That was the last of him so far as I was concerned,' wrote Leeson, 'until I received a letter from his brother saying he had died in America in 1914.'

There is no discrepancy in the respective statements of Leeson, Sir Basil Thomson and Vassilyev, but only Vassilyev asserted that Peter the Painter was a Czarist agent. Gerald Bullett suggested that the probable reason Peter was not arrested was 'that he escaped with the other inmates, and *with the knowledge of the* [British] *police*'. The suggestion here is clearly that the British police connived at the activities of Czarist counter-espionage in order to trap the real Anarchists.

Peter Straume was in all probability used as a useful decoy to detract attention from Jacob Peters, or some other revolutionary. It would be interesting to know if Stalin was at this time playing a double rôle, both agent for the Ochrana and master-mind of the revolutionaries. 'Josef Georgi' was certainly the name by which Stalin was known to Bolsheviks in London and, according to the Ochrana files which found their way to Paris after the revolution, 'Josef Vissarionvich Dzhugashvili', Stalin's other name, was listed as 'a member of the Foreign Agency' in 1909.

Mr Edward Ellis Smith, of San Francisco, who has conducted considerable documentary research into the question of Stalin's pre-1917 affiliations with the Imperial Police, takes the view that, while much of the evidence is circumstantial, it is clear that Stalin had an intermittent relationship with the Ochrana. In the Hoover Institution there is a monograph written by Mr Ellis Smith based on an interview he had with a certain Veselgao, who was the last surviving employee of the St Petersburg headquarters of the Ochrana. Veselgao stated that Colonel Eremin, chief of the Special Section, told him that in 1913 Stalin was affiliated with the Ochrana.

The idea of staging, or rather inciting to be staged, the burglary of a jeweller's shop in the cause of espionage may sound so unnecessarily complicated and devious that no Intelligence chief would have sanctioned such a charade. Yet it must be stressed that this bizarre technique was typical of the Czarist Secret Service. If Azeff had been permitted to murder a Grand Duke and a Minister of the Interior, as we now know was the case, then anything was possible.

Peter Stolypin, the Russian leader accused of deceit and treachery by Lopuchin, was a curious mixture of devious politician and courageous statesman. He would probably have described himself as a conservative royalist, but he also had the foresight to acknowledge that Russia was in mortal danger of catastrophe if radical measures to assist the peasants were not introduced. An attempt on his life was made in 1906, his son and daughter being badly wounded, but Stolypin himself escaped. From that time he set himself to exterminate the revolutionaries everywhere. He handed over supreme control of the Police Service to General Kurloff.

But Stolypin's deviousness proved his undoing. The extremer revolutionaries regarded him as their chief enemy now that Plehve had gone and they also realised that his land reforms were an effective palliative to Russia's troubles which, if allowed to continue, would rob their propaganda of much of its point. So in 1911 a revolutionary agent named Bagroff insinuated himself into the confidence of the Kiev police with a story about a revolutionary plot. The police foolishly failed to make full inquiries into Bagroff's background and gave him a ticket for a gala performance of Rimsky-Korsakoff's *Tsar Sultan*, which Stolypin was to attend. Bagroff shot Stolypin dead.

In the feverish years of war preparations among the great powers of Europe prior to 1914 Russia was being steadily supplied with intelligence gathered by Colonel Alfred Redl, who by this time had been appointed Chief of Staff of the Eighth Army Corps in Prague.

Redl's information proved its true value when war broke out and was largely responsible for the Austrian defeats in Galicia in the early part of the war. The Russians had full details of the entire railway system of the Austrians, their forts and installations, while the military code Redl had given to St Petersburg enabled them to tap all the secrets of the Austrian military radio until the code was changed in November 1914.

It was not until 1912 that Redl was suspected. Then in March 1913 came some surprising clues to his treason. The Austrian secret censors opened two envelopes addressed to 'Opera Ball, Poste Restante 13, G.P.O., Vienna' and posted from Eydtkuhnen in East Prussia, close to the Russian border. They contained banknotes totalling 14,000 Austrian kronen. The letters were sealed up again and the Austrian Secret Police waited to see who would collect them. The clerk on duty at the Poste Restante office was told to press a button which would set off a warning call in the nearby police station the moment anyone arrived to claim the letters.

Not until twelve weeks had passed did anyone call for the letters. The postal clerk pressed the alarm button, but the waiting detectives were out of the room at the time and thus valuable seconds were lost. When they reached the post office the man who had collected the letters was just leaving in a taxi.

Luck often plays a useful rôle in espionage and sometimes an initial error can lead to detection. The detectives should have reported the incident to their superiors at once. Instead they waited outside the post office more in fear than in hopefulness for half an hour, at which time they saw the taxi return.

'Where did you take your last passenger?' they asked the taxi-man.

'The Café Kaiserhof,' was the reply.

Without delay they drove there, too. In the taxi they found the sheath of a pocket-knife. There was no trace at the Café Kaiserhof of the man they were looking for, but a taxi rank nearby provided the confirmation that he had taken another taxi to the Hotel Klomser.

At the Hotel Klomser the detectives found their man. The pocket-knife sheath had provided the clue. All they had to do was to ask the hotel receptionist to find out if anyone staying in the hotel had lost it. To their astonishment they learned that the person who claimed it was Colonel Redl.

At first the detectives were embarrassed and believed that what they had stumbled across was some top secret operation by the former spy chief. Nevertheless the Austrian Intelligence decided that Redl must be shadowed. The latter's training quickly made him realise that he was being watched and as he tried to elude his pursuers he was seen to tear up some scraps of paper and throw them away. The detectives picked up the scraps, took them back to headquarters and had them pieced together. They revealed receipts for the dispatch of money to an officer of the Uhlans and for registered letters to addresses in Brussels, Warsaw and Lausanne. It was soon established that the addresses abroad were those of Russian Intelligence officers.

Panic was widespread in the upper echelons of the Austrian Army. Redl's treachery threatened the Austrian War Plan and dishonoured the officer caste. It was decided that though the traitor must be punished, his treachery must be covered up. Four senior officers were sent to call on Redl, to kill him if necessary, but preferably to enable him to kill himself.

Redl spared them from murdering a brother officer. 'I realise why you have called,' he told them coldly and without a trace of panic. 'I have ruined my life and I am prepared to go. At this moment I am writing some letters which I should be glad if you would take.'

Redl was given a revolver and the officers bowed and withdrew from his presence. They kept vigil on the hotel until the morning and then sent a detective to Redl's room. The master-spy was dead: he had shot himself through the brain, standing in front of a mirror. He had left a letter which read:

'Levity and passion have destroyed me. Pray for me. I pay with my life for my sins.'

The receipts for the registered letters posted by Redl suggested that the leakage of Austrian military secrets might have extended to Russia's allies as well as to St Petersburg. One address – that in Brussels – was that of the Franco-Russian Intelligence Centre in that city, an organisation developed for co-operation in the event of war. The address in Warsaw was that of Dr Katz, the No. 1 Russian Intelligence chief in Poland. As a result of the detection of Redl Dr Katz closed down his Warsaw bureau and moved to Copenhagen.

An investigation into Redl's affairs by the Austrians revealed that he had made considerable sums of money out of his spying activities. He had a luxuriously furnished house in Prague, an estate in the country and a large house in Vienna. He possessed four motor-cars, a cellar containing wines of the rarest vintage and many costly art treasures. How much money Redl had received from the Czarist Secret Service over all these years is hard to assess. It was established that he had obtained nearly 80,000 kronen from them in the past year alone.

Despite the Army's attempts to hush up the scandal, news of Redl's suicide eventually leaked out and to silence all gossip a denial that he had been guilty of betraying secrets to the Russians was issued to the press.

The extent of Redl's treachery was appalling. He had even denounced personal friends and brother officers to the Russians, sending them a complete list of every Austrian spy on Russian territory and causing some of them to be summarily executed. He had given every assistance to Russian spies coming into Austria and had himself helped to build up a network of espionage for St Petersburg in Vienna, Prague and elsewhere. He had been even more helpful in trapping Russians who had tried to sell secrets to Vienna, luring them to his office and encouraging them to talk, then notifying St Petersburg. The investigation of his home at Prague and the documents in his safes revealed that he had pro-vided the Russians with maps, police records, codes, ciphers, details of armaments and armament factories, Army orders and mobilisation plans. But his most valuable contribution was to pass on the full details of 'Plan Three', the detailed scheme for action in the event of war against Serbia into which years of planning had been devoted by the Austro-Hungarian General Staff. When war came Marshal Putnik, Chief of Staff of the Serbian Army, was able, with information supplied by the Russians, to counteract the Austro-Hungarian advance and with his tiny force of relatively ill-equipped soldiers to take heavy toll of the invading army.

Count Apponyi, of the Austro-Hungarian General Staff, stated later that Redl had also prevented intelligence reports being obtained by the Austrian Secret Service: he had suppressed them the moment they arrived on his desk. Thus, added Apponyi, 'if we had known of the existence of those Russian Army corps, our General Staff . . . would have recognised the hazard of a quarrel with Russia and would have been able to prevent our statesmen from driving us into war in the summer of 1914. . . . That black-guard Redl denounced every Austro-Hungarian spy in Russia, suppressed reports that leaked through in spite of him, and delivered our own secrets to the Russians.'

No sooner had the Redl scandal broken in Vienna than another spy scare was raised. The chief of the Cipher Department in the Government Offices in Vienna decided to make some checks on his own account and when he examined the safe in which the master code and cipher book was kept he found a book which appeared externally to be that work, but which, when opened, was found to be filled with blank pages.

Inquiries elicited that the Russian military attaché had informed the Austrian Secret Service about a man who had offered to sell him the code-book for 400,000 roubles. The man was eventually found and as a result the Austrian Intelligence traced the thief, an Italian countess who had become the mistress of an Austrian officer on the General Staff. She had found an excuse for getting into the office in which the safe was kept and, when her lover's back was turned, exchanged the dummy for the real code book.

But the Russians had already obtained a copy of this very code book from Redl, so when the countess approached them and offered to sell the book they dismissed her and informed the Austrians. The countess guessed this was what the Russians would do so she returned the code-book and hurriedly left the country.

Meanwhile Sidney Reilly himself managed to combine his espion-age on behalf of Russia and Britain with some interventions in the highly technical sphere of armaments with a skill and impudence that brought him large sums of money. Yet though some of the Reilly anecdotes are apocryphal, one frequently finds that his most legendary and extraordinary feats are usually supported by in-dependent testimony and fact. He first of all organised the St Petersburg Flying Week to obtain information on German aircraft developments. Reilly, whose experience of commercial enterprise had been largely confined to timber in the Far East and patent medicines in Britain, now blossomed forth as an expert in the largely unknown field of aeronautics. Then he got himself the job of sole agent in Russia for the German firm of Blohm and Voss of Hamburg, and by this means was able to see all the blueprints, plans and specifications of the latest developments in German naval construction. Details of these were passed both to Russia and Britain. Few other spies, and almost no other double-agent, could have got away with this in the peculiar circumstances in which Reilly found himself. For this was practically stealing the potential enemy's plans from under their nose while actually working for them. Such espionage must have made the Russians, British and Germans almost equally suspicious of Reilly. He took an incredible risk when one considers that only a few years previously he had murdered a German to silence him while working as a spy for the British in Krupps' works in Germany.

The Germans, while having no idea that Reilly was an agent of the Russians or the British, were sufficiently suspicious of his name to have him watched day and night; yet still he copied the plans. Meanwhile he was providing Russia with orders from a German firm that he might more easily have obtained from a British firm, and when the British colony in St Petersburg heard about the British subject who was so enterprisingly obtaining orders for the Germans some of them protested vigorously to the British Ambassador about Reilly. The British Secret Service must have had some anxious moments, too, for Reilly was drawing large sums in commission from the Germans. Reilly's reply to this was the same to the British as to the Russians – that he was saving each Secret Service the cost of his salary! The plea was accepted, but the truth was that Reilly was earning more than double in commissions what either side could have afforded to pay him.

By this time Reilly was having serious marital problems. His British wife, Margaret, was an unsuitable spouse for any spy: she was an hysterical alcoholic, though until this period Reilly had insisted to his British superiors that she was no hindrance to his work. But though the British may have accepted this the Russians took an altogether different view when she unexpectedly turned up in St Petersburg. It was pointed out to Reilly that she was a security risk as far as the Russians were concerned. Certainly Margaret Reilly posed a threat to her husband while he was working for Blohm and Voss and he offered her a large sum of money to divorce him. The British appear to have been against his attempt to persuade her to divorce him, taking the view that a scorned woman would be more of a menace than an awkward wife. The Russians, being somewhat more ruthless, suggested that if Margaret Reilly did not acquiesce she should be liquidated. Then Reilly proposed to ingratiate himself further with the Russians by marrying bigamously the divorced wife of a naval officer in the Russian Marine Ministry.

Reilly warned the Russians that their own War Minister,

Suchomlinoff, was in collusion with Sir Basil Zaharoff on various nefarious deals. Raffalowitsch, the former financial attaché in Paris, aided and abetted by Zaharoff and Suchomlinoff, paved the way for the Russian Government to give to Vickers what was a virtual monopoly of the manufacture of guns, despite the fact that Vickers' prices were higher than Le Creusot's. Zaharoff scored over Reilly when he managed to inspire an official message from St Petersburg that the Putiloff works required another two million pounds, which they would be grateful if the Schneider-Creusot company could deliver to them. On the surface it looked as though Zaharoff was handing the deal on a plate to his rivals. In fact the French firm immediately put the required capital at the disposal of Putiloff, and at the same time a new Russian loan of £25,000,000 was raised in France. Vickers were able to obtain their share and *The Times* Paris correspondent was able to announce that during the preceding months orders to the amount of £6,500,000 had gone to Britain.

Cynic, opportunist, double-agent, murderer and fomenter of plots Reilly may have been; a spy licensed to kill, a ruthless operator who showed little mercy, womaniser, bigamist he undoubtedly was. Yet he was one of the most likeable rogues of this or any other generation. Though his mind and his professional skill were pledged to Britain, his heart, his romantic soul were committed to Russia. I asked the late Prince Serge Belloselski, who spent the last quarter-century of his life in Britain, in what way he thought Reilly wished to serve Russia and in what manner his service to that country different from the work he did for British Intelligence.

'If I could answer that completely, then I could probably solve the final mystery of Sidney Reilly,' replied the Prince. 'You have got to understand that he felt his first loyalty lay with England because England had given him a name and work when he was more or less down and out. He loved England in a romantic way. But when he returned to Russia as a successful man his love for Russia returned to him. In his own way I imagine he wanted to change Russia. But how? That is the question, because Reilly never entered into political controversy in ordinary conversation.'

Russian military intelligence had benefited to a remarkable degree in the few years before the First World War by the revelations of Colonel Redl and relied greatly on his advice on espionage and counter-espionage techniques. In intelligence circles it had been a decade which was known as the cryptographers' war. Every power devoted immense sums of money to capturing the codes and ciphers of its rivals. Soon the cryptographers' war threatened to become at best an uneasy stalemate, with everyone knowing everyone else's secrets.

Thus the conflict was speeded up. The aim was to change codes and ciphers frequently so as to be always a step ahead of the spies. But, bureaucracy being what it is, a slow-moving, conservative instrument of human machinery, such swiftly changing action often led to errors that outweighed the advantages of fending off the spies. Colonel Redl's advice was that even if a nation's codes had been captured, this could be turned to the advantage of the nation robbed rather than to that of the robber.

The Russians put this theory into practice. They knew long before the war came that the Germans either had obtained their ciphers, or would shortly obtain them through their spy network. But they made no attempt to change them. They carried on as though they suspected nothing. But they took the precaution of working out a new secret cipher that was partly a code. One copy of this was made and locked away in a safe in St Petersburg. Then the day war was declared in 1914 the cipher was issued to General Jilinsky, the commander of the Northern Army Group.

This comprised the crack forces of the Czar: the First Army under General Rennenkampf and the Second under General Samsonoff. Both were supremely confident of victory, not only because they were the best equipped of all the Russian forces, but also because the Russian Secret Service had obtained from a German staff sergeant named Wolkerling plans of the important German frontier fortress of Lötzen. Thus General Rennenkampf was not only expected to take Lötzen swiftly and without serious loss, but to make a speedy advance into German territory.

But a series of disasters on both the Prussian and the Austro-Hungarian fronts soon offset the initial advantage which the Russians possessed from the coup of the Lötzen plans and Redl's intelligence. General Jilinsky by some mischance gave the single copy of the new secret cipher to Rennenkampf, but did not make a copy of it for Samsonoff. The Germans soon noticed that the signals from Rennenkampf to Samsonoff were in a new cipher which they did not understand. Initial panic changed to perplexity when Samsonoff sent messages in the old cipher which they had already obtained. But Samsonoff could not understand Rennenkampf's messages any more than the Germans could, while Rennenkampf could not read Samsonoff's messages because he had followed orders to destroy all copies of the old cipher.

Perplexity changed to triumphant amusement for the Germans when the two commanders started to send panic messages in the clear. Then they realised that someone had blundered.

There is no doubt that the Military Intelligence of the Russians intended one or other of the commanders to continue to use the old cipher to mislead the Germans, while keeping vital field orders in the new cipher. This could have caused havoc in the German armies. Now the Germans had a clear picture of the muddle in Russian communications and knew everything they were planning to do. By 26 August 1914 the Germans had seized the initiative once more. The Battle of Tannenburg resulted in the total defeat of Samsonoff's army with the loss of a hundred thousand men. The commander, regarding the defeat as a personal blunder on his part, shot himself. Rennenkampf held out a little longer, but within the next month his forces were also defeated.

The Russian High Command, who had expected to drive back the initial German advance, felt convinced that treachery must be the reason for this defeat. An inquiry into the whole affair was instantly set afoot, but, without waiting for it to be completed, wholesale arrests were made. An officer of the Czar's Gendarmerie, Colonel Sergei Miasoyedoff, was executed for espionage, particularly for having betrayed to the Germans details of the Russian movements in East Prussia. Miasoyedoff's fatal error had been his friendship with Madame Suchomlinoff, the wife of the Minister of War. She was suspected of having communicated with the Germans, using the Colonel as a go-between.

Without doubt Miasoyedoff was made a scapegoat for other men's blunders. Some of the 'evidence' against him was later disproved and just how unsure the prosecutors were of their case against him can be judged from the fact that they introduced a relatively trivial charge that he had stolen two statuettes from an abandoned house in East Prussia. The Colonel continued emphatically to deny his guilt right up to the last. He had been an officer of the Intelligence Service and his record was beyond reproach. One court martial acquitted him, but a second trial was demanded and he was found guilty and hanged within two hours of the passing of the verdict. It would seem that his accusers were afraid of his being reprieved at the last moment.

The other great blunder by the Russian Intelligence Services was not merely their failure to replace Redl with a spy of equal calibre, but their ridiculously complacent belief that the Austro-Hungarian war plans would not be changed. For Redl had not only himself hidden information about Russia from the Austro-Hungarians, but had caused the Austrian Intelligence to be provided with false reports about the strength of Russian forces. As these reports came in from sources apparently outside the control of Redl they were accepted as the truth long after Redl was unmasked. But the Serbs had made better use of Redl's information than the Russians, while the Austro-Hungarians changed their plans and dispositions after Redl's treason was discovered. When the Russian attack came it was launched in the wrong direction, thanks to the Redl plan, and again it proved disastrous.

It was ironic that the one coup in the early part of the war which Russia achieved in the field of intelligence was brought about through the initiative of the Navy and that it brought greatest benefit to Britain. During a fog the German light cruiser, *Magdeburg*, ran aground in the Baltic while raiding the Russian coast. When the fog cleared the Russian fleet was seen sailing towards the cruiser and the German captain gave orders for the code-books to be taken in a rowing boat as far away as possible from the ship and dropped in deep water. This was done, but the water in which the books were dropped could hardly be called deep. When the Russian navy arrived the captain of their leading ship ordered the bodies of the Germans to be recovered so that they could be given a proper burial with honours.

That, at least, was his excuse for giving the order, though in fact he was probably determined to try to find the code-books, for he demanded that the ship's divers went down to look for the bodies, not being content with retrieving those corpses floating on the surface. The code-books were found and, as Britain was looked upon as the leading naval power among the Allies, Naval Intelligence in Whitehall was informed right away about the discovery. The books were sent to London where Admiral Hall's celebrated team of de-cipherers quickly found the key to them.

While Colonel Redl was Russia's 'ace' spy in the Austro-Hungarian empire prior to the war, it must not be thought that he was the only one of any note. The Russians had long ago realised that the most fruitful field for their espionage lay in Vienna rather than Berlin. Vienna held the key not only to Austro-Hungarian-German secrets, but to those of the whole of the Balkans and Turkey as well, and the Balkans were still regarded as Russia's most vital sphere of influence. Not only this, but the Austro-Hungarian empire contained intriguing minorities drawn from many nations and each one of these groups, dissident Poles, Czechs, Croats and Slovaks as well as Italians, had their own miniature secret services, some of them working to bring about a dissolution of the Austro-Hungarian empire.

The presence in Austro-Hungary of Polish anti-Czarist revolutionaries also posed a special problem. These people were freely given political sanctuary in Austro-Hungary, doubtless partly to embarrass the Russians, and the Russian Secret Service was ordered to keep a special watch on them. But soon the Russians began to realise that their need for espionage in this part of the world was so great that it was worthwhile recruiting some of the Poles as agents, regardless of their revolutionary background.

If wealth of intelligence counted for most in war Russia would have crushed the whole of the Balkans in the first twelve months of the 1914–18 War and been knocking at the gates of Constantinople. No nation in the world had so powerful an espionage service in this area at that time. It cost a fortune and it embraced a variety of nationalities and a host of callings. Russian Orthodox priests, lawyers and teachers spied for the motherland; in Ruthenia even the schools were organised into cells.

Redl must have been well aware of the widespread ramifications of the Russian Secret Service in Austro-Hungary and it must have caused him many anxious moments. Perhaps it is surprising that he was able to operate for so many years without being detected. Possibly in the end the strain of contending with it made him lose his nerve. Yet in the early years his quick brain saved him on a number of occasions. His first test came in 1903, only a short while after he had started to work for the Russians. Hekailo, a clerk in the military service at Lemberg, was arrested, ostensibly on a charge of using Army funds for his own ends. After inquiries were carried out the Army decided not to proceed with the case and Hekailo was set free. Almost at once he left the country. Redl then berated the authorities for letting Hekailo go, alleging that he had betrayed secrets to the Russians. The Austrian Intelligence chief then revealed that Hekailo had gone to Brazil where he was living under the name of Karl Weber and still an active Russian agent.

It was not, of course, possible to have Hekailo extradited on the grounds that he was a spy, but, following persistent pressure from Redl, Austro-Hungary demanded his extradition from Brazil because he was involved in a series of thefts. The charges were unsubstantiated; indeed they had been concocted by the Austrian Intelligence Service. Hekailo was brought back to Vienna and under intensive cross-examination revealed the names of two of his confederates, both Russian agents, named Wienckowski and Acht. All three men were tried and sentenced to lengthy terms of imprisonment.

Redl had cynically used the case of Hekailo to impress both the Austrians and the Russians with his talents as a spy-master. He wanted to appear omnipotent to each. The top secret plans which it had been alleged that Hekailo had passed to the Russians had actually been betrayed by Redl himself. But, knowing the scope of the Russian spy system in Austro-Hungary, he feared that some hint of his implication in this might leak out. For it should have been obvious to the Austro-Hungarians that only someone very high up in the Army could possibly have had access to these secrets. To draw suspicion away from himself he had trumped up charges and faked evidence against Hekailo and made the Austrians believe that this Russian agent was the guilty man. Hekailo was only a minor figure in the Russian espionage set-up and he had certainly not provided information comparable to that supplied by Redl, but the 'evidence' Redl produced was sensational and detailed, even including the name and address of a governess to a senior staff officer of the Russian Army in Warsaw, claiming that she was Hekailo's intermediary.

The greedy Redl had also told the Austrians that it had cost him 30,000 kronen to obtain his 'evidence', a sum which was paid to him as expenses. Thus his treachery cost both the Austrians and the Russians a great deal of money.

To safeguard his own position Redl had asked the Russians to co-operate by giving him the information which would enable Hekailo to be caught in Brazil. The Russians had no objection to betraying one of their own men, who was only a minor agent and of no use to them there. But they had not reckoned with Hekailo, in a desperate attempt to save himself from imprisonment, revealing the names of Wienckowski and Acht. These two men were among the Russians' best agents in Austro-Hungary and their arrest seriously interfered with the Russian espionage system.

Thus while the Austro-Hungarians were delighted with Redl the Russians were less pleased and thought that Redl had over-reached himself. Their military attaché in Vienna called on Redl and demanded that he should find some means of freeing Wienckowski and Acht.

It is not surprising that Redl should develop a dislike of military attachés after this visit. There was nothing he could do to help the Russian agents without bringing himself under suspicion, nor was he in a position to arrange for the men to escape. The spies must remain in prison, he said, but he would compensate for this loss by betraying to the Russians the top agent serving the Kundschafts Stelle. This top agent was a major in the Russian Intelligence who had long been secretly serving the Austro-Hungarians and was a close friend of Redl. The major paid the penalty with death.

The immediate effect of war was to bring to Russia a great wave of patriotic feeling and a spy scare that, said Vassilyev, 'ran through the whole Russian population like a plague'. As in Britain, everyone with a German-sounding name, anyone of German descent or married to a German, was immediately suspected of being a spy in the cause of the Kaiser. In the Duma an anti-

German group was formed for the purpose of counteracting what they called 'German influence' and for unmasking spies. Its leader, Chvostoff, was one.

In the ranks of the Ochrana General Junkovsky became the chief of the 'German-hunters' and his misplaced enthusiasm for this task resulted in his prosecuting as spies a number of innocent Russians. One man was sent to Siberia merely because he had lived in Germany for two years, another was arrested solely because he walked around with his coat-collar turned up and popular rumour had it that two secret aides of the Kaiser were living in St Petersburg unmolested and that they habitually walked the streets with their coat-collars turned up.

Vassilyev blamed military interference for many of these blunders. 'During the war,' he wrote, 'much disorder was created by the independent action of the military authorities, who had had conferred upon them the right of removing, without formality of any kind, from the war zone all persons whom they deemed to be suspect. Governors representing the Civil Power were obliged, in matters of this kind, to submit to the instructions of the military commanders and to carry out their orders. The officers commanding the various Army groups would send whole bands of people away from the territories under their jurisdiction.'

Vassilyev was scathing in his denunciations of Military Intelligence officers, alleging that they perpetrated 'the most incredible blunders, so that they were hardly distinguishable from the ignorant country-people in their panic fear of spies'.

On the other hand while the Army Command and its Intelligence Branch showed over-enthusiasm in arresting and detaining people whose innocence they had not troubled to ascertain, they were incredibly lax on occasions in dealing with real spies and enemy agents. Once they discovered five Jews who had been employed by the Austrian Secret Service in a Galician village. Instead of bringing them before a court martial they merely expelled them from the war zone.

Grigory Efimovitch Rasputin was an enigma in his lifetime and after his death became a legendary figure, endowed with a great deal of extravagant fiction about both his private and his public life. He was the son of a peasant, born in the eighteen-sixties, in Pokrovskoe, not far from Tobolsk. He was a bright child, but had little schooling and preferred an open-air life to studying. But all are agreed that even as a child he had one outstanding quality – the gift of second sight, or at least an amazing power of intuition.

Many of the peasants of Western Siberia, whence Rasputin came, were from time to time seized by religious fervour. Rasputin was no exception: he left home to wander all over Russia as a pilgrim and also became interested in a strange and heretical sect (many years previously proscribed by the Ochrana) known as the Chlysty. They had an odd belief that the way to salvation was through the commission of sin and the Chlysty put this into practice by flagellation, rape, adultery and in some extreme instances by murder.

Yet the familiar portrait of Rasputin as a charlatan, lecher and disreputable scoundrel is merely achieved by portraying only his warts, by concentrating on his vices and the malicious and often totally untrue stories put about by his enemies. His religious beliefs may have been unorthodox, but it is not without significance that he made a deep impression on leaders of the Orthodox Church. He may have indulged in bogus mysticism, often for his own sensual ends, but he possessed remarkable gifts such as today we should call extra-sensory perception, a talent for interpreting character and for prophecy and without question the powers of spiritual healing and hypnotism. Eventually he came to St Petersburg and, despite his lack of formal learning and his peasant habits, he attracted the interest of the Grand Duke Nicholai Nicholayevitsh. It was the latter's wife who introduced him to the Czarina.

From then on Rasputin's rise to power was rapid and from about 1905 onwards he was unofficial spiritual adviser to the superstitious and introvert Czarina and invariably called in to 'cure' the Czarevitch's illnesses by his faith-healing. Not surprisingly the advent at Court of a moujik monk, associated with the Chlysty sect, attracted the attention of the Russian Secret Service in all its branches and Rasputin was kept under close surveillance and a lengthy dossier compiled on him. But at the same time Rasputin himself was not without influence inside the Intelligence Services, being on close terms with such diverse characters as Peter Alexandrovitch Badmayev, the Far Eastern expert, and Manasevitch-Manuiloff who had for so many years worked under Ratchkovsky.

It is probable that Rasputin's entry into the sphere of intelligence and intrigue was prompted by men like Badmayev and Manasevitch-Manuiloff more than by any ambitions of his own. In short, the politicians themselves, through intermediaries like these, used Rasputin to obtain influence at Court. For there he had a unique position, the confidence and protection of the Czarina and, through her, a direct link to the Czar himself. He was well placed to obtain a great deal of secret information because, whereas the Czar and Czarina mixed less and less with the people at Court, Rasputin was frequently admitted to their private apartments and the Czarina, having great faith in his powers of observation and his extra-sensory perception, often discussed political

135

problems with him and sought his advice.

When Stolypin had been Prime Minister he had been disturbed about rumours of Rasputin's influence with the Czar and he called for a report on the moujik. The report stated that Rasputin was a member of the Chlysty sect and the fact that sexual orgies were part of the Chlysty rites explained his licentious behaviour. Stolypin ordered Rasputin to leave St Petersburg, an action that in no way enhanced his standing with the Czar and the moujik did not return to the capital until just before Stolypin's assassination.

Others tried to remove the moujik from the Czar's influence, but without success. Anyone who spoke ill of Rasputin had to bear the wrath of the Czarina: so vehement was her defence of the man that it is not surprising that gossips alleged that she was Rasputin's mistress. The moujik himself grew in confidence and started to make suggestions to the Czarina as to who should be given posts and who should be dismissed from them. He was not only responsible for the sacking of the police chief, Belyetsky, but even instrumental in reinstating him later. Vassilyev wrote that Rasputin's 'intelligence and insight enabled him sometimes to form a tolerably shrewd judgement with regard to persons he had once met. This, too, was known to the Czarina, and therefore she would ask him sometimes what he thought of this or that candidate for some high Government post.' Vassilyev himself admitted that the chief of the St Petersburg Ochrana called on him every morning with a report in which was a detailed list of everyone who had appeared at Rasputin's quarters the day before, and of everyone he had visited.

It is not quite clear how the whispers of Rasputin's pro-German sentiments started. Probably it was due to the fact that about 1908 he had warned the Czar that he must avoid war with Austria because if he embarked on such a campaign it would be 'the end of Russia'. No doubt the German Secret Service was well aware of these rumours and they may even have fostered them to create confusion, but no evidence had ever been produced to show that he received bribes from the Germans or the Austrians, or that he ever worked for them. But the rumours were sufficient for the Ochrana to maintain a constant watch on the monk, though for fear of incurring displeasure at the Court the reports never referred to Rasputin by his name, but always as 'The Dark One'. Those reports read more like an erotic novel than anything else: they contained all the lurid details about his peccadilloes, his seductions of young girls hardly in their teens, his adulteries with the wives of the famous and his rapes of servant girls and other women whom he was called in to 'cure' of some nervous ailment and whom invariably he would hypnotise into submission to his will. Extracts from the reports were gleefully published by the Bolsheviks after the Revolution to demonstrate to the world at large the corruption and decadence that flourished in the Czar's entourage:

'On the night of 17 January, Maria Gill, wife of a captain in the 145th Regiment, slept at Rasputin's'; 'On the night of 25 November, Varvarova, an actress, slept at Rasputin's'; 'Rasputin came home in the motor-car . . . with the prostitute Gregubova. He was blind drunk, kissed Gregubova passionately and stroked her cheeks'; 'Rasputin, accompanied by the twenty-eight-year-old wife of the Burgess Yazininski, left in a car . . . the pair, in a very tipsy state, then proceeded to Madame Yazininskaia's flat, from which Rasputin did not return home until midday.'

Meanwhile the new head of the Police Department, General Dzhunkovsky, took a much less lenient view of Rasputin's activities than did the Ochrana. He put in a report about Rasputin's habitual lechery which resulted in the monk being temporarily out of favour with the Czar so that even the Czarina had to meet him secretly outside the palace. Shortly after this General Dzhunkovsky had Rasputin arrested in a notorious night haunt in the capital, alleging that he had not only created a disturbance but indecently exposed himself to public gaze. Rasputin got his own back by complaining to the Czarina about Dzhunkovsky, saying that he was trying to smear him with false reports and that he had deliberately neglected to prosecute men who had been sent to try to kill him. The Czarina spoke to her husband and Dzhunkovsky was dismissed. It was then that Belyetsky was restored to his job.

All this time enemies of the War Minister were building up a formidable case against him. This was not difficult for Suchomlinoff had made error after error since war broke out. But his enemies were not satisfied with merely finding fault with Suchomlinoff's conduct of the war; they were determined to prove he was a traitor and to concoct evidence to this effect. The War Minister was suddenly charged with treason. The so-called 'proof' was a letter posted in Carlsbad and addressed to the War Minister's wife by a merchant named Altschiller. It was an innocent enough letter, merely stating that there had been excessive rain in Carlsbad, that the roads were in a bad condition and that long walks were impossible. But it was alleged that these words contained a hidden meaning. Yet there was no proof whatsoever that the War Minister had received vast sums from the Germans, which was what the prosecution had alleged.

Suchomlinoff was nevertheless found guilty and sentenced to imprisonment. He had been imprudent, foolish in failing to check his wife's extravagances and friendships with Germans, but it does not seem that he ever actually committed treason or anything approaching this. Discussing the question of the allegations that Suchomlinoff had received huge bribes from the Germans, Vassilyev said he was utterly unconvinced by such statements because long years of experience had shown him that often 'amounts of money were entered as having been paid to certain individuals without those persons having actually received them'.

An uneasy period in the Ministry of the Interior and the Police Department ensued for several months. With Belyetsky as chief of police and Chvostoff as Minister of the Interior corruption was widespread and more time was spent in intrigues for personal greed and aggrandisement by both men than in maintaining security. Chvostoff and Belyetsky appeared on the surface to be the closest of confederates; in fact neither ever really trusted the other and each spent his time frustrating plots the other had embarked on. At the same time that Chvostoff and Belyetsky were pretending to play along with Rasputin both men were plotting together to kill him. Rasputin was trying to prevent Chvostoff from becoming Prime Minister, while Chvostoff was scheming to oust the current Prime Minister, Goremykin. In the end Goremykin was dismissed and Rasputin's choice, the incompetent and sycophantic Sturmer, was appointed Prime Minister at the instigation of the Czarina.

The appointment of Sturmer aroused a wave of hatred against Rasputin and infuriated the Duma. Chvostoff continued to make various clumsy attempts to have Rasputin murdered, but without success. There was something farcical about Chvostoff's plots against Rasputin; certainly some of them had farcical endings. One was to have Rasputin poisoned, but it was Rasputin's cat which died, not the monk. On yet another occasion an Ochrana agent saved Rasputin's life!

Later Belyetsky and Chvostoff seemed to reach an accord that Rasputin must be destroyed and they prepared an elaborate dossier on his seductions and rapes, together, so it is said, with actual photographs of sexual orgies in which the lascivious monk was shown with a number of women indulging in group coitus in oriental fashion. But Chvostoff either lost his nerve at the last moment when going to present this latest evidence to the Czar, or he decided to double-cross Belyetsky, for on this occasion he failed to give the Czar the dossier, but instead demanded the removal of Belyetsky as chief of police.

The Czarina, hearing of these plots, warned the Czar that Rasputin must be protected at all costs, that he was 'the only man who could save Russia from disaster' and the extent of her superstitions was such that she insisted that her husband should use Rasputin's comb on his hair before he made any important decisions.

Chvostoff was dismissed and once again Rasputin's advice was sought. The man whom he urged should be made Minister of the Interior was Protopopoff, a choice which was as preposterous as it was naïve.

Now Rasputin had come to the pinnacle of his power: behind the scenes he was the most influential man in Russia, urging the Czar and the Czarina to cling to their belief in absolute monarchical government and deriding the power and authority of the Duma to them. Rasputin had an annual allowance of ten thousand roubles from the Czarina's private funds and while Protopopoff was Minister of the Interior he received various payments for intelligence provided to the Ochrana. Vassilyev stated that during the time that he was head of the Ochrana no larger sum than a thousand roubles at a time was paid to Rasputin.

While there is no question of Rasputin having been a German agent, or indulging in treason, he continued to assert that a continuance of the war would mean the end of the Czarist régime and he constantly urged the Czar to make a separate peace with Germany.

II

Dzerzhinsky Seizes Power

It was perhaps only poetic justice that if Russia had its Colonel Redl spying for them inside the Austro-Hungarian Intelligence Service, Austro-Hungary should have its own key man on the Russian side. The defection was perhaps the worst blow the Russian Intelligence machine suffered in World War I.

Colonel Victor Kaledin served as a member of the Russian Military Intelligence as Agent K. 14 of the Seventh Section of the General Staff. Like most competent double-agents he was a cool, objective operator who worked dispassionately for financial gain. While serving the Russians he was at the same time selling their secrets to Austro-Hungary and Germany. He even became a trusted member of the *Nachrichtendienst*, the top section of the German Military Intelligence Service. In addition Colonel Kaledin set up a secret section of the German spy network at various addresses around St Petersburg from which information was passed back to Germany by means of Heinrich Schtaub, a German parachute spy who landed several times behind the enemy lines.

If the counter-espionage of the Russian Army was not very impressive, the actual field organisation of the Secret Service in putting spies in enemy territory was extremely efficient. Indeed when the Soviet started to recruit for its foreign network in the early twenties it managed to persuade some of these former Czarist agents to work for them on the grounds that their ability was so great they could not be ignored. Some refused and were imprisoned but others willingly changed masters.

Meanwhile the double-agent, Sidney Reilly, had proved himself almost indispensable as a source of information to both the Russian and British Secret Services right up to the outbreak of war. At the same time the Germans, who still had no idea of Reilly's rôle as a spy, were hugely delighted with the orders he had been winning for Blohm and Voss and had no inkling of the fact that Reilly was making photostat copies of their naval construction blueprints behind locked doors in his Potchtamsky Street apartment. Reilly was also used by the Russians to report on Rasputin. This he did, not by the conventional tactic of following the moujik and noting his multifarious peccadilloes, which he rightly considered to be a waste of any intelligence agent's time, but by maintaining a close liaison with one of Rasputin's women friends who regaled him with news of goings-on at Court.

Captain Mansfield Cumming, the head of Britain's M.I.6, said of Reilly at this time that he was 'a man of indomitable courage, a genius as an agent, but a sinister man whom I could never bring myself wholly to trust.' On various occasions in Reilly's life he had shown a ruthless disregard for life in circumstances quite unrelated to espionage. As an agent in the field he never hesitated to kill when necessary. He had killed men in Germany to ensure their silence, including a night watchman at Krupps' factory when he stole some blueprints there, and there was also the mysterious death of his wife's former husband which left grave doubts as to Reilly's rôle in the affair, as well as his behaviour towards Margaret when her hysterical conduct and alcoholism proved a hindrance to him. There is no doubt that he threatened her life when she refused an offer of £10,000 to divorce him, for she fled from Russia immediately afterwards. The British Secret Service must have been perpetually worried as to whether Margaret would 'blow' Reilly as an act of revenge. They must have been even more concerned at his determination to marry Nadine Massino, the wife of the Naval Assistant to the Russian Minister of Marine. The latter had agreed to divorce his wife to enable her to marry Reilly, so one must assume a similar offer of payment was made to him.

Reilly married Nadine Massino bigamously in 1916 at the Greek-Orthodox Cathedral in New York, describing himself as a widower. In fact Margaret Reilly was still alive, though she kept moving around the continent of Europe to avoid her husband's efforts to trace her. That way at least she stayed alive.

Grigori Rasputin's rise to a position of power had aroused the fiercest hatred and resentment among many at the Russian court, but among none so much as Prince Felix Yussopoff.

The Prince, a popular figure in St Petersburg, had disliked Rasputin intensely on his first meeting with him and these feelings had grown to the point that he was openly asking other courtiers what could be done to rid Russia of such an intolerable nuisance. The fact that the Czar, his wife's uncle, favoured the monk made no difference. Yussopoff conceived it as his patriotic duty to rid the nation of a licentious rascal and a pro-German. Finally he decided to kill Rasputin.

The killing was done on 16 December 1916 at the Prince's palace in Moika Street. It was a clumsy affair, the most remarkable feature of which was the seeming invincibility of the moujik to all attempts to finish him off. The monk was lured to the palace on the pretext of a party. He was given cakes and drinks which, it is reputed, had been dosed with potassium cyanide. This seemed to have no effect whatsoever. The suggestion has been made that Rasputin was suffering from acute alcoholic gastritis which had so thickened the lining of the stomach that it took a long time for the poison to act. The plotters in consternation retired to discuss the situation and first talked of strangling Rasputin, then of shooting him. Finally Yussopoff shot him in the back and the monk fell to the ground. A doctor was summoned and he proclaimed Rasputin to be dead. Shortly afterwards the 'corpse' rose from the floor, made the sign of the Cross, crawled up the stairs and burst open a locked door. In a state of near panic Purishkevich, one of the other plotters, fired four shots at the monk, missing him with two, but hitting him with each of the others. They carried the dying man to the river and he was still alive when they pushed him into it. But the cold water aroused him and he once again made the sign of the Cross before he died.

The Ochrana's attention was drawn by the censorship authorities to two telegrams sent by the Czarina's sister, the Grand Duchess Elizabeth. The first was addressed to the Grand Duke Dimitry Pavlovitsh:

'Just returned very late after week in Sarov and Divyeyev. Prayed for you all. Please send letter with particulars. God grant

Felix necessary strength after patriotic deed.'

The second was sent to Princess Yussopoff, mother of the Prince, and stated: 'My earnest heartfelt prayers for you all after your dear son's patriotic deed.'

Even the hardened men of the Ochrana were somewhat shocked by the callous attitude of many of the boyars and their families to the murder and the sympathy they openly expressed for the killers. Prince Yussopoff gave officialdom no assistance in solving the crime and the investigation dragged on in desultory fashion. It was not until a month later that Trepoff, President of the Council of Ministers, at the instigation of the Czar ordered Yussopoff to be cross-examined. Shortly afterwards the Czar instructed the Prince to retire to his own estate in Kursky and to remain there under a relatively mild form of supervision.

Vassilyev had many more important problems with which to grapple at this time. He was mainly concerned with combating the threat of revolution, organising watches to be kept on terrorists as far afield as Warsaw and Paris, Zurich and Capri. Maxim Gorky, under his pen name Pyeshkoff, had founded a training school for revolutionary activists on the island of Capri and it was from this establishment that the Bolsheviks recruited some of their ablest agents. It was Vassilyev's job to be kept informed every time one of the trainees arrived back in Russia. The system of detecting this was well nigh perfect as far as the Capri revolutionaries were concerned. Vassilyev had the trainees stopped at the frontier and brought to St Petersburg for interrogation. Now while the Ochrana could and, as we have seen, did many things that were illegal, they adopted a curious stance of bureaucratic correctitude in dealing with the trainees. They referred each case to the Public Prosecutor and, ironically in a country where law and justice so often had little meaning, the Public Prosecutor's Department decided that no legal measures could be taken against the arrested persons because they had not committed any offence on Russian territory.

During the early part of the war Vassilyev had been second-in-command of the Political Section of the Police Department. He came to hear of a plan for the leaders of all the various Russian socialist organisations to meet and thrash out a campaign for revolutionary action. The Ochrana knew the aims of the conference, they had a list of all those attending it, but they could not discover the time and place of the meeting.

In a desperate effort to gain this information the Ochrana ordered its agents to shadow every person on the list. The shadowing was carried out efficiently, but the agents made one elementary error: they ceased watching when the suspected revolutionaries retired for the night and did not take up their watch again until early the following morning. One day the agents all reported back to Ochrana headquarters that the suspects had left their homes or lodgings before they arrived. Contact with each revolutionary had been completely lost.

But what saved the Ochrana on that occasion was their talent for always having a revolutionary on their pay-roll. A message came from the chief of the Moscow Ochrana that one of his informers had received an invitation to the conference, giving the address where it was being held. A squad of police was rushed at once to this address, which turned out to be the home of a workman. He insisted that the guests had come to celebrate his birthday, but this time the Ochrana were not to be fooled. They arrested the lot and packed them off to Siberia.

But the battle against the revolutionaries was nevertheless slowly being lost by the Ochrana. Just as the Ochrana had infiltrated the revolutionary ranks, so the revolutionaries placed their agents in Government departments, in the Police, the War Office, in units of the Army and in the Ministries of the Interior and of Justice. These agents were the men who were to take over the Secret Service work of Russia after the revolution.

By the autumn of 1916 Vassilyev was promoted to head of the Police Department under the new Minister of the Interior, Protopopoff. Vassilyev's predecessor, Klimovitsh, had not got on at all well with the previous Minister of the Interior, Sturmer, and had frequently carried out investigations without consulting his chief. Vassilyev therefore was confronted with the task of bringing about some kind of mutual trust between the Ochrana and the new Minister. He also undertook certain reforms in the Ochrana organisation, mainly concerning a better system of consultation between various sections and fuller powers of action in the light of the war and the national need. Incredibly, these reforms had to be presented to the Duma and solemnly debated. Yet, day after day, the question of the debate was removed from the Orders of the Day and so the reforms were postponed.

Meanwhile the Ochrana's chief agent in Germany, Krassilnikoff, had sent back disturbing reports of the propaganda which Germany was disseminating inside Russia. Krassilnikoff had tracked down the source of this propaganda machine and found that the main aims were to foment revolution in Russia and at the same time to spread rumours that the Czarina was pro-German. It was swiftly apparent from Krassilnikoff's findings that Germany was far better informed on the efficiency of the revolutionaries' organisation than was the Ochrana. Even worse, the revolutionaries had established contacts inside the High Command of the Russian Army.

From that moment Czarist Russia was doomed. It was only a matter of time before the whole edifice tumbled down, Army, Navy, Ochrana and Civil Service. The Imperial Adjutants-General, Russky and Alexeyev, paying more attention to maintaining good relations with certain liberal members of the Duma, neglected to take any positive action against the now widespread distribution of revolutionary tracts inside the Army. Inertia seemed to have entered the hearts and minds of many of the military leaders who were away from the fighting lines. Discipline in the Forces melted away so swiftly that the police were constantly arresting soldiers who had deserted and turned pickpockets in the large cities. Strikes broke out in several factories and Ochrana headquarters became the target for revolutionary attack. Vassilyev gave instructions that books with addresses of officials and agents should be burned at once. This was only partially carried out, but the revolutionaries themselves captured the Criminal Register and destroyed all records of their members, photographs and fingerprints included.

Sheer inefficiency helped the revolutionary cause. For example no attempt was made to safeguard the telephone exchanges and other sections of the Ochrana made no attempt to retrieve the situation. The abdication of the Czar swiftly followed. Protopopoff was arrested by the revolutionaries and Vassilyev was seized and asked to provide information about the Ochrana. When he refused he, too, was put under arrest.

Yet despite the chaos and anarchism that followed the outbreak of revolution in Russia and lasted for the next few years, the organisation of the new Secret Service was begun by the Bolsheviks almost immediately.

It has been suggested by some writers that the new espionage and counter-espionage machine did not come into being until 1921. This is totally incorrect. Lenin, as early as December 1917, gave the task of rebuilding the Secret Service to one of his fellow Bolsheviks, Felix Dzerzhinsky, the son of a Polish aristocrat who had had a long career of revolutionary activity.

Dzerzhinsky had started his career as a student when he joined the Socialist Revolutionary Party, but he soon grew impatient with their aims and switched to the Social Democratic Labour Party and then, when the split between the Bolsheviks and the Mensheviks came in 1903, he joined the Bolsheviks and soon attracted the attention of Lenin. He was ruthless, cold, clear-headed, gifted with organisational talents and insisted from the start that he must have full powers and not be subject to any supervision. Such was the regard Lenin had for the man that he was given these powers without reservation.

Of course the plans for this new Secret Service had been discussed in some detail a few months before while the Kerensky Provisional Government was still in being. On 25 October the Bolsheviks staged their own revolution and not a single regiment in the St Petersburg garrison made a stand against the revolutionaries. Kerensky fled and the Bolsheviks took over.

Dzerzhinsky ordered the arrest of many Ochrana officers and agents, but some of them, under threats of death or life imprisonment, were forcibly persuaded to work for the Soviet régime. Even Vassilyev himself a few years later was approached while in exile in Munich and asked by an agent of Dzerzhinsky if he would enter the service of the Bolshevik Government as a spy. 'The sum of money offered as a bribe was quite considerable,' he stated, 'but I have seldom in my life experienced such satisfaction as I felt at the moment when I had the privilege of throwing that gentleman downstairs.'

For the first few days of its existence the new Secret Service of Russia was largely a one-man operation. Dzerzhinsky first imposed a communications blanket between the Soviet Government and the rest of Russia. Post, telephones, telegraphs, even messengers were banned to all non-Bolsheviks. Dzerzhinsky maintained this secrecy for weeks, sealing off all possibilities of communication between what he termed 'the enemy' and the Soviet Government.

On 20 December 1917, six weeks after the Bolsheviks had seized power, Dzerzhinsky was ready for the next move in setting up his Secret Service. He now had a considerable amount of information to work on and he turned his hastily improvised Security Sub-Committee into the more pretentious sounding title of Extraordinary Commission for the Struggle against Counter-Revolution and Sabotage. Its full Russian title was *Chrezvychainaya Komissiya po Borbe s Kontr-revolutisnei i Sabottazhem* and from the first two initials of the first two words this body became known for short as the Cheka.

Clearly from its title Dzerzhinsky was sufficiently realistic to put first things first: its prime aim was to build up a counter-espionage body to put down any attempts at counter-revolution and to organise an Intelligence Service which would keep a close check on all enemies of the régime. Dzerzhinsky sought to discredit the Ochrana in every way possible and to use all its misdeeds as a form of propaganda against the old régime. It was for this reason that the Extraordinary Commissions of Inquiry were set up to probe the use of *agent provocateur* tactics by the Ochrana. At the same time

Dzerzhinsky wanted to find out how many revolutionaries had been acting as police agents.

The task of the Cheka was made much easier because of Kerensky's refusal when he set up the Provisional Government to preserve the Ochrana as an institution. Muddle-headed liberalism was the key-note of the Kerensky administration and because of this incredibly lax attitude in the face of the Bolshevik threat the Kerensky Government fell. V. Burtsev, the man who had unmasked Azeff, had urged the Kerensky Government to maintain the Ochrana. But Kerensky demurred: the Ochrana, he said, was a despised institution, belonging to the Czarist régime and an instrument of repression. Thus the Bolsheviks' task was made even easier because the Kerensky Government had demolished all the Ochrana sections that survived the initial revolution, and had either sent the Ochrana agents and officials to join the Forces or put them in prison.

Dzerzhinsky ordered wholesale raids to be made in St Petersburg to round up counter-revolutionaries. He was at one and the same time hunter of spies, police chief, judge and jury. Mass arrests were made by the Cheka and, without troubling to have even the semblance of trials, sentences were passed and carried out immediately, execution being usually preferred to imprisonment.

Lenin himself spelt out the full meaning of Bolshevik terror when on 27 January 1918 he told the Presidium of the Petrograd Soviet: 'We can achieve nothing unless we use terror, and shoot speculators on the spot.' A few months later he was declaring that 'the Council of People's Commissars, having heard the report of the Chairman of the All-Russian Extraordinary Commission [the Cheka] on its activities, finds that in the given situation the safeguarding of the rear by means of terror is a direct necessity.'

Dzerzhinsky chose for his chief lieutenants men as brutal and callous as he was himself: he ensured that there would be no mercy shown to opponents of the régime. Though the Ochrana had been guilty of many atrocities on occasions the magnitude of their crimes never was as great as those of the Cheka. And it was not only in the Civil War period of 1917–20 that terror was used as a positive weapon to cow the people and preserve the Bolshevik régime. As late as June 1921, the powers of the Cheka to carry out 'extra-legal repression' in certain areas were explicitly confirmed by Government decree.

Whereas the Ochrana had been responsible directly to the Minister of the Interior and he in turn responsible to the government of the day, the Cheka was in the privileged position of not being under the direction of any Minister or Ministry, but responsible directly to the Soviet Government. This gave Dzerzhinsky supreme power.

When the Soviet Government moved to Moscow the Cheka transferred its headquarters to Lyublyanka Street, while its chief office in St Petersburg was moved to Gorochovaya Street, where the section chief was a bloodthirsty character named Uritsky. The latter acquired such a notorious reputation as a tyrant that he was eventually murdered by a Revolutionary Socialist named Kannegiesser. After that Dzerzhinsky tightened up control of all Cheka sections and ruled them like a dictator, allowing none of his leaders much scope for individual judgement. On the whole the men he selected, though brutal and often barely educated, were efficient in carrying out their duties and made up for their deficiencies in administration by their considerable experience as pre-revolution conspirators.

After the first wave of arrests and executions the Cheka was divided into two main divisions, the Counter-Espionage Section, comprised of the most trusted men, and the Secret Operative Section, designed principally in its early stages as an economic espionage unit. The Counter-Espionage Section followed somewhat conservatively at first in the steps of the Ochrana by employing a vast army of informers and sub-agents. But in forming this nation-wide army of informers they used the terror weapon as the chief inducement to recruitment. Thousands of ordinary citizens were compelled on threats of death or imprisonment to inform on their fellow citizens. Officers in the armed forces, priests, factory workers, peasants and women were all coerced to work for the Cheka.

By building up a vast army of informers and sub-agents Dzerzhinsky was able very quickly to extend the Cheka network to all parts of Russia. Within a year he had established branches in almost every small town in the country as well as in the large cities, and in some cases there were even village branches. At the same time he ensured that a watch was kept not only on known or suspected enemies of the Bolshevik régime but on the People's Commissars and Bolshevik district leaders as well. It was also Dzerzhinsky's idea that as and when the Soviet set up embassies abroad the diplomatic representatives should also be Cheka members, or, failing this, under observation by the Cheka.

When the Bolsheviks came to power the surviving members of the Kerensky Government with others set up a White Russian Government in exile and tried to continue the war against Germany and to defeat the Bolsheviks at one and the same time. But the White Russians lacked the one thing which the Bolsheviks were

147

beginning to build up – a Secret Service. For information, in the early stages at least, the White Russians had to depend on assistance and information from the secret services of Allied Governments. It was then that foreign spies began to appear again inside Russia.

At first these were mainly British, for the British Secret Service had maintained a few high quality agents in Russia after the revolution. One such was Paul Dukes who had gone to Russia as a youth to study music at the St Petersburg Conservatoire in 1909. During the war he was working in Moscow, attached to the American Y.M.C.A., though nominally in the service of the British Foreign Office. One day he was summoned back to London where he found himself recruited as a member of the British Secret Service. He was told to return to Russia and to report on the situation under the Bolsheviks. In November 1918, under the identity of Joseph Ilitch Afirenko, a member of the Soviet Secret Police, he was infiltrated over the Russian border from Finland.

In Whitehall Dukes was known simply as Agent ST 25; in Russia he had several aliases and proved himself to be a master of the arts of disguise. He not only gathered considerable information but built up an effective spy ring and linked up with counter-revolutionaries in an attempt to steal back some of the art treasures which the Bolsheviks themselves had already plundered.

In order to escape detection Dukes frequently had to undergo facial transformations and for months he was completely isolated from the outside world, for although he found couriers to carry his dispatches none of them returned to him and he was left in ignorance as to whether his messages were being delivered.

Dukes posed on various occasions as an official of the Cheka, having obtained a Russian passport which showed him to be one of their agents, and he also enlisted in the Red Army and became a Communist Party member to provide himself with satisfactory aliases.

In 1918 Robert Bruce Lockhart, then a young man in the Diplomatic Service, was appointed head of a special British Mission to the Soviet Government with the rank of acting British Consul-General in Moscow. Protests against this appointment were made to the Foreign Secretary, Lord Balfour, on the grounds that this was granting recognition to the Bolsheviks. In fact the post was a cover for one of Britain's most percipient agents who had proved himself highly efficient in gathering intelligence from inside Russia. The move did not for one moment deceive the Bolsheviks who regarded Lockhart as a spy first and a diplomat second.

It was the British Secret Service more than any other factor which kept the Cheka tied down in the first few years of its existence to containing the counter-revolutionaries. Yet it was in this 'honeymoon' period of world Communism, when the Russian fever spread over Europe, that revolution on an international scale became a possibility. In the minds of the visionaries world Communism – in Europe at least – seemed only a matter of six weeks distant at one period late in 1918. Yet the question of making this dream an actuality had to depend on fortuitous circumstances. The Russian Secret Service could do little about it. Perhaps for this reason Britain became the arch enemy, for the Cheka were pinned down by the British Secret Service to a defensive rôle.

Thus the defensive battle which the Cheka was forced to wage was a severe blow to Lenin's plans for world revolution. The best that could be done was the setting up of the Communist International, or the Comintern, which did not come into being until 1919. The danger period had passed by that time. But in the long term it was the best institution Russia had for creating the nucleus of a Secret Service capable of operating on a large scale abroad.

Bruce Lockhart spoke Russian fluently and he knew some of the Bolshevik leaders intimately. Some in the Foreign Office were jealous of Lockhart's success, others disliked his mixing of diplomacy and spying, while there were some who ridiculously dubbed him a 'pro-Bolshevik'. Unlike Dukes, who believed the revolution would not last, Lockhart insisted it had come to stay and that there could be no question of putting the clock back to Czarist days. He made friends with Trotsky, then War Minister, because he thought it would be possible to drive a wedge between Trotsky and Lenin.

The gist of Lockhart's advice was that the Russians were entirely at the mercy of the Germans and that demanding their intervention against Germany would only make them more obdurate. He was not anti-interventionist, but he believed that through Trotsky and one or two others the Soviet should be shown it was possible ultimately to win back from Germany what they had lost. Trotsky had actually asked for a British naval mission to reorganise the Russian fleets and offered to put a Briton in charge of the Russian railways. But the British ignored Lockhart's suggestions.

One of the worst features of the Terror was the Cheka's system of taking hostages. They had no scruples about arresting the wife, parents or children of a wanted man and keeping them in prison until the man gave himself up. Indeed this system of hostages was even used against Cheka officers who disobeyed orders or made mistakes. Dzerzhinsky was determined never to allow a dissatisfied or dismissed agent to go alive.

It was Dzerzhinsky who insisted on carrying through his policy of isolating Russia from the rest of the world, of preventing contacts with the non-Communist countries. For this reason the Secret Service adopted far more stringent censorship precautions than the Ochrana had ever done. The Bolshevik secret police were installed in every post office in the land and the closest surveillance was given to all mail coming in from abroad. It was imperative that .no news from outside should leak into Russia about the extent of the Terror. Similarly the importation of newspapers, magazines and books was rigorously controlled. Every Russian who wished to go abroad had to give the names and addresses of all members of his family living in Russia before he obtained a permit to travel. It was made clear to him that if he made any criticisms of the Soviet and conditions in the country while he was abroad his relatives would be seized as hostages.

But if the Cheka were ruthlessly efficient at the top, the vast majority of their members were of poor calibre, illiterate and unable to distinguish between an innocent citizen with no concern in politics and a counter-revolutionary. Many could not read what was written on identity documents: all they could recognise was the Cheka stamp. Thus, when in doubt, they frequently made an arrest on the principle that it was safer than letting a man go.

It was because of his contempt for the intellectual poverty of the vast majority of the Cheka that Sidney Reilly back in London conceived the idea of infiltrating the Russian Secret Service and defeating it from within. Reilly's idea was to build a new, counter-revolutionary Secret Service. He was an out-and-out interventionist and extremely critical of the procrastination of the Allies, and of Britain in particular, about mounting a counter-offensive against the Bolsheviks.

Lloyd George was always lukewarm on the subject of actively opposing the Bolsheviks, but under pressure from his colleagues in the British Cabinet he asked Captain Mansfield Cumming, head of the Secret Service, if he had any suggestions for attempting a coup against the Soviet régime. It is doubtful whether Lloyd George seriously expected to receive any suggestions, but Cumming unhesitatingly put forward the name of Reilly as the one man who was capable of organising this. Perhaps Lloyd George did not expect anything to come of it, for his doubts on the subject of intervention remained. Reilly was a known sympathiser with the Social Revolutionaries, though it had been kept discreetly quiet during his previous stays in Russia and had never prevented him from co-operating with the pre-war Russian governments. But he was seemingly implacably opposed to the Soviet régime and one of his bitterest complaints against the Soviet Council Executive

Committee was that it was not the Russians who made the revolution possible who reaped the harvest, but alien Jews, Poles and Armenians who usurped them.

It was in the spring of 1918 that Reilly, bearing a pass from Litvinoff, the Bolsheviks' representative in London, went to Russia with something like a free hand to make what contacts he could with both the Bolsheviks and the counter-revolutionaries.

Litvinoff must have been well aware of Reilly's antecedents and he took a risk in sponsoring him. One suggestion is that Lloyd George himself misled Litvinoff as to the motives of Reilly's visit, but the Soviet may well have thought it worthwhile giving Reilly some scope in order to find out what his plans were. It should be stressed that Reilly went out under his adopted name of Reilly and not under any of his Russian aliases or his original name. He made straight for Moscow, lost no time in going to the Kremlin and boldly demanded to see Lenin. He was informed that Lenin was away, but he managed to see Bonch-Brouevich, a close associate of Lenin, and told him that he had been sent out specially by Lloyd George to obtain a more honest report of the situation in Russia than Britain had received to date. According to Robin Bruce Lockhart, Reilly added that 'the British Government was not satisfied with the reports it received from Bruce Lockhart'.

This seems an unnecessarily mischievous comment to make to a leading member of the Soviet. To begin with it cast doubts on Lockhart and could have jeopardised his position with the Russians. It will remain a mystery why Reilly adopted these tactics with the Russians unless he was even then playing some devious game. The Russians immediately suspected that Reilly had come to Russia as a spy rather than as an envoy of Lloyd George. Being equally mischievous, and seeking to embarrass Reilly, they reported what he had said to Bruce Lockhart.

At this stage Reilly went underground again and reappeared in Petrograd as a Mr Constantine, a Greek from the Levant. Here he made contact with his old friend, Sasha Grammatikoff, and with Vladimir Orloff, who had infiltrated the Cheka under the name of Orlinsky. Thus Reilly was in indirect contact with the Cheka's headquarters in Petrograd and managed to learn a good deal about their organisation.

The Terror was at its height at this period. Torture had been specifically legalised by command of the Communist Party Central Committee who stated that they considered 'physical pressure should still be used obligatorily to known and obstinate enemies of the people as a method both justifiable and appropriate.'

On 5 September 1918 the central Cheka and local Chekas were authorised to shoot class enemies and isolate them in concentration camps. They continued to have legal and administrative powers and it has been estimated that they must have shot more than 50,000 people and committed hundreds of thousands to prisons and concentration camps.

Thus Reilly's activities were fraught with extreme danger and only a very brave or extremely reckless man would have risked what he did. It is appropriate that his nickname was 'Reckless Reilly', but he seems to have acquired by this time not only a feeling of being indestructible, but of being a man of destiny as well. He certainly aimed to build up a White Russian Secret Service.

When visiting Moscow Reilly used the name Constantine, establishing himself in the flat of a dancer at the Moscow Arts Theatre named Dagmara, and two other actresses. Here he started to plan an alternative government which could take over when Lenin was toppled from power.

Reilly did not envisage his future rôle merely as that of a go-between. He actually had the audacity to see himself not only as the man to pick the future government but to be at the head of it as well. His old friend Badmayeff was to be put in charge of Eastern Russian affairs, another friend, Grammatikoff, was to be Minister of the Interior, and a business acquaintance, Chubersky, Minister of Communications and Transport. The former Czarist General Yudenich was assigned the task of head of the Army.

All this was no pipe dream. Reilly was far too much a man of action to be content with dreams. Despite the care he had to take to remain hidden he moved around the country organising counter-revolutionary cells and arranging various 'safe' addresses. To make travelling safer for himself he obtained identity papers which showed him to be 'Comrade Relinsky', a member of the Cheka.

Dzerzhinsky gave orders that the Cheka were to adopt the tactics of the Ochrana and employ *agents provocateurs* to smoke out the counter-revolutionaries. A special section of the Cheka was set up to recruit and organise former Social Revolutionaries to do this work. The section was small at first and concentrated mainly in Moscow and Petrograd and close to the Finnish border, but towards the end of the year a few agents were sent abroad to make contact with counter-revolutionaries in France, Britain and U.S.A. One of the first blows struck was by Michael Vladimir, head of the Cheka in the area along the Finnish border. He infiltrated anti-Bolshevik groups and as a result rounded up no less than three hundred counter-revolutionaries in the Kronstadt district.

Yet it was the counter-revolutionaries who played the Bolsheviks at their own game and scored a tactical success. In July 1918 Blumkin, a Social Revolutionary, assassinated the German

Ambassador, Count von Mirbach, in the belief that this would force the Germans to attack Russia once again and so bring about a collapse of the Soviet. This proved to be the signal for a rising of other anti-Soviet revolutionaries in Moscow. They had planned to kill leading Bolsheviks at the Moscow Opera House by planting bombs there, but the Cheka had infiltrated their ranks and warned the Soviet hierarchy to stay away.

Reilly was furious that this counter-attack had been launched too soon, for he had been making plans to capture Dzerzhinsky himself. The head of the Cheka heard of the plot and instantly swept into action. The man who was such a fanatical Communist that he had even had his own mother executed ordered a 'salutary bloodbath to cool the ardour of the criminal bourgeoisie'. Hundreds of people were hauled out of their beds and taken straight to the firing squads and within ten days the Czar and his family were killed and their bodies hurled down the shaft of a coal mine.

12

Trotsky Forms the G.R.U.

IT WAS an extremely foolish propaganda move on the part of the British to put about the story that both Lenin and Trotsky were German agents and that they had maintained liaison with the German High Command. True, Lenin was aided and abetted in his return to Russia by the Germans who saw that revolution was the quickest means of putting Russia out of the war, but Trotsky was strongly anti-German and, as Bruce Lockhart saw clearly, could, if handled properly, have been persuaded to carry on the war against Germany.

Trotsky took the view that unless Germany was totally defeated by invading Allied armies, she would eventually arise again and confront her enemies. He would have preferred the Allies to do the job for him, but he wanted to see the Russian borders extended, to crush German militarism and have a Communist dictatorship installed there. It was primarily for this reason, whatever apologists may say, that Trotsky created the new Red Army and he made a first-class job of it, when one considers that what he took over was an undisciplined, ill-fed, ill-clothed, demoralised and shabby rabble. Discipline was restored, the salute, which had been abolished in the first flush of the Revolution, was brought back, as were the badges of rank.

Dzerzhinsky had been one of the first to suspect, then to fear that Trotsky, given enough power, would mould the Soviet revolution into a one-man dictatorship. With the Army behind him, Trotsky might easily have achieved this. But there was one other vital factor that held the balance of power: Dzerzhinsky, through the Cheka, controlled intelligence and dominated the day-to-day running of the country. To grasp the reins of power Trotsky needed a similar instrument, which he acquired when he set up the Fourth Department of the General Staff of the Red Army, more generally known as the G.R.U. There was nothing markedly revolutionary about this development: it was almost entirely concerned with military intelligence and in the beginning was based on the military intelligence systems of other great powers. But naturally the creation of a rival organisation, albeit a complementary one, irked Dzerzhinsky and he saw it as a possible challenge to his own supremacy in the field of intelligence.

It was then that Dzerzhinsky began to build up a dossier on Trotsky. He learned of his relationships with Bruce Lockhart and suspected that, though dedicated to the Communist revolution, Trotsky might well consider foreign adventures if he could turn his developing Army against the remnants of the Germans. Then Cheka agents informed Dzerzhinsky that Trotsky had established a secret liaison with Captain George Hill, a member of the British Military Intelligence. Hill had undertaken many secret missions during the war and Trotsky had invited him to become his adviser on air warfare, a secret post which Hill accepted with alacrity in order to find out about Russian plans. It did not take Dzerzhinsky long to discover that Captain Hill had also helped Trotsky with advice on the creation of the G.R.U.

Meanwhile Captain Hill had been encouraging the development of bands of guerrillas consisting of White Russians who were employed to attack the Germans. Dzerzhinsky was determined that, though George Hill was no direct threat to the Soviet, he must be liquidated and gave orders for his arrest. Hill was tipped off by friendly agents and managed to escape.

So the G.R.U. owed something of its constitution to British influence, but it never achieved any real power as a branch of the Russian Secret Service. Dzerzhinsky was determined from the very beginning that it should not acquire supremacy and it says much for his insistence on civil control of intelligence that the G.R.U. has remained even until today as a subordinate agency.

The Cheka not only dominated the G.R.U. but demanded the right to screen the personnel of the military organisation.

Trotsky and his Army generals disliked this attempt to control the G.R.U., but they were overruled. Not only did the Cheka screen G.R.U. personnel but they infiltrated the organisation and even formally insisted on having Chekists inside the ranks of the Trotsky intelligence body. At the same time they denied the G.R.U. any right to have their men inside the Cheka. It was a one-sided arrangement, but it has lasted right down to the present time and only in the emergency of World War II did the G.R.U. come into its own.

Late in 1918 Dzerzhinsky, suspecting an Allied plot against the régime, ordered his Cheka to raid the French Secret Service head-quarters in Moscow. He had long suspected that Colonel de Vertement, head of the French Intelligence in Russia, was hatching some plot and a tip-off had indicated that de Vertement was in touch with the British and had accumulated an enormous stock of bombs and explosives for sabotage. The raid was successful and the Cheka not only captured a quantity of explosives but arrested six French agents whom they immediately accused of working with certain Letts to overthrow the Soviet Government. De Vertement escaped capture by climbing on to the roof-tops and making a get-away.

At this very moment Sidney Reilly was engaged in working out a plan to arrest Lenin and Trotsky and other leading Bolsheviks when they attended a meeting of the Soviet Central Executive Committee. The implementation of his plan to set up an alternative government was drawing near and all key members of it had been warned to stand by for instant action. But the Cheka raids were intensified after the swoop on the French headquarters and this meant that three of Reilly's agents were put out of action. Then on 31 August Dora Kaplan, a Social-Revolutionary, shot at Lenin at point-blank range as he was leaving a meeting in Moscow. The wounds did not prove fatal, but they were severe enough and the incident possibly shortened Lenin's life. Dzerzhinsky then decided to launch counter-attacks in all directions with the utmost vigour and ferocity. Dora Kaplan was shot by the Commandant of the Kremlin before Dzerzhinsky could have her interrogated, but Dzerzhinsky himself ordered the immediate shooting of five hundred people in Moscow and sent orders to Petrograd for a further seven hundred to be executed there. Instructions also went out that all Social-Revolutionaries were to be exterminated. It was estimated that close on seven thousand persons were shot following the attempt on Lenin's life.

Bruce Lockhart was arrested at gun-point and removed to

Cheka headquarters. The news was blazoned in the Soviet press that the attempt on Lenin was a plot by Bruce Lockhart and attacks were launched on the 'Anglo-French criminals and enemies of Russia'. Reilly's master-plan for arresting Lenin and Trotsky and setting up an alternative government was ruined by this series of mishaps, but he bravely remained in Moscow in disguise and still carrying his Cheka pass. He, too, was made a scapegoat for the attempt on Lenin's life and his photograph was reproduced on countless posters and in the newspapers beneath an offer of 100,000 roubles to anyone who would capture him alive or dead.

There was a touch of farce in the Cheka's drive to find Reilly. Though the spy himself eluded them, they arrested eight women known to have associated with him. Each of the eight, when interrogated, claimed to be Reilly's wife and not even fear of the dreaded Cheka robbed them of the pride they took in these confessions! As all eight were placed in the same cell there was some considerable argument and even fighting among them about the question of who really was Mrs Reilly.

When Bruce Lockhart was arrested and kept in prison by the Cheka the British Government immediately informed the Soviet Government that Litvinoff, their representative in London, would be held as a hostage until Lockhart was released. Litvinoff was kept in Brixton Prison and only when Lockhart was freed was he allowed to return to Russia.

Reilly, frustrated in his attempts at a counter-revolution, escaped back to London.

In November 1918 Germany collapsed and the war was over. Meanwhile in Moscow the Bolsheviks put on one of their show trials and announced to the world that Bruce Lockhart and Sidney Reilly had been tried in their absence, found guilty of organising the plot against Lenin and that they would be put to death if ever they came to Russia again.

In his counter-revolution plans Reilly had co-operated not only with the French Secret Service, but with Kalamatiano, an American of Greek origin, who was head of the American Secret Service in Russia. By planting an *agent provocateur* in the ranks of the plotters the Cheka had been able to track down the conspirators; Kalamatiano had been caught, put on trial and executed and so, too, had Colonel Friede, who had been a member of the Russian General Staff.

In 1966 an account of the Cheka's work in what was called the 'Lockhart Plot' was given in *Nedelya*, the Sunday edition of *Izvestia*: 'Only forty-eight years afterwards has it become possible to name the person who played the leading rôle in capturing

156

Lockhart's counter-revolutionaries,' stated the article. It then referred to the *agent provocateur* mainly responsible for this under the name of 'Schmidhen'. 'In 1918, to maintain the fight against the counter-revolution . . . and find out from what direction the enemy's main efforts would come, F. E. Dzerzhinsky entrusted to a small group of Chekists the task of infiltrating into one of the counter-revolutionary movements . . . One of them went under the surname of "Schmidhen".'

Basically the *Nedelya* account of the Cheka's operation is reasonably factual and a good deal of it is substantiated by independent evidence. 'Schmidhen', together with a man named Sprogis, gained the confidence of Captain Cromie, the British naval officer, who explained to them that he was remaining in Petrograd to try to prevent the Russian Fleet being seized by the Germans. Cromie introduced the Chekist spies to Sidney Reilly who asked them to hand over a letter to Bruce Lockhart. The letter was shown to Dzerzhinsky before it was taken to Lockhart.

Sir Bruce Lockhart, in his book *Storm Over Russia*, appears to confirm this story when he tells how one night when he was dining in Moscow 'my servant told me of the arrival of two people. One of them was a pale young man of small stature, who was called "Schmidhen". Schmidhen brought me a letter from Cromie, which I carefully checked.' Schmidhen pretended that he was a second-lieutenant of the Czarist Army and to be in touch with the influential commanding officers of the Lettish Rifles.

Dzerzhinsky directed the Chekist agents, urging them to encourage Lockhart to establish contact with General Poole, who was in Archangel, to discuss with him a scheme for the defection of the Lettish Rifles. By this means the two plotters gained a greater insight into the thinking of the counter-revolutionaries and were able to report their plans to Dzerzhinsky.

Nevertheless the *Nedelya* account of these events contains many gaps. The 'Lockhart Plot' was always more of a fiction in the minds of the Bolsheviks than anything concrete. True, Lockhart was plotting, but the major plan against the Soviet at this time was that of Reilly, whereas *Nedelya* pays scant attention to him, and much more to Lockhart. And the man who betrayed the Reilly plot to Dzerzhinsky was not a Chekist agent but a French informer named René Marchand.

Nedelya, however, revealed that Schmidhen was really Jan Janovich Buikis, a Lett and a member of the Communist Party. He joined the Cheka in March 1918, and was still alive up to 1966 at least.

The campaign waged by the White Russian armies against the Bolsheviks was by the early months of 1919 severely handicapped by Dzerzhinsky's non-stop drive against the counter-revolutionaries inside Russia. The Cheka had wiped out tens of thousands of these within a few months of the attempt on Lenin's life.

One of the earliest of the Soviet intelligence agents operating in enemy territory – in this case in territory held by the White Russian forces – was Grigori Galaton, a young Cossack from the Kuban, who was popularly known as the 'Black Captain'. This was because he dressed himself up in the smart, black uniform of the élite Markov Regiment.

Galaton established himself in the Black Sea port of Novorossisk in 1919. His aim was to spy on the White Russian forces and to rescue Communist sympathisers. In this way Galaton had something of the panache and daring of Sidney Reilly and an undoubted talent for winning friends and supporters. He gathered around him a dozen Communist Partisans – they certainly were not Party members, nor were they as yet accustomed to Soviet methods – and he proceeded to imbue them with his own enthusiasm for the cause of the revolution. Somehow or other Galaton had managed to steal the uniform of a captain in the Markov Regiment and, wearing this, he marched into a depot and ordered uniforms of the same regiment for his men. He appears to have had great influence inside this regiment as he drew his own personal bodyguard from their ranks.

One day the heir to the throne of Serbia visited Novorossisk and the nobility of the area, together with refugees from the north, attended a gala performance at the city theatre in his honour. Galaton and eight of his men entered the theatre which was ablaze with lights. The Serbian prince, accompanied by General Denikin, the White Guard leader, was in a box. The 'Black Captain' deployed some of his men to the pit, others to the balcony. Suddenly all the lights went out and shots were fired. There was general pandemonium, but nobody, according to reports, was killed. Galaton's aim was to strike terror into the hearts of those present, to remind them of the long arm of the Soviet, not to kill.

On another occasion a black Rolls-Royce drew up outside the home of General Denikin's chief quartermaster, Colonel Morozoff. Out of the car jumped the dashing 'Black Captain', boots superbly polished, uniform immaculately smart, looking every inch an exceptionally handsome Markov officer. He rang the doorbell and the maid admitted him. With complete composure and splendid gallantry Galaton greeted the Colonel's wife, bowed and explained that he had come for her daughter whose presence was required at a reception for some visiting British officers.

Madame Morozova was charmed by the 'Black Captain's' gallantry, but she was somewhat hesitant about letting her daughter go. However, the young girl, equally charmed with the 'Captain', begged to be allowed to accompany him. Soon she was seated beside Galaton in the Rolls and they headed away to the 'party'.

Next day Galaton, still in his uniform, politely insolent and still playing the rôle of an officer, called on Colonel Morozoff.

'Where is my daughter?' demanded the irate Colonel, his hand on his sword.

'Ah, dear sir,' replied Galaton. 'Put away your sword. Let us behave like civilised beings. Your daughter is well and comfortable and she sends you this letter. Please read it before you say any more.'

The Colonel, nonplussed, read the note, which was in his daughter's handwriting, stating that she was being well treated, but requesting that he should provide the 'Captain' with whatever he wanted. Morozoff stormed and shouted and threatened, but all to no avail. The 'Black Captain' was suave, but firm.

'I do not have to remind you, surely, Colonel, that if you don't grant your daughter's wish, it will be unfortunate, to say the least, for her.'

Morozoff capitulated and agreed to let the Red Partisans have three freight cars full of foodstuffs, British uniforms and ammunition. But Galaton, unlike the Cheka, was sufficiently civilised to keep his word: the Colonel's daughter was restored to her family, unharmed, and a few weeks later she and her family sailed away from Novorossisk. Nor, curiously enough, did the daughter bear Galaton any malice. 'He was always a charmingly polite rogue,' she told her friends. 'I should like to meet him again.'

In organising this kind of political kidnapping Galaton was carving a new chapter in the sphere of intelligence. His final coup was the freeing of a group of Bolsheviks from Novorossisk Prison by presenting the prison authorities with a forged order to deliver the prisoners to him and his men for execution. Shortly after that the Red Army entered and took Novorossisk.

During the period of the Terror the member of the Cheka next in importance to Dzerzhinsky was its vice-president, Jacob Peters, who came to the fore in 1919–20. It will be recalled that Jacob Peters had been suspected by many of being the 'Peter the Painter' of the Sidney Street Siege in London's East End some few years before World War I. Certainly Jacob Peters had been arrested in December 1910, on suspicion of being concerned with a number of others in the wilful murder of three police officers at Houndsditch, but at the trial at the Central Criminal Court the judge said there was an element of doubt in the evidence and Peters was accordingly acquitted.

Jacob Peters was born at Courland in 1886. He came to Britain in 1909 and secured employment as a presser in a second-hand clothing business. After the trial he returned to the firm who had previously employed him and remained with them until the spring of 1917. In 1913 he married an English woman, a Miss Freeman, of Worcester. In fairness to Peters it should perhaps be mentioned that he told his wife-to-be all about his trial and his association with the Sidney Street terrorists. Then in May 1917 Peters was sent back to Russia by the London Russian Delegate Committee, needless to say a revolutionary body. From that time he became a Bolshevik and after the Revolution in October of that year was given a post in the Russian Foreign Office.

He was, in fact, put into the Foreign Office as a spy, with orders to make a detailed examination of records and secret dossiers and to report back personally to Dzerzhinsky. Soon he was drawn into the Cheka and made its vice-president. Soon Peters was to become almost as notorious as Dzerzhinsky. In September 1918 M. Dosch-Fleurot, the *World*'s correspondent in Petrograd, wrote in a dispatch from Stockholm that 'the most awful figure of the Russian Red Terror, the man with the most murder on his soul, is the present Extraordinary Commissioner against Counter-Revolution and Sabotage, a dapper little blond Lett named Peters, who lived in England so long that he speaks Russian with an English accent.'

Despite his reputation Peters was a gregarious fellow who was known and liked by the American correspondents in Russia because he seemed more cultivated than the rest. To the Americans he showed quite a different face than he did to the counter-revolutionaries, whom he often ordered to be shot without sending them before Krylenko, the president of the Revolutionary Tribunal.

But to portray Peters solely as a monster is to give a one-sided picture of the man. He was a dispassionate operator, dedicated more to efficiency and speed than to sadism. He was quite unlike some of the animalistic executioners of the Terror: he took no pleasure in his grim work and indeed he often berated his men for prolonging torture and death as a needless waste of time. Those who knew him testified to many small kindnesses which he performed when off duty: he delighted in speaking English on every possible occasion and, in fact, his pro-British and pro-American prejudices caused suspicion among his colleagues.

Nevertheless, even so ardent a Bolshevik as Peters was regarded as something of a security risk among some of the Bolshevik leaders. He owed his strength to the support he received from Dzerzhinsky and few would go against the head of the Cheka. It may have been his Lettish origins which had something to do with this, for many Letts were to be found among the counter-revolutionaries. Or it may have been his pro-British sentiments, or the fact that he had an English wife who was still safe in England. Or even that somebody had heard him make unfavourable comments about the 'untidy revolutionary men'. Then again his record as a 'police butcher' may have made him enemies, as they did to that other Cheka killer, Uritsky.

By the summer of 1919 he had been made Chief of Internal Defence and *Pravda* of 14 June of that year printed an order by Peters that the wives and grown-up children of all officers escaping to the anti-Bolshevik ranks should be arrested. The following day he ordered the disconnection of all private telephones in Petrograd and the confiscation of all wine, spirits, money above £500 and jewels.

His success in putting down revolt in Petrograd led to his later being sent to Turkestan in complete control of the counter-espionage organisation. At some time during 1919 he must have suddenly fallen under a cloud for it was freely reported that he was out of favour and a report from Reval in October of that year stated that he had been killed in Moscow. This proved to be false and after that it was authoritatively stated that he had been given another assignment elsewhere in Russia.

One of Peters' special interests was in organising spies to discover hidden counter-revolutionary loot and to steal art treasures from museums to raise funds for the Soviet at a time when currency was in short supply. Then in October 1920 came a report that Peters, 'with his friend, Miss Krause', had left Russia, taking with him a large quantity of valuables which had been entrusted to his care by the Bolshevik Government. He was believed to have gone to Germany and, according to a report in a Petrograd journal, several Bolshevik Commissioners had set out to look for him.

A few years later Peters was reported to have been engaged in counter-espionage work directed against certain officers in the Red Army. Then in 1937 it was reported from Warsaw that he had been executed for plotting against Stalin, along with Valery Meshlauk, head of the State Planning Commission, and Ivan Meshlauk, General Commissioner of the Soviet Pavilion at the recent Paris Exhibition.

The mystery of Jacob Peters lasted until almost the end of World War II. Then Peters' British wife's brother, Mr D. Freeman, stated that the rumour that his brother-in-law had been executed was not true. 'I know Peters is alive and holds a high position in Moscow,' he told the London *News Chronicle*. According to him, Peters' wife and daughter had gone out to Russia to join their husband and father some years before this.

From the time of the 'Lockhart Plot' trial the Cheka began to build up an impressive dossier on Sidney Reilly. British Intelligence prided themselves that the secret of Reilly's origins was theirs alone. They forgot two things: the Ochrana's pre-war probes into their own agents, and the women friends of Reilly who were imprisoned by the Cheka. How much the last-named knew is problematical, but it is significant that all these women escaped execution and at the 'Lockhart Plot' trial were partially exonerated by the State Prosecutor.

This love-hate relationship which the Soviet has always had for its most formidable enemies is curious only if looked at by Western eyes: from the Russian point of view it is a mixture of fear, admiration and expediency, a kind of emotional logic that is more Oriental than anything else. To the Soviet, Sir Basil Zaharoff was perhaps the ultimate 'fascist beast', a multi-millionaire monster who made fortunes out of war and the fomenting of wars. Implacably opposed to the Soviet régime, Zaharoff was in World War I actively encouraging right-wing Germans to stamp out Communism, but Zaharoff's main interests at this time were concerned with the Middle East and Greece. To gain his own way in this area Zaharoff was prepared to do some horse-trading with the Russians.

Suddenly the Bolsheviks brought off a neat diplomatic coup by publishing the secret Sykes–Picot Agreement of May 1916, which shared out the territories of the then unconquered Turks among the powers of the *Entente*. Under this agreement Russia was to have the Dardanelles, Constantinople and a large area around Erzerum and Trebizond. Charles Maurras, one of Zaharoff's most virulent critics, swore that Zaharoff himself had indicated to the Soviet Government through Kapp, the German *putsch* leader, where the document was to be found. Sir Basil Thomson, when head of Britain's counter-espionage team after the war, in the course of his investigations into Bolshevik activities discovered documents which incriminated servants of the Crown as secret agents of Sir Basil Zaharoff and learned that Zaharoff, who had been so lavish with his presents to members of the Russian royal family, had established links with the Bolsheviks. He sought to divert munitions supplies intended for the White Russians to Greece for ultimate use against the Turks.

For Zaharoff the issues were clear, if his methods were complex and devious. If the White Russians won, they might demand Constantinople as their right in accordance with the terms of the secret Sykes–Picot agreement. Zaharoff's dream was the creation of a Greek empire, with Constantinople in the hands of the Greeks. So, by underground methods, he obtained from the Soviet an assurance that they would make no claim for this city, if Zaharoff would help to check arms supplies for the counter-revolutionaries.

Ironically, the Soviet's arch enemy now was that former fiery and ruthless revolutionary, Boris Savinkoff, the colleague of Azeff, and for so many years the most dedicated and active supporter of revolution. Savinkoff had come into his own as Minister for War under the Kerensky Government and had immediately thrown himself wholeheartedly into the task of giving the Russian people democratic government. For at heart Savinkoff believed in democracy, in liberty and tolerance. It was for the establishment of these things as a permanent feature of Russian life that he had risked his life for a quarter of a century, assassinated, organised terrorist attacks and co-operated with killers. For him the end was greater than the means, but he soon found that for the Bolsheviks the end was merely the perpetuation of the means – terror as a permanent policy of holding down the people. So Savinkoff the bomb-thrower and revolutionary became the hero of the White Russians and the most determined of counter-revolutionaries.

No ordinary man could have survived such a transition. That Savinkoff did so and surprised his former enemies by his courage and integrity, and won the admiration of such men of other nations as Winston Churchill and Marshal Pilsudski of Poland, was a tribute to his personality and his ability.

The loss of Savinkoff from the revolutionary ranks was a serious blow to the Soviet. Dzerzhinsky said sadly that it was as though the Red Army had lost three divisions and he was personally as much disposed to win back Savinkoff as to see him assassinated. Nadel, a Soviet agent in Paris, was consulted as to how a permanent watch could be kept on Savinkoff. 'The only way to do it,' he reported back to Moscow, 'would be to control the man who keeps Savinkoff supplied with morphine.' The fatal vice of the former revolutionary was that he was addicted to morphine, a drug he had taken to keep up his courage in his days as a terrorist. From the moment Dzerzhinsky received this advice he decided that Savinkoff must either be kidnapped, or lured back to Russia where morphine would be given to him, or withheld according to the degree to which he agreed to co-operate with the Soviet authorities.

One of the earliest tasks of the Russian Secret Service from 1919 onwards was the creation of an organisation through which the luring back of supporters of the counter-revolutionaries could be achieved. It was an uphill, seemingly impossible task at first sight and called for great patience, much detailed planning and absolute security. It was Dzerzhinsky's greatest achievement.

In the meantime the White Russians were slowly but surely crushed and the civil war was brought to an end, but it was typical of Dzerzhinsky's thoroughness that he never regarded the ending of the civil war inside Russia as the final defeat of the counter-revolutionaries. Nor did the Supreme Soviet. The fight against the counter-revolutionaries became a 'cold' and silent war waged by the Secret Service in such far-off places as Paris, Berne, New York, Stockholm and Helsinki.

The first stage in this new battle overseas was the setting up in 1921 of the Foreign Department of the Cheka, the I.N.O., under the supervision of the old Bolshevik fighter, Meyer Trilisser. The I.N.O.'s first task was to destroy the remnants of the exiled White Russians wherever they formed. But on the suggestion of Dzerzhinsky this policy was changed to include scope for the infiltration of *agents provocateurs* in the White Russian ranks and to recruit spies among them. At the same time the I.N.O. kept a close watch on the activities of the Trotsky-created G.R.U. and had orders to establish close links with foreign Communist Parties.

In December 1921 the Bolshevik Government ordered a re-organisation of the Cheka with the aim of substituting trials for the practice of instant execution of the death penalty. Then in February 1922 the Cheka was abolished by a decree and in its place was created the G.P.U. (State Political Administration). Such changes of titles have been frequent in the history of the Soviet Secret Service, but they have hardly ever marked any real change in the *status quo* and have represented partly an attempt at greater administrative tidiness and sometimes a rather naïve effort to alter the image of the Intelligence Service.

The G.P.U., like the Cheka before it, retained the right to screen G.R.U. personnel and the Red Army was filled with G.P.U. informers, never less than one agent to a battalion and sometimes more. The G.P.U. remained as supreme in its controlling rôle and as ubiquitous as ever the Cheka was.

The G.P.U. came under the N.K.V.D. (People's Commissariat of Internal Affairs) in rather the same way that the Ochrana came under the Ministry of the Interior, but in practice it went its own way unhindered by a higher authority. If any proof of this were needed it could be found in the fact that Dzerzhinsky became not only the head of the N.K.V.D. as Commissar for Internal Affairs but controlled the G.P.U. and later became chairman of the

O.G.P.U. (Unified State Political Administration) when this successor to the G.P.U. was created in November 1923.

The O.G.P.U. differed very little from the G.P.U., but it tidied up the work administratively and brought all sections of the G.P.U. under a more efficient system of national control. It was not a part of the N.K.V.D. and the Militia, which had been under the control of the N.K.V.D., was eventually placed under the O.G.P.U., though this did not take place until 1932.

Dzerzhinsky was insistent on professionalism in his agents and made it a cardinal rule that every agent must always observe every rule of security, however irksome and in all circumstances, on penalty of death. The agent who deviated in the least respect from his cover story was immediately liquidated however good he may have been. To ensure that agents followed out the prescribed drill on each occasion Dzerzhinsky would have them watched. It had been the habit among Soviet spies in Paris to pass information written on cigarette papers which would be rolled into cigarettes and then smoked. One day an agent, having read his message and memorised it, rolled his cigarette and then found he had no match with which to light it. He screwed up the cigarette and dropped it into a drain. His action was reported, he was ordered back to Russia and shot.

Technical advances in the sphere of espionage were rapid among the Western powers after World War I, but Russia, due to lack of contact with technological experts in other parts of the world, lagged behind for some years. Most progress was made in the use of micro-photography, mainly owing to the ingenuity of a former Ochrana photographic expert who joined the G.P.U. The use of radio came much more gradually and Lenin was apparently disturbed about the delay in adopting radio techniques in espionage, for on 19 May 1922 he was writing to Stalin about a report in *Izvestia* that the British had invented a device for keeping telegrams transmitted by radio secret: 'if we could buy this invention, communication by radio-telephone and radio-telegraphy would achieve greater importance in the military field.'

Meyer Trilisser was an energetic and capable head of the I.N.O. and one of his prime aims was to develop industrial and scientific espionage in the Western world. He had direct encouragement from Lenin to achieve this and set about it in a circuitous but nonetheless disarmingly effective manner. Trilisser had the utmost contempt for the 'worker-spy' in industry, maintaining that he was unprofessional, too closely allied as a rule to the Communist Party of the country in which he operated, and with insufficient technical knowledge to know what to look for. So he decided that if Russia were to obtain the West's scientific and technological secrets she

165

must employ dedicated scientists who could be trusted to serve the cause.

One such promising scientist was available. He was a dark-haired, square-faced young man of considerable talent and an almost fanatical desire to explore hitherto unplumbed scientific fields. His name was Peter Kapitza, the son of a Czarist general and the grandson of another general of the pre-revolution régime, one whose background represented everything the Bolsheviks rejected and detested. Normally he could have expected little mercy from them. As it was, the Communists had confiscated his family's property and he was too poor to go to university or to take a degree.

Trilisser had heard reports of the young man and decided that Kapitza's background, however 'unsafe' from a narrow security point of view, might have the virtue of making him more trusted in the outside world. What better choice for an agent to worm out the scientific secrets of the industrial and capitalist Western world than one who could be looked upon as a refugee from Communism. A hint was passed down the ranks of the Bolshevik hierarchy and Kapitza was awarded an industrial research scholarship, enabling the eager student to go to Britain from Leningrad in 1921 and to study at Cambridge University.

This marked the modest beginning of what was to become a steady infiltration of Cambridge University by Soviet Government agents over the next fifteen years. It was to provide the Russian Secret Service with hundreds of thousands of pounds worth of intelligence and to give them such agents as Kapitza himself, Lev Landau, Allan Nunn May, Guy Burgess, Donald Maclean, Kim Philby, Julian Bell and John Cornford – to name only a few. But, as will be seen later, the penetration of the cloisters of the university city had to be organised from within as well as from without.

Kapitza at once attracted attention as one of the most promising of students and perhaps because he appeared to be the underdog, or even because of his Czarist background, he was given special privileges. Soon he became a doctor of philosophy and his scientific work came to the attention of Lord Rutherford, the man who split the atom, who made Kapitza his assistant at the Cavendish Laboratory in Cambridge. In fact Kapitza was present when Rutherford first split the atom.

Shortly after Kapitza's departure for England Trilisser discovered yet another promising scientist in embryo, the son of an engineer who had entered Baku University at the age of fourteen. Young Lev Landau gave every indication of becoming another Kapitza. When he was sixteen he was sent to the University of Leningrad on the instructions of the head of I.N.O. and required to study foreign languages. Three years later he was engaged in research at the Leningrad Physico-Technical Institute and two years after this he was sent abroad.

Already speaking several languages fluently, young Landau made a tour of universities and scientific institutions in various European countries, arriving in Cambridge where he made contact with Kapitza. On the latter's advice he decided to concentrate his attention on Denmark where Professor Niels Bohr of Copenhagen had the reputation of being one of the most advanced nuclear scientists of the day.

These two men were scientists first and foremost and intelligence agents secondly, but they would never have been given the opportunities for advancement unless they had taken their espionage seriously. The Soviet Secret Service, though lagging behind in many of the technical developments of their professions, had realised the importance of such scientific espionage long before the other Western powers. Agents in the West had never seriously looked much further ahead than the latest type of gun or ship when it came to supplying intelligence. Heads of the major European intelligence services were apt to look upon reports of new secret weapons as the madcap schemes of cranks and to pay them scant attention in consequence. But such men as Kapitza and Landau, working under scientifically-minded spy-masters, looked twenty years ahead to the time when nuclear science could be put to the most terrible and devastating concepts of warfare.

Peter Kapitza was given a rare honour for a foreigner at Cambridge: he was elected to a Fellowship of the Royal Society. Then at a cost of £15,000 the Royal Society built for him the Mond Laboratory at Cambridge to carry on research in ultra-low temperatures.

In October 1934 Kapitza went to Moscow 'for a holiday'. He never returned. The official reason given was that the Russians refused him an exit visa. What else could they be expected to do? For six months his wife and two children stayed on in Cambridge. Then they, too, joined him in Moscow. Visitors from Russia described how the laboratory the Russians had provided for him was four times the size of his Cambridge laboratory. In Britain he had two assistants: in Russia he had a hundred. What is more the Russians had been prepared for his homecoming; they had started work on the laboratory *before* he returned. They had even built him an English-style cottage at the side of his laboratory, and, when he returned, they imported specially for him the English tweeds to which he was devoted. He became Director of the Institute of Physical Problems at the Academy of Sciences in Moscow.

His days as a spy were more or less ended: the fruits of his espionage were now to be put to the test.

Yet when Kapitza left Britain some scientists said his loss was unimportant. Professor Henry Armstrong, senior Fellow of the Royal Society, said: 'I fail to see any signs of severe shock to the scientific world. Cambridge has put too high a value on Professor Kapitza. There are hosts of young men who can do his work.'

If this were so, why did the Cambridge University authorities and Lord Rutherford in particular make such strenuous efforts to induce the Soviet authorities to allow Kapitza to return to them? The truth is that it was only when they learned of the laboratory the Russians had given Kapitza that they began to take such a keen interest. In 1935 Kapitza offered to purchase the special apparatus on which he was working at Cambridge. It was then announced that his offer had been accepted, that not only would the apparatus be sent to him, but that two Cambridge assistants would be loaned to him for three years. The more important pieces of apparatus consisted of a large generator for producing an intense magnetic field and plants for making liquid helium and liquid hydrogen.

Lev Davidovich Landau was at the age of twenty-two developing a theory of diamagnetism of metals and had already learned much from such celebrated nuclear specialists as Bohr and Edward Teller, later to become the driving force behind the American H-bomb. He went back to Russia in the mid-thirties and it was his work in this period which led up to the experimental discovery of 'second sound' in 1944 by Peshkoff working in Moscow. Landau had something of the reputation of an *enfant terrible* and was fond of practical joking in an age when such humour was regarded by the Stalinists as showing a true lack of respect. At any rate he joked once too often and in one of Stalin's purges was imprisoned as a suspected German spy. On the intervention of his friend Kapitza he was eventually freed.

13

'The Trust' Lures Savinkoff back to Russia

WHEN DZERZHINSKY set about building up an organisation for luring important counter-revolutionaries back to Russia he had to tread very warily indeed. It was essential that any such organisation should have a base firmly established in a foreign country that would be suitable for the purpose. Switzerland was ruled out because the revolutionaries themselves had used this country for their operations for too long. Germany offered greater possibilities in the sense that there were many pro-Soviet sympathisers there at the time, but it was dangerous as well because there was an equal number of counter-revolutionaries and Czarists.

Britain was ruled out because it was regarded as the base of the most feared of the counter-revolutionaries and, in Soviet minds, Britain had the most efficient Secret Service of all the powers. This was not altogether a correct assessment, but the legend of British pre-eminence in the field of intelligence lived on for many years. France was ruled out mainly because the Soviet Secret Service had formed a very doubting and critical opinion of the French Communist Party as an ally. It was felt that French Communists were far too independently-minded and not therefore reliable material for building a foolproof *agent provocateur* movement. It was well known that the rank and file of the French Communist Party were in the main loyal Trade Unionists and as such they regarded anything in the nature of espionage as something practised only by capitalist powers and totally indefensible.

After making a careful survey of all possibilities Dzerzhinsky, aided by Trilisser, decided to use two bases rather than one – the United States, to which many Czarists had fled, and Finland. The U.S.A. had the disadvantage of being a distant base, from which communications would obviously be difficult, but in the atmosphere of democratic freedom which America possessed it was felt that people would talk more freely and therefore be more susceptible to overtures by *agents provocateurs*.

In June 1966 the usually unforthcoming Soviet authorities suddenly and surprisingly permitted a tiny part of the curtain of secrecy to be lifted on their Secret Service intrigues between 1919 and 1926. What the purpose of this was remains a matter for speculation, though it would seem that it was part of a positive campaign to represent to the Russian people that their Secret Service was not merely a matter of secret police and oppression also, but one of glamorous heroes ever eager to keep their country safe from enemies abroad. What was even more surprising in this instance was that they revealed that the one member of the counter-revolutionaries they most desired to capture at that time was not, as one would have thought, Boris Savinkoff, but Sidney Reilly.

Two skilled operators were chosen by Dzerzhinsky to carry out this work, Yakushev and Opperput, who operated inside Russia under the cover of an organisation calling itself the Moscow Municipal Credit Association. Ostensibly it was a trading organisation permitted by the Soviet Government to carry on its work, but its real purpose was secretly to pose as an under-cover agency for assisting the counter-revolutionaries. Naturally any such body inside Russia, known to have the permission of the Government to carry on its trading, was at first regarded with grave suspicion by all but the most inexperienced of anti-Bolsheviks. So it required several months before word got around that 'The Trust' (as it was known) might be genuine. Once 'The Trust's' controllers knew that the bait was arousing if not confidence then at least keen interest, the next stage of the operation was launched.

Genuine anti-Bolsheviks outside Russia decided to put 'The Trust' to the test. They asked for its aid in smuggling some of their supporters out of hiding in Russia to the safety of the Western world. At first this experiment was undertaken with much doubt and head-shaking by the veteran anti-Bolsheviks who had experienced *agent provocateur* tactics, but gradually the mistrust disappeared as several opponents of the Soviet were rescued from Russia and then a few emissaries from the West were smuggled in and out of Russia after making contact with the leaders of 'The Trust'.

More than a year passed and the counter-revolutionaries marvelled that not once had they been betrayed. Their returning emissaries brought enthusiastic reports that 'The Trust' was preparing to stage a counter-revolution.

It was Boris Savinkoff who was the first to be inspired with confidence in 'The Trust'. He was given to understand that all the plotters inside Russia were waiting for was an assurance of massive support from the anti-Bolsheviks outside Russia. Soon Savinkoff's own agents were being smuggled in and out of Russia.

Savinkoff, with his long experience of revolutionary tactics, his own knowledge of the treachery of such *agents provocateurs* as

170

Azeff, should perhaps have been more wary of 'The Trust'. It was not that he did not realise there was a risk of deception, but that he had become desperate in his quest for a solution to the problem of defeating the Bolsheviks. His impatience caused him not merely to take a cautious gamble but to risk his life in the cause of counter-revolution. What appeared to have convinced Savinkoff of the reliability of 'The Trust' was the fact that the White Russian General, Kutyepoff, who had escaped to Finland, was a member of it. But by this time 'The Trust' had won over many unsuspecting anti-Bolsheviks into its actual network: without realising it, they were being used to defeat their own eventual aims.

Those who saw Savinkoff in these last days before he took his fatal decision were shocked at the change in the man. He was drugging himself heavily and it was obvious that somebody was actively encouraging him to do so. He was full of madly defiant schemes of action at one moment, deep in depression the next. Whether 'The Trust' ensured that drugs should play a part in the breaking down of Savinkoff one cannot be sure, but they knew from the dossier on Savinkoff that under the influence of morphine he could be persuaded to perform deeds of quixotic daring. At any rate it was 'The Trust' who persuaded him to return to Russia, give himself up and 'confess' his 'crimes' and announce that he supported the Soviet Government. But, he was assured, because he would make this renunciation of the White Russian cause, his life would be spared and he would be inside Russia ready to take over the reins of power the moment 'The Trust' launched their counter-revolution.

On 10 August 1924 Savinkoff set off for Russia. Nineteen days later *Izvestia* announced that Savinkoff had been arrested. Rumours persisted for days. First it was reported that Savinkoff had been condemned to death, then came news that he had been completely acquitted and was free.

But the Russian version of Savinkoff's return to his fatherland is somewhat different. This states that Reilly had approved of Savinkoff's mission to Moscow, having changed his mind after he and Savinkoff had failed in their attempt to engineer the assassination of Chicherin, the Soviet Foreign Minister, at The Hague. Indeed the Soviet version – and it is contained in the book *Troubled Waters* – is that Reilly actually paid for Savinkoff's trip to Russia.

The report from Moscow of Savinkoff's renunciation of the cause of the White Russians and his statement that he 'honoured the power and wisdom of the G.P.U.' shocked his supporters into silence and dealt a devastating blow to the counter-revolutionaries. Small news items given out by *Izvestia* seemed to confirm the worst suspicions that Savinkoff had indeed betrayed his cause, and when Sidney Reilly received a letter from Savinkoff stating that he had 'met men in the G.P.U. whom I have known and trusted from my youth and who are nearer to me than the chatter-boxes of the foreign delegation of the Social-Revolutionaries', this seemed the final straw.

Undoubtedly drugs had played havoc with Savinkoff's state of mind and drugs were to be used by the G.P.U. finally to crush his spirit once he was safely in Russia. Savinkoff had tried to play a devious game which he could not possibly win. But it is also possible that this letter, which the G.P.U. had allowed him to send, was a forgery. The Foreign Section of the G.P.U. had a special department known as *Kaneva* which spent their time forging letters and documents. Indeed, the *Kaneva* was not only an important adjunct of the I.N.O., but one of the most useful agencies the Soviet Secret Service possessed at this time for obtaining foreign currency with which to pay their spies. *Kaneva* was more a factory than an intelligence department, turning out forged documents by the score, and most of these were given to agents to take abroad and sell to foreign governments for pounds, dollars and, in some cases, French gold.

Savinkoff was not kept in prison, but confined to what was in effect comfortable house arrest in Loubianka Square. The G.P.U. needed to keep Savinkoff alive in order that the outside world should be convinced of the fact that 'The Trust' was still influential. Yet the very fact that the Soviet Government showed such mercy to Savinkoff, who had long been on their 'death list', should have put other counter-revolutionaries on their guard. Far from confirming that 'The Trust' was dependable, it should have told them that the organisation was probably controlled by the G.P.U.

It is all the more surprising that Sidney Reilly should have appeared to have been deceived by all this. But Reilly was the man Dzerzhinsky most wanted and 'The Trust' now swung into action in the United States, to where Reilly had now gone.

Reilly had now divorced his Russian wife, Nadine, though as this was in effect a bigamous marriage the divorce was superfluous and necessary only to hide the truth about his first marriage from Nadine. He had fallen in love with a young actress named Pepita Bobadilla, who was the widow of Charles Haddon-Chambers, the playwright. But in between pursuing his normal love life of having at least two or three women around him at the same time he was playing a somewhat ambiguous game in the world of espionage. There were certain things that Reilly did about this time that made even the admiring British Secret Service a little chary of him. For example, Reilly, who had always insisted on being a freelance spy and not being tied to any single intelligence service, suddenly asked to be put on the full-time staff of M.I.6, the British foreign espionage department. The request was refused, much to Reilly's dismay. Then again while in London Reilly had established contact with Krassin, the Soviet representative to the British Government. It was suggested that Reilly and Krassin were engaged in currency smuggling, and it is a fact that Reilly helped Krassin to send personal funds out of the country and that years later Krassin's 'crime' was discovered by the Soviet authorities who demanded his recall. What worried the British was Reilly's apparent belief in 'The Trust' despite the sinister implications of the Savinkoff betrayal. Reilly's answer was that 'The Trust' included some members of the Soviet Government who were secretly biding their time until that government could be overthrown.

The Soviet version of what happened next is that in 1924 – some time after his marriage to Pepita Bobadilla in London – Reilly set up in business in the United States as a trader named Sidney Berns and that while there he received a letter from a friend telling him of the arrival in Paris of a married couple named Krasnostanoff. The implication was that this couple represented 'The Trust.'

Soviet State documents assert that the name of Krasnostanoff was a 'cover' for Maria Vladimorovna Zaharachenko Schultz and her husband, George Radkevich: 'to none of the leaders of the emigré organisations did it occur that the emissaries Maria Zaharachenko and her husband had been sent by the G.P.U. in Moscow. Zaharachenko and others who were also sent as emissaries fully believed that they were preparing for a counter-revolution.'

This is a startling admission by the Soviet, but it all fits into the story of how Sidney Reilly was lured back to Russia: the question is how much does it still hide? Reilly had every confidence in Maria and her husband. He was a man not easily fooled. There is also no reason to suspect that this couple betrayed Reilly; they were merely the unwitting and unsuspecting puppets manipulated by the G.P.U. What more brilliant stage-managing in espionage could one have than an intelligence organisation using its enemies as its unconscious agents? Trilisser even succeeded in putting one of his own female agents in Reilly's New York office, hoping she could play on the spy's well-known weakness for women. But from all accounts Reilly accepted her as his secretary because he suspected she had been planted on him and wanted to learn more about her.

It was Maria who finally convinced Reilly of the reliability of 'The Trust'. He was always something of a romantic and it was Maria's legendary career in the war that appealed to him. Though the daughter of a general, she had joined the Russian Army as a private and spent most of the war in this capacity. Such quixotry should have warned Reilly that she might easily be duped, but he had been equally impressed by the fact that she was one of the first to join the White Russian resistance to the Bolsheviks after the Revolution. Her reports on 'The Trust', carefully fed to her by Trilisser through such people as Vladimir Orloff, who had penetrated the Cheka and then been used by them, by Alexander Yakushev and others, had spoken eloquently of the growing strength and influence of the organisation.

Reilly decided that 'The Trust' was a potentially sound organisation for overthrowing the régime and that, given support from outside, it might fulfil its promises. He also took the view that if 'The Trust' had saved Savinkoff's life, it might equally save his, if he were captured. That might appear as a somewhat naïve belief, bearing in mind that in May 1925 it was reported that Savinkoff had committed suicide by throwing himself out of a window, but, curiously, Reilly fell into this error by divining the truth about Savinkoff's death. His colleagues all insisted that the Soviet had murdered Savinkoff and then pretended he had committed suicide. Reilly rightly believed that they wanted Savinkoff to remain alive because he was more useful to them that way and that he committed suicide probably as a result of his drug-taking.

So Reilly decided, on the prompting of Yakushev, acting on G.P.U. orders, to go to Russia. He was given a forged passport in the name of Nicolas Steinberg and on 25 September 1925 crossed the frontier into Russia from Finland.

What happened after this has been the subject of many conflicting and contradictory reports. Commander Boyce, of the British Secret Service, received a postcard from Reilly, dated 27 September, franked in Moscow, indicating that he had arrived safely. Then, a few days later, a news item appeared in *Izvestia* to the effect that on the night of 28–29 September, 'four smugglers attempted to cross the Finnish border. Two were killed; one, a Finnish soldier, taken prisoner, and the fourth, mortally wounded, died on the way to Leningrad.'

Piecing together these two items of evidence it would seem that Reilly arrived in Moscow, which was his intention, and that somehow the G.P.U. had discovered him and followed him back to the Finnish border. For it had been Reilly's intention to return to Finland on the very night that the four men were reported to have been caught.

From that moment the British Secret Service seemed anxious to disclaim all interest or responsibility for Reilly. They even refused information to Pepita Reilly, who was quickly given to understand that her calls were an embarrassment to officialdom. In desperation, hoping that the move would attract some attention to the mystery of her husband's disappearance, she had the following notice published in the deaths column of *The Times* on 15 December 1925: 'REILLY – On the 28th Sept., killed near the village of Allekul, Russia, by G.P.U. troops, Captain Sidney George Reilly, M.C., late R.A.F., beloved husband of Pepita N. Reilly'.

The announcement had the effect of stimulating a spate of press articles about Reilly and his exploits in British newspapers, but still the Foreign Office and the Russians maintained a total silence.

It was not until a year later that the awful truth, which some had suspected, became apparent – that 'The Trust' had been used as a 'front' by the G.P.U. Opperput, one of the leading members of 'The Trust', went to Finland and admitted that he was a member of the G.P.U. counter-espionage section. His confession was the most horrifying of all to 'The Trust's' supporters outside Russia, for he had not only been an officer in the Czar's army but had been nominated as Minister of Finance of the anti-Bolshevik Government which aimed to take over from the Reds.

Dzerzhinsky, Trilisser and Artuzoff, head of the G.P.U.'s counter-espionage section, were the trio who first urged that *agent provocateur* tactics should be adopted to lure back the White Russians to infiltrate their ranks. Trilisser planned the organisation abroad and nominated the chief agents (he had a genius for selecting the right men) and Artuzoff was the executive planner, filling in the details, master-minding the structure of the counter-espionage operation and building up 'The Trust' himself.

But only because this trio worked in unison and refused to be hustled into hasty, ill-considered action did the plan succeed. They did not merely react to events, they created the events to which other people reacted. In the main much of this planning was undertaken by young men. Artuzoff was only thirty-three, but he had the experience of a man twice that age, while Staroff, one of his chief assistants, was twenty-eight.

But let us examine the Soviet version of what happened when Reilly crossed the border into Russia. The journal *Nedelya*, describing these events in June 1966, stated that 'in January, 1925, the G.P.U. gave Yakushev the assignment of investigating the possibilities of luring Sidney George Reilly to Helsinki and thence to Moscow'. It had all been most carefully planned: Reilly was to be allowed to cross the border, to be smuggled to Moscow and there to take part in discussions with 'The Trust' Council. Having learned all that Reilly had to tell them, the plotters would allow him to return safely to Finland on this first occasion, thus convincing him finally that 'The Trust' was not a ruse for trapping him. Then at a later stage Reilly was to be brought back into Russia and held there.

The vital intermediary was a man named Bunakoff, who had also been lured into believing in the power and reliability of 'The Trust'. From him a complete picture of Reilly's plans for alternative government in Russia was formed: there should be a monarchist dictatorship with the Grand Duke Nicolai Nikolaievich as the titular leader. There seemed to be no doubt that Reilly, like Savinkoff before him, had weighed the risks of being arrested against the probability that 'The Trust' was influential enough to ensure his being freed.

According to the *Nedelya* version of what happened next – and it must be assumed that this is also the Soviet official version – Reilly crossed the border safely, was met by a Soviet agent, Toivo Vjahi, who posed as an emissary of 'The Trust', and taken by train to Leningrad. There he was met by another Soviet agent, Schukin of the G.P.U., who passed him on to Yakushev. That same night Yakushev brought Reilly to Moscow where he was met by Staroff, who introduced himself as 'Representative of the Monarchist Society'.

Now to the Bolshevik plotters the mystique of Czardom was still an effective weapon. They could not conceive of any anti-Bolshevik organisation being effective unless it was Czarist in principle. Therefore in building up 'The Trust' they had been careful to make it clear that this was not a mere democratic movement, or a Savinkoff- or Kerensky-style organisation, but one that was committed to the principle of the monarchy. Only by making 'The Trust' appears one hundred per cent royalist and respectable did they expect to win confidence. It must therefore have come as a considerable shock to them to learn that Sidney Reilly himself did not give a damn for monarchist principles, only for the defeat of the Soviet, and that as far as terrorism was concerned he was more bloodthirsty than Savinkoff.

Reilly's plan was to raise funds by raiding museums and art galleries and selling the works of art thus acquired abroad. Another step was to infiltrate the British Secret Service and earn money this way by selling them forged documents and, if necessary, by feeding them with false information. He confessed that he had already made money in this way by selling to the British the notorious forged Zinovieff Letter which incited British workers to sedition, and the publication of which had brought about the downfall of the first British Labour Government. He urged new and terrible measures of terrorism, saying that they must not be scrupulous, but stoop to any methods, however brutal, to achieve their ends. 'You will never succeed if you observe the rules of morality.'

The plotters listened in silence and in horror. Nor was it a feigned horror. They just could not believe that Reilly was sincerely as ruthless as they were themselves. The myth of 'the English gentleman' was shattered in an hour. What Reilly was urging in effect was the use of G.P.U. and Bolshevik tactics; wistfully they began to wish he was on their side. And indeed every tactic he had suggested could have been applied just as much in the Soviet cause as against it, in some respects more so.

The Soviet account of Reilly's stay in Russia on this occasion confirms the posting of a postcard from Moscow to Commander Boyce on 27 September. 'It had been planned to arrest Reilly in the car while on the way to Moscow [the council meeting of 'The Trust' had taken place outside Moscow], but he wanted to send a postcard to his friends abroad and to put it with his own hand into the pillar-box to prove that he had visited Moscow. In order to find out to whom the card was to be addressed, Reilly was taken to the apartment of one of the G.P.U. agents taking part in the operation.'

After this Reilly was taken to G.P.U. headquarters and arrested, and, according to *Nedelya*, 'locked up in solitary confinement. . . . He hoped that the Intelligence Service would insist on his release by the Soviet Union. . . . As an experienced intelligence agent himself Reilly had to acknowledge the accomplished skills of Yakushev and Staroff.'

Some of the *Nedelya* article is obviously propagandist and aimed at presenting the Russian Secret Service in an heroic light. But the most interesting part of it contains 'the protocol of interrogation of S. C. Reilly'. In this Reilly described himself as a British subject, born in Connemara. Now it is certain that the G.P.U. knew this was not true and that he had been born in Odessa. It may be that for the purpose of the *Nedelya* article they did not wish to reveal that Reilly was himself half Russian, that for propaganda purposes he must seem to be completely a 'foreign villain'. The interrogation statement included an admission of his links with Savinkoff, his work for the British Secret Service (there is enough detail in all this to suggest he had given away a good deal of information), and the revelation that 'I have always been actively engaged in anti-Bolshevik matters and to these I have given much time and my personal funds. I can state that the years 1920–24, for instance, cost me at a very minimum calculation fifteen thousand to twenty thousand pounds.'

Then on 13 October 1925 Reilly wrote to Dzerzhinsky that he was ready to co-operate with the Soviet: 'After prolonged deliberation I express willingness to give you complete and open acknowledgement and information on matters of interest to the G.P.U. concerning the organisation and personnel of the British Intelligence Service and, so far as I know it, similar information on American Intelligence and likewise about Russian emigrants with whom I have had business.'

In capturing Reilly the Soviet Secret Service had brought off its most successful coup to date. At one single blow they had not only the means to destroy the morale of the counter-revolutionaries and blast their hopes, but to infiltrate the British and American Secret Services. From this date Russia managed to acquire a foothold inside the secret services of both these powers which has never since been completely eliminated. The names of all British and American agents remaining in Russia were delivered to the G.P.U. From being the Cinderella of all spy services the Soviet was from this date onwards a potential threat to every other major power in the field of intelligence.

Officially the Russians have likewise made no statements on Reilly and inquiries put to them to reveal the truth about his last days have drawn no response. What has appeared in the Russian press has had no official blessing, but it can safely be assumed that it would only have been published with the approval of the authorities. The *Nedelya* article states that Reilly was executed on 5 November 1925. But this is almost certainly not the truth. It can be said now that the story that he was shot trying to escape back into Finland was a false report, deliberately circulated by the G.P.U. through 'The Trust'. When Opperput went to Finland and confessed his own rôle in 'The Trust' in 1927, he stated that the border shooting incident was faked, that Reilly had gone to Moscow where he had been 'kept under observation, with limited freedom' by the Soviet, but had finally been executed that year.

It is worth noting that in September 1927 *Izvestia* reported that Reilly had been executed in June of that year, so that Opperput would seem to have been putting over the account the G.P.U. wished to publicise. Now there was an excellent reason for putting out the border shooting incident story in 1925. The G.P.U.'s original intention was to allow Reilly to come to Moscow, attend a meeting of 'The Trust', find out something of his plans and then to let him go back to Finland and to bring back more detailed information the second time. It was Reilly himself by his revelations of what he proposed to do which made the G.P.U. change their minds and decide he must be arrested then and there. But at that stage it was vital that counter-revolutionaries outside Russia should not lose faith with 'The Trust', which the Soviet still intended to utilise. If it appeared that Reilly had been shot while crossing the border after having been to Moscow, 'The Trust' would not come under suspicion and the shooting might look like an accident. But by 1927 there was no point in covering up any longer because 'The Trust' had outlived its usefulness.

It is certain that the G.P.U. would not have gone to such immense trouble and expense to lure Reilly back to Russia merely to shoot him. Reilly, it is true, would be of less propaganda value to the Soviet than Savinkoff. When the latter appeared to go over to the Soviet the very name of Savinkoff was something to play with. But Reilly was known mainly in intelligence circles, among the rank and file of White Russians he would be almost totally unknown. Reilly's value was that he could supply the Soviet with intelligence worth hundreds of thousands of pounds. His intimate knowledge of the workings of other intelligence services made him worth far more to the Soviet than either to Britain or U.S.A. To shoot Reilly without obtaining that intelligence was unthinkable.

When reports trickled through from various parts of the world, the mystery of Sidney Reilly's fate deepened. A White Russian who escaped from a Soviet prison to Tientsin in October 1927 said that Reilly was alive in Orlovsky Prison, but was insane. Then a Latvian by the name of Brunovski, who had been released by the Russians after four years in a Moscow prison, said that he had learned that 'an important British spy lay in the hospital at Butyrski Prison'. While he was in prison Brunovski made secret notes on strips of linen he brought out with him. But the stresses and strains of incarceration made him forget the significance of many of these notes. One such series of notes read: 'British officer Reilly – Persia – father-in-law' when translated from Russian. But he could not recall the significance of the words 'Persia' and 'father-in-law'. Pepita Reilly, while not throwing any light on the meaning of Persia, suggested that Brunovski had misread the Russian for father-in-law, *testi*, for 1' S.T. 1, which was her husband's code name in the British Secret Service.

There were many rumours that Reilly was still alive and the silence of the Soviet Government led some people in M.I.5, the British counter-espionage service, to suspect that he had made a deal with the Bolsheviks. Perhaps he had sold out to them because there was no prospect of settling his debts. His old friend, Captain George Hill, was certain that Reilly was alive long after 1927. With the rank of Brigadier George Hill remained in Intelligence during World War II, when he was in Moscow as a liaison officer with the N.K.V.D., as the G.P.U. became known after the mid-thirties. He learned from an N.K.V.D. agent that Reilly was alive in 1944, though still kept under surveillance. Again, this is no proof that Reilly was in fact alive, but there is some confirmation

179

of this in Robin Bruce Lockhart's *Ace of Spies*, in which he stated that 'an N.K.V.D. man did tell another member of the British Mission that Reilly was still alive, in prison but insane.'

One former Intelligence officer of Czarist days, Peter Alexanderovitsh Badmayeff, the authority on the Far East, is said to have recommended to the Cheka that an effort should be made to engage Reilly in the Russian Secret Service. Badmayeff was regarded as an enemy of the régime, but for some curious reason his advice was still sought by the Cheka. He even offered to try to persuade Reilly that the Russian Revolution must be accepted and that his duty lay in co-operating with the Soviet. Thus it seems possible that the G.P.U. not only wanted to capture Reilly, but possibly to win him over as an agent as well. There is no doubt that overtures were made to Reilly by G.P.U. agents quite distinct from those under-cover moves made by 'The Trust'. It was because he had had information of a Soviet attempt to seduce Reilly's loyalty that Captain Sir Mansfield Cumming, the head of M.I.6, regarded with some suspicion Reilly's request to be made a full-time, permanent member of the British Secret Service. If the Russians wanted to infiltrate the ranks of British Intelligence Reilly was the ideal man to employ, if he could be persuaded, for he had not only been a top man in M.I.6, but an adviser to M.I.5 as well, an irregularity in the sphere of Intelligence which normally would not have been tolerated.

On the surface Reilly was essentially a man most at home in the drawing-rooms of London and Paris, with thirty years of proven loyalty to the British Secret Service to his credit, and as he appears to have admitted to the G.P.U., he had contributed large sums out of his own pocket to the counter-revolutionary cause. But one has only to probe beneath the surface to find that this picture is too fragile a façade and that there are many grounds for doubting Reilly's integrity. During many of these years he had been working as a double-agent, first for Japan, then for Russia, and to some extent latterly for the Americans.

To solve the enigma of Sidney Reilly one must find the answers to these questions: (1) did Reilly make up his mind, while in America, that he would go over to the Soviet side, either to save his dwindling finances, or because he was angry with the British Secret Service for turning down his request for permanent membership? (2) did the Soviet Government make overtures to Reilly and win him over, first of all having leaked information to the British suggesting that Reilly was on their side? (3) did Reilly go to Russia, knowing the risks, but prepared to play a devious game, possibly pretending to be pro-Soviet, while at the same time spying on them? (4) was he asked by the Soviet to apply for full-time membership of the British Secret Service? (5) did he go to Russia as a sincere White Russian agent but, when captured, pose as a friend of the Soviet to try to save his own skin? (6) did he simply collapse under interrogation and decide to co-operate to save his own skin? (7) did he die without giving any information away?

One cannot answer all these questions satisfactorily, but to some of them hard answers can be given. It is certain that Reilly was fully alive to the risks of going to Russia in 1925, and, as an experienced agent, he must have made careful plans as to what action he would take if captured. Those plans included an attempt at least to pretend to co-operate with the Soviet. He knew that, to save his skin, he would have to produce vital information. The Soviet dossier of his interrogation suggests that he did give them a great deal of information. Even the inaccuracies in his statement to the G.P.U. ring true, for they were essentially the kind of inaccuracies he would have introduced deliberately. Mr Robin Bruce Lockhart points to the fact that the Russian dossier mentions that Reilly used the name of Sidney Berns in the U.S.A. and denies that this was so. Presumably Mr Lockhart is relying on British Intelligence knowledge of Reilly's activities in this period, but during this particular sojourn in the U.S.A. Reilly was not working for the British so they would not know what cover-names he might be using. Curiously Walter Krivitský, the G.P.U. agent who defected from Russia in the thirties, supplied some confirmation of the use of the Berns pseudonym when he informed the Americans in Washington that the Russians had first penetrated the American Secret Service through a man known as Sidney Berns and that 'this code-name was carried on by a substitute until 1936'.

There is some incriminating evidence that, stemming from Reilly's last trip to Russia, the Soviet forged the first link in the chain that led to the Canadian spy ring, Philby, Maclean, Burgess and Blake. With Reilly's disappearance the British Secret Service lost the nucleus of a small but useful network inside Russia. It took several years to build up any comparable network and even then it never achieved the pitch of efficiency or was anything like as comprehensive as in the years 1918–25. Yet within a few years of Reilly's reported death the Russians had started to build up a new clandestine organisation inside Britain and begun to infiltrate the British Secret Service and the Foreign Office.

How Reilly's information enabled the Russians to penetrate the Secret Services of the West will be shown in later chapters. Reilly was without question the first link to be forged in that long chain of traitors inside the British Secret Service, a chain that remained unbroken for more than forty years. Partly through this, and partly independently of it, Reilly's information enabled similar infiltration to be made of the U.S. Secret Service.*

14

Menzhinsky, Yagoda and Ignace Reiss

THE STRUCTURE of the counter-espionage and police forces in Russia under the Soviet régime has always been a matter of conjecture as no official statistics of these bodies have ever been published. Nor have the actual duties of the various forces ever been clearly spelt out, though up to about 1930 Soviet laws gave a broad picture of what they did and how they functioned. Since then secrecy has been intensified.

The Border Troops of the Cheka comprised the first attempt to link Intelligence with defence. Then in 1922 the G.P.U. was given the task of assuring the political security of the frontiers of the U.S.S.R. and a year later a Border Guard of the O.G.P.U. was formed. These have since been developed into three distinct types of Border Troops – Maritime, Land and Aviation. From 1934 onwards these came under the control of the N.K.V.D. The 1941 State Plan revealed that twelve small ships were being supplied to the N.K.V.D., indicating that the Maritime Border Troops of the G.P.U. were responsible for the prevention of illegal immigration to the U.S.S.R., keeping a watch on coastal movements and stamping out smuggling.

There was no real power struggle within the G.P.U. while Dzerzhinsky was in control: that developed only after his death. But there were signs of an attempt to jockey for positions of supremacy in the directorate of the Cheka at the time of its formation. Though Dzerzhinsky had the ear of Lenin and therefore almost unlimited authority, an attempt was made at the end of 1918 by Jacob Peters to enhance his own position. Peters was more devious than Dzerzhinsky, a born intriguer who kept in close touch with all shades of opinion within the Bolshevik Party. Soviet

* In an article in the Russian emigré press (*Russkaya Mysl* of Paris) in June, 1972, it was alleged that Reilly was an agent of the Cheka almost from the beginning of the revolution.

records reveal, though they do not explain, how at one stage in December 1918, Peters became provisional chairman of the Cheka, a position which would seem to rival Dzerzhinsky's authority as its chief. However, a compromise seemed to be reached by which Dzerzhinsky retained overall control, while Peters became vice-president of the Cheka, but at the same time President of the Revolutionary Tribunal which tried and sentenced counter-revolutionaries. In 1923 Peters was elected a member of the Central Committee of the Communist Party and became extremely influential in intelligence circles. But he was never regarded by the hierarchy as being an absolutely reliable Party man, however fanatical a Communist he may have appeared to Western observers. His Lettish background counted against him, so, too, did his fondness for wining, dining, and visiting Westerners, and it was suspected by some inside the Cheka that his close watch on the G.R.U. was not entirely disinterested. In short, it was believed that Peters did not simply organise a watch on the G.R.U. but secretly worked with them.

The full truth about Peters will probably never be known. That some of the allegations made against him were totally untrue cannot be doubted. His last known position was that of Commandant of the Kremlin and he held this post at the time of his arrest in 1937 during the great Stalinist purge. With scores of others he disappeared during this purge and presumably was shot.

Yet it is significant that after Stalin's death Peters was post-humously rehabilitated and regarded as one of the early heroes of the Revolution. The Soviet have an oblique method of making amends posthumously for anyone who was wronged at the time of the purges. This is to commission some State writer to compose a work of fiction around the character of the person they seek to rehabilitate and in this way to demonstrate the excellence of his qualities. Vassily Ardamatsky was th writer who fulfilled this task for Peters. But no account has ever been published as to how Peters met his end and though the Soviet have since praised him for his rôle in luring counter-revolutionaries to Russia, they never revealed that he was the one Chekist above all others who believed that Sidney Reilly could be persuaded to work for the Soviet Union and who urged that Reilly alive was worth twenty times more than Reilly dead.

Felix Dzerzhinsky died suddenly on 20 July 1926 and, according to the *Greater Soviet Encyclopaedia*, 'three hours after he delivered a fiery speech unmasking the foul enemies of the people, Kamanev, Pyatakoff and others'. The Central Committee of the Party issued a brief announcement that 'Comrade Dzerzhinsky died suddenly from a heart attack'.

He was succeeded as head of the G.P.U. by Vyacheslav Menzhinsky, with Meyer Trilisser controlling the organisation of foreign espionage. Trillisser had learned the arts of administration when, as a revolutionary, he had been in charge of the Party's archives. Thus when the Bolsheviks came to power he had the tremendous advantage of a ready-made Intelligence Library in miniature. Trilisser had made a habit of compiling biographies and dossiers of a very wide range of people from politicians, generals and merchants trading overseas down to their wives and families. His filing system was made so that there were cross-references on every person to his or her wife, or husband, parents and children. And on each filing card the recreations and vices of the people were carefully noted. Sexual aberrations, if they existed, were always noted. 'Blackmail is one of the prime arts of extracting intelligence,' said Trilisser, 'and a card-index system that is not intended for this purpose is useless.'

Many of the people inside the G.P.U. (and the G.R.U. too, for that matter) had spent years of exile in Switzerland and knew that country well. For this reason Switzerland was chosen as one of the first bases for espionage. It was used as a 'letter-box' territory and as a base for spying first on France and secondly on Germany. In consequence the Soviet spy section operating in Switzerland acquired over the years a curious autonomy of its own, with much wider powers of discretion and action than was normally granted to any similar section elsewhere.

Britain and France were the powers feared most by the Soviet in the early twenties of this century. France was looked upon as the chief enemy, being not only the greatest military power in Europe but the country that had most actively supported the counter-revolutionaries and the war of intervention, 1918–22. As Communism had far more adherents in France than in Britain, the first major espionage drive of the Soviet Union was against that country, with the Second Directorate also seeking to use the French Communist Party as an ally. Their chief difficulty was the quietly independent line which the French Communist Party then pursued. This was something which Trotsky, much more of an internationalist and with far wider experience of foreign affairs than most of the other Bolsheviks, appreciated, and he attempted to put the brakes on blatant attempts to use the French Communist Party as an annexe of Soviet Intelligence.

However, when Trotsky was eliminated from the leadership of the Party, the situation with regard to France changed perceptibly. The coming to power of Stalin led at first to a loosening of the rigid rules of professional espionage and for a demand that foreign Communist Parties must give greater assistance to Russia in intelligence matters. Thus it was that Jean Cremet, a leading member of the French Communist Party's Central Committee, became chief of the Soviet intelligence network in France. This appointment was made on Stalin's insistence. At the same time Moscow displayed a certain caution in its dealings with the French Communist Party and it was decided that the experiment of using Cremet should be regarded as a test case, while to safeguard against any dependence on French Communists both the G.P.U. and the G.R.U. maintained their European control centres in Berlin rather than in Paris. German Communists were much more disciplined and obedient than French Communists. It was not until about 1924 that Moscow began to send out trained professional spies of Russian nationality, people who were given false passports, and new identities to operate abroad.

Stalin possessed a peasant's instinct for character-reading. His intuition was rarely wrong when it came to assessing people and reading political trends. While he mistrusted most of the French Communist leaders he had great faith in Cremet. As secretary of the St Nazaire branch of the Shipbuilders' Union, as well as being secretary of the Metalworkers' Union, Cremet was powerful in the French trade union movement and, unknown to his French colleagues, with great skill organised a network of spies in the armaments industries. But Stalin was still realist enough to know that often the blindly loyal supporter can, through his more limited brain, make mistakes which the more erratic but highly intelligent agent would never make. Stalin feared that Cremet's militancy might prove a liability. In June 1926, Stalin gave Cremet the official title of Head of the French Section of Soviet Intelligence, a job he had unofficially held for two years. The appointment was kept secret from the French Communist Party. But Stalin's suspicious nature caused him to keep a close watch on Cremet, so he put his own man in the Soviet Embassy in Paris, a G.R.U. operative named Meslanik, and sent to Paris as Resident Director of Soviet Espionage a G.P.U. officer, Uzdanski-Yelenski, who had just been expelled from Warsaw by the Polish Government.

While Meslanik maintained overall watch from the Soviet Embassy, Uzdanski-Yelenski went underground and under the name of Abraham Bernstein set himself up as an artist in Paris.

This sudden burst of activity in France was determined mainly by the fact that the Russians wanted the maximum amount of intelligence on French armaments. Uzdanski-Yelenski's task was to see that Cremet delivered this information and to check it and supplement it in every way he could. The new Resident Director confirmed Stalin's hunch: he reported back to Moscow that Cremet's spy network was thorough, extensive and productive.

'That is excellent,' was Stalin's cautious reply. 'It bears out all I felt about Cremet's capabilities, but if his network fails, it will be because a Communist betrays him, not because of the French counter-espionage system.'

What he foretold came about. Cremet was betrayed by a fellow Communist, a trusted Party man named Cochelin. The latter had been asked by Cremet to provide information on tanks and explosives being manufactured in an arms factory at Versailles. Cochelin at first refused to give this information, which should have alerted Cremet to the risk he had taken. Instead Cremet doggedly played on the necessity for Cochelin to do his duty for the cause and Cochelin then agreed to make a report. In the meantime, as Cremet should have suspected, Cochelin had given the French War Ministry details of Cremet's approach to him.

From then on the French counter-espionage took charge of the situation. What they uncovered gave them a clear-cut view not only of the workings of Soviet espionage, but of the exact nature of the information they were seeking. It also taught the Russians a lesson from which they benefited considerably over the next twenty years. For the tactics of the twenties laid the Russians wide open not only to discovery of their espionage techniques but to the destruction of their networks. Each leading spy, such as Cremet, was supplied with detailed lists, drawn up by Soviet engineers and scientists, of questions concerning armaments, explosives, methods of production and plans of new weapons. These questions were so highly technical and precisely worded that they could not be understood, let alone memorised, by the military attachés at Soviet Embassies. In Paris the military attachés usually passed them on either unread, or not understood, to Uzdanski-Yelenski, who translated them, made several copies and handed them to Cremet. The latter made further copies which he gave to his agents, including, of course, Cochelin. Thus a large number of these secret questionnaires must have been passing around the factories of France.

The French counter-espionage were thorough. By following Cremet they tracked down Uzdanski-Yelenski and his intermediary, a man named Grodnicki, and within a short time they arrested Cremet, Uzdanski-Yelenski, Grodnicki and various others, including Louise Clarac, who had been Cremet's mistress and had herself indulged in espionage.

What it took the Russians longer to realise was that some of the information on armaments they had been given over the previous few years had been furnished by the French counter-intelligence and was totally false. The publicity given to l'affaire Cremet was a major blow to Soviet prestige and set back Franco-Soviet relations, which had been improving, for a long time to come. When sentences were passed at the trial of the spies the following statement was made in the terms of the summing-up:

'Since at least 1924 an espionage system has been set up in France under the direction and for the benefit of a foreign power, the seat of which is in Moscow. A foreign government sends to us its agents and money to obtain from the workers, even from Government workers, the most complete and secret data on the production and operations of our important defence machinery.'

Later Cremet and his mistress went to Moscow and Cremet worked for Soviet Intelligence for some years. In 1936 he was sent to Shanghai on a secret mission. Shortly afterwards he was reported 'missing'. In fact he had been killed by Soviet agents in Macao because his mistress was suspected of being politically unreliable and it was thought that she had subverted him. Louise Clarac had been ordered to leave Russia and return to France two years earlier: presumably she was still watched by the G.P.U.

Meanwhile the Soviet completely re-organised its intelligence system in France and ordered its operatives to lie low for a long time. One minor network, which had not been detected by the French counter-espionage, however, was allowed to continue. This was a group of spies inside the printing-works of the College of Military Studies at Versailles, which had first been established by Cremet. The typesetters in this printing-works dealt with a large quantity of confidential material and because of this they were obliged by the terms of their employment to maintain absolute secrecy. Nevertheless there were ten Communists employed on the work and they passed out proofs of all material that went into the works, for which they were paid quite handsomely. This cell lasted for two years. Then in November 1927 a corporal had his suspicions aroused and reported to the authorities. Rougaeyres, the intermediary, was arrested and under interrogation he not only confessed to his own rôle in passing on the information but gave the names of most of the cell. Eleven people in all were rounded up and received sentences ranging from six months to five years.

The graph of Soviet Intelligence in these early years would have revealed seismographic tremors both in its successes and failures. It was an uneven course, but its very unevenness is a measure of its effectiveness. If there were many failures, resulting in the breaking up of networks, they merely testified to the extent of Soviet espionage and the results that were being achieved. There can be no spectacular successes without some defeats and the early failures showed the Russians that the use of foreign Communists in espionage was not nearly as effective as employing professionals, even when the latter were apolitical. The Comintern, founded in the first flush of Bolshevik successes with the aim of spreading revolution throughout the world, failed miserably in its prime objective, though it provided the means of developing and extending the espionage system. It was as a result of all this that the I.N.O. section of the O.G.P.U., as the G.P.U. had now become, took control of all Comintern agents and imposed a ruthless, harsh but nevertheless efficient discipline on what had become an amateurish scramble for information regardless of the risks.

The principals directing espionage from the Comintern Secretariat had been men as diverse as Zinoviev, Pyatnitzky, Radek, Kuusinen and Manuilsky. They made great use of information obtained from Sidney Reilly to build up a spy network in the United States, the planner of which was Ludwig Karlovich Martens, a Russian of German ancestry and a dedicated Communist. At this time the Russians were not specially interested in American military or naval matters, regarding U.S.A. not as a threat to the Soviet Union but rather as a useful territory in which to spread Communist propaganda. Thus, traditionally, there was for more than thirty years a far closer link between the Soviet Secret Service and the American Communist Party than between the former and any other Communist Party in the world.

Other spy-agents of the Comintern were Pogany-Pepper and Miroff in Berlin, Mikhail Borodin in London, Ho Chi Minh, of Indo-China, then known as Nguyen-ai-Quoc, and the Bulgarian Communist, Georgi Dimitroff, later associated with the Reichstag fire. But slowly the G.P.U. took control over more and more of the Comintern activities and in some cases eliminated whole networks and rebuilt them with new members. The Comintern headquarters were originally in the Kremlin itself, then they moved to premises in Machovaya Street in Moscow until the early nineteen-thirties, when the G.P.U. (by this time renamed the N.K.V.D.) took complete charge.

Dzerzhinsky had always shown a preference for revolutionaries with proved experience in subversion and espionage in choosing his staff. Both Trilisser, head of the I.N.O., and Dzerzhinsky's deputy, Josef Unshlikht, came under this category, the latter having been an active revolutionary in Poland who had played a rôle in the abortive rebellion of 1905. But when Stalin came to power he frequently urged Dzerzhinsky to accept recruits he personally recommended, always stressing that they should be given swift promotion. In this way Stalin managed to infiltrate his own cronies into the Secret Service, one of them being a young, prematurely balding man named Lavrenti Pavlovich Beria, who had made his name as an organiser of the Communist cells among the oil workers of Baku.

The attempts to stir up trouble in Europe had been crude and unprofessional. They often went to such extreme methods that they threatened to destroy Russian attempts to establish diplomatic contacts, friendship missions and trade headquarters in foreign territories. Thus the offer of funds to the British miners during the 1926 General Strike caused Winston Churchill, then Chancellor of the Exchequer, to threaten to break off trade relations with Russia. This caused Dzerzhinsky to insist on having one of his most trusted agents posted to London to keep an eye on party hot-heads who might cause the break-up of his base, the Soviet Trade Delegation in Moorgate in the City of London. This man was N. K. Jilinsky, who put an end to open subversion and instead concentrated on getting jobs for Communist seamen in British Merchant Navy ships and using them as spies.

A staff of more than three hundred was set up in the Moorgate offices of the Russian trade delegation, which went under the name of Arcos. It should have been obvious from the beginning that a personnel establishment of this size implied undercover espionage on a large scale. Jilinsky may have realised that time was not on his side, for he worked with incredible speed in building up a spy network, mainly through his planting of seamen agents in British ships, but also by suborning key technicians in the Air Ministry. He co-operated with Ernst Wollweber, one of Dzerzhinsky's chief agents in Hamburg, in selecting trusted Communist seamen, and methodically set about choosing ships which used particular routes and setting specific tasks for the agents.

The Russians were at first surprised by the ease with which they were able to operate in Britain and confidence made them careless and over-ambitious. Their first warning came when a British technician serving with the Royal Air Force was arrested and charged with the theft of top-secret documents. During his trial the British authorities were alarmed by the revelation that these documents had been transmitted to the Moorgate offices of Arcos. Almost immediately afterwards news came from Paris that a Soviet spy, posing as a former officer in the Czarist Navy and an anti-Bolshevik, had organised an espionage network concerned solely with aircraft development. Not only had he obtained blueprints of the new French military planes, but he and Wollweber had secured the services of a former British Army officer named Stranders.

Even with this information the British authorities seem to have been singularly slow in reacting to the Soviet threat in London. The matter came to a head only when the Air Minister, Sir Samuel Hoare, informed the Cabinet that a top-secret document on strategic plans for aerial bombardment had been purloined. At last it was obvious that the Arcos offices were being used as an espionage headquarters and on 12 May 1927, the offices were raided by members of the Special Branch of the Metropolitan Police. In the basement they found Russian officials burning papers. The Russians had already been tipped off about the raid for the simple reason that they had an informant in Metropolitan Police headquarters. But the vital proof that diplomacy and espionage were both involved was the presence among the persons burning the papers of Anton Miller, the chief cipher clerk in the Soviet Embassy. He attempted to resist arrest, but when searched was found to possess a list of agents and addresses covering many countries in the world and details of secret 'letter-boxes' in France, Germany, U.S.A., Australia, New Zealand and South Africa. Stanley Baldwin, then British Premier, stated in the official report of the affair on 27 May 1927, that 'military espionage and subversive activities throughout the British Empire and North and South America were directed and carried out from the Arcos and Soviet Delegation offices'.

This was a severe blow to the Soviet both in the field of espionage and in diplomacy, for it was proved beyond doubt that Arcos had been the cover for spying on a wide scale and that Jilinsky's agents had penetrated not only military centres at Aldershot and elsewhere but the Air Ministry and dockyards at Plymouth and Chatham. Despite the search of the Arcos offices the Russians managed to escape with several documents and secret information, for they had constructed an underground tunnel through which their agents entered and left the Moorgate premises and much material was smuggled out of here when the raid was made. The discovery of the tunnel was not made until considerably later.

The British Government reacted firmly to these revelations: the Arcos offices were closed down and the trade delegation ordered back to Russia, with whom diplomatic relations were suspended, and for the next few years no Russian was allowed into Britain.

Jilinsky had laboured effectively and built up a powerful organisation, but its size soon made it too obvious. For Jilinsky himself this did not matter, because he moved on and utilised what remained of the network from Paris, but his successor in London, Igor Khopliakin, was swiftly aware that Arcos had drawn attention to itself by reason of its huge staff. It was he who urged that steps should be taken to link the network with Paris before it was discovered and, as he feared, inevitably destroyed. Moscow confirmed his recommendations and Maxim Litvinoff, Deputy Commissar for Foreign Affairs, received a dispatch from Arkady Rosenholtz, the *chargé d'affaires* in London, stating that as 'a very useful measure of precaution' documents in future would be forwarded by 'friends and neighbours from London to Moscow'. 'Neighbours' was the Russian code-word for the French network and the man entrusted to see this salvage operation was carried out and to link up with the British network was Lavrentia Beria, who was sent to Paris for this specific purpose.

The main effect of the expulsion of Trotsky from the Communist Party at the instigation of Stalin was, as far as Intelligence was concerned, to tighten control of the G.R.U. by the O.G.P.U. It also meant a long period of screening of all Soviet agents, especially those operating in foreign territories. Menzhinsky, the new head of the O.G.P.U. was, like his predecessor, Dzerzhinsky, a Pole. It was astonishing to find such a man at the head of the Secret Service in this period of mistrust, but Menzhinsky not only displayed his contempt for the Party rank and file, but gloated over his delight in luxurious living. He was in almost every respect the antithesis of the men with whom he worked and he behaved in the manner of an idle dandy. He would even conduct interrogations lying on a settee draped in rich Chinese silks, manicuring himself while he put his questions. Yet he had inspired trust and was tolerated with amusement by Lenin, who called him 'my decadent neurotic', and maintained in office by Stalin who dubbed him 'my amiable, but watchful Polish bear'.

He surrounded himself with trusted Polish agents, was more interested in counter-espionage than in spying abroad and hated being bothered with unnecessary detail. He took the view that the only worthwhile intelligence abroad was in the field of science, dismissing all else as 'so much waste of time that the information our spies bring in is two years out of date by the moment it comes to my office'.

The son of a lawyer from an upper-middle-class family, his background alone made him an incongruous choice for the post of head of the O.G.P.U. at this period. Brusque, efficient and completely detached in his attitude to his work, he had an almost effortless command of the complexities of the job. Yet, though eminently fitted in many ways to succeed a man like Dzerzhinsky, he was perhaps doomed from the beginning to succumb to his enemies, not least because of his intemperate remarks. He referred to 'the riff-raff proletariat who clutter up the machine of government' and dubbed the working-class more wittily than tactfully as 'a stupidity discovered by the intelligentsia'.

Menzhinsky was quick-witted, an opportunist and a realist, but he was certainly not a typical Communist – though he dyed his finger- and toe-nails red.

It would be difficult to know what his ultimate aims really were.

In some ways he could be described as a Ruskin-style reformer, more at home in the world of William Morris and the early arty-crafty socialists than in a power struggle between one set of revolutionaries and another. While despising the proletariat, he wanted the Russian people to have and to enjoy culture. Off duty he constantly talked of the need for saving the proletariat from themselves by artistic education. It is little wonder that he was nicknamed 'The Poet of the Cheka'.

His offices in a small building in Kaljayev Place in Moscow were filled with every beautiful object he could collect, icons, paintings, oriental works of art and statues. In this unreal atmosphere he spent his time signing death warrants and writing and translating poetry.

With the minimum of fuss he kept his subordinates on their toes and, with prodding from Stalin, ordered a re-organisation of the collecting of foreign intelligence. The manner in which he did this suggests a certain amount of cynical indifference to the task. He called a meeting of departmental heads and let them talk unprompted while he continued with his manicuring. Each man gave his own views on where Russian espionage had gone wrong, analysed failures and suggested plans for the future. Then Menzhinsky nodded to a young man in the drab uniform of a Party worker.

'Comrade Yagoda,' he said, 'will now address you. He has the full confidence of Stalin.'

The departmental heads were flabbergasted. They had never heard of Comrade Yagoda before, let alone seen him. Who was this upstart who enjoyed the patronage of Stalin?

Yagoda immediately attacked the whole espionage set-up, declared that Stalin was extremely annoyed by the way things had been handled and demanded that many of the names of key agents mentioned during the conference should be struck off the lists. He then announced what appointments he would make in their place.

Genrik Yagoda was a complete contrast to the aristocratic Menzhinsky. He was of peasant origin from Latvia, lacking in education, uncouth in manners and speech, but possessed of an obstinate streak that refused to take 'no' for an answer and a ruthless determination not to allow any man who served under him to make a mistake more than once.

From the beginning Yagoda took the keenest interest in the Special Division of the Second Directorate, the section which liquidated enemies of the régime by murder. This section was for a time run by Nicolai Yezhoff, but it was Yagoda who ensured that the organisation was to be devoted entirely to dealing with Stalin's enemies. 'The enemies of Stalin are the enemies of Russia,' said

Yagoda. 'The enemies of others are of less account and can be dealt with by others. The Special Division is to ensure that no enemies of Stalin continue to live.'

A continuing and curious feature of Soviet Intelligence has been that following a period of diplomatic successes and actual gains in prestige Russia has ruined her relations with other countries by taking grave risks in espionage and in having her spies captured and her networks destroyed. But in periods when Russia has been forced back on the defensive, when she has had to rebuild her networks from scratch and has been engaged in war her Intelligence services have brought off her greatest coups.

Yagoda had much purging of over-confident and unprofessional agents to carry out in the early thirties. Matters had come to a head by the arrests of three key agents, Rudolph Gaida, a Czech Legionnaire, in Prague in 1926, of Daniel Vetrenko, the head of the Polish network, in 1927, and of Bue and Euphony by the Swiss Police shortly afterwards. Every counter-espionage service in Europe was alerted to the peril in its midst: the Austrians closed in on the Vienna network and in May 1927, discovered that its leader was an official of the Soviet Legation named Bakony.

Orders for tightening security went out to all networks and to Soviet embassies in Europe. The latter were instructed to divorce themselves from any direct contact with local Communist Parties and to take steps to ensure the safety of intelligence material they had gathered. Such was the panic that in the summer of 1927, according to G. S. Agabekoff, a former G.P.U. official in Iran, the Soviet Embassy in Teheran was instructed 'to examine all their archives and destroy documents which could compromise Soviet activities abroad. The Embassy started immediately to examine the archives and selected huge piles of papers for destruction. For a week these papers were burning in the yard of the Embassy.... The employees of the embassies and consulates were strictly forbidden to maintain connection with members of the local Communist organisations.'

New rules were laid down for espionage overseas. Yagoda ordered a total reversal of the tactics which had been used by Comintern espionage, which had been based on the belief that agents should be natives of the countries in which they operated. He insisted that whatever had been the custom before, and however well such tactics might have worked in individual cases, henceforth all key men and Resident Directors of espionage must be Russians and that professional agents must never be employed in their native countries.

Yagoda was responsible for selecting some of the best spies Russia was to possess during the next decade. A new director of espionage was appointed to France, a commissar who was given the cover name of 'General Muraille' and who quickly settled down in his new surroundings, proving to be a good mixer and a man of resource and enterprise. It was a curious cover name to choose because the rank of general had not then been re-introduced into the Red Army, while the name itself was French. But the aim was for Muraille himself to pose as something of a mystery man, to appear to be too blatant an adventurer to be mixed up in espionage.

'General Muraille' set about building up a new espionage network in the armaments field. He established agents in Lyons, Marseilles, Paris, Toulon and Havre and instead of relying on the previous practice of maintaining a group of agents in a single arms factory, or at a naval base, he employed itinerant spies who moved from place to place under the pretence of carrying on some innocent business. For some years 'Muraille's' methods worked splendidly and he acquired a mass of information on new types of naval vessels, torpedoes, guns and aircraft. But in 1931 he was betrayed by one of his own agents, arrested and put on trial. He was given the relatively light sentence of three years' imprisonment. Expelled from France when he left prison, he returned to Russia where it was later whispered that he had been liquidated.

One of the most tragic spies of these early days of the Soviet Union was Ignace Poretsky, more generally known as Ignace Reiss. He was a Pole who in his earlier years had been a sympathiser with the ideals of the early revolutionaries. According to his wife, Elisabeth, he joined the Polish Communist Party in 1919 and, like many of the younger revolutionaries, found himself part of the Third International, 'without realising the long-term implications – into the service of the Comintern and ultimately of the Soviet Union.'

Soon he was selected for work as a spy under Joseph Krasny-Rotstadt, director of propaganda for the Comintern in Poland. His first assignment was to obtain military intelligence in Poland. He was arrested and after a brief trial given a sentence of five years' imprisonment. But he escaped and made his way to Germany. Here he was brought into the German network of Soviet espionage by Miroff-Abramoff, head of the O.M.S., the international liaison department of the Comintern.

The story of Ignace Reiss is in effect the history of the demoralisation of many ardent, idealistic revolutionaries under the Stalin régime, how they became aware of the atmosphere of repression, mistrust and brutality in the Soviet hierarchy, were disillusioned by it and hunted down and ultimately liquidated when they made even the mildest protests. Stalin was seriously concerned by the creation of a Trotskyite alternative brand of Communism. He made his first priority the hounding of Trotsky and the liquidating of anyone who took a Trotskyite line, regardless of whether he was a good Communist or otherwise.

Elisabeth Poretsky, Reiss's wife, had this to say about the Russian Intelligence system in the late twenties: 'In those early days it was common practice for members of these sections [the N.K.V.D. and the Fourth Department] to switch back and forth between the Red Army and the Comintern. The N.K.V.D., on the other hand, had scarcely any contact with the European parties and took its orders directly from Moscow. From the earliest days of the I.N.O. the N.V.K.D. made strenuous efforts to recruit personnel from the Fourth Department and the Comintern, but only succeeded when intrigues in those organisations became policy and their staffs were completely overhauled.'

The O.G.P.U. had been associated with the trials of deviationists and the deportations that occurred after the collectivisation drive of 1929. Their activities resulted in millions being either sent to prison, banished or forced into labour battalions. Perhaps because the O.G.P.U. had acquired such a sinister reputation, but more probably because Stalin wanted to centralise authority to a greater degree, in July 1934 the O.G.P.U. was absorbed into the People's Commissariat of Internal Affairs, the N.K.V.D., and for the next seven years the N.K.V.D. was in effective control of all espionage and counter-espionage and police forces.

This was Stalin's greatest achievement in the field of control of espionage and it greatly strengthened the Soviet Secret Service, enabling it to acquire a degree of co-ordination such as before had existed only in theory. The tentacles of the N.K.V.D. extended far beyond espionage and counter-espionage, but effectively controlled such diverse sections as the Border and Internal Guard, the Forest Guard, the administration of State Surveying and Cartography (still considered of prime importance in an intelligence and security sense), the transport system of the Soviet Union, anti-aircraft defence and all archives.

That a greater degree of unified control was necessary is exemplified by Ignace Reiss's own experiences. When he went on a trip to Dresden with another agent, Piatakoff, and they registered at the same hotel it was discovered to their mutual embarrassment that each carried a forged passport asserting that he was an Austrian citizen named Reinhold Hauer. They passed off this discrepancy by pretending that Ignace, who was much younger than Piatakoff, was the latter's nephew and that they had been born in the same town.

Similarly the use of too many cover names by individual agents created confusion. Often three agents were using the same cover name at one and the same time, which sometimes resulted in one of the agents coming under suspicion for playing a double game and even being unfairly liquidated on the grounds of better making sure than being sorry. On other occasions it resulted in an agent being arrested because the cover name had been used so often it was already well known to the German police.

Ignace Reiss was later transferred to Vienna where he worked under Ivan Zaporozhets, the N.K.V.D. representative, who gave him various assignments in the Balkans. Later he was sent to Prague and Amsterdam so that he acquired an all-round experience of espionage in all parts of Europe. It was perhaps unfortunate for him that in these days he became slowly associated with men who were later to be liquidated in the Stalinist purges of the thirties – Miroff-Abramoff, who was accused of using Soviet funds to finance Trotskyite movements in Europe, Zaporozhets, later deputy chief of the N.K.V.D. in Leningrad, who with his chief, Medved, was arrested in 1934 and sentenced to three years' imprisonment, and Walter Krivitsky, who eventually defected and was hunted down and killed by Soviet agents in the U.S.A.

But contact with the non-Communist world made Reiss increasingly conscious of the fact that there was a tremendous gap between the hard-liners in Moscow and left-wingers, even Communists, in Europe. In Holland he was surprised to find that the Dutch Communists considered themselves first as loyal Hollanders and only secondly as supporters of the Soviet Union. He noted with amazement that Dutch Communists were so devoted to the Royal House of Holland that they gave Princess Juliana a wedding present. Not unnaturally Reiss became friendly with a number of deviationists. Holland was being used at that time by the Soviet Intelligence as a base for espionage in the British Isles and Reiss was ordered to make contacts with the Irish Communist Party. He found their members to be concerned with Ireland first and foremost and quickly and rightly judged that they would be more of a hindrance than a help to the Soviet Union. Britain's M.I.5, however, took the Irish Communists rather more seriously, shadowed two of them who went over to Holland to meet Reiss and made sketches of Reiss which were reproduced in the British press.

Reiss returned to Moscow where he remained until 1932, becoming disillusioned with Stalin and deeply depressed by conditions inside Russia after the freedom of Europe. Grumbling in subdued undertones was replaced by peasant uprisings and in some Communist Party cells inside Russia there were even secret demands for the removal of Stalin.

Despite making enemies easily owing to his impulsive tongue,

Menzhinsky remained head of the O.G.P.U. until 1934, when, again according to the *Greater Soviet Encyclopaedia*, 'he was atrociously murdered upon the orders of the chiefs of the anti-Soviet counter-revolutionaries, a bloc of Trotskyites and Rightists.' It should perhaps be pointed out that this quotation comes from an encyclopaedia published before the de-Stalinisation campaign and that it was only repeating the assertions made at the political trials of the late nineteen-thirties. But no explanation of Menzhinsky's death has ever been offered and, though he appears to have got on well with Stalin, it is possible that he was nevertheless liquidated on the orders of Stalin himself. G. S. Agabekoff, who was his assistant, later fled to Germany.

A purge was made in the Fourth Department itself. Two Stalinists were brought into that department and Ignace Reiss suddenly realised that before long he, too, might well be next on the list for liquidation. He had been loyal to the Soviet Union, he had carried out all tasks assigned to him with efficiency and devotion, but, though not a Trotskyite, he was the friend of Trotskyites and opposed to the anti-Trotsky campaign. One by one he saw his friends compromised on some trumped-up charge, arrested and then either executed or allowed to disappear for ever.

When Reiss returned to Europe he must already have known that he had little choice in future: either he must defect to safety, or he must carry on working until he himself was liquidated. He had become known to the police and intelligence authorities of Britain, France, Austria, Holland and Germany, and latterly was one of the Resident Directors of Soviet espionage in France. When men with whom he had been intimately associated, such as Bukharin, Kamanev, Rakovsky and Zinovieff, had been executed or imprisoned, the writing was on the wall. In July 1937 he was warned that if he did not go back to Moscow at once he would be 'treated as a traitor and punished accordingly'.

It was then that Reiss courageously wrote his now celebrated letter to Stalin by which he signed his death warrant. The letter, which was handed to the new Resident Director in Paris, Zinitzin, stated:

' . . . Up to this moment I marched alongside you. Now I will not take another step. Our paths diverge! He who now keeps quiet becomes Stalin's accomplice, betrays the working class, betrays socialism. I have been fighting for socialism since my twentieth year. Now on the threshold of my fortieth I do not want to live off the favours of a Yezhoff. I have sixteen years of illegal work behind me. That is not little, but I have enough strength left to begin everything all over again to save socialism. . . . No, I cannot stand it any longer. I take my freedom of action. I return to Lenin, to his doctrine, to his acts.'

The gesture was empty because it led nowhere: Reiss did not disagree with the Communist revolution, only with how Stalin had interpreted it, so he did not betray any secrets to the Western powers, nor did he seek political asylum. Instead he laid himself wide open to instant retribution from the N.K.V.D.

An elaborate and costly operation for assassinating Reiss was put in motion. The man given the task of planning this was Colonel Mikhail Shpiglglas, a commissar who had been engaged in making reports on the French network of Soviet espionage. He decreed that three special mobile commando units of Russian Intelligence should be detailed to seek out Reiss. The leaders of these three groups were Roland Abyatt, London-born former Resident Director in Prague, known under the alias of 'François Rossi', Vladimir Konradyev, a Soviet cultural attaché in Paris, and Serge Efron, an agent who was sent to Paris under the cover of a Russian newspaperman.

Meanwhile Reiss, using a Czech passport in the name of Hans Erhardt, had disappeared to Switzerland, leaving his wife and child in Paris. Laboriously the Soviet man-hunt team went into action: Swiss agents were ordered to keep a look-out for Reiss, while others trailed his wife and child. It was not long before Elisabeth Poretsky was discovered travelling to Switzerland where she was tracked down to an hotel in Montreux.

It was at this stage that the Soviet Intelligence brought into action a Swiss teacher named Renata Steiner who had joined the Swiss Communist Party as a student and, following an Intourist visit to Russia in 1934, had been enrolled as a minor agent. Two years later she returned to Moscow and was given full-time work in Soviet Intelligence, being sent to join the French network in a cover job in an antique shop in Paris. The shop was used as a clearing-house for information.

Renata Steiner was employed with discretion; she was often given assignments without being allowed to know their true purpose. Thus, when she had been ordered to shadow a Monsieur and Madame Sedoff, she had no idea that M. Sedoff was the son of Trotsky, and that he had been marked down by Konradyev's organisation for assassination. Having shadowed the Sedoffs to Switzerland, she reported to her superiors that Ignace Reiss had contacted Sedoff. The discovery that Reiss was probably actively conspiring with Trotskyite circles caused the Soviet to redouble their efforts to locate and then liquidate him. Renata Steiner was assigned to Efron's organisation and succeeded in tracing Reiss to a village in the Alps. She was then ordered to trace Ignace's wife.

On 5 September 1937 a saloon car was noticed to be parked in the Boulevard de Chamblandes in Lausanne. Inside it was found the body of a man riddled with machine-gun bullets. In his pocket was the passport of 'Hans Erhardt, of Prague'. The Swiss police were baffled because they had no record of 'Hans Erhardt'. It was only when Ignace Reiss's widow called on them and said she was afraid the murdered man was her husband and formally identified the body that they realised a Soviet murder gang was operating in their midst.

It was then that Renata Steiner walked into a trap. She had been told to hire the car in which Reiss's body had been found and had paid the deposit on it. When she failed to trace Madame Poretsky and could not establish contact with her superiors she foolishly went to the garage to find out what had happened to the car she had ordered.

The Swiss police were waiting for her. Renata Steiner, not having read the papers, or learned of the murder of Reiss, could not at first understand why she was being interrogated. Even the Swiss police were quickly convinced that she was just a dupe of the killers and had no knowledge of the plan to murder Reiss. Nevertheless she was arrested, closely questioned, tried as an accomplice, receiving a sentence of only eight months' imprisonment.

Ignace Reiss had been liquidated, but at serious cost to at least two networks just because a vital witness had been allowed to fall into the hands of the police. Elisabeth Poretsky stated that 'they left behind a witness who could identify them all and reveal the well-guarded secret that White [Russian] organisations were used in the services of the Soviet Union. The killers themselves got away.'

The technique of 'The Trust' had been re-created to combat the Trotskyites in particular, but Stalin's enemies in general. White Russians were again used to spy on both anti-Bolshevik and Trotskyite agents and at a given order to kidnap them or kill them. Sometimes kidnapping proved more effective, especially when it was a case of obtaining information. There was the case of General Eugene Miller, former chief of staff of the Czarist Fifth Army, who had gone to live in Paris. He was chairman of the Union of Russian ex-Combatants, an anti-Bolshevik White Russian organisation that had been founded by the exiled Grand Duke Nicholas. General Miller had been advised by the Union's secretary, Lieutenant-General Scoblin, that the best means of ousting the Soviet régime was to back Hitler and encourage him to wage a 'liberating' war against Russia. At Scoblin's behest Miller agreed to meet two German secret agents to discuss plans. On 22 September 1937 General Miller set out to meet the Germans at a café on the outskirts of Paris. He was never seen again.

For a long time the Soviet Intelligence had marked down the Union of Russian Ex-Combatants as a dangerous group. It was perhaps one of the strongest remaining White Russian organisations with a membership approaching 80,000. Seven years earlier the Russians, disguising themselves as French *gendarmes*, had kidnapped the former head of the Union, General Kutyepoff. No trace of him had ever been found.

It was the same with General Miller. Inquiries by the French police, prompted by strong representations from the Union, revealed that Miller had gone to Le Havre. There the trail ended, but coincidentally a Soviet cargo ship, *Marya Ulyanova*, left Havre the night he arrived there.

Almost always there is the sinister figure of a 'White' Russian among the men controlled by the *Innostranny Otdyel* (the dreaded Executive Branch for Terror and Diversion). In the case of General Miller it turned out to be Lieutenant-General Scoblin, who had posed as a right-wing reactionary, sympathetic to Hitler and anxious for a 'liberating' war against Russia. The two 'Germans' who Scoblin had arranged should meet Miller were Soviet agents as indeed was Scoblin himself. He denied any knowledge of a plot and indignantly defended himself before a committee meeting of the Union, but shortly afterwards he disappeared from Paris and later was heard to be in Moscow. The interesting fact emerges from this story that Scoblin had been a friend of Sidney Reilly and an active Soviet agent from a date shortly after Reilly was arrested in Russia.

15

Infiltration

INFILTRATION OF Britain and the United States by the Soviet Intelligence did not begin on any worthwhile scale until the late twenties and early thirties. As far as Britain was concerned it was generally conceded by the directorate of the Russian Secret Service that premature attempts to build up a network in Britain at the end of World War I and during the war of intervention by the Allied powers against the Bolsheviks had met with almost total failure.

This had been due in part to a belief that the British Communist Party could undertake espionage and that the trade unions could be effectively infiltrated. As we have seen, Russia learned the hard way that national Communist Parties were not the best means of building up networks and that the British trade union movement – at that period at any rate – was solidly socialist, but in the main mistrustful of Communist policy and intrigues. But Russia also learned that British counter-espionage was a force to be reckoned with and that it was safer and certainly more professional to mount spying operations against Britain from a base in Holland. Elisabeth Poretsky has gone on record as stating that her husband (Ignace Reiss) was in 1927 given 'a much more important assignment; he was to direct operations aimed at obtaining information in Great Britain. The headquarters were not to be in England, but in the Netherlands. . . . Britain was greatly respected and envied in those days, especially for its intelligence service; and as one of the foremost capitalist powers, it was considered the most dangerous enemy of the Soviet Union.'

Britain was, therefore, somewhat of a challenge to the Soviet Secret Service and if the latter had an inferiority complex in relation to British Intelligence, it at least stimulated them to find the best method of circumventing the difficulty. Amsterdam was used as a centre for gathering the scientific intelligence supplied by such agents as Lev Landau and Peter Kapitza. From them it was learned that the likeliest place from which to recruit professional agents of British origin was Cambridge University.

Menzhinsky had been very impressed by Kapitza's reports. He had always been contemptuous of the working class as a recruiting ground for agents and, though he was not normally particularly interested in overseas intelligence, the idea of penetrating one of Britain's key universities appealed to his fastidious mind. It also bore out what Dzerzhinsky had been told by Sidney Reilly – that 'the only true Radicals in England are not in the working classes, but in the universities'.

There were at least two Marxist, pro-Soviet dons at Cambridge at that time: J. D. Bernal, who was awarded the Stalin Peace Prize in 1953, and Maurice Dobbs, who had written many works touching on the Communist régime in Russia, comparing it favourably with the capitalist world. Trinity College, Cambridge, became a focal point for pro-Communist sympathisers and it was to this breeding ground for the 'New Left' that the Soviet Intelligence paid special attention.

Two men in England at that time were vital to the cause of Soviet Intelligence. One was a don at another Cambridge college, avoiding debates and controversies but secretly a supporter of the Soviet for some years. He had acted as an intermediary courier for intelligence reports since about 1927 and was personally vouched for by Igor Khopliakin, of the Soviet Embassy in London. This don was chosen as recruiter-in-chief for the Russian Secret Service at Cambridge. The Russians were more cautious than usual in this attempt to infiltrate Cambridge and applied the orthodox rules of espionage vigorously. All direct contact between Khopliakin and the don was ended and communications were established by using a hidden code in chess games played by correspondence. It will be noted that just as the Soviet had ruled that a spy in one country must be the native of another, so the recruiting agent briefed to find prospective agents in Trinity must belong to another college.

The second man who was of great value to Soviet Intelligence at this time was Reginald Orlando Bridgeman, the first fanatically pro-Soviet figure in the British Diplomatic Service, from which he retired on pension in 1923. He had served in the Diplomatic Service in Spain, France, Greece, Austria and Persia and in 1931 contested Uxbridge Parliamentary Division first in the Labour Party's interests, later as a Workers' Candidate. Bridgeman was in his way an honest idealist with revolutionary sympathies and had been nauseated by what he had seen of the darker and more disreputable side of British Intelligence in Greece in World War I. It was this that made him become a member of the British-Soviet Friendship Society and secretary of the League against Imperialism.

Bridgeman's wide knowledge of the workings of British diplomacy was of value to the Soviet, but the difference between Bridgeman and the Cambridge don was that the former was an open sympathiser with Russia, anxious mainly to show the Soviet where they could expect to find latent support in the British diplomatic ranks, yet still a loyal British subject, whereas the don was a calculating traitor, or perhaps worse, an instigator of treachery in others.

Somewhere between the sphere of espionage and that of tacit approval of the Soviet lay the one man the Russians both admired and feared, Professor J. D. Bernal. They feared him because Bernal was not merely a brilliant physicist who supported the Communist cause, but because he was in that intellectual tradition that accepted Marxism, but retained a humanist belief in the possibility of human perfection through the use of reason. Bernal was Irish of Spanish extraction, a Catholic who had become an atheist while at university and had early on embraced Communism. Yet he continued to be part of the British Establishment, while expressing his pro-Soviet views by belonging to no fewer than sixty Communist front organisations. Despite this – and despite the advice and information which he frequently passed on to Russian colleagues in the scientific world – Bernal was appointed scientific adviser to the Research and Experimental Department of the Ministry of Home Security in Britain. At the same time he helped to form an Anti-War Group of scientists at Cambridge and expounded his radical views at luncheon parties at All Souls at Oxford. Sir John Anderson, later to become responsible for air raid precautions in the wartime Government, was so impressed by Bernal that he said he would have Bernal as his adviser 'even if he were red as the flames of hell'. And, as the war progressed, and as the idea grew that the Russians and British were devoted allies, so Bernal was given more and more secret work to do. He made a secret expedition to the Normandy coast before D-Day and was an adviser on artificial harbours. He was without question a man with a foot in both camps and after World War II became a close friend of Ilya Ehrenberg in Moscow and Kuomeijo in Peking. This remarkable man, nicknamed 'The Sage' at Cambridge, died in September 1971.

First results in obtaining recruits for the Soviet Secret Service in Cambridge were slow in coming. Not all the pro-Soviet undergraduates were spy material. They were political extroverts and only too anxious to advertise their sympathies and flaunt them in public. As Julian Bell wrote to the *New Statesman* in December 1933, 'in Cambridge . . . by the end of 1933 we have arrived at a situation in which almost the only subject of discussion is politics and in which a very large majority of the more intelligent undergraduates are Communists or almost Communists'.

Thus the don acting as a spy recruiter had to proceed very cautiously and dared not make an approach except in an oblique manner. Indeed it is possible he merely explored the talent available, sifted it and tested it, made discreet inquiries on his own account and then passed on the information on which others could act. General Walter Krivitsky, at one time the head of Soviet Military Intelligence in Western Europe, where he posed as an art dealer in Amsterdam, when he defected to the U.S.A. shortly before World War II, referred to this Cambridge set-up. One of Krivitsky's oldest friends and a man primarily responsible for his defection was Captain van Narvig, a Finnish subject who had served for a time on the staff of General Mannerheim in Finland. Krivitsky told van Narvig that there was a 'recruiting agent in academic circles in Cambridge who found suitable candidates for the Russian espionage networks' who tipped off British Communists to initiate them.

Cambridge University in the thirties produced a number of Soviet agents of varying ability and temperament, some of whom lasted the course, while others dropped out. A majority of these came from Trinity. Apart from Peter Kapitza there were Allan Nunn May, the atom spy, Kim Philby, who infiltrated the British Secret Service on Russia's behalf, Guy Burgess and Donald Maclean, the two Foreign Office men who defected to Russia. There were many others who did not become Soviet agents but who were nevertheless proclaimed Communists, such as David Haden-Guest, son of a Labour M.P., James Klugman, later to be a leading member of the British Communist Party, Julian Bell, the poet, and John Cornford, the last two named going out to Spain to fight on the Republican side in the Spanish Civil War.

But Trinity was the principal breeding ground for Communism and perhaps no university college in the world has such an unenviable record for producing traitors. In 1932 there was an attempt to co-ordinate Communist student activities in all universities in Britain. It was a premature movement and never achieved much outside of Cambridge, and even there mainly in Trinity. There the Communist students infiltrated an organisation called the Apostles, a curious semi-secret society which drew its membership almost exclusively from Trinity and King's College. Guy Burgess was one of its members.

In addition to this there was an inner ring, or secret Communist cell in Trinity of which two dons were members. The system for vetting those undergraduates who were earmarked as potential agents was to encourage them to go to the Continent where they were given introductions to local Communists who took care of them in the sense of observing their behaviour, movements, temperament and character generally. A number of them were declared unsuited to the rôle of agents, but it has been estimated that at least ten undergraduates were enrolled in this way and of these at least six proved highly successful. Donald Maclean had been an open, compulsive Communist sympathiser and had even indicated to his mother that when he left the University he intended to go to Russia 'to help the revolution'. But he came of a family with strong liberal traditions (his father had been a Liberal Cabinet Minister) and no one suspected just how deep his feelings really were. Incredibly, it was only a short time afterwards that he appeared to change his mind and decide to enter the Foreign Office, where he was accepted without question.

As for Guy Burgess and Kim Philby they, too, underwent a metamorphosis. The former visited Russia, returned to Cambridge and described himself as being only mildly impressed with what he had seen and with many reservations about the Soviet experiment. He left the Communist Party shortly afterwards and adopted the life of a bohemian *enfant terrible* with no firm political convictions. Philby went off to Vienna in 1933 and a few years later was posing as a pro-German right-winger, attending dinners of the Anglo-German Fellowship, a society which had among its members some of the leading reactionaries of the day.

Yet by this date one, if not all three of these men, was already a Soviet agent. Isaac Levine, who wrote Krivitsky's memoirs, recalled that Krivitsky had once made a reference to the presence of a 'second traitor' in the British Foreign Office, whose name was Scottish and whose habits were bohemian, a description which could have fitted Donald Maclean. Kim Philby had stated that he was first recruited into the Soviet Intelligence 'in Central Europe in June 1933', adding that 'all through my career I have been a straight penetration agent working in the Soviet interest. The fact that I joined the British Secret Intelligence is neither here nor there. I regard my S.I.S. appointments purely in the light of cover jobs.'

Krivitsky knew all about Philby because it was in Vienna where he and Philby both met their future wives and all four were members of the same underground Communist cell in that city. The girl Philby encountered in Vienna was Elisabeth Kohlmann, the daughter of a Polish Jew and she had already been married and divorced by the time she met the Englishman. Elisabeth was by then a deeply committed Communist and on 24 February 1934, at Vienna Town Hall, Philby married this attractive girl only two years his senior.

Ostensibly, the reason for the marriage was that the Austrian police were busily hunting down Communists and that Philby was thus able to give her a British passport, enabling her to go to England with him.

From then on Philby certainly gave the impression in Britain that he was a non-Communist, even though he was clearly regarded by his friends on the Continent as a Party member. He did all the correct things from the Establishment point of view, maintained friendly contacts with Government and Whitehall circles, joined *The Times* and even covered the Spanish Civil War on the side of Franco's forces. He had, of course, one great asset: his father's reputation. Harry St John Bridger Philby, though an eccentric individualist in many ways, was still an Establishment figure with the background of the Indian Civil Service, the authority of a Middle East expert and distinguished Arabist.

No doubt Philby dropped hints and put out feelers from time to time to be recruited into the British Secret Service. But it was not until the summer of 1940, when he was still working for *The Times*, that a direct approach was made to him. In his own words he 'watched various irons I had put in the fire, nudging one or other of them as they appeared to hot up'. Then came a telephone call asking if he was available 'for war work'. Within a few days he and Guy Burgess were both interviewed for work with the British Secret Service.

Russia had at last successfully infiltrated not only the British Foreign Office but the Secret Service as well. The Italians at this time were apprehensive about considering even as a remote possibility some rapprochement with Britain as they had discovered that there was already a traitor in the British Foreign Office. One of their agents had been regularly burgling the safe of the British Embassy in Rome and had provided the Italians with the key to the British diplomatic ciphers. This agent, unknown to the Italians, had also worked for the Russians who had fed him with a certain amount of information to pass on to the Italians. But it is highly unlikely that such information included what he gave his Italian contact – the news that the Russians had one of their own agents actually working in the archives section of the British Foreign Office and another in a British Embassy overseas. At first the Italians refused to believe this, but later they found it to be correct.

This raises the question of who was the fifth man in the British Diplomatic and Secret Services who was a traitor, the man who preceded Philby, Maclean, Burgess and Blake. The agent in London just mentioned certainly could not have been Maclean, who was then at the British Embassy in Paris. But the other one at 'a British Embassy overseas' could very well have been Maclean. The answer seems to be that either there was a sixth traitor, which is strongly suspected, but not yet proved, or that the 'fifth man' was Captain John Herbert King. If King was not the man the Italians were told about, then there was almost certainly a sixth Russian agent working inside the British Foreign Office or Secret Service.

The case of Captain John Herbert King is a peculiar one. In June 1956 Isaac Levine, an anti-Communist writer, gave evidence to a United States Senate Investigation Committee that in 1939 the British executed a Soviet agent named King who was found working in the cipher room of the Imperial War Council. This was the same Isaac Levine who had written Krivitsky's memoirs and he revealed that it was Krivitsky's testimony about the presence of spies in the British Foreign Office when he defected to the West that enabled the Americans to tip off the British.

A day later the British Foreign Office revealed for the first time that on 18 October 1939 Captain John Herbert King, a retired

Army officer, was sentenced to ten years' penal servitude for passing information to the Russian Government. King worked in the Communications Department of the Foreign Office (this was not the same as the archives section, though the Italian agent could have made a mistake), which handled messages in code and cipher. King was then fifty-five and the trial was held in secret under the Emergency Powers Regulations. The Foreign Office statement added that King was 'believed still to be alive and in Britain. He had remission for good conduct and did not serve his full sentence.'

The case of Captain King seems to have been curious in a number of ways. The trial was held in the No. 1 Court of the Old Bailey before Mr Justice Hilbery in conditions of great secrecy. King was the first spy to be tried in Britain in World War II and the M.I.5 agents who trapped him went to the Old Bailey in a curtained car. All corridors were cleared. But though it is customary in wartime for such trials to be held in secret, normally the result and sentence are publicised. In the case of Captain King no details were published and everything was hushed up. Indeed, when Levine gave his evidence in the U.S.A. in 1956 it was at first officially denied that there had been a spy named King. The Foreign Office statement followed only when it was obvious that awkward questions were going to be asked by at least one Member of Parliament.

The question arises as to whether King was given preferential treatment despite the enormity of his offences. By mutual agreement the truth about them was kept a secret when he went to prison and other prisoners in Maidstone and Camp Hill jails, where he was sent, thought he had merely been convicted for a passport offence. Spies in British jails – at that time, if not today – were the most hated of prisoners except for those guilty of offences against children. King was popular with his fellow prisoners and he played the violin in the prison orchestra along with a professional violinist who had been jailed for distributing seditious literature.

It was also curious that he was frequently moved from prison to prison as though the authorities were afraid of other prisoners getting to know his secret if he remained anywhere too long.

There was a definite link between King and Sidney Reilly: the two men had known one another and had kept in touch in the early twenties when King was attached to the British Embassy in Paris. Even though Reilly had disappeared in Russia more than twelve years previously, his contacts in Britain were still being used.

But if this alone should have warned the British, Krivitsky's testimony should have alerted them to further dangers. The

Americans had paid scant heed to Krivitsky's warnings about the extent to which the Russians had penetrated some Western Intelligence Services. They had passed on the information to the British Embassy in Washington, who in turn informed London. Krivitsky was sent secretly to Britain and it was his information that led to M.I.5 watching King and finally having him arrested by the Special Branch. But there were some in London who were suspicious of Krivitsky, and felt that he had not told all he knew. This was true. Krivitsky had a premonition that somebody in London had informed Moscow of his visit and that this had sealed his fate.

'When Krivitsky got back to New York,' van Narvig told me, 'he was certain that he had made a great error in going to London. I asked him why and he replied, "One just cannot trust the British. The Soviet Union has spies there in very high places. One never knows who is a friend or an enemy." I told him not to be foolish and he added, "You know the agent Reilly? It was his information which enabled the Russians to penetrate the British network. He thought that by telling us a little he could help Britain and save himself. In the end he did not help Britain and he did not save himself."'

One of the items of information Krivitsky gave the British pointed clearly in the direction of Donald Maclean. He also stated that the Soviet had spent a sum of more than £70,000 trying to infiltrate key Government posts in London. Yet nothing was done to locate the 'young Scotsman with bohemian tastes' in the British Foreign Office.

Van Narvig's comments on all this were equally shrewd. 'There never was any chance that the Soviet Union would make any agreement with Britain when talks began in the early summer of 1939. They knew that in the British Foreign Office and the Secret Service were men of influence who were predominantly anti-Bolshevik and pro-German. They knew this because their own agents inside both the F.O. and the S.I.S. told them. They knew perfectly well that these forces would like nothing better than to see Germany and Russia engaged in war while Britain and France looked on from behind the Maginot Line.'

The case of Captain King remains one of the enigmas of Russian penetration of Britain. John Herbert King joined the Artists' Rifles in World War I and went out to the Middle East where he became a cipher officer. After the war he joined the Foreign Office in a similar capacity. He was first posted to Paris, where he met Reilly, and then in about 1926 to Germany. It was about that time that he separated from his wife.

King was not a member of the Communist Party. When he was

arrested a top-secret message was found in his possession: he was on his way to a tea-shop in Whitehall to meet his Russian contact.

In 1956 King was traced by journalists to a West London block of apartments where he was living in obscurity. He declined to throw any further light on the matter other than to say that 'I never really understood the charges. But when you are up against the powers that be there is nothing you can do. Trial is a formality. I pleaded guilty and the trial took only a matter of minutes.'

Mrs King was more forthcoming. She said: 'I gathered that when he was asked for more information after the last war started he refused because his country was at war. That refusal led to his denunciation.'

It was following the assumption of centralised direction of the Soviet police forces and the Secret Service by the N.K.V.D. in 1934 that the Soviet Union suffered a period of repression and purges that was in many respects worse than that of the Cheka era. Kiroff's murder in Leningrad in December 1934 became a signal for mass arrests and purges throughout the Red Army and the Secret Service.

Yagoda had taken over from Menzhinsky on the latter's death in 1934. His special contribution to the N.K.V.D. was his ability to choose talented agents, for which he had a singularly judicial mind in weighing up their qualities, their weaknesses and strengths. Yet in a practical sense even this contribution was perhaps outweighed by his organisational genius for financing the work of the Soviet espionage machine by forgery. Russia had been short of currency in the early thirties because of the large quantities of mechanical equipment and goods that had to be purchased to carry out the Five-Year Plan. Yagoda, a realist if nothing else, decided that from a Communist standpoint it was perfectly ethical to finance the Secret Service by organised forgery. Otherwise, as he pointed out, there simply was not the money to undertake the full-scale spying abroad which Stalin desired and Russia needed. Yagoda put his scheme directly to Stalin who approved it without demur. After all it was not dissimilar to the tactics employed when they had been revolutionaries in exile.

The forgery experts in the Secret Service decided that pounds sterling were too difficult to forge and that the detective system of the Bank of England was too clever to be caught out this way. So they concentrated on dollars and it was largely through the forgery of dollars that Yagoda was able to organise the penetration of the United States at a time when America was insufficiently vigilant to the menace of Soviet espionage. Yagoda used Beria as his chief instrument in organising the distribution of forged dollar bills mainly through small banks in Germany run by crypto-Communists. It was the existence of such banks and the knowledge that they passed forged money in their import-export business that later played into the hands of Hitler in his propaganda drive against the Jews. One of the leading operators was a pro-Communist Jew in Berlin. Most of this distribution of forged dollars was carried out in 1928–29, the years of the depression and the bankers' slump. It was an ideal time in which to launch such an operation and it was not discovered until 1930, by which time the members of the espionage chain responsible had been broken up. Walter Krivitsky himself was one of the chief organisers of this forgery ramp when he was Resident Director of Soviet Espionage in Vienna and he later declared that more than nine million forged dollar bills had been passed on to the market.

Though Yagoda succeeded Menzhinsky he never achieved complete power even in his own sphere. Stalin began to intervene personally in all Secret Service matters more and more, even dictating operations and demanding the removal of personnel who had displeased him. What brought about Yagoda's arrest and dismissal remains somewhat of a mystery, but there is some evidence that Stalin thought he had compromised Soviet security by his forgery transactions, despite the fact that Stalin himself had originally approved them.

Yagoda was superseded in July 1936 by Nicolai Yezhov, the Secretary of the Central Committee, who was given full authority to purge the Secret Service.

If Yagoda had been ruthlessly oppressive, Yezhov was even more drastic in his measures. He not only appointed more than three hundred new heads of departments, executives and agents, but ordered a drastic purge of the overseas networks of the Soviet Secret Service such as had never been carried out before. It was an attempt, mainly inspired by Stalin, to ensure that the last of the old-time revolutionaries with independent views were liquidated. Stalin developed a phobia against the internationalist Communist and at the same time also turned against the Jewish agent.

Yet the truth is that until 1948 the Jews remained Russia's best agents. However much Stalin sought to destroy their influence, Hitler's highly publicised persecution of Jewry ensured that they remained the allies of international communism: many of them saw it as their only hope. In the United States especially the Jews helped to provide the best espionage machine that Russia possessed and as soon as one cell was destroyed another sprang up.

When Hitler came to power, there was a real attempt to infiltrate the Nazi Party and the Soviet military attaché in Berlin had sought to compromise leading Nazis, including Ernst Roehm and Gregor Strasser. The G.R.U. was heavily involved in attempts to obtain a secret understanding with the Nazis and this alarmed Stalin, not so much that he was opposed to doing a deal with the Nazis, but enough to make him aware of the fact that such manoeuvres were in danger of getting out of hand.

Thus it was that the Soviet Intelligence pounced first on those of its own members who had either independently or too enthusiastically sought to bring about a deal with Nazi Germany. But, apart from this, the German Intelligence had planted false information on the Russians suggesting that many of their own generals were plotting with the Nazis. Anyone with Stalin's obsessive mistrust of those around him only needed to hear such rumours to carry out a further purge. This time the purge nearly ruined Russia: it certainly robbed her of many of her ablest generals and left her desperately short of field commanders. General Putna, the Soviet military attaché in Berlin, and Marshal Mikhail Tukhachevsky, together with six other generals, including some of the best military intelligence experts, were tried in 1937 on charges of high treason and collaboration with the Nazis. They were all executed.

Stalin himself took charge of Intelligence. He probed, checked and counter-checked his executives and the fact that he had originally appointed them was not always in their favour. Nobody could have carried out Stalin's orders more faithfully than Yezhoff, but he cracked under the strain. In Stalinist Russia the man at the head of affairs either in the Secret Police or the Secret Service needed to be not merely obedient, but efficiently obedient. Few could live up to this test. Walter Krivitsky, before he defected, became convinced that Yezhoff was insane: 'in the middle of an important and confidential telephone call he [Yezhoff] would suddenly burst out in crazy laughter and tell stories of his own life in the most obscene language . . . this was the man to whom Stalin had given the task of purging the Party.'

Thus in 1938 Yezhoff was removed to a mental asylum. His place was taken by Beria, probably one of the ablest men who ever controlled the Soviet Secret Service. As long as Stalin lived Beria was safe and this was no mean tribute when one considers what happened to Menzhinsky, Yagoda and Yezhoff. Beria, as we have seen, had acquired his reputation for quiet efficiency in a wide range of jobs both inside Russia and abroad. He was a Georgian, which counted for a great deal with Stalin. Born in Tiflis in 1898, Beria was the son of a civil servant but came of a peasant family. He had been educated in a teachers' training college and had served in the Czar's army in World War I despite poor eyesight.

211

He had, however, played down his Army service and in the typical fashion of Russian revolutionaries of his epoch had conjured up a picture, albeit fictitious, of an earlier career devoted to active revolutionary zeal in the underground. There is no documentary evidence of this and it would seem that Beria was far too young for such activities. He first attracted attention when he organised the Baku oil workers in 1918, and the following year he escaped from the anti-Bolshevik forces and found his way into Siberia.

At the age of twenty-three he was already a Soviet secret agent and successful work in Prague was followed by equally effective and diligent service in Paris and elsewhere. He was a gifted linguist, unostentatious, though he had a weakness for night life in the capitals of Europe, a trait that might have been fatal to most agents, but which as far as Beria was concerned he developed into a strength. A good mixer in all classes of society, he used many aliases abroad and was particularly effective in gaining the confidence of exiled White Russians in whose restaurants and night-clubs he posed as a moderate Socialist intellectual who was opposed to the Soviet régime. This enabled him not merely to keep watch on White Russians who continued to plot against the régime, but to track down the movements of Trotsky in exile. It was this quality for patiently infiltrating the enemy's ranks which made him so indispensable to Stalin.

The mass arrests of the early thirties were bad enough, but what followed after 1934 was so extensive that it purged the whole apparatus of the Secret Service of individualism. Only a few brilliant individuals escaped. Those who were left were reduced to cringing, frightened robots, blindly following the policy switches of their masters. In August 1936 sixteen executions were carried out, following the trials of Zinoviev, Kamanev, Smirnoff and Mrachkovsky. In the following January thirteen prominent Communists were executed, including Piatakoff who had been one of the ablest of Soviet agents in Europe.

Altogether during 1937 there were no fewer than fifty-six executions of notable Communists, many of whom had played important rôles in one or other of the branches of the Secret Service. The blood bath continued until 1938, when in March at the 'Trial of the Twenty-one' eighteen executions were ordered, including that of Yagoda. It has been estimated that more than 30,000 members of the Red Army and Navy forces were executed and more than 500 members of the Secret Service.

Thus Beria's task amounted almost to rebuilding the Secret Service, bringing it under a much tighter central control, and creating hundreds of new agents to take the places of those who either had been liquidated or had escaped from the Stalinist tyranny. A lesser man might have been so appalled at the magnitude of his task that he would not have had the courage to see it through, or by reason of the lack of trained agents been unable to provide the intelligence which Stalin demanded. But Beria was, as we have seen, something of a cosmopolitan and his wide experience of other countries and his flair for grasping essentials made him *par excellence* the right man in the right job at the right moment.

Beria insisted on much higher educational qualifications for his agents. He sought for these among the new school of technically educated Russians, preferably men with scientific knowledge who could evaluate new techniques in the military sphere. Also, to please Stalin, he gave a certain preference to men from Georgia, Stalin's native territory. Soviet agents abroad were expected to obtain Post Office and trade directories, reference books, lists of personnel in various Ministries in their area, lists of refugees and immigrants, guide-books, maps, plans of docks and airfields, up-to-date records of new technical publications and specialist books and invariably all books published about Russia or any aspect of Russian life. Dossiers were kept on authors, journalists, inventors, university professors and in some instances on students.

The G.R.U. underwent a drastic purge in its higher levels and suffered accordingly. Jan Berzin, its chief, was executed along with his assistant, Alexander Korin. Scores of agents were recalled 'to report for further orders' only to find themselves dismissed, if they were lucky, but more often deported, imprisoned or executed. The draining off of experienced personnel in addition to the weeding out of incompetents meant that Russia was for two years at a grave disadvantage in the field of intelligence. The German network, which had once been so strong, was broken up and had to be built afresh and Beria himself decreed that this was to be done primarily from Switzerland, but to a lesser degree from Denmark, Holland and Belgium. Geneva became temporarily the headquarters for spying operations directed against Germany.

But for two years prior to the war it is estimated that there were less than forty professional, full-time agents in Germany, only ten in Holland, but more than fifty in Switzerland. These figures do not take into account the much larger numbers of informers. To some extent it was Stalin's realisation of the weakness of Russian espionage in Germany that made him so eager for the German-Soviet Pact of 1939. Only Ernst Wollweber of the earlier German network survived and he was based in Copenhagen and given the rôle of organising Scandinavian espionage, a task he undertook until his arrest in 1941.

The 'Execution Squad' of the Secret Service was kept busy with many other planned murders apart from that of Ignace Reiss. By using this squad Stalin sought to frighten potential traitors in any part of the world and to make them realise that nowhere were they safe from the long arm of Soviet retribution. Dimitry Navachin, a former Soviet diplomat, was killed in the Bois de Boulogne in Paris in January 1937, shot down by two gunmen while taking a walk. He had declared that he was willing to give evidence before any independent tribunal in Western Europe about the truth behind the purge trials in Moscow. No arrests were made.

Soon it was clear that the 'Execution Squad' was on the trail of Trotsky himself. The N.K.V.D. had learned that Trotsky had deposited secret papers in the Institute of Political Science in Paris before he moved on to his exile in Mexico, hoping that the New World would be somewhat safer than the Old. Soviet agents infiltrated the Institute and one night a burglary occurred there and several cases full of Trotsky's papers were removed. The next move was an attempt to poison Trotsky's son, Leo Sedoff, who had become influential in exiled Russian Socialists' circles in Paris, generally known as the Mensheviks. Leo Sedoff's 'crime' was that he was concerned in the publishing of a bulletin called *Vestnik*, which was printed in Russian and carried much material about conditions inside Russia. After the poisoning attempt Sedoff was taken to a hospital in Paris where he slowly recovered. As a safety precaution he was given a night nurse who was supposed to be in constant attendance on him. By some means the nurse was enticed away from Sedoff's bedroom and shortly afterwards he had a sudden and unexpected relapse and is alleged to have been found staggering along a corridor, shouting: 'Help! I have been poisoned again. This time they have got me.'

Soon after this Sedoff died. The mystery of his death has never been completely cleared up. The forensic pathologists came to the conclusion that 'Sedoff's death could be explained by natural causes', but they recommended an open verdict.

The killings of Trotskyites, or suspected Trotskyites, continued. Rudolf Klement, Trotsky's secretary, who had been unable to get a visa to Mexico, remained behind in Paris. He had been a close friend of Sedoff and in July 1938 he was sent on a mission to Brussels. But Klement never reached his destination: on the sixteenth of that month a headless body was recovered from the Seine. The *Sûreté* could not identify it, but two men who had been associated with Klement confirmed that the torso was his.

Even during the Spanish Civil War, when the Soviet intervened on the side of the Republicans the 'Execution Squad' carried on its activities in Spain, the aim being to eliminate all deviations from the Soviet line. Support for the Spanish Republicans was not enough: anyone who deviated, however slightly, from the official policy of the Soviet in Spain, or belonged to a splinter group, was marked down. Thus Andreas Nin, a Spanish Communist who had fled from Spain to Moscow in 1920, but had switched his allegiance to Trotsky, founding the P.O.U.M. (Workers' Party of Marxist Unity), was detained by the 'Execution Squad' in Spain and was never again seen alive. The Spanish branch of the 'Execution Squad' was known as the Assault Guard of the Spanish Mobile Group. They included among their victims Professor Jose Robles, Marc Abramovich, son of a Menshevik, Bob Smile, a Briton who was a member of the Independent Labour Party, and Hamilton Gold, a radio operator for the Republican Government, who was kidnapped and taken to Russia.

At the same time nearly fifty overseas agents of the N.K.V.D. were recalled to Moscow and shot without trial. There were some Resident Directors of espionage among them, including Milhail Kholtzoff, who had been in charge of the Spanish network, and two Red Army generals who had been to Spain, assisting the Republican Army as advisers on tactics.

16

Richard Sorge

FOR CENTURIES Muscovite Russia and China of the Ming dynasty were separated by two thousand miles of desert, mountains and steppes, an area sparsely inhabited by nomads. Then in the latter part of the nineteenth century, as we have seen, Czarist expansion towards the Far East and Manchu excursions into Central Asia brought the two nations into much closer contact.

Russian espionage in the Far East increased as trading posts sprang up and reached its peak about the time of the Russo-Japanese War. After about 1906 it declined rapidly. Soviet Russia's intelligence drive early on had been mainly directed towards Europe in general and Germany in particular, where it was thought there was the best chance of furthering revolution on the Communist pattern. But by the early thirties it was realised that there was little hope for a worthwhile revolt inside Germany and attention was turned to China.

A small network of agents had been established in China in the late twenties, but this had produced scant results and it was decided to set up a completely new China unit. The man earmarked for organising this was Richard Sorge, who had worked at the Comintern headquarters in Moscow for three years.

Sorge became one of the greatest Russian spies of modern times. After his death he was described by the senior political commentator of *Pravda*, Victor Mayevsky, as 'a man whose name will become the symbol of devotion to the great cause of the fight for peace, the symbol of courage and heroism'.

Mayevsky was commenting on the posthumous award given to Sorge, that of Hero of the Soviet Union. He was the first of the spies to be glorified by the Soviet, articles in his praise proliferated throughout the Russian press in 1964 and a film entitled 'Who are you, Richard Sorge?' was co-produced with the East Germans.

Sorge was by any standards a first-class spy. He was also a remarkable and even likeable man, admired and respected by his enemies just as he was venerated and trusted by his friends. General MacArthur said that Sorge's story 'represents a devastating example of brilliant success of espionage – its evolution, techniques and methods'.

Born in Baku in Southern Russia in 1895, Sorge was the son of a German engineer working for a German oil firm in the Caucasus and a Russian mother. According to Mayevsky, Sorge's grandfather had been active in the abortive German revolution of 1848 and was a friend of Marx and Engels. When he was three years old young Richard was brought to Berlin by his family and educated in Germany. In World War I he joined up as a private in the German Army and was wounded on the Western Front. He had a lengthy spell in hospital and was eventually discharged. It says much for his pertinacity that he re-enlisted in 1916, by which time the authorities were not so particular about disabilities in recruits, and served on the Eastern Front. After the war he studied at the universities of Berlin, Kiel and Hamburg. By this time he had become interested in Socialism and Marxism and he sought actively to win converts to his opinions among the students.

Sorge received a doctorate of political science at Hamburg in 1920 and gradually moved further to the left in politics. Wanting to learn more about the workers, he became a coal miner for a spell and then in 1922 undertook occasional work as a teacher and a journalist. Either consciously or subconsciously he was preparing himself for a career in espionage by gaining as much experience as possible in a wide field of activity. He had joined the Independent Socialist Party as early as 1917 but now became a member of the German Communist Party, attached to the Hamburg branch.

Sorge had been tremendously influenced by his mother and, despite the fact that he was educated in Germany, spoke Russian fluently from childhood. He was, in fact, a natural linguist and later learned new languages within a matter of months, including English, French, Japanese and, to a lesser extent, Chinese.

His devotion to the Communist cause, efficiency and zeal, as well as his intellectual abilities, soon attracted the attention of the Soviet Intelligence. In 1925 Sorge was summoned to Moscow. He resigned from the German Communist Party, joined the Soviet Communist Party and was enrolled first as an agent of the Comintern.

For three years he was on probation and received training for a career in espionage. In 1928 he was admitted as a fully-fledged G.R.U. operative ready for work in foreign territory.

The official Bulgarian news agency, B.T.A., revealed on 30 January 1971 that the spy instructor who taught Sorge the arts of espionage was 'engineer Nikolai Yablin, who lived in a quiet street in the Lozenets district of Sofia and who was publicly known only as a former director of the Bulgarian Radio'. Yablin, who survived his pupil and is still alive, was a Soviet Intelligence officer of high standing prior to and during World War II. He trained many intelligence radio operators from the Soviet Union and other countries, including Max Klausen, who became Sorge's radio operator in Tokyo. Klausen was a German seaman who was recruited by the G.R.U. in 1928 and given training at the Red Army Radio School near Moscow. Yablin was born in Bulgaria and emigrated to the Soviet Union in 1923. He later became a member of the scientific and technical council of the Red Army Signals Corps.

In 1927 Sorge had been sent out as a fully-trained professional agent for the first time, a trial run in effect, since one of the jobs given to him was to stay in Los Angeles to make a detailed report on the Hollywood film industry. He used the cover of a German magazine reporter. During these few years he visited Scandinavia, the Balkans and Britain, where, in 1928, he stayed at a Bloomsbury boarding-house. Despite the fact that at this very time the hierarchy of the Soviet Secret Service was insisting that professional agents should keep their contacts with foreign Communist Parties down to a minimum, Sorge was actually given a dual rôle, carrying out the work of a spy and at the same time establishing contacts with such parties and giving them advice.

Sorge disliked the implications of the double rôle, feeling that the risks he ran could easily jeopardise his reputation at the outset of his career as a professional agent. He feared, not without good reason, that someone who might have remembered him as an openly avowed Communist in Hamburg would eventually recognise him. This was what actually happened in London where he was visited and questioned by Special Branch officers; someone in London had undoubtedly found out his antecedents and the officers demanded to know whether he had ever lived in Hamburg. M.I.5 did not believe his denials so his visit was terminated. 'England knows more about spies than any other country,' Sorge reported back to Moscow.

It is probable that, though Sorge's talents were much appreciated in Moscow, some of his superior officers were suspicious of his German ancestry and that the plan to send him to Britain and Scandinavia was an attempt to test his loyalty. Sorge had always been independent-minded, though well-disciplined, and he had been the friend of many agents who were shortly to be liquidated. Possibly, too, Sorge had scented the dangers to himself if he remained tied to the much criticised Comintern, for he made an immediate request to be transferred to the Fourth Bureau of the Red Army General Staff.

Had Sorge not joined the Fourth Bureau, the man who was to become Russia's ablest agent might have been liquidated in the purges of the thirties. Elisabeth Poretsky, who, with her husband Ignace Reiss was one of his friends, has said of him: 'Accounts of Sorge's later activities in the Far East picture this "formidable" secret agent as a hard drinker and a woman chaser, with a wife in Russia, another one, "a school-teacher", in the United States, and some twenty women around him in Japan. I do not know how many women he knew in Japan, or anything about a Russian wife, unless that was a girl in Moscow who attached herself to him and whom he suspected of having been sent by the N.K.V.D. to watch him. But the "school-teacher" in the United States was his real wife, Christiane, a distinguished-looking, reddish-blonde German girl whom Sorge met when they were both at university.' Sorge was rarely seen with his wife and in fact she was living in Britain when he was in the Far East, moving to the U.S.A. when World War II broke out.

Sorge was allowed to choose his own agents when he formed the China Unit. His original brief was simply to organise the collection of information on Chiang Kai-shek's growing Nationalist Army, but he went far beyond this, arguing with great prescience that the greatest menace to Russia in the Far East was Japan, due to her preoccupation with military adventures and expansionism. He was given a list of existing agents in the Far East and most of these he discarded when he set up his headquarters in Shanghai. He also laid it down that the primary task of the Unit was to obtain intelligence on Japan and that intelligence about Chinese matters was of secondary importance.

In Shanghai Sorge's cover was that of correspondent for *Soziologische Magazin*. He set about recruiting agents all over China, in Canton, Nanking, Hanchow, Peiping and even in Manchuria. Meanwhile he sought to master the Chinese and Japanese languages and spent long hours studying the politics and literature of each country. He was not merely a first-class agent, but a supremely good director of intelligence with a real flair for selecting the right type of agent. He seems to have avoided using Russians, but to have employed a number of Americans, Germans, Japanese and Chinese. His radio operator was a German named Weingart and some of his most trusted agents were Americans, of whom there were a number in China at this time with strong pro-Soviet views, largely produced by their dislike of what they had seen of the imperialism of the big European powers in China.

While Sorge was personally deeply committed to the Soviet revolution and experiment he seems to have had reservations about many of the Russians with whom he had to work. Perhaps his experiences of being shadowed by the N.K.V.D. and the knowledge that even the genuine revolutionary idealist could find himself liquidated had made him this way. But he decided early on that the China Unit was going to be completely in his hands and that there should be no question of the N.K.V.D. or anyone else having an agent in China to send back reports on him to Moscow, if he could help it. Six months after he went to Shanghai his Russian chief in China was recalled to Moscow at Sorge's request and from then onwards he was to all intents and purposes Resident Director in the Far East.

One of the Americans who worked closely with him over a long period was Miss Agnes Smedley, a Communist sympathiser, who arranged for her apartment to be used as a base for the network's secret radio. Agnes Smedley, whose writings on China had attracted wide sympathy in liberal circles, also supplied Sorge with a number of Chinese and Japanese contacts, of whom perhaps the most notable was Ozaki Hozumi, a graduate of Tokyo University who came from a wealthy family, and who in due course became Sorge's most trusted assistant.

Ozaki Hozumi worked as a journalist after he left university and though he never joined the Communist Party his sympathies in that direction were marked in his early days. In 1927 he went to Shanghai as correspondent of the celebrated Tokyo newspaper, *Asahi Shimbun*. He only spent three years in that city, but during this time established close links with Sorge. However, it was Agnes

219

Smedley who really recruited Ozaki Hozumi into the Soviet spy service. When he returned to Japan in 1932 it was as a key agent of the Fourth Bureau in Osaka.

About this time Sorge changed his name for a short period and adopted the identity of William Johnson, an American journalist. It was not until six years later that Ozaki Hozumi discovered the true identity of 'William Johnson' even though they had been working closely together. While in Shanghai he never knew whether Miss Smedley or 'Johnson' was the head of the network.

Back in Japan Ozaki Hozumi energetically set about extending the Soviet spy network himself, closely following Sorge's instructions that any Communist who was recruited into the network must give up active membership of the Party. This brilliant young man soon proved himself to be the most gifted of all Sorge's agents, his journalist's grasp of the intricacies of Far Eastern politics giving him an insight into the relevance of items of information which would have meant little to the average spy. One thing saddened him: on Sorge's orders he was told he must not see or correspond with Agnes Smedley again. If the Japanese secret police became aware of their friendship, warned Sorge, the whole network inside Japan might be endangered.

By the mid-thirties Soviet Russia had by far the most efficient Secret Service of any of the powers in the Far East. The Americans lacked experienced operators and men knowledgeable about the politics of the area. Even their intelligence officers innocently believed that the Chinese Communist Party was not really Communist at all, but simply an agrarian organisation aiming to give the peasants a fair deal. This belief lasted in many quarters until after World War II, by which time it was far too late to put matters right.

Yet it was due almost entirely to Richard Sorge that the Soviet network achieved such success. Before he arrived on the scene Russia had relied to some extent on the Tass (official Russian news agency) correspondent in Japan. Captain Malcolm D. Kennedy, writing about three successive Tass correspondents in Tokyo, has this to say: 'Unlike his predecessor Slapec, whom he had succeeded as Tass correspondent a year or so previously, Romm was a well-trained and highly intelligent journalist. It seemed extraordinary therefore that, when Soviet hopes and wishes conflicted with rational reasoning, he always tended to give priority to the former in his assessment of any particular situation by believing what he wished to believe. During my years as a foreign correspondent in Japan, I came to know him and Nagi, his successor, well, and I developed a real liking for both of them; but time and again I was struck by this curious dichotomy in the reasoning of these two extremely intelligent, well-informed and likeable men. Slapec, Romm's predecessor, on the other hand, was a very different type, a slimy, shifty little creature, who seemed more fitted for the rôle of a communist agitator than for that of a foreign correspondent.'

Romm and Nagi were both liquidated during the Soviet purges of the thirties.

Prior to the arrival of Sorge in Japan in 1934 Russia had been almost as contemptuous as Britain in its regard for the Japanese armed forces. Colonel Rink, the Soviet military attaché in Tokyo, took the view that the Japanese military standards were far lower than had previously been imagined, and Golkovich, the local O.G.P.U. representative, was equally optimistic that Japan posed no real threat to the Soviet Union. Perhaps this was the reason why both Rink and Golkovich were liquidated in the Russian purges of 1937 like Romm and Nagi. On the other hand Sorge himself must have put in some extremely critical reports on these men. The international situation was changing rapidly in the mid-nineteen-thirties and it was clear that Germany was turning from her traditional friendship towards China in favour of an alliance with Japan. This posed a danger to Russia on two fronts, the east and the west.

Sorge warned that Japan would attack wherever the great powers were weakest and that Russia needed to build up her defences in the east. He also forecast that sooner or later Japan would strike a blow against the British Empire and that the British were far too complacent about their defences in the Far East. 'Singapore,' reported Sorge, 'is a symbol of British unpreparedness. It is not a citadel, but an open invitation to an adventurous invader and can be taken with comparatively small casualties in less than three days.'

On the strength of these reports the Soviet Secret Service recalled Sorge to Moscow and both the Fourth Bureau and the N.K.V.D. took joint action to improve still further their Far Eastern intelligence system. Colonel Beldin, who had been a Director of the Centre in Moscow, was promoted to the rank of General and ordered to organise a special intelligence section for Far Eastern affairs. From Sorge's point of view the important factor was that the direction of Far Eastern Intelligence continued to come under the Red Army. Beldin was an imaginative man and he understood rather better than the other military personnel of the G.R.U. the value of political as distinct from purely military intelligence. On this question he and Sorge were in accord. Ulitsky succeeded Beldin as head of the Fourth Bureau. He was a much more cautious man than Beldin, always tending to cover his every move by referring even trivial details to the Party leaders before making a final decision. But he was friendly towards Sorge, even welcoming his adventurous spirit, and he acquiesced with something like enthusiasm to Sorge's request that he should establish relations with the German Embassy in Tokyo and infiltrate the ranks of Japan's one and only European ally.

Sorge's proposal was that he should go to Germany and establish contacts with the leading Nazis, aiming to join the ranks of the Gestapo or some other powerful German agency. The plan was so outrageous that it was considered unsafe to agree to it without first consulting Stalin himself. The Soviet leader nodded silent approval and in May 1933 Sorge set out for Berlin. Elisabeth Poretsky has stated that Sorge 'could not be bothered with safety and the little details that were essential to such work', and that 'his joining the Nazi Party in his own country, where he had a well documented police record was hazardous, to say the least. Such actions were typical of . . . his superb self-assurance.'

Sorge was a strange mixture of the reckless and the methodical, the masterful and the humane. When it came to organisation he was almost without a peer, cautious in the extreme, following out all the rules and never missing a detail. Yet left to himself he would sometimes take incredible risks that were totally alien to one of his profession. His true sympathies were with his many friends who mistrusted Stalin and detested the purges, but he never allowed the deaths of his friends or the outrages perpetrated in the name of Stalin to sway him from his belief in the ultimate triumph of 'the system' and the survival of the Soviet Union. He did not approve of all that was done in Stalin's name, but he had complete faith in Stalin as the one man able to control and direct the juggernaut that was the Russian people.

Perhaps it was Sorge's charm which misled the Nazis. His application to join the Nazi Party was successful and he returned to Tokyo as correspondent of the *Frankfurter Zeitung*, a newspaper which also had, without realising it, another Soviet agent as their correspondent in Shanghai – Agnes Smedley. From the moment of his return to Tokyo he quickly became established in the highest German circles in Japan, being *persona grata* at the German Embassy.

His closest confidant in the German ranks, Lieutenant-Colonel Eugen Ott, an artillery expert attached to the Japanese Army, later became the Major-General Ott who succeeded von Dirksen as German Ambassador in Tokyo. Ott had such trust in Sorge that he showed him copies of secret reports he sent to Berlin, details of which Sorge passed back to Russia. At the same time Sorge joined the German Club and generally conducted himself as a fervent believer in the Third Reich, but with sufficient good manners and lack of arrogance to make himself agreeable to a wide range of acquaintances.

Sorge was shortly joined by another Soviet agent, Branko de Voukelitch, a Yugoslav who had been living in Paris. Together with Ozaki he became one of the key agents in Sorge's carefully built-up Japanese network. Sorge's aim was to penetrate the German Embassy, to ingratiate himself with everyone there and to find out at one and the same time both German and Japanese plans and the degree to which these two nations were working together. Voukelitch had only become a Communist as recently as 1932, and his cover in Japan was that of special correspondent for a French newspaper. It was Voukelitch's job to set up the clandestine radio station in his apartment.

Sorge's ability to glean so much military intelligence through Ott naturally endeared him to the Fourth Bureau and in due course he secured the post of press attaché in the German Embassy. Each morning at breakfast Sorge would regale the German Ambassador with gossip and information about Japanese affairs and in return the latter would tell him all manner of things about his own relations with the Japanese. Often, almost under the nose of the Gestapo agent in the Embassy, Colonel Meissinger, the Soviet agent would photograph documents with his pocket camera.

It is interesting to note Sorge's instructions from the Fourth Bureau and see how much more professional was this outfit in comparison with the cruder and sometimes rather less comprehensive planning of the N.K.V.D. Sorge himself listed the subjects on which he was asked to concentrate:

(1) Japan's policy towards Russia following the invasion of Manchuria. To ascertain whether Japan intended to attack the Soviet Union; (2) The battle order of the Japanese Army and Air Force and organisational details of both services; (3) Japanese-German relations and how these affected Russia; (4) Japan's policy towards China and her activity there; (5) Japan's relations with the U.S.A. and Britain and the possibility of her waging war on either; (6) The influence of the Japanese war lords on the purely political front; (7) All intelligence and details of operations and movements in Manchuria.

It can be seen from this that Sorge was not merely a collector of information, but an analyser and an evaluator as well. He always maintained that his job as a writer for newspapers and magazines helped him enormously in his quest for intelligence. 'A shrewd spy,' he declared, 'will not spend all his time on the collection of military and political secrets and classified documents. Also, I may add, reliable information cannot be procured by effort alone; espionage work entails the accumulation of information, often fragmentary, covering a broad field, and the drawing of conclusions based thereon. This means that a spy in Japan, for example, must study Japanese history and the racial characteristics of the people and orient himself thoroughly on Japan's politics, society, economics and culture.'

All the time he was in Japan Sorge was being watched by the Japanese police and his maid and laundryman were often questioned by them, his house being searched when he was away on a visit to China. It required a strong nerve to operate under these conditions, but Sorge said he came to the conclusion that the Japanese police were too interested in little things and not sufficiently alert to the more important aspects of counter-espionage.

Whenever Sorge wanted to see his chief agents – men like Ozaki, Voukelitch and his telegraphist, Klausen – he gave a noisy party in a most ostentatious manner, inviting geisha girls along to entertain the guests as well as many people who were totally ignorant of Sorge's real activities. The noise of these goings-on was alone guaranteed to attract the attention of the secret police, but they would naturally never believe that anything of a clandestine nature could be carried on at so blatantly orgiastic a gathering. What the Kempeitai (Japanese secret police) agents failed to notice was that long after the geishas and the other guests had gone Sorge's key agents remained behind until dawn. It was in the early hours of the morning that plans were discussed and information exchanged.

Drink and women were Sorge's method of baffling the Japanese secret police. He realised that what he appeared to do in his spare time was what they would be most interested in. And if they merely reported that he indulged in drinking bouts, gay parties and that he changed mistresses like another man changed his suits, nobody would begin to suspect that he was a spy. And, of course, his links with the German Embassy gave the impression that he was pro-Japanese.

His first major coup was obtained for him by Ozaki. A special report on Japan's economic problems and political plans for 1936 was prepared by the Japanese Foreign Minister and Ozaki, who was a counsellor of the Japanese Government, was shown the papers and asked to give his opinion on those sections that related to China. Ozaki, regarded as an authority on Chinese affairs, was trusted absolutely by the Japanese Cabinet. He photographed the whole report and as a result Sorge was able to report back to Moscow that Japan had no plans for an attack on Russia in the immediate future and that the invasion of South China depended on how soon the Japanese could get their factories in Manchuria into full production.

In 1939 Sorge warned Moscow that the German invasion of

Poland was scheduled for 1 September. Again in April 1941 he reported that 150 German divisions were being concentrated on the Soviet border and gave a general résumé of Hitler's war plans. In a subsequent message he even spelled out the exact date of the invasion, 22 June. Mayevsky, his biographer, states: 'Analogous information reached Moscow through other channels. But Stalin disregarded it. How many thousands and millions of lives would have been saved had the information from Richard Sorge and others not been sealed up in a safe! Alas, we paid in full for this mistrust and disregard of people which was an inseparable part of the personality cult.'

In the autumn of 1941, when the Nazis were pounding at the gates of Moscow, Sorge and his comrades provided the Russians with priceless information that the Japanese were preparing to make war in the Pacific and were concentrating their main forces in that area in the belief that the Germans would defeat the Red Armies. This intelligence made it possible to transfer some divisions from the Far East to help defend Moscow. Thus, says Mayevsky, Sorge made a vital contribution to saving the Russian capital and helped the Russians to give the Germans their first major set-back.

'But by then,' wrote Mayevsky, 'the hero-intelligencer was already languishing in prison. The Japanese secret police had long suspected something was amiss within the German Embassy walls. But even these shrewd and skilful opponents were unable to discover anything. And there is no knowing how it all would have turned out, had it not been for a traitor who called himself a Communist. Sorge's friends were picked up one by one and in mid-October he was arrested.'

Mayevsky was not exaggerating the importance of Sorge's intelligence. The ace agent realised that the Soviet Union was engaged in a fight for survival with the Nazi hordes hammering close to Moscow. His information that for the foreseeable future the Japanese would honour their 1940 neutrality pact with the Soviet Union while they planned for an attack against the Philippines enabled the Russians to switch troops from the Far Eastern front. His last message to Moscow was to the effect that Japan would shortly attack Britain and the U.S.A. in the Far East.

But in paying tribute to Sorge one must not forget his equally brilliant assistant, Ozaki. He was all along Sorge's chief informant and, like Sorge himself, he was able to evaluate what he had heard and to explain the implications of Japanese policy. When Japan's drive into China was slowed down Ozaki was made unofficial adviser on China to the Japanese Cabinet. He held this post until the fall of the Konoye Cabinet in 1939 and was then made adviser to the South Manchurian Railway, which again gave him links with the Cabinet and put him in an excellent position for furnishing further intelligence to Sorge.

Major-General Charles A. Willoughby, General MacArthur's chief of intelligence, said of Ozaki: 'He never passed on undigested information. He stored up his knowledge, weighed it against other relevant data, and made a preliminary evaluation. He discussed his conclusions with officials, his associates and friends. . . . He presented only final evaluations in answer to Sorge's questions.'

At his subsequent trial Ozaki stated that his success 'lay in my attitude to my job. By nature I am a sociable person. I like people, I can make friends with most people. Moreover I like to be kind to people. . . . The important thing is to ascertain the general trend rather than to know exactly what has been said, or what has been decided.'

And, of course, Ozaki's close links with Prince Konoye's circle provided him with a great deal of information on Japan's plans for war against the U.S.A. and Britain.

It was part treachery and partly two fatal errors by the masterspy himself which brought about the arrest of Sorge and the destruction of his network. He had been aware for some time that the Japanese were convinced there was a spy inside the German Embassy and that they were watching him more closely than usual. He had achieved great things and his wisest plan would have been to close down the network except for a handful of trusted agents and to have left the country. The secret police had suspected an illegal radio transmitter was being used by the Russians in Tokyo and, in case any surprise search of apartments in the city might reveal something, he had the radio placed in the cabin of a fishing boat which he had hired: here Klausen tapped out his messages to Moscow.

But Sorge wanted to ascertain the exact date and place from which the Japanese would launch their attack on the Americans. While waiting to get this information from Ozaki, instead of lying low Sorge conducted a liaison with a new Japanese girl he had only recently met. What he should have realised was that the girl had been planted on him by Colonel Osaki of the Secret Police. This girl, Kiyomi, was herself a trained spy and she did not miss the fact that a waiter dropped a tiny ball of rice paper on the restaurant table they were sharing and that Sorge smoothed out the paper and read the message on it.

The message was a warning to Sorge that the secret police's watch was being intensified. Little did he know that his mistress had straight away telephoned the dreaded Kempeitai, informing them of the incident.

Meanwhile Sorge received the news he had hoped for – the date of the proposed Japanese attack against the Americans at Pearl Harbor, scheduled for 6 December. Perhaps he was too elated at this success, for he rejoined Kiyomi the next day, which was a fatal error. The girl was now on the look out for further screwed up balls of rice paper and sure enough the waiter dropped one on the dance floor while they were dancing. Sorge picked it up and learned that the Kempeitai were hot on his trail and that he was urged to escape immediately.

Official instructions to Russian spies were that all such secret messages should be burned at the first opportunity. It was an elementary rule. But Sorge, possibly nervous by this time, bungled the job. He tried to make his lighter work on the pretence of lighting a cigarette while he and Kiyomi were in a car. When the lighter failed him he asked Kiyomi for a light, but she pretended she could not give him one. Finally, and apparently exasperated, he threw his cigarette and the rice paper out of the window and drove off. That was his second fatal error. Kiyomi later asked Sorge to stop the car so that she could warn her parents that she was staying out for the night. He foolishly agreed and she rang up the secret police and told them exactly where the papers had been dropped. They were immediately recovered and from that moment Sorge's doom was sealed.

Next day Sorge was arrested and Voukelitch, Klausen, Ozaki and Miyagi, an artists' agent, were swiftly rounded up. Altogether thirty-five members of the network were arrested in connection with the Sorge affair. Most of them were Japanese. By the end of October 1941 the Soviet spy system in Japan was virtually destroyed.

The real culprit in all this was undoubtedly a Japanese Communist, Ito Ritsu, who had been arrested by the Kempeitai in June 1941, on the grounds that he was suspected of underground Communist activities. To save his skin Ito Ritsu pleaded that he had already seen the error of his ways and offered information about other members of the Japanese Communist Party. This led the police on the trail first of Miyagi, then of Ozaki and Sorge.

The Germans were dumbfounded at Sorge's arrest for they obviously knew nothing of the Kempeitai's suspicions and believed the Japanese had blundered in putting their own man in prison. They made strenuous efforts to have Sorge released but without success. Possibly Sorge was over-confident and convinced that the Germans would bring pressure on the Japanese to release him, but of course he had no knowledge of the uncovering of the network by the Kempeitai. He merely thought they were shadowing him.

Branko de Voukelitch received a life sentence for his part in the spy network and he died in 1945. Max Klausen, the radio operator, also had a life sentence, but was released in 1945. Ozaki and Sorge were both hanged on the same day, 7 November 1944, after their appeals had been rejected. Both men faced death with courage and dignity, Ozaki spending his last days writing exceptionally beautiful love letters to his wife, one of which was later made into a book entitled *Love Was Like A Falling Star*. Sorge thanked the prison officials 'for all your kindness', but made no other statement before walking to the death cell.

17

The Belgian and the 'Lucy' Networks

IF THE practice ground for World War II was in the arena of the Spanish Civil War, it can also be said that Spain, too, was the testing ground for the new type of intelligence agent who had been superseding those purged by Moscow.

The 'Execution Squad's' rôle in Spain was threefold: to find out and eliminate those agents of the old school suspected of Trotskyite leanings, or having other deviationist proclivities; to report on the reliability of the new agents in the field, about the only occasion on which the Squad was employed in this way; and the organisation of the plot to kill Trotsky.

A number of new key intelligence chiefs were switched to Spain about this time. One of these was Otto Katz, the son of a textile manufacturer in Prague, who, because of his friendship with Kafka, decided he wanted to become a figure of importance in the literary world, so with help from his father he started a highbrow periodical. In the late twenties Katz was launching out in theatrical production and started a left-wing theatre group in Berlin. It was through this theatre, the *Volksbuehne*, that he first made contact with the Russians, inviting a company from a Moscow theatre to come to Berlin.

Katz might well have remained no more than a dabbler in the arts and the founder of a theatre for revolutionary plays but for the fact that he lost his chief backer when his father became a bankrupt during the slump. His theatre collapsed for lack of funds and Katz asked his Communist friends if they could find him a job. In 1929 he was invited to go to Moscow, ostensibly to discuss theatrical productions, but in fact to be asked to join the Secret Service. It was a deliberate choice on Moscow's part. The N.K.V.D. were highly suspicious of the German Communist, Willi Muenzenberg, who ran a Communist publishing business in Berlin, and they believed he had lined his pockets with the profits of a business which, they felt, rightly belonged to the Party. Therefore, they ordered Katz to join Muenzenberg's publishing house in order to watch its proprietor and report on his activities.

When Hitler came to power Katz was moved to France, where he was given the job of screening Communists who fled from Germany to escape the Nazi purges. Katz's task was to seek out *agents provocateurs* who might be infiltrated into France in this manner. He must have performed this work satisfactorily because in 1936 he was given an assignment in Spain. The official reason for this was that he had been selected to act as N.K.V.D. liaison officer between the Spanish Republican Government and their embassy in Paris. By using this official status with the Republicans as a 'cover', Katz was a link man with the 'Execution Squad', shadowing suspects and with the power to recommend to the Squad any Russian agent or Spanish Liberals who, in his opinion, needed to be liquidated. It was at this time that Katz was brought into the network specially built up to track down and liquidate Trotsky.

Katz adopted various aliases, frequently posing as a Frenchman. He was promoted to the rank of colonel in the N.K.V.D. and shortly before the war returned to Paris using the name of M. André Simone. It was ironical that Katz, a Czech Jew, should become practically immune from arrest by the Gestapo. What was truly horrible was that during the brief honeymoon period between Germany and Russia after the signing of the German-Soviet Pact, he was also responsible for sending a number of Jews to their deaths. When the Germans occupied France Colonel Katz had the full protection afforded to him by the terms of the Pact and he used it to inform the Gestapo of any Jewish Trotskyite the Russians wanted executed or put behind bars. Among those who escaped from the Gestapo was Willi Muenzenberg, his former employer, but Katz tracked him down in France and had him murdered.

Meanwhile in Spain Kim Philby had been under observation by the N.K.V.D. As a war correspondent attached to the Franco forces he was already being tested as an agent of the Russians. Philby's biographers state that 'he was never content with knowing the general details of troop movements. He insisted on numbers, divisions, regiments – information far more detailed than any of the readers of *The Times* would have required. What was he doing with it? . . . there seems little doubt that it was in Spain that Philby made his first careful, tentative contacts with the Intelligence Service he was later to dominate.'

Another British-born agent of the Russians was also being tried out in Spain. He was Alexander Foote, then an officer of the International Brigade on the Republican side. He was a left-winger with strong Communist sympathies, but more in his support for the idea of forming a Popular Front for a war on fascism than in any ideological sense.

The manner in which the Russians recruited Philby and Foote is worthy of study if only to throw light on Soviet methods in finding new agents and testing them at this period. It took much longer for Philby to prove himself because he had been set the harder, if not the more courageous rôle, of infiltrating the British Secret Service on behalf of the Soviet. The Russians were clever enough to realise that Philby had excellent contacts and that for this reason he needed to be given a freer hand, but there were initially grave doubts as to whether he would ever make a really professional spy. Philby was quixotic and contemptuous where Foote was discreet, self-effacing, cool and imbued with common sense. Foote had the advantage over Philby that he had never been a member of the Communist Party. The Russians' initial fear about Philby was that he would never be able to hide his earlier Communist associations and that, in posing as a pro-German and acting as a war correspondent with the Franco forces, he would cause questions to be asked in the ranks of British Intelligence. The swing from one political extreme to the other was surely enough to cause even the most obtuse eyebrow to be raised. Had Philby been a person of no social significance, questions might well have been asked, but in those days to belong to the 'right class' was regarded as a guarantee of patriotism and moral rectitude in Britain.

The fact that Foote had never been a member of the Communist Party counted in his favour with the Russians. They were impressed by his sincerity and his efficiency as an officer and by the relative anonymity of his middle-class background. It was noted with approval that while more extrovert members of the International Brigade often took an independent, even a critical attitude, to their superiors, Foote carried out orders without demur. No fewer than four N.K.V.D. members had reported favourably on him.

Even then his recruitment was organised in a roundabout fashion. He was first tested for his capacity for obedience. Foote was told that, though an officer, he would be required to act as driver of a Red Cross truck travelling to and from Britain. Without any questions he agreed with alacrity. In London he had to report to the Communist Party headquarters in King Street. There he was informed that he had been recommended for a special and dangerous mission overseas. No details were given to him, but he accepted the proposition. He was then told to report to a certain address.

'It was an autumn day in October 1938. The leaves were still on the trees lining that pleasant road in St John's Wood, and there was still something of summer in the air as I walked towards the house with the green door – the door of the flat where I was to be recruited into the Russian Secret Service,' declared Foote.

Yet, as will eventually be seen, it was the upper class, public-school-educated Philby who became the traitor to his country, while Alexander Foote ultimately helped the British cause from inside the Russian Secret Service.

The advent of the Gestapo and its relentless purge of Communist elements had forced the Soviet Union to re-create its Secret Service networks outside Germany at almost feverish speed. The few agents left inside Germany were often isolated from any contact with their network controllers for weeks, if not months on end. One advantage of the German–Soviet Pact was that it gave Russia a chance to complete network building before it was too late. There was much to be done in those months of the 'phoney war' period. Each control base had to be supplied with short-wave radio equipment, operators had to be trained, new codes distributed, couriers arranged and 'letter-boxes' fixed. Resident Directors of networks were allowed very little scope for independent action and the new centralised total control ensured that the Centre in Moscow was no longer hampered by the problems posed when the N.K.V.D., G.R.U. and the Comintern operated separately.

Yet Russia, like Britain, still suffered severely when Germany launched her all-out *blitzkrieg* in 1940. When Belgium, part of France, Denmark, Holland and Norway were occupied by the Nazis all networks in these countries were disrupted. The Dutch network was ordered to remain passive and to take no action when Hitler invaded Holland other than the reporting of German troop movements. On the other hand the head of the Belgian network, Leopold Trepper, a Polish Jew, was for a period put in charge of all networks in this part of Europe. He had a reputation of being one of the most skilled operators in the Soviet ranks and was highly regarded by Stalin himself. In consequence he was given a greater freedom of action than any other Resident Director. Trepper was assisted by Viktor Sukuloff, a Latvian, and linked to him in the enlarged network were another Polish Jew, Sophie Pozanska, who was the cipher expert, Mikhail Makaroff, a relative of Molotoff, the Soviet Foreign Minister, and Rita Arnould, a German who ran the network headquarters.

This headquarters, which was intended to link up the networks in Holland, Denmark, Belgium and France, was situated in a house in the Rue des Attrebates, in a suburb of Brussels. It was cunningly hidden for the agents who controlled it were tenants of an aged Belgian widow who occupied rooms in the house and she had no suspicion of the nature of their work. Trepper also set up a 'front' for his network in the firm of Simexco, which was nominally a supplier of building materials. Most of the latter were sold to the Germans and in this way Trepper sought to infiltrate his way into the Todt (German construction) Organisation.

Trepper had had a variety of jobs before he came into espionage. For a brief spell he had been at Cracow University, then he worked as a locksmith (a useful apprenticeship for any spy), a steel worker in Poland where he was imprisoned for Communist activities, spent some time in Palestine and at the age of twenty-eight went to Russia and received training as a spy. In 1940 he managed to get himself invited on a Nazi-sponsored conducted tour of France to be shown how the Germans organised their invasion of that country. As a result he was able to give Moscow a detailed report of the whole operation.

At last Russia had a distinct advantage over the Germans in radio transmitting techniques and as a result they were able both to monitor German military radio and to get their own messages back to Moscow without detection. But Berlin soon became aware of what was happening and orders went out both to the Gestapo and the *Abwehr* that the radio station of the Soviet network in Belgium must be tracked down.

Believing that they had completely fooled the Germans, the Russians became careless. Instead of restricting their traffic, or changing their headquarters, they stayed in the house in the Brussels suburb and increased both the length of their transmitting time and the frequency with which they used it. By constant observation in that painstaking manner for which German Intelligence agents are famed the *Abwehr*, always keener than the Gestapo when it came to tackling the Russians, eventually pinpointed the area in which the radio set must be situated. Finally on 13 December 1941, No. 101, Rue des Attrebates was raided, the radio transmitter was found and Rita Arnould, Sophie Pozanska and Makaroff were caught.

Trepper was saved by adopting, curiously enough, a ploy used during the Civil War by the White Russians when avoiding arrest. He arrived at headquarters while the *Abwehr* were conducting

232

their search, but had the presence of mind to pretend to be a salesman. It was lucky for him that the *Abwehr* and not the Gestapo were conducting the raid for they let him go. He escaped to France and continued his work from there.

But the discovery of the headquarters in Brussels was a serious blow for Russia. Makaroff was tortured and died without giving away any information. Sophie Pozanska swallowed a cyanide tablet before the Germans could interrogate her. But Rita Arnould told all she knew and even gave away the names of Trepper and Sukuloff. This treachery did not save her: she was executed almost as soon as the *Abwehr* learned all she had to tell them.

Quick thinking by Trepper salved something from the wreckage, but the Belgian network was virtually destroyed, for no one could be sure how many people Rita Arnould had compromised, and all the codes had to be changed though in fact on this occasion the Germans had not obtained them.

When Trepper and Sukuloff fled from Belgium a Finn named Konstantin Yefremoff took charge of what remained of the Belgian network. It was a brave thing to do for the Germans were desperately trying to round up the remainder of its members and Yefremoff could not be sure whether he was on the list of suspects. His instructions were to lie low while information was diverted to France, but to obtain at all costs a radio operator to set up a new transmitting station. He solved this problem in desperation by bringing in Johann Wenzel who had been in charge of the Dutch network. He was skilled in radio techniques and had operated a station in Holland which had kept the Russians well supplied with information on German troop movements. In selecting Wenzel Yefremoff made a grave error. Rita Arnould had given the Germans details about Wenzel's activities and, though he operated successfully for a time, the Germans were searching for him. When they learned he had left Holland it was not difficult to guess he had moved to Belgium. In June 1942 the *Abwehr* located the new radio station and Wenzel was arrested.

At first Wenzel refused to tell the *Abwehr* anything. Eventually they gave him a choice: death, or collaboration. To counter-espionage authorities a live radio operator who is prepared to collaborate is an invaluable asset not only because of what he can reveal, but also because of how he can be used to put out false messages. This was the proposition the *Abwehr* set before him.

' . . . the police intercepted a great number of wireless messages which they succeeded in deciphering by means of the key revealed by Wenzel after an exhaustive interrogation by the police,' stated the Gestapo report of 21 December 1942. 'From these messages important indications of the existence of a Soviet intelligence organisation in Berlin were obtained.'

This was the Germans' first success against what came to be known as *Rote Kapelle* (The Red Orchestra) to the *Abwehr*. In Soviet espionage terminology a radio operator was a musician and the short-wave radio transmitting set was known as a 'musical box'. This much the Germans knew, which was why as much in admiration as in anger they dubbed it *Rote Kapelle*. For it had been apparent in Berlin for a long time that many German military secrets were being radioed back to Moscow.

It was Moscow's insistent pressure on the radio operators, of course, which had increased the risks of using it and in the end enabled the *Abwehr* to close in on the transmission stations. The Centre in Moscow had bombarded the Belgian network with inquiries. The Gestapo reports of this period – 1941–42 – indicate from messages intercepted that Moscow was asking for such information as the disposition of German troops in Belgium, the size of the Swiss Army, the anti-aircraft defences in Holland and Belgium, production figures from various arms factories and details of troop-movements in Holland.

Eventually Wenzel capitulated to German threats and agreed to co-operate. From that moment *Rote Kapelle* was doomed. As Wenzel revealed who the intermediaries were so the Gestapo or the *Abwehr* interrogated them and this led to further betrayals. Finally Yefremoff was caught. He withstood all threats by the *Abwehr*, who were much more subtle than the Gestapo in their methods of interrogation, until they hinted that if he still refused to collaborate they would notify his family in Russia that he had betrayed the network. Yefremoff was devoted to his family and could not bear the thought of their believing he was a traitor. He, like Wenzel, began to give away information, and from his admissions the Germans effectively destroyed the whole network in Belgium and that in Holland, too.

In the years immediately preceding these incidents the Russians had been busily engaged on the other side of the Atlantic tracking down their three remaining most important enemies, Léon Trotsky in Mexico, the defector, Walter Krivitsky, and Alexander Orloff, who had been head of the Economic Section of the Cheka.

Orloff alone escaped. He had been sent to Spain to obtain economic intelligence and, learning at first hand something of the operations of the 'Execution Squad', cast caution to the winds and published articles about the 'Soviet terror in Spain'. Orloff blamed Stalin personally for the work of the Squad, declaring that 'the decision to perform an "execution" abroad, a rather risky affair, was up to Stalin personally. If he ordered it, a so-called mobile brigade was dispatched to carry it out. It was too dangerous to operate through local agents who might deviate later and start to talk.'

Much of the activities of the 'Execution Squad' were later described by Orloff in his book *The Secret History of Stalin's Crimes*.

Krivitsky, as we have seen, became a figure of great importance in the Soviet espionage networks before the war. He was frail-looking, pale and whimsical with a childish smile, but in serious mood he awed people with his fixed stare from beneath bushy eyebrows. He had lived in Vienna and the sophistication of that capital had to some extent caused him to look with a critical eye on the Bolshevik hierarchy. He regarded himself as much more politically mature than they were and did not always take care to hide the fact. He had been Resident Director of Soviet espionage in Vienna during the forged bill racket of the thirties and was later Resident Director in Holland.

As early as 1935 Krivitsky told Ignace Reiss's wife that 'they do not trust us'. It was quite obvious who 'they' were. 'They need us,' he added, 'but they can't trust us. We are International Communists. Our time is over. They will replace us with Soviet Communists, men like Zarubin to whom the revolutionary movement means nothing.'

Yet Krivitsky took a long time to make up his mind to defect. He still hoped that a miracle would happen, that Stalin might disappear and that repression would be ended. When Ignace Reiss was murdered he seemed to make up his mind: he sent an enigmatic message to Elisabeth Poretsky that he had 'broken with my employers'. He added, 'If you receive this letter answer it by inserting an advertisement in *L'Oeuvre* and sign it as I do, Krusia.'

Krivitsky defected first to France and then went to the United States. His revelations have already been mentioned in some detail. For the rest they were over-sensationalised by the interpreters and ghost writers he employed, leavened with a good deal of inaccuracy, but in part at least of great value.

Krivitsky was given an American passport and lived comfortably enough in the Bellevue Hotel on Capitol Hill in Washington. Then on 11 February 1941 a maid found him in his room with his head blown off, a blood-stained revolver by his side and four ambiguous farewell notes.

Suicide was the official verdict, but his friends did not believe he had killed himself. They said that Krivitsky was safe and financially secure, that he was not the type to commit suicide and that the farewell letters had been dictated at gun point. U.S. Intelligence circles suspected that the 'suicide' was staged and that the Soviet Secret Service had plotted his death. Louis Waldman, his lawyer, stated that he was convinced that 'Krivitsky's death was not simple suicide. He had been informed by a messenger that a notorious G.P.U. assassin named Hans Bruesse had arrived in New York and towards the end he was grey with fear. Also he had further very damaging evidence to offer the British Government.'

Certainly Hans Bruesse was a member of the 'Execution Squad' and actively engaged in tracking down Trotsky. But the killing of Trotsky was made a more difficult operation because Beria had himself laid it down that Trotsky must be killed without anyone being able to attribute his death to the N.K.V.D. Possibly because of this, almost certainly through poor organisation, the assassination of the former Soviet War Minister was most clumsily carried out and resulted in two bungled attempts on his life before he was finally silenced for ever. This was partly due to the removal of the key Soviet agents planning the operation shortly before the first attempt was made on Trotsky's life. A crude attack was launched on the Trotsky villa by Spanish and Mexican Communists disguised in Mexican Army uniforms. This failed in its main aim, but the would-be assassins kidnapped and later murdered Trotsky's secretary, the American, Robert Sheldon Harte. The Mexican police were unable to prove anything, but they suspected that Harte was involved in the plot and that he had been killed in case he talked.

In May 1940 a similar team of ill-assorted assassins attacked Trotsky's villa with sub-machine-guns and incendiary bombs, but Trotsky and his wife saved their lives by hiding under their beds. Meanwhile Trotsky's bodyguard engaged the attackers and eventually drove them off. The Mexican police gave chase, but never caught or identified the gang. Now fully aware that Moscow was prepared to go to any lengths to liquidate him, Trotsky ordered his villa to be strengthened against any future attacks.

Beria was furious at what he regarded rightly as incompetent bungling. No doubt he had every reason to fear Stalin's displeasure. But, luckily for Beria, he was able to prove that a direct assault on the Trotsky villa had never been his intention and that more than a year before he had himself selected a man who was to infiltrate the Trotsky entourage and to be personally responsible for killing the leader of the anti-Stalinist Communists.

Beria had asked Mihail Shpiglglas, the officer in charge of the Spanish section of the 'Execution Squad' to submit names to him for this purpose. 'It will not be easy,' replied Shpiglglas, 'for Trotsky is prepared for attacks on his life and he is well protected.

If he is to be killed, it must be done by somebody who has won his trust and can gain admission to his villa. I would suggest a Spaniard or a Mexican.'

One of the first to be consulted was a Spanish female agent of the G.P.U., Maria Caridad del Rio Mercader. This fanatical devotee of Communism, inspired with all the hates and passions of her race, had been born of devout Catholic parents and at seventeen had developed mystical religious tendencies, for a short time entering a Carmelite convent as a novice. But this phase passed and at the age of nineteen she was married to Pablo Mercader in Barcelona. There were five children of the marriage.

In 1925 Caridad left her husband and took her five children to France where she lived first in Toulouse and then at Bordeaux. Here she fell in love with a young airman who was a Communist and persuaded her to accept its doctrines. Caridad did nothing by halves: just as mysticism had driven her into a convent so conversion to Communism drove her into service with the G.P.U.

She joined the G.P.U. in about 1927 or 1928 and during the Spanish Civil War became secretary of the Union of Communist Women in Catalonia. She saw service in the front line at Aragon and was wounded from aerial bombardment. It was about this time that she came to the attention of Shpiglglas who regarded her as a dedicated professional agent who had amassed a great deal of information on the Trotskyite circle and close friends of the Trotskys.

Beria was taken aback when Caridad declared that she would trust nobody for such an assignment as the killing of Trotsky except herself.

'Impossible,' she was told. 'It is quite out of the question for a woman to undertake this task.'

'Then,' replied Caridad, 'if you will not accept me, you must take my son and I will vouch for him personally.'

Rarely in the history of espionage can a woman have made such a strange request. She must have known that she was risking sending her son to his death.

As Shpiglglas supported Caridad, Beria somewhat reluctantly at first acquiesced in the plan. Caridad's son, Ramon Jacobo del Rio Mercader, had already done some work on behalf of the Comintern. He was now ordered to adopt the name of Jacson and, briefed by his mother, to mix in Trotskyite circles in Paris. But was it Caridad's lover who really pressed her son into this assignment? Nicolas Khokhloff, the former Soviet agent who defected to the U.S.A. in the fifties, asserted that the assassination of Trotsky had been organised by G.P.U. agent, Léonide Eitingon, 'the lover of Caridad Mercader', and that it was he who 'recruited a

Spaniard who received minute instructions from Moscow to go to Mexico under the name of Mornard'.

Young Mercader used both the names Jacson and Mornard from this time onwards. He struck up an acquaintance with Sylvia Ageloff, a friend of Trotsky's wife, pretending to be a Canadian of French origin. In 1939 Sylvia Ageloff went to New York, Mercader followed her, having been given a Canadian passport in the name of Antoni Babich, a Yugoslav who had become a naturalised Canadian in 1929. Babich had left Canada in 1937, ostensibly to return to Yugoslavia for a holiday but in fact to join the International Brigade in Spain. The N.K.V.D. became interested in him and confiscated his passport and all his identity papers. This was a tactic often employed by the N.K.V.D. to obtain passports for their agents during the Spanish Civil War period; sometimes those robbed of their passports were liquidated. On this occasion Babich was shortly afterwards announced to be 'killed in action' and his papers were given to Mercader.

But, having arrived in the U.S.A. under the name of Babich, Mercader contacted the Soviet Resident Director in New York and received new passports in the names of both Jacson and Mornard. He once again met Sylvia Ageloff, followed her to Mexico City and eventually persuaded her to introduce him to Trotsky. The latter was always suspicious of strangers and took some convincing before he agreed to a meeting. But he seems to have taken a liking to Mercader, who had an attractive personality, and several visits followed the first, but always with others, including Trotsky's bodyguard, present.

The bungling of the two attempts on Trotsky's life, however, had changed the situation. Until May 1940 Beria had been prepared to play for time and to await the right moment for Mercader to play his rôle. But Stalin was getting impatient and Beria knew that any further failures would have serious repercussions. For there was now an awful suspicion in the Kremlin that Trotsky himself might have engineered the two attacks on his life. Beria was in a quandary: he was faced with two possibilities, first, that his own men had blundered, secondly, that Trotsky had made a fool of the G.P.U. And he had no means of establishing the truth. The Mexican police were certain that Harte, Trotsky's secretary, had been involved in the first plot, and they were even less impressed when Trotsky insisted his secretary was guiltless.

There is some evidence that Trotsky deliberately staged both the first and second attempts on his life, mainly to discredit the Stalinists, but also to bring pressure to bear on the Mexicans to give him better police protection. In 1939–40 Trotsky believed himself to be the only geniune Communist leader in the old revolutionary tradition. Despite his German origins he had always pointed to Germany as the real enemy of Soviet Russia and the German–Soviet Pact gave him the opportunity to announce to the world that Stalin was a traitor to Communist ideals and a truckler with fascism. As a former War Minister he also knew how Stalin's purges had bled the Red Army of some of its best generals. He half believed that it was not too late for him to be called from exile to lead a great crusade against German militarism. To stage an attack on his own life and to pin the blame on Stalin would have been a splendid propaganda ploy for him. As to the kidnapping and murder of the secretary, Harte, the Mexican police were convinced that Harte knew of his master's imbroglio and was killed by Trotsky's bodyguard to prevent him from revealing the truth.

All this caused intensive pressure to be put on young Mercader. It was pointed out to Beria that Mercader had been given a good deal of money during the past year and that he had acquired an expensive American car and was living in comparative luxury in the rôle of a businessman. He was reputed to have given Sylvia Ageloff considerable sums of money, having seduced her under promise of marriage. Members of the 'Execution Squad' who had kept Mercader under observation warned that he was leading a soft life and that he appeared hesitant about the task before him, making excuses that it was almost impossible to see Trotsky alone. No doubt Mercader realised that after the two murder attempts Trotsky was far too well guarded for him to be able to kill his selected victim and make good his escape.

So the threats were stepped up as Moscow became more apprehensive about the whole affair. Mercader was told he must kill Trotsky forthwith or else his mother and his brother would be held hostages until he accomplished the deed. He argued that he had carried out the essentials of his assignment, that he had won the confidence of Sylvia Ageloff with a promise of marriage and had got himself accepted into the Trotsky ménage, but that he must be allowed to choose the right moment for carrying out his main objective. But to ensure that he was fully conscious of his filial duties the N.K.V.D. had, while using the ultimate weapon of threatening to make his mother a hostage, sent her to Mexico in company with her lover, Léonide Eitingon, at the end of the Spanish Civil War. The noose was being slipped slowly round Mercader's neck: the N.K.V.D. believed that only her fanaticism and her devotion to Eitingon would ultimately force Mercader into action. Both Caridad and Eitingon came under the direction of Dr Gregor Rabinovich, the Soviet director of Intelligence in New York, known by the code name of 'Roberts' and ostensibly a Red Cross officer in that city. Rabinovich was the real organiser of the murder of Trotsky. He arranged a conference with Mercader at which both the latter's mother and Eitingon were present. It was again made plain to Mercader that he must kill Trotsky and then either kill himself or make good his escape; if he failed to kill Trotsky or was caught actually killing him, his mother and brother would be made hostages to ensure his silence.

In such circumstances it was hardly surprising that Mercader only partially carried out his assignment. He went to see Trotsky again on 20 August 1940 and asked for his advice on an article he had written. Trotsky took him into his study and, as he pored over the manuscript, Mercader took from his raincoat pocket an ice-pick and hit him on the head. Trotsky's screams brought his bodyguard running into the room and Mercader was seized. It was then that he told them: 'I had to kill him, because they forced me to do it . . . they are holding my mother prisoner.'

Trotsky died the following day. Mercader was interrogated by the police who had great difficulty in establishing his identity. They knew him only under the name of Mornard and his story was that he hated Trotsky because he was an enemy of true socialism and had even tried to persuade him to go to Russia to kill Stalin.

The N.K.V.D. had hoped that Trotsky's bodyguard would kill him, but Mercader had failed to kill Trotsky instantaneously and that had saved his life. For Trotsky had just sufficient strength to tell them: 'Don't kill him. He must be made to talk first.' Convicted of the murder of Trotsky, Mercader was for years terrified that the G.P.U. would plan his death even inside a prison. He was afraid to eat his food in case he would be poisoned and he refused to have visitors. What happened to his mother is somewhat of a mystery, but at the end of World War II she was allowed to go to Mexico and to visit her son in prison.

His life meanwhile had been comparatively pleasant. He was allowed to start a radio business in his prison cell and to keep the money he made out of it. Gradually he lost his fear of the outside world, no doubt reassured by his mother, and he had a regular girl visitor to his cell, eventually marrying her while he was still in jail. In due course he was released and, still somewhat fearful of his ultimate fate, left by Russian ship for an unknown destination.

As the *Abwehr* and the Gestapo closed in on the Russian networks in Occupied Europe in 1940–42 so the Soviet Union came increasingly to rely on its Swiss espionage group for acquiring intelligence.

The network in France had been taken over by Trepper when he escaped from Belgium. Next to the Swiss section it was easily the most important in Western Europe at that time, but its size (there were at least three sub-sections), its vulnerability to being infiltrated by unreliable Communist Party members and the fact that it was still in the process of reorganisation were distinct disadvantages. Then again the Russians had taken a grave and unprofessional risk in allowing Trepper to take control of the French network, knowing that the network he had previously controlled in Belgium not only had been destroyed by the Nazis, but some of its members had been forced into collaboration with the Germans.

In October 1942 when the *Abwehr* officers in Belgium came to Paris with some of the defecting Soviet agents they rounded up about twenty Russian agents. Their prime aim was to capture Trepper, on whom they now had a complete dossier, and two former Soviet agents were offered absolute freedom if they would lure Trepper into their clutches.

Meanwhile the Swiss network was absolutely vital to the Centre in Moscow. It had been reorganised after the assassination of Ignace Reiss and put on a war footing. Small, highly efficient, well equipped with radio transmission facilities, this network had grown out of the tiny G.R.U. section which operated in Switzerland up to about 1937. Its leader was a woman, Ursula-Maria Hamburger, generally known by her code name of 'Sonia'. She and her husband, Rudolf, were both members of the German Communist Party and before coming to Switzerland they had operated on behalf of the Soviet Union in Poland and China.

When Alexander Foote was recruited into the Russian Secret Service his first instructions had been to present himself 'outside the General Post Office in Geneva. . . . I was to be wearing a white scarf and to be holding in my right hand a leather belt. As the clock struck noon I would be approached by a woman carrying a string shopping bag containing a green parcel; she would be holding an orange in her hand. . . . The woman would ask me, in English, where I had bought the belt, and I was to reply that I had bought it in an ironmonger's shop in Paris. Then I was to ask where I could buy an orange like hers and she was to say I could have hers for an English penny.'

The woman he actually met outside the G.P.O. in Geneva was 'Sonia'. The briefing for this meeting may seem more like something invented by a novelist than fact, but complicated details such as these are standard procedure in the Russian Secret Service. Rendezvous places like a general post office or a museum are favoured because they are not unusual meeting places and so many people are normally waiting for friends outside such places that an additional loiterer does not attract much attention. On the other hand many professional spies dislike such a rendezvous because they are always afraid that any one of the other people waiting could be a counter-spy, or a plain-clothes policeman. The tremendous detail worked out for identification has two purposes: one is to make misidentification almost impossible, the other is to test the spy's memory.

Foote was informed that the network in Switzerland had been set up primarily for mounting espionage against Germany and he was soon detailed to go to Munich. There he had to pose as a tourist, for which he was given enough money to last him for three months at which time he was to return to a rendezvous in Lausanne.

One of the advantages of Switzerland as a centre of espionage was its traditional neutrality. This worked two ways in favour of the spying power operating within its borders. The strict neutrality laws meant that there was no discrimination against any one country and, if anything, the Swiss preferred to turn a blind eye to espionage rather than to act against a foreign power.

'Sonia's' cover in Switzerland was that of a smartly but un-ostentatiously dressed woman of independent means, living with her two children and a maidservant at a villa at Caux, high up above Montreux. The home was an admirable vantage point for a short-wave transmission station for sending messages to Moscow.

She had received orders from the Centre to pull back her agents inside Germany as soon as war started and meanwhile to build up the small network in Switzerland. About fifty agents in all were eventually attached to the network. In the main these were dedicated Communists working for the cause either without any pay at all, or for very low salaries. Some were Germans, two were Frenchmen and four Britons also joined the network, two of whom were actually infiltrated with the knowledge of the British Secret Service.

The importance of the Swiss network after 1939 can be gauged from the amount of money spent on it between then and 1944. The Swiss police discovered some papers relating to the finances of the network towards the end of the war and these revealed that expenses rose from 2,500 Swiss francs in 1939 to more than 20,000 francs in 1943. Alexander Foote threw some light on this when he stated that he spent 21,730 francs in two years and that his salary, which started at 650 francs a month, rose eventually to 1,300 francs.

The Regional Director of the Swiss network was Alexander Rado, an experienced agent of the G.R.U., Hungarian by birth,* who at one time had operated a news agency in France as a cover for his work. But it was in Switzerland that he made his name as

* His real name was Alexandre Wassilijewcz Kuliczew.

a skilled and discriminating spy chief. He had originally been a member of Bela Kun's organisation and at the age of nineteen, when Kun's rebellion in Hungary petered out, escaped to Moscow. He had been appointed in charge of the Swiss network at the time of the purges in 1936–37.

Rado's greatest asset was his personal charm, which won him a wide circle of friends, none of whom suspected his true rôle but all of whom in some way or other unwittingly served his purpose. He had a genius for drawing intelligence out of/unsuspecting friends. In Geneva he lived an outwardly respectable life with his wife, a German named Helene, and his two sons. His weaknesses were a love of luxury and, consequently, a tendency to play fast and loose with the network's funds. He was also rather too much of an individualist for Moscow's tastes and did not always keep strictly to the rules laid down for Soviet agents.

One of the somewhat demoralising factors with which the Swiss network had to cope was that the Centre in Moscow only belatedly realised how vital it was to their interests. This was a bad error of judgement on the part of the Centre, and it was reflected in a certain meanness in supplying the network with regular funds. To some extent this explained the irregularities which Rado used to practise, for as the war continued and as expenses grew so the Director of the network had to seek other means of acquiring funds to carry on the work. This was sometimes achieved by obtaining money from other networks, particularly from the U.S.A.

In the end the Swiss Intelligence acquired a complete picture of how the whole network was operated and financed and there were clear indications that some of the monies belonging to the network were used by Rado in promoting his numerous love affairs. Rado foolishly mixed work and pleasure and though this might give him an excuse for devoting espionage funds to financing mistresses who became his agents, it was a gross breach of all the rules.

The network was supposed to operate independently of and to be unknown to the Swiss Communist Party, but in fact Rado again broke the rules by establishing contacts with two of the most prominent members of this Party, Karl Hofmaier and Léon Nicole.

Despite these shortcomings, Rado succeeded for a long time because of the quality of the intelligence he provided. He also ensured that this was passed on to Moscow by the speediest possible method of communication – radio.

The most valuable intelligence supplied by Rado's ring was that concerning German military moves. While not detracting in any way from the ability of the network to organise its own intelligence, it must be conceded that to a considerable extent they owed much to indirect aid from the British and a degree of infiltration of the

Soviet network by the British. At this time Britain had most to gain by doing everything in her power to ensure that Soviet Russia realised that Germany was planning to invade her. Russian mistrust at the highest level made this extremely difficult, but fortunately there were some Soviet agents who, not being themselves Russian, and therefore not narrowly suspicious of British motives, were prepared to co-operate. But the real problem was how to help the Russians without the Russians themselves knowing who was helping them.

Thus it was essential for the British to pass intelligence on German movements to the Russians by devious means. In their book *La Guerre a été gagnée en Suisse* Pierre Accoce and Pierre Quet have described how the 'Lucy Ring' in Geneva made all the difference between a Russian victory and defeat. Through this unique clandestine Secret Service set-up, plans and orders of the German High Command on the Eastern Front right down to brigade level were transmitted to Moscow daily after the invasion of Russia by the Germans. It was a remarkable feat, certainly one of the most efficient radio transmission feats in espionage history and probably the most effective single intelligence operation of the war. It saved countless Russian lives and eventually helped to stabilise the Soviet Union's defensive positions.

'Lucy' was the code name of Rudolf Roessler, a German publisher who moved to Switzerland after the Nazis came to power, and started up a firm called Vita Nova Verlag in Geneva. He was eventually employed by Brigadier Masson, of the Swiss security organisation, in the Bureau Ha. After the fall of France, when the Swiss were temporarily concerned about the possibility of a German invasion, his job was to assess military intelligence relating to Germany. Roessler soon proved to be a highly competent analyser of such information and also provided extremely accurate forecasts of what the Nazis would do next. But what he did admirably for the Swiss he supplied in even greater detail to the Russians. His information was so valuable that the Soviet eventually gave him a retainer equivalent at the time to £350 a month plus various commodity emoluments.

Yet Roessler, despite having twice been convicted of spying by Swiss courts, continued long after the war to deny that he had ever indulged in espionage for any power. He was the most cautious of spies and he managed to keep his true identity well hidden even from those he was serving. For a time Rado himself had no idea who was supplying such accurate information and Alexander Foote recorded that ' "Lucy" produced the "goods" ' and that on all occasions save one 'these were accurate, speedy and complete. The war on the Eastern Front was fought largely on them, and the intelligence produced led to victories for the Allies. . . . ' And he added that 'he produced the answers and protected his sources, and one asks no more of a secret agent'.

Roessler's work as a spy for the Russians was certainly known and connived at by both the Swiss and the British. Not unnaturally, the Centre in Moscow was at first highly suspicious of the intelligence he supplied, but so swiftly did he prove himself that they had to admit that their original hunch that he was a plant by the *Abwehr* was wrong.

The authors of *La Guerre a été gagnée en Suisse* suggested that ten Bavarian officers who served with Roessler in World War I became anti-Nazis, but joined the German Army and, having reached high rank, were jointly able to send Roessler in Geneva by German radio channels intelligence of all operations on the Eastern Front. It only requires a cursory examination of this theory to realise that it defies belief. The ten Bavarians are never named, nor is it explained how they could continue to use official channels for sending such information.

More plausible would be the theory, not previously put forward by anyone, that a major source of the Russians' intelligence out of Germany came direct from Martin Bormann, Hitler's deputy. In September 1971 a former German General's daughter was reported as having stated that she saw Martin Bormann alive in the hands of Soviet soldiers in mid-June 1945. She made this statement to a notary because she had read about the claim made by General Reinhard Gehlen, former West German Intelligence chief under the Adenauer régime, that Bormann actually became a Russian spy as early as 1941 and that at the end of the war he defected to the Russians.

This claim was greeted with some scepticism in official West German sources and General Gehlen's allegations were seen by some as part of a campaign to discredit certain sections of post-war German Intelligence. On the other hand some Western Intelligence Services in Berlin believed as long ago as 1947 that Bormann had gone over to the Russians. Since then he has been variously reported as being in Uruguay, Paraguay, and Brazil, yet not even the intensive and highly skilled tracking operations of the Israelis have revealed any real clue to his whereabouts.

But whether or not Bormann played any rôle in the 'Lucy' network, it was the most extraordinary example in history of the use made of one Secret Service by another. If infiltration of the British Secret Service by the Russians had been effective, the penetration of the latter by the former was on this occasion no less so. In order to pass intelligence to the Russians without its being suspected that they were doing this, the British used a Soviet spy as their link-agent, aided by two other agents. It was perhaps the best use made of a double-agent in any war and undertaken in such a way that it helped both the Russians and the British.

Foote made it quite clear in his book, *Handbook for Spies*, that 'Lucy was . . . our link with the German High Command . . . whose identity was known only to another link, the recruiter of "Lucy", named "Taylor".' Though 'Lucy' was Roessler, Foote declined to reveal his true identity as long as Roessler was still alive. Foote stated that 'Lucy' frequently answered queries the Russians put to him and that when he was asked for information about a German force on the Eastern Front, he would come back with details of its composition, strength and location. 'In effect, as far as the Kremlin was concerned,' wrote Foote, 'the possession of "Lucy" as a source meant that they had the equivalent of well-placed agents in the three Intelligence Services, plus the Imperial General Staff, plus the War Cabinet Office.'

In passing 'Lucy's' information to Moscow in the early stages, the agents of the Swiss network were risking their own careers. It was the persistence of Foote, as the chief radio-operator for the Russian network in Switzerland, that enabled this intelligence to be forced on an unwilling Centre. It is almost certain that Brigadier Masson, who was both pro-French and pro-British, knew what was going on and that he connived at it. Only in November 1943, when the tide of war had turned in the Allies' favour did the Swiss start making arrests of the Soviet spy network and even then they were extremely lenient to Foote who had a relatively comfortable time in prison and was released the following year. Roessler was even more leniently treated. He was not arrested until some time later and then released after three months with a certificate from the Swiss General Staff.

Stalin had refused to believe information given to him by the British Ambassador in Moscow about German plans for invading Russia. He had treated all intelligence from British sources with the utmost suspicion. It is also reported that he took a lot of convincing that Sorge's reports from Tokyo had not been the result of baited information from the Germans. Yet 'Lucy' had succeeded where others had failed.

Suspicion initially soon turned into amazement, amazement into incredulity, incredulity into delight and loud praise for their agent. Alexander Foote was one of the coolest spies of all time. In two years he sent more than six thousand messages to Moscow by his radio set. He was an indefatigable worker, staying up all night to tap out his messages and spending his days gathering information and making contacts. He made a small circle of friends in Lausanne where he lived and some of these wrote about him years later in the *Gazette de Lausanne*, when his book *Handbook for Spies* appeared. 'We kidded him about being a British spy,' wrote one of them. ' "Listen, where are your secrets, your messages in invisible ink . . . " we used to ask him. He enjoyed the jokes immensely and took part in the game with dry humour. Someone asked him once: "In fact, what are you doing for a living?" Unperturbed, he answered: "Don't you know? I am a spy." '

Rado did not trust Foote and suspected he was a British agent. He may well have been right, for Foote was certainly in effect serving two masters, unwittingly for a while, but later quite deliberately. Yet while Rado was ultimately sentenced to ten years in Siberia, for incompetence, Foote escaped the Soviet espionage net and returned to Britain. When he left prison in Switzerland Foote went to Paris and from there to Moscow. The Russians wanted him to go to Mexico and to operate from there against the U.S.A. But Foote had had enough. When he reached East Berlin he crossed over to the West and contacted British Intelligence. Eventually he settled down as a civil servant in the innocuous-sounding Ministry of Agriculture and Fisheries. He had served Russia loyally and well and, perhaps, over the whole period he had served Britain even better. Of the Russian Secret Service he had this to say: 'The faults were many and manifest. The Centre were frequently foolish, frequently unco-operative and frequently inefficient. They were often dilatory when speed was essential and rash when caution was the better course.'

The story of the 'Lucy' Ring admirably illustrates both the strengths and the weaknesses of Soviet espionage at this time. Full advantage was taken of the leniency of the Swiss; indeed, but for the Swiss turning a blind eye the constant stream of radio messages between Switzerland and Moscow could never have continued so long undetected. Yet it should be noted that the Soviet agents were not only taking great risks in using prolonged periods of transmission, but were repeating the very errors that led to the break-up of the Belgian network. As will be seen, even when these agents began to become frightened of discovery, the Centre would not permit other and safer methods of communication. There is no doubt that 'Lucy' was protected by the Swiss security and that he was fortunate in that Brigadier Masson was strongly in favour of the Allies. Some small proportion of 'Lucy's' information possibly came from Germany, but the bulk of it was routed to Roessler through British Secret Service channels. The Swiss would never have connived at receiving intelligence directly from Germany, a menacing neighbour (that would have been far too compromising to their precious neutrality). The bargain the Russians engineered with the Swiss was that Roessler's intelligence would be passed on to them only if the Swiss permitted its transmission to the Russians. Nobody, of course, spelt it out as brutally as that, but the niceties of espionage are often as courteous as those of diplomacy, despite beliefs to the contrary. The Centre would, of course, have been horrified to realise such a bargain had been struck. Back in England the cipher-crackers had already got to work tapping German field radio transmission. Consequently a day-to-day analysis of German intelligence, interlarded with intercepted signals from the *Oberkommando der Wehrmacht*, was sent to Switzerland, which was an ideal centre for disseminating it and concealing its British origins. Then Roessler did the rest. This does not mean, of course, that the resourceful Roessler had not other and more direct means of supplementing his intelligence from inside Germany.

Both the Centre and Rado blundered at this time. Rado erred when he failed to heed Foote's suspicions that their network was being compromised by two of their own agents, George and Joanna Wilmer. Rado retorted that he was a much older hand at espionage than Foote and that the Wilmers had been trusted agents for many years, having served in Japan before Richard Sorge went there. Rado should have known that the pre-Sorge set-up in Japan was no recommendation for a reliable agent. Foote, not getting any support from Rado, told the Centre that he suspected the Wilmers, but they took the same view as Rado. Foote was right. By May 1943 it was learned that the Wilmers were collaborating with the *Abwehr* and it was this that led eventually to the breaking up of the Swiss network. The Wilmers also anonymously denounced Foote to the Swiss police. But it was not until the *Abwehr* showed themselves interested in breaking up the Soviet network and putting pressure on the Swiss security that the Swiss, somewhat reluctantly, acted. Rado panicked and instead of burning his papers and code-books put them in the apartment of another agent who was shortly afterwards arrested. This was a gross breach of Secret Service regulations.

The Centre blundered by showing a dumb, bureaucratic lack of initiative and by sticking rigidly to the rules. Foote recorded that in 1942 Rado had in his hands certain documents that would have been of great value to the British as well as the Russians, they were too bulky to pass safely by radio, and he suggested they be handed over to the British. But the Centre's reply to this suggestion was to order Rado to burn the documents forthwith. Later, in October the same year, Rado sent this urgent request to Moscow by radio:

'Since general situation in regard to unhampered continuation of work is getting more and more unfavourable and there is the danger of destruction through police action, I suggest after serious consideration getting in touch with the British and continuing work from there in a new camouflaged way . . . [we] can only be saved by contact with the British.'

Rado was told that this proposal was 'absolutely unacceptable'.

When the Swiss police closed in on the network and made their arrests Rado fled to Paris where he was ordered eventually to return to Moscow on the same plane as Foote. As it was wartime the plane was routed via Cairo and when they stopped in the Egyptian capital Rado immediately disappeared. Foote made no effort to join him and it is possible that Rado's decision to defect helped the Englishman in his subsequent interrogation in Moscow. Certainly the fact that he had stayed on to face the inquiry into the breaking up of the Swiss network counted in his favour at a time when some in the Centre had their suspicions about Foote's loyalty. The Russians brought pressure to bear on both the British and the Egyptian authorities, claiming that Rado was an Army deserter, and demanding his extradition. Eventually their request was granted and Rado returned to Moscow. After a secret trial he was sent to Siberia, released after Stalin's death and is now a professor in Budapest.

Foote was remorselessly cross-examined by his spy chiefs. He was left with the impression that he was lucky not to have met the same fate as Rado. Yet, as Foote somewhat whimsically remarked, once they had cleared him of suspicion of being a British spy it was clear that he was no longer regarded as of much importance.

18

Atomic Espionage in the U.S.A.

SOVIET INFILTRATION of the United States really began in the early twenties when 'The Trust' was being engineered to lure anti-Bolsheviks back to Russia. It was the discoveries made as a result of 'The Trust's' machinations which led to the second wave of agents being sent over to the U.S.A., not least to make use of the contacts initiated by Sidney Reilly.

It was, as we have seen, a slow and unspectacular build-up, especially as the American Communist Party was mistrusted even more than had been the French Party. One of the first organisers of espionage on the Russian side in America was Lydia Stahl, Russian-born, who had emigrated to the U.S.A. about the time of the Revolution. She went back to Europe in 1920 and settled in Paris where she not only became a Communist, but agreed to spy for the Soviet Union. A skilled photographer, she returned to the U.S.A. and undertook the photographing of documents which other agents obtained. Lydia was assisted by one Alfred Tilton who became the Resident Director of this early Soviet network in the U.S.A., a post he shared with a Russian, Sergey Gusev, the object being for each man to keep a check on the activities of the other. In fact neither of these joint-Resident Directors possessed anything like the acumen or resourcefulness of Lydia Stahl who was very much more than a mere photographer of documents. It was Lydia who first made contacts for the Soviet Secret Service in U.S. governmental circles.

Her methods were to make casual acquaintances with civil servants and Army officers, then to ensure that these purely social contacts enabled her to extend her circle of friends to higher circles both in the Government and the Civil Service. Lydia Stahl was recalled to France in 1932, two years after Alfred Tilton, and both of them continued to work for the G.R.U.

Yet even by this date Lydia had laid the basis for future espionage operations in the U.S.A. on a modest scale. Eventually she found two Americans, one an embittered civil servant, the other an anti-German Army officer, whom she persuaded to work for the Soviet Union. These two formed the nucleus, if only in embryonic form, of a spy cell inside the U.S. Establishment. They not only made reports for Lydia Stahl but advised her on the weaknesses, the secret vices and the foibles of a score or more of senior civil servants and Army officers. From them grew what came to be known as the 'Ware Ring', named after Harold Ware, a civil servant, comprising a Soviet spy network actually inside the U.S. Government administration. Whittaker Chambers, not perhaps the best witness, estimated that by 1936–38 there were as many as seventy-five Government officials involved in espionage on behalf of Russia.

The psychological background for the creation of this network in the years immediately before Roosevelt came to power was, of course, ideal. Huge unemployment, widespread poverty, the slump, the discrediting of the capitalist system and the Wall Street disasters and hysteria of the Stock Market all helped to condition the minds of men who were already questioning the political set-up of the democracies. The idea of a proletarian-controlled Utopia began to have its attractions. As the spy cell developed so one after

250

another the ripe plums of discontent with the *status quo* dropped into the Soviet lap. Apart from Harold Ware there were Frank Coe, Lauchlin Currie, Laurence Duggan, Alger Hiss, Nathan Silvermaster and Harry Dexter White.

Naturally the advent of the Nazis made recruitment in the U.S.A. much easier among the Jewish emigrants: among these people during the late thirties and early forties were to be found a wide range of Soviet agents. In a country such as America, created out of so many races, it was easy to find those who were sufficiently lacking in any conception of patriotism to spy for a foreign power.

It was perhaps unfortunate that the first real attempt to unmask the Communist espionage in the U.S.A. was made by so discreditable, vulgar and despicable a character as the late Senator Joseph R. McCarthy. His crude methods of interrogation, his use of the 'smear technique', so outraged liberals throughout the world that much of the good he undoubtedly achieved was obscured by his own unpleasant personality. These very methods in the long run aided the Russians: he ensured sympathy not merely for his victims but for those who had not yet been unmasked.

For years infiltrations went on unchecked. The Russians used similar tactics to those employed in London when they created Arcos. They established the Amtorg Trading Company which was financed by the sale of Romanoff jewels smuggled into America by merchant seamen in the pay of Wohlweber's Seamen's Union. Nicholas Dozenberg took the place of Lydia Stahl. He had been a Latvian emigrant to the U.S.A. and hit on the brilliant idea of establishing the American–Rumanian Film Company with a view to providing cover for spies in both countries.

Amtorg was manned by Soviet spies who were given the job of recruiting agents in the U.S.A. Robert Pitcoff in the House Committee on Un-American Activities investigation of Communist propaganda activities hearings of 14 October 1938 stated that he had been asked to become an agent and was sacked when he declined: 'A member of the party who had been sitting on the same committee with me asked whether I would be interested to become a secret service agent for the Soviet Government in the navy of some foreign country. . . . I didn't think my qualifications warranted such a job because I was not so familiar with it, and he said that would be taken care of; that I would be sent to Russia for two years to be trained. . . . I declined the offer.'

While the G.R.U. controlled all effective espionage in the U.S.A. in these early days the N.K.V.D. operated Amtorg. A great deal of the espionage was purely commercial and industrial. Some was entirely scientific and often so confined to theoretical science of an advanced kind that at that time it hardly passed for espionage, but almost came under the innocuous heading of a thirst for scientific knowledge.

The greatest feat of Soviet espionage in these early days was its quest, hardly then grasped by those who were organising it, for atomic secrets. The origins of this were the early attempts at scientific espionage organised from Moscow and directed at Cambridge University and Copenhagen. The ground work had been laid by Lev Landau and Peter Kapitza: they had impressed on Moscow the need for extending this work and the hint that ultimately it would lead to the creation of a super-bomb. In assessing the future prospects of atomic science the Russians were ahead of the Germans and the British in theory if not in practice. Orders went out to obtain intelligence on such matters from Britain, Denmark, Germany and the United States. There had even been a plan to try to kidnap the celebrated scientist, Einstein, in order to find someone capable of explaining the possibilities.

In the earliest stages atomic espionage was directed by Amtorg, which established study groups for various branches of industry and science. As counter-espionage in America was in its infancy and as the serious nature of such espionage was not grasped — indeed it was hardly looked upon as espionage — much of the work was blatantly carried out by visiting commissions from Russia. 'Almost every industry was studied by these commissions,' testified Robert Pitcoff.

One man, however, began to realise what was going on under his very eyes. He was Basil W. Delgass, an Amtorg vice-president, who, when resigning from that office in 1930, charged that he had 'seen information regarding the Army and Navy defences of the United States that has been gathered by Amtorg's agents and transmitted to Russia'.

But even such a warning as this failed to bring home to the American authorities the danger that lurked in their midst. Another counterfeit money scandal was, however, exposed in 1933 and led to the arrest of Dr Valentin G. Burtan, a Soviet agent. Notwithstanding this, President Roosevelt invited Litvinoff, the Russian Foreign Minister, to the U.S.A. and shortly afterwards the U.S.S.R. was given official recognition in America. This move resulted in an order from Moscow that the new base for espionage activities directed against the U.S.A. was to be in Ottawa.

Gradually the G.R.U. was ousted from its previously strong position in the U.S.A.: the new fields of espionage were regarded as essentially a matter for the N.K.V.D. It was a wise decision, for atomic espionage called for prompt and frequent reassessments of intelligence received and policy decisions in the Kremlin itself.

The damage wrought by the Soviet Secret Service in America

in these early years was appalling in its extent, its stranglehold on certain sections of officialdom and in its long-term results. No nation in the world has been so thoroughly and devastatingly infiltrated by Russia as the U.S.A. There were so many important Soviet agents operating in America in the Roosevelt era and even before that a whole chapter could be occupied in naming them and their main exploits. Apart from those mentioned there was Tschatzky, who served as a member of the Amtorg staff from 1925 until 1928, Mark Zilbert, who specialised in obtaining naval secrets, Pavel Mikhailoff, who came to the U.S.A. in 1929 and stayed to help organise atomic espionage, and Mikhail Gorin, who, as manager of Intourist, the Soviet State Travel Agency, blackmailed an American Intelligence officer into betraying naval secrets by hinting at reprisals against the latter's relatives who were still living in Russia. Gorin was eventually caught by the F.B.I. and sentenced to six years' imprisonment in 1939.

Already in the late thirties there was a closely guarded but largely autonomous team of experts in Moscow sifting, assessing and interpreting scientific intelligence reports. It was, luckily, immune from the purges and only because of this did it ultimately become the most important intelligence unit in Russia. Information came in that Germany was desperately trying to make an atomic bomb. From this moment atomic espionage was regarded as almost a matter of life and death for the Soviet Union.

It was Lev Landau who, acting on this tip-off, suggested that inquiries should be made from Lise Meitner, a Jewish professor of mathematics from Vienna, who worked in Berlin with Professor Hahn, the man after whom the element hahnium was named. Though she was Jewish, it was pointed out, the Nazis regarded her work as so important that they refused to let her leave the country.

Lise Meitner had studied theoretical physics in Vienna before World War I and in 1907 went to Berlin to study at the Kaiser Wilhelm Institute. During the First World War she served as an X-ray nurse with the Austrian Army, afterwards returning to her research in Germany. In the pre-Nazi era in Germany she paid frequent visits to Vienna and the Russians learned that during this period she had made close contacts with a number of Russians, including the poet and Communist leader, Fischer. Slowly, from various contacts which Lise had had with Russian scientists and Communist Party members, a dossier was built up on her. It revealed that she was not only working on similar lines to Niels Bohr in Copenhagen but that she had gone a long way towards developing a new weapon based on nuclear power. More important, in 1935 she had joined forces with Hahn to study the transformation of uranium nuclei under neutron bombardment. From then on it was only a matter of time before Lise was drawn into the Soviet espionage net, never through any direct contact (that was far too dangerous), but mainly by agents acting under the guise of friends from neutral countries and scientific researchers.

As a Jewess she was, of course, bitterly opposed to the Nazis and hated working under them, dreading even more giving them the benefit of her work only to see it turned into weapons of destruction. By this time she was determined that the Germans should not reap the benefits of her research any longer. The Russian Secret Service went into action: orders were given that Lise Meitner was to be 'rescued'.

The first idea was that she should be kidnapped and taken to Russia. This, however, was vetoed on the grounds that the operation was too hazardous and also because Landau insisted that her work was still far from completed and that it was essential she should be able to co-operate with Niels Bohr and finish it off. 'No one person can discover the secret of the super-bomb,' asserted Landau. 'Only a team can do that and we must be sure we are in a position to learn the team's findings.'

There have been various stories about how Lise Meitner escaped from Germany first to Denmark and then to Sweden in 1939. One story is that Professor Hahn obtained permission for her to visit Niels Bohr, but the truth is that Soviet agents prepared the escape route in advance and ensured that she could slip across the border, a certain amount of money having been spent in bribing one or two German officials. From that day on, details of Lise Meitner's research were passed on to the Russians. Thus from about 1939 the Russians knew exactly what they had to find out to complete their dossier on the creation of a super-bomb.

The Russian code name for Lise Meitner was 'Terese'. Curiously this was the name by which she was known to the Hungarian branch of her family, but it was a code name which was never broken either by U.S. Intelligence or the Germans, though British Intelligence in 1945, when investigating some intercepted signals, suspected that it might refer to her. The signal that caught their attention was one that had been sent to Ottawa in March 1944. It read:

'Tell Gisel's parents that Terese has heard from Washington that her letter has been received safely. This means that Terese's situation has improved.'

This caused inquiries to be made by British military Intelligence in Vienna immediately after the war into the activities of Lise Meitner. But nothing ever came of these inquiries as it was wrongly assumed that a female cover name such as 'Terese' must indicate a male agent. Translating this message from Soviet code jargon it ran: 'Tell G.R.U. in Ottawa that Lise Meitner has heard from Washington and that she has new information.'

It has long been thought that the Soviets became interested in atomic secrets only as late as 1943, but the Soviet Union could never have grasped the importance of this at that time unless they had accumulated a vast amount of background intelligence covering the preparatory ground to atomic development in the twenties and thirties. By 1942 they were fully in possession of as much intelligence as the British had, somewhat less than the Germans possessed and almost all that was coming out of Sweden on the Lise Meitner discoveries. But they knew that the real developments were taking place in the U.S.A. and it was for this reason that the drive for atomic espionage was switched to the comparative security of Canada. All information gained was passed swiftly back to Moscow where it was assessed by such Russian nuclear physicists as Kapitza, Ivanenko, Seminoff and Tamm.

The chief planner of atomic espionage in Moscow was Peter Bukhanoff, an M.V.D. colonel who controlled the filing cabinets containing dossiers on foreign agents, 'contact men' and sympathisers of the Soviet régime. Bukhanoff was teaching higher mathematics at the Technological Institute in Kiev when he was asked to organise a special foreign intelligence service for the Soviet in the early thirties. He was specially chosen because of his knowledge of mathematics and science and, though his work covered general espionage, his special task was building up a team of scientific spies.

Bukhanoff started a file on scientists in all countries. Having built this up he started to look for likely spies among them. Having found a man with specialist knowledge of the type in which Russia was especially interested, he would then find out all he could about the man, his family, his background, his interests, his position, his vices and prejudices. For many years Bukhanoff never left his Moscow office. He was given a general's uniform, but he looked like a civilian and spoke with a soft, quiet voice and made a virtue of being polite to his subordinates.

Bukhanoff had the task of choosing the spies who were to concentrate on atomic espionage. When the pressure to obtain atomic secrets was at its height in 1942 Bukhanoff checked his filing system for the record cards of foreign scientists who were potential traitors. He turned up the names of Dr Klaus Fuchs and Dr Alan Nunn May. Orders to contact these men secretly were sent to Washington and London.

Klaus Fuchs, the scientist who worked for the British on atomic research, was already working for the Russians at the end of 1942 and one of the charges later brought against him was that 'at some time in 1943' he 'did pass information to representatives of a foreign power in the City of Birmingham'. In July of that same year Douglas Frank Springhall, a Soviet agent recruiter in Britain, was sentenced to seven years' penal servitude for obtaining information from Olive Sheehan, an Air Ministry employee, 'for a purpose prejudicial to the interest and safety of the State'. The case was heard *in camera*, but on 7 November 1943 the War Office issued a statement that Captain Ormond Leyton Uren had been tried by court martial on a charge of communicating to Douglas Frank Springhall 'information of a highly secret character which was calculated to be useful to an enemy'. He was found guilty and sentenced to be cashiered and given seven years' imprisonment.

Uren had become a Communist sympathiser and a friend had introduced him to Springhall. As a result of this he had been asked to pass on confidential information about military operations.

At this time, taking advantage of the fact that Britain and Russia were allies, the Soviet Secret Service suddenly stepped up its activities inside Britain. Its main aim was to create a new network under ideal conditions, but first and foremost was the demand for all and any intelligence on matters relating to the creation of a super-bomb. From Springhall's contacts one vital piece of information had been obtained – that the committee presided over by Sir George Thomson had reported on the feasibility of a bomb dependent on atomic energy and that uranium was being sought from the pitchblende deposits of Canada.

Meanwhile the need to obtain more atomic secrets had been made even greater by the fact that the German advance across Russia had resulted in the temporary closing down of their own laboratories. Thus in a matter of a few weeks the Soviet Union was far behind the West in atomic research. Pavel Mikhailoff undertook the work of spearheading the drive for this intelligence from the Soviet Consulate in New York. He linked up the Canadian and U.S. networks and gave the orders to Major Sukoloff, who was in charge of the Canadian set-up. But it was not until Colonel Nicolai Zabotin arrived in Ottawa as military attaché in 1943 that the somewhat loose and unco-ordinated arrangements for collecting specialised intelligence were overhauled and new impetus given to the Canadian network.

Zabotin was a man of great drive and within a few months of his coming to Canada had developed a specialist network comprising twenty-two local agents and a team of fifteen Soviet specialists, the latter being all given covers as members of the Russian Mission in Ottawa. Key people in this network were Sam Carr, national organiser of the Labour-Progressive Party in Canada, and Fred

Rose, a member of Parliament and an organiser of the same party in Quebec. Others brought into the network were David Gordon Lunan, editor of *Canadian Affairs*, Dr Allan Nunn May, a British physicist, P. Durnford Pemberton Smith, of the National Research Council in Ottawa, Kathleen Willsher, Assistant Registrar of the Office of the United Kingdom High Commissioner in Ottawa, and Edward Mazarall, of the National Research Council. It was a formidable list of traitors and it may well have included other notable names for when the network was finally broken up several escaped and not all of these were identified.

With such varied talent among the key members of this network it was not difficult for them to organise a vast amount of intelligence from other contacts. One of the most valuable of the latter proved to be Professor Raymond Boyer, of McGill University, who provided the information that a plant for the production of uranium was being set up at Chalk River and that experiments had proved that uranium could be used for making a new type of bomb.

Moscow was highly excited at this piece of news and, to put the issue to the test, immediately asked the U.S. Government for sixteen tons of uranium to conduct urgent experiments of their own. It was a risky move in that it might have alerted the U.S. Government to the extent of Soviet espionage, but it was intended to probe U.S. intentions. The United States gave their own game away when they refused the Soviet request on the grounds that the supply of uranium was not sufficient to spare any of it.

Security on the Allied side was quite appallingly bad. The British had failed to ascertain that Dr Allan Nunn May was a secret Communist. He, too, had been at Trinity College, Cambridge, and had been a member of the team working at the Cavendish laboratories on nuclear fission. He had been sent to Canada and the U.S.A. to co-operate with American and Canadian scientists working on the project. He had been working for the Russians for years. So, too, had Dr Klaus Fuchs, a German who had fled to Britain from the Nazis, and been recruited into the British atomic research team without M.I.5 having discovered that he had been an underground Communist in Germany and had made contact with the Russian military attaché shortly after he came to Britain. Both these men were colleagues of Bruno Pontecorvo, an Italian physicist, who was working in Canada and the U.S.A. on the super-bomb, and who later defected to Russia.

Meanwhile in the U.S.A. Anatoli Yakovlev, under the cover of vice-consul in New York, had been given the task of co-ordinating atomic espionage from there. His key spies were four dedicated

Communists, Harry Gold, David Greenglass and Julius and Ethel Rosenberg. Gold was selected because of his proved skill in stealing industrial chemical secrets, Greenglass because he was working on the Manhattan District Project at Oak Ridge, Tennessee, and had access to official secrets, while the link with the Rosenbergs was that Ethel Rosenberg was Greenglass's sister. By the latter part of the forties Soviet Intelligence had penetrated into every vital sector of atomic research and bomb development – at the Radiation Laboratory in California, at Oak Ridge, McGill University, and had even tried to suborn Dr J. Robert Oppenheimer, who eventually became director of Los Alamos, the chief U.S. atomic plant. The effects of all this might have been even worse but for the surprise defection of Igor Gouzenko, a cipher clerk in the Soviet Embassy in Ottawa.

The story of Gouzenko is well enough known, but it provides an example of the gravest danger which must always confront Russian Intelligence as long as the Soviet Union remains a totalitarian, police state. A trusted servant of the Soviet state is sent abroad, he contrasts the freedom and luxuries of the democracies with life at home and he suddenly wishes to opt out of the horrors of Communist tyranny. So it was with Gouzenko. He went to the Canadian Mounted Police and handed over documents which showed beyond question the extent of Soviet espionage in Canada. The Russians indignantly insisted that Gouzenko was a thief who had stolen documents and money from the Soviet Embassy and demanded that he be handed back to them. The Canadian authorities refused, though at one time there was a real risk that they did not realise the seriousness of the situation and Gouzenko was nearly returned to his embassy.

The revelations of the Canadian spy trials that followed are well enough known. Allan Nunn May had returned to London, but he was quickly identified as the man known as 'Alek' in the Soviet network and in March 1946 was sentenced to ten years' imprisonment. Most of the Canadian spies were caught within weeks, but Fuchs was not finally detected until after he returned to Britain, and then only on a tip-off from the F.B.I. in 1949. But the Americans suspected treachery or criminal negligence when the British failed to act on their information that Pontecorvo was implicated in the atomic spy ring. Two years after the British had been told of Pontecorvo's activities he was allowed to go to the Continent with his family on holiday. He immediately defected to Russia.

It is only recently that a document has come to light in Canada showing that Britain had positive information as early as 1945 about a Russian agent who had penetrated its Intelligence Services. This man could have been either Kim Philby or the mysterious 'fourth man' of the Burgess-Maclean-Philby affair, who has never been uncovered.

This information is contained in a memorandum written in 1952 by Igor Gouzenko for the Royal Canadian Mounted Police at the request of British Counter-Intelligence. It is dated 6 May 1952, and addressed to Superintendent George McClellan, then with R.C.M.P. Intelligence. It is important not only for the light it sheds on the penetration of British Intelligence by the Russians but on what it reveals of Soviet methods of espionage.

Gouzenko referred to a 'person in British M.I.5'. He was probably confusing M.I.5 and M.I.6, the former being counter-espionage and the latter the British Secret Service overseas. 'I forget the cover name,' wrote Gouzenko. 'However, the cover name is not so important in this case. Moscow quite often changed the cover name and there is great probability that it had changed the cover name of the person in question during the last ten years. . . . The case of the member of M.I.5 was, in my opinion, much stronger and there was much more to go on. . . . In the first place I was not told by somebody, but saw the telegram myself concerning this person, and then, as a second confirmation, I was told by Lieut. Lubimov. With these two pieces of evidence there is not the slightest doubt in my mind that there was a Soviet agent inside M.I.5 during the period 1942–43, and possibly later on. . . . The telegram dealt with the description of a contact through a *dubok* [a hiding place]. It was clear that the person mentioned (and it was stated, I remember) was one of Five of M.I. It was evident that personal contact with the man from M.I.5 was avoided. The place of the *dubok* in that particular case was at some graveyard – in a split between certain stones of a certain tomb. I remember that the telegram struck me as unusual and we had a short talk about it. It is most probable that Lubimov deciphered it since he usually was working on telegrams from London. . . . Lubimov said: "This man has something Russian in his background." I understood that he had learned this from previous telegrams. The words "something Russian" could be understood in different ways. The man himself (White Russian, of noble origin, etc.), or his relatives came from Russia or are Russian. He could be 100 per cent English but was in Russia before the revolution or during the 1919–21 civil war, or later on official duties. Or, less probable, he has some friends of Russian origin. . . . From what I saw with my own eyes this man was contacted not personally but through a *dubok*. This showed that Moscow took special precautions in dealing with him. A *dubok* contact may have taken place once a month or even once every two months. The place of a *dubok* can be changed often. In 1944 Zabotin received from Moscow a long telegram of a warning

259

character. In it Moscow informed him that representatives of British "Greens" (counter-intelligence) were due to arrive in Ottawa with the purpose of working with local "Greens" (R.C.M.P.), to strengthen work against Soviet agents. Now it could be that Moscow just invented these representatives . . . in order to make Zabotin more careful. On the other hand it might be genuine, in which case it would mean that Moscow had an inside track in British M.I.5. . . . The mistake (in my opinion) in dealing with this matter was that the task of finding the agent was given to M.I.5 itself. . . . The result, even beforehand, could be expected as nil.'

Gouzenko also gave interesting information on the organisation of *duboks*. 'The favourite places for a *dubok* are telephone booths [behind the phone box], inside the water tank [of lavatory cisterns], some abandoned stone structure with plenty of splits between the stones, old fences, graveyards. In most cases all places are selected in such a way that access to them is easy but not conspicuous. . . . Watch every movement of the hands of contact men. Sometimes they may use a trick such as this: the contact man sits down on a bench in a casual and relaxed pose. Unnoticed, he may pin a letter under the bench with thumbtacks, then, minutes later, leave the place. Agents may come half an hour later and pick it up. So those who are watching the agent's every movement – even the most unsuspicious and relaxed movements – should check them right away.'

Those who know Gouzenko say that he did not always distinguish between various British Intelligence services and that he might have been confusing M.I.5 with M.I.6. But this seems to me merely an excuse for trying to identify the agent he mentions as Philby simply because Philby worked for M.I.6. But Gouzenko seemed quite clear in his own mind that the Soviet agent in the British ranks worked for Counter-Intelligence, which was clearly M.I.5. In any case Philby had close links with M.I.5 at one period in the war.

Two facts point to the traitor actually being in M.I.5. First, the warning from Moscow that Britain was sending a counter-intelligence team to Canada, secondly the failure of M.I.5 to act on America's warning that Pontecorvo was suspected of being a Russian agent. In a later chapter I shall attempt to show that there was not only a 'Fourth Man', but a 'Fifth' and possibly a 'Sixth' working for the Soviet Union under cover of British officialdom. Strictly speaking, the 'Fifth Man' was really the 'First Man' in that it was he who paved the way for Guy Burgess, Donald Maclean and Kim Philby, not to mention George Blake later on. Much more dangerous was the 'Fourth Man' who was still operating for Russia as recently as the early sixties.

Unquestionably atomic espionage was Russia's supreme coup and it enabled her within a few years to wipe out the lead the West had obtained in possession of the A-bomb. Before long she had all the secrets of the hydrogen bomb as well, and enough scientific data to enable the Soviet Union to mount a highly successful programme of missile development and space exploration.

19

Ilya Svetloff Foils the Nazis

CHANGES IN the structure of the N.K.V.D. were made during World War II, but they resulted from political manoeuvres rather than serious reorganisation. In February 1941 the N.K.V.D. was split up into two sections, the one retaining the title of N.K.V.D. being responsible for internal affairs and that for State Security being designated N.K.G.B. Then, after Germany invaded Russia, the N.K.V.D. was once again put in supreme control of the whole espionage and counter-espionage networks.

Obviously there was a good deal of jockeying for position in the whole Secret Service hierarchy in these war years, for in April 1943 the N.K.V.D. and N.K.G.B. were again restored as separate commissariats. After the war the N.K.V.D. and the N.K.G.B. were remodelled into the M.V.D. (Ministry of Internal Affairs) and the M.G.B. (Ministry of State Security). But none of these changes in any way affected the essential work, methods or duties of those engaged in Soviet Intelligence. And, more important, after so many changes in the leadership of the Secret Service Beria not only survived the purges, but the war as well, and remained as co-ordinator of the M.G.B. and the M.V.D. The former was directed by Merkuloff and the latter by Krugloff.

While Russia had chalked up several espionage victories in her penetration of British and American secrets and in the Sorge network in the Far East, the Soviet Union had been heavily mauled in Europe during the war years. True, there had been the short-lived triumph of the Swiss network, but the Belgian and Dutch networks had been completely destroyed and the French networks seriously compromised. Treachery by individual agents played havoc in the French networks and torture by the Gestapo, or the mere threat of torture, broke down agents whose loyalty to the Soviet Union had never previously been in question.

There were many factors playing a part in creating an atmosphere of treachery and moral decay. The Stalinist purges had not helped; there was the inevitable feeling that failure through no fault of one's own, even capture by the Gestapo or the *Abwehr*, would be regarded as a crime by the Centre. So there was little choice: execution or imprisonment ordered from Moscow, if one escaped, or survived, or collaboration with the Germans. Then again the swift advance of the German armies across Russia in 1941–42 had demoralised many a lonely Soviet agent who must have felt defeat was closing in on him.

When the Russians had learned their lesson about over-dependence on Communist Party members for espionage in France they experimented with agents with agreeable social backgrounds. Two such had been Henry Robinson, the son of a German merchant with an English name, and Vasili Maximovich, a Russian of noble birth who had turned Communist. Each man sought to exploit his social background in his quest for intelligence and quite independently of one another set up networks which eventually came under the direction of the elusive Trepper.

The case of Vasili Maximovich and his sister, Anna, is a classic of the strange love-hate often to be found among White Russians. By background, parentage, education and environment they represent the very antithesis of Communism, yet they are irresistibly drawn towards the very thing they detest because it envelops their romantic conception of an eternal, powerful and splendid Russia. It was the same with the Maximovich brother and sister; Chekhov would have understood them. They never joined the Communist Party, never made any protestations of political faith in Communism, but they slowly slipped into the Soviet espionage net, a net always held out in the knowledge that a certain type of White Russian will be lured into it.

Maximovich, under instructions from the N.K.V.D., proposed marriage to a middle-aged German woman who was one of the secretaries in the German military administration in Paris. He was accepted and soon found himself in a position to acquire plans and moves of the German administration and even documents of a confidential character. Meanwhile his sister, Anna, who was a psychiatrist by profession, set up a clinic on the border of the Occupied and Unoccupied Zones of France and through her work she was able to elicit a great deal by questioning her German patients, especially the officers. This pair comprised one of the best intelligence teams the Russians possessed in France.

But when Trepper's identity had been revealed by agents trapped or tortured by the Gestapo his days were numbered. He was eventually arrested in the dentist's chair. The *Abwehr*'s tactic with the man they regarded as their prize captive was to threaten to hand him over to the Gestapo if he did not talk. The threat worked: Trepper not only talked, he betrayed his secretary, Henry Robinson, Vasili and Anna Maximovich, and even collaborated with the *Abwehr* in misleading other networks by radio. The treachery of Trepper played havoc with some Resistance groups and resulted in scores of people being arrested, French patriots as well as Soviet agents.

For several months afterwards the whole French Communist Resistance network was put out of action. Mistrust ran like a contagious disease through its ranks. When the network started to rebuild itself countless innocent members were brutally and unjustly murdered merely because they were suspected of being traitors.

Trepper was always kept under close guard by the Germans, but in June 1943 he managed to escape from the private house in the Avenue Foch, where he had been permitted to remain with his mistress. He returned to Russia after the war where surprisingly he survived.

One of the great feats of Soviet espionage during the latter part of the war was that in which the Russians foiled a Nazi plot to kill the 'Big Three' – Roosevelt, Churchill and Stalin – at Teheran. The Russian version of this, taken from the N.K.V.D. archives, is that Soviet agents infiltrated the German Secret Service, thus gaining news of the assassination plot and thereby taking steps to prevent it.

One day in November 1943, Major Walter Schultz of the Eastern Department of German Military Intelligence, was summoned by Admiral Canaris, head of the *Abwehr*, to a conference at which was discussed 'Operation Long Jump', a daring attempt at a coup to turn the tide of the war then flowing fast against Germany. News had been leaked to the German Secret Service through their agent Cicero, who was valet to the British Ambassador in Ankara, that Churchill, Roosevelt and Stalin were to meet in Teheran. The man who had been chosen to lead the operation was Schultz himself. The plan, he was told, was to fly two plane loads of German specialist troops to Teheran. The soldiers would break into the city and kill the three Allied leaders.

The details of the coup were worked out with care. Schultz was to go ahead to Teheran to prepare the ground several weeks beforehand. He would fix secret landing sites for the planes, arrange for them to be guided in and then give the soldiers details as to where to attack.

The plan might have worked splendidly but for one factor. Major Walter Schultz was none other than Ilya Svetloff, a Soviet double-agent. He had been born on a collective farm near the Russian port of Baku, about a hundred miles from the Persian border. Not only did he speak Persian fluently but in his early days had lived among Germans in Baku and soon acquired perfection in speaking their language. Because of his linguistic ability and keen intelligence he had been picked out as a young man to be trained as a G.P.U. agent. But there was another reason for Svetloff being selected for espionage work: he had been a close friend of one Friedrich Schultz, whose uncle in Munich ran a sausage factory. This uncle, Hans Schultz, had met Hitler in 1920 and had been one of the founder members of the Nazi Party and a contributor to its funds. Then the ageing Schultz, who had lost his only daughter in a car accident, recalled that he had a nephew in Baku and wrote offering to adopt him and give him a real chance in life.

Friedrich Schultz was not enthusiastic about this proposition. He was engaged to a Russian girl and preferred to stay in Baku. Svetloff urged his friend to delay replying and to think matters over. In the meantime he reported the uncle's offer to his G.P.U. superiors. Soon after this he was told to report to headquarters at Aliev and instructed to take on the identity of Schultz's nephew and to go to Germany.

'You speak German fluently,' he was told. 'You know everything about the Schultz family and there is the advantage that Schultz senior does not know what you look like. Also you have the talents required for an important espionage assignment. If Schultz's uncle is a power in the Nazi Party, you should be able to join it as an under-cover agent without any difficulty. But first of all you must send a photograph of yourself to Herr Schultz and say you are prepared to join him.'

Svetloff went to Germany, was welcomed as the long-lost nephew Herr Schultz had never seen since he was a baby, and lived in the family mansion in Rumfordstrasse. Before going to Germany, however, he received an intensive course of training in Secret Service techniques, codes, ciphers, radio-telephony. The G.P.U. were taking no chances: even after their new agent arrived in Germany they had him under observation. For one development the G.P.U. were not prepared: anti-Sovietism among the Nazis was at that time so prevalent that Hans Schultz decided to engineer yet another change in identity for his 'nephew'. He felt that the fact that Friedrich Schultz had lived so long in Russia and associated with Russians might not only compromise the young man but his own reputation in the Nazi Party. So he covered up all traces of Friedrich Schultz and turned Svetloff into Walter Schultz, the name of a younger member of the Schultz family who had lived in Hamburg and had never been to Russia. Walter Schultz had, in fact, committed suicide in circumstances that had been hushed up.

This further change of identity made the Russians' task easier. There was now little risk of anyone probing into Walter Schultz's background and finding incriminating evidence about his associations in Baku. It also presented no difficulties later when Walter Schultz became an agent for the Germans.

Ilya Svetloff in the rôle of Walter Schultz not only joined the Nazi Party but became a Storm Trooper. He became engaged to the daughter of a German Foreign Office official, Gustav von Mikk, and, by means of coded postcards, sent details to the G.P.U. about German rearmament and foreign policy.

He had arrived in Munich in 1930 and by the mid-thirties was sending through a steady stream of information to Russia by various means. He had enrolled himself in the Department of Oriental Languages at Berlin University and studied Persian and Turkish. He began to make himself an authority on Turkish and Iranian affairs and even made friends with the chief of a nomadic tribe on the Turkish–Iranian borders.

There were no great difficulties about his being given a job in Military Intelligence in Germany. His specialist knowledge and talent for languages were noted and as his uncle was a friend of Admiral Canaris he obtained a recommendation for him to enter the *Abwehr*. It was then that he decided that marriage might compromise his career as a double-agent and he broke off his engagement to the daughter of the Foreign Office man.

Ilya's first big assignment for Canaris was to infiltrate the Iranian road and rail services and to make arrangements for the mining of tunnels and bridges should the Soviet attempt to move into Iran. While in Iran he operated under yet another alias, that of Samuel Sulzer, a Swiss representative of a textile firm. He had to make the trip to Iran in a hurry and was therefore concerned in case Soviet Intelligence thought he had gone off the air or defected. However, they were still keeping close watch on him and while on the train to Teheran he was contacted by another Soviet agent who de-briefed him while they played a game of chess.

For his services on this occasion Svetloff was awarded the Order of the Red Star and promoted to the rank of major. The Russians today claim that German sabotage plans were not implemented because Svetloff had not given the order to move the explosives closer to the sites chosen for their use. Instead he sent a radio signal, warning the Russians and giving them the location and names of his group of saboteurs. The group was captured by a special Russian unit sent into Iran.

No doubt this claim is true in part, but Svetloff must have proved himself to the Germans with some successful work, or he would not have been retained for even more important missions later.

When he undertook the Operation Long Jump Svetloff was, however, shadowed from the moment he left Count Schellenberg's office. He had been told by the Germans to use the same Swiss alias as before, but this time he was to be accompanied by another German agent, named Anna, who was to pose as his wife. The 'Sulzers' went to Iran and here Svetloff managed to escape from his shadowers to pass information to the Russians. He was lucky in that future shadowing was to be left entirely to Anna. As it was, Anna did not suspect that his absences from her company meant anything sinister, but she was angry nevertheless, because she thought he was seeing another woman. Out of revenge she thought of informing Berlin of Svetloff's absences, but she was unable to do this as he had seen to it that her radio set was put out of action. This she only discovered when they both went to the ancient tomb where their radio had been hidden. Svetloff made an excuse and dashed back to Teheran. Anna, who could not give the radio instructions to guide down the German aircraft, followed him by car. She was chased by the Russians who forced her into the parapet of a bridge and she died in the crash. Meanwhile a German transport plane was shot down near the Soviet–Turkish frontier by a Soviet fighter aircraft and another German transport was forced to turn back. The Soviet Intelligence rounded up the network of German agents in Teheran and the lives of the 'Big Three' were saved.

Roosevelt himself admitted that he had stayed in the Soviet Embassy in Teheran because the existence of a German plot had become known to Stalin. In 1968 the former German Commando ace, Otto Skorzeny, admitted some of the details of Operation Long Jump. 'My part in the whole damned thing was to turn it down rather bluntly,' he said. 'The basis of an operation is information and we had no information. Schellenberg had two agents in Teheran . . . but we had nothing to go on.' A French journalist, Laslo Havas, however, in a book entitled *The Long Jump*, confirmed the story of the plot to kill the 'Big Three' and stated that it was foiled by the Russians. Sir Alexander Cadogan, then Permanent Under-Secretary at the British Foreign Office, makes one reference in his diary to the fact that 'the Russians are supposed to have discovered a plot', an entry that was made when he was staying in Teheran.

Poland was for the Soviet Union a key country, like Czechoslovakia, in her post-war policy of creating a bloc of satellite Communist states in Eastern Europe. It was a policy forged during the war, strengthened by Secret Service intrigues, sealed at the Yalta Conference and consolidated in 1945. I. Modelski, the wartime Deputy Minister of Defence in Sikorski's Polish Government in Exile, somewhat reluctantly agreed to be military attaché of the Warsaw Communist régime in Washington in 1946. Two years later he resigned and testified to the U.S. Congressional Committee for Un-American Activities as to the extent of aggressive espionage by Poland and the U.S.S.R. in the U.S.A.

'When I first came to Poland,' he said, 'it was difficult to find any Poles in the new Government sponsored by Soviet Russia. Many officers I saw wore Polish uniforms, but they were certainly Russians. I was told that Russia and Poland would try to separate America from all other peoples and stand against the U.S.A. alone. My primary object as military attaché in Washington was to extract from American leaders all valuable military and political information which would be transmitted to the Warsaw Military Intelligence H.Q. and thence to its central H.Q. in Moscow. I was warned that I should only serve as a "cover" for Alef-Bolkoviak, an N.K.V.D. officer who was first parachuted into Poland in 1942 to set up Communist cells. He was to be my master.'

Modelski also added that late in March 1946, when he was about to leave London for Washington, he was handed a sealed envelope which contained detailed instructions as to how to set up a ring of spy cells all over U.S.A. and how to obtain the necessary military secrets. These instructions were written in Polish but contained many Russian expressions, undeniable proof that the Warsaw Communist Government was under Moscow's orders.

Modelski's instructions were indeed comprehensive. They required him to ascertain details of chemical and nuclear warfare, the nature of Army education, habits, weaknesses and the morale of troops, secret fortifications, location of bases and airfields and the type and character of military colleges and lists of various societies, both cultural and political, with a significant demand that information should be provided as to how best such societies could be infiltrated and what such infiltration could yield.

20

The Anti-N.A.T.O. Spy Rings

THERE WAS not even the semblance of a honeymoon period between Russia and her Western Allies when Germany was finally defeated. The Soviet Union promptly made it absolutely clear that she was unremittingly committed to maintaining her control over all those Eastern European countries which she regarded as within her sphere of influence.

Where Communist governments had already been established in those countries there was no problem; where the governments were non-Communist it soon became evident that Russian policy was to ensure that these were swiftly overthrown and Communist governments installed. The Intelligence Services were used as one of the main weapons in bringing this about.

Under Beria the Russian Secret Service had put itself in the forefront of the world's greatest espionage services. It had blundered on occasions, it had suffered from purges, defections and from treachery, especially in Europe. But overall it had succeeded brilliantly by 1945. Both the British and U.S. Intelligence Services had been penetrated, the former to a lesser degree, but possibly in a deadlier fashion. Resounding successes had been scored with the Sorge spy ring in the Far East and the 'Lucy' ring in Switzerland and atomic espionage had yielded results the planners had never dreamed of a few years previously.

All this had cost large sums of money and the urgent need in 1945 was for even larger amounts to finance post-war espionage which, the Kremlin had decided, must be maintained on a war footing. To find such huge sums of money it was decided that a search must be made for any German securities the Soviet could negotiate. A special Red Army Intelligence unit was sent into the vaults of the Reichsbank after the fall of Berlin and, it is believed, removed from there something like £30 millions worth of German securities comprising Government 5½ per cent Gold Debt Bonds, industrial bearer bonds and mixed bearer bonds. These were smuggled out of Berlin into East Germany and eventually sent to New York, almost certainly with the object of financing Russian Secret Service activities in the Western World. How much gold bullion and jewellery were removed as well is a matter of conjecture. The master mind behind this coup was an intelligence officer of the Fourth Bureau named Feodor Novikoff.

In 1951 U.S. Intelligence officers in Wiesbaden were startled by the sudden appearance of a former U.S. Air Force lieutenant, Herbert William Brann, who offered to sell £30 millions worth of German bonds at forty per cent of their face value, admitting that he was acting on behalf of a Soviet agent who ran a business from an apartment in the Avenue de Marigny in Paris. His offer was declined, but the American Intelligence authorities set about tracing the history of the bonds. Ten years later large quantities of the bonds appeared in Tangier at the American and Foreign Bank in that city: it was said that they were en route for Panama, but after that all trace of them was lost.

The Soviet Secret Service in 1945 was mainly staffed by Stalinists: few of the former Cheka or G.P.U. remained. Beria retained a tight grip on the organisation after the war and this was to some extent strengthened by the death of Zhdanoff, generally regarded as Stalin's successor, for Beria had been alarmed at the proposal to give Zhdanoff complete control over atomic espionage. The M.G.B. leadership changed from Merkuloff to Abakumoff in 1946, but Krugloff continued to preside over the M.V.D. The last-named was popular despite his calling, liked by those of the Allies who met him and efficient in a quiet unfussy manner. To all intents and purposes he filled a rôle similar to that of Menzhinsky in the days of the Cheka.

Sergei Nicoforovich Krugloff was made an honorary Knight of the British Empire by the British and awarded the Legion of Merit by the U.S.A., presumably as a token of gratitude for the foiling of the German plot to kill the Allied leaders in Teheran, as he was in charge of security arrangements for the Yalta conference. Krugloff had one endearing quality: in revealing that he had inside knowledge about all foreigners with whom he came in contact he would make a social grace out of this information.

He informed one astonished American officer that the latter's wife practised ballet steps in front of her dressing-table mirror. It was quite correct, but not even her husband knew about it.

Perhaps his most astonishing revelation was to greet an Allied interpreter with the comment that 'Your daughter has expressed a wish to study ballet in Russia. I shall be happy to arrange this.' The father in question had no idea his daughter was interested in ballet, let alone her desire to go to Russia. Nevertheless a visit was arranged.

Krugloff survived perhaps because after the war the M.G.B. extended its influence at the expense of the M.V.D. and was therefore less restricted in its activities. But Krugloff was not simply an intelligence officer. He was also a supremely good public relations officer, something which the Soviet Secret Service had not possessed before. He exploited the plot to kill the Allied leaders with the skill of a supreme propagandist, even urging Stalin to send a letter to Roosevelt telling him that Teheran was 'teeming with German agents' and would he please come and stay in the Soviet Embassy for safety. Krugloff's aim was to publicise the fact that the Soviet Secret Service had saved Roosevelt's life.

Beria, however, made one grave mistake from the viewpoint of his own security of tenure. He neglected to make friends with the Army and they continued to resent the part he had played in liquidating so many generals in the late thirties.

It was Beria who directed and controlled the attempts to establish a Czech Communist Government after the war and who planned the death of Jan Masaryk, the Czech Foreign Minister, who had aimed to keep Czechoslovakia neutral and maintain close ties with the West as well as with the Soviet bloc. On 10 March 1948, Masaryk's body was found sprawled on the flagstones of the courtyard of the Czernin Palace in Prague beneath his apartment. This occurred just two weeks after the *putsch* in which the Communists had seized power in the country. The official verdict on his death at the time was suicide: it was alleged that he threw himself out of a window. A probe into this affair was launched under Dubcek's government in 1968 and revealed many discrepancies in the evidence.

Jan Masaryk was the son of Thomas Masaryk, the founder of the Czech republic, a member of the Czech Government in Exile during the war and an admirer of the Western way of life. He had immense prestige in the West and it was solely because of this that the Communists asked him to stay on as Foreign Minister in their government. Reluctantly Masaryk accepted, but he later had grave doubts as to the wisdom of this and planned to escape to London. The Russians soon had news of this proposed move through their agents inside the British Secret Service. Orders immediately went out to N.K.V.D. agents that Masaryk was to be liquidated.

As to exactly how Masaryk was killed there is still no proof. The Communist security police moved in and took control the moment his body was discovered. Within hours at least twenty-five people who could have testified about his death were arrested and put in jail, and fourteen of these were later executed. But the evidence which points to murder is substantial. Masaryk's body was found some twelve feet away from the wall of the building; if he had jumped to his death he would hardly have landed so far away. Everything pointed to murder by the N.K.V.D.

270

Soviet espionage was stepped up in all the countries of Eastern and Central Europe during the years of the 'cold war'. Nowhere was this more pronounced than in Vienna in those twilight days of the occupation when many rather crude individuals, members of the Austrian Communist Party and fellow-travellers, spied on almost everyone who was not a Communist and made the 'Third Man' city into a whispering gallery of intrigue.

Of course it was not the Russians alone who did the spying and their repulsive methods were copied by the intelligence services of the Americans, British and the French. Telephones were tapped, kidnapping in broad daylight was a regular feature of N.K.V.D. activities. People also mysteriously fell out of trains. The truth was that Russian thuggery in the sphere of espionage was often provoked to extreme measures by the insensate aggressive espionage of the American C.I.A. Soviet Intelligence was well aware of these provocative activities of the C.I.A. and sought to teach the Americans a lesson by selecting agents for rough treatment. A much favoured method of treatment was to seek out a C.I.A. agent travelling by train and to throw him out on the line while it was passing through a tunnel.

When in October 1955 the last of the occupying troops left Austria, Russian mayhem and espionage as far as Austria itself was concerned largely came to an abrupt end. However, the Russians decided to 'keep a white waistcoat', as the saying is in Vienna, and to use as its unobtrusive agents in Austria the intelligence officers of the satellite countries and the officials of the several 'World Federations' which had their headquarters in Vienna. These were subversive organisations and the rather rash, if brave, Austrian Minister of the Interior, Oskar Helner, decided to banish them from the Austrian capital. One by one they were outlawed and forced to move to new headquarters behind the Iron Curtain, though for some time afterwards the Austrian State Police kept a wary eye on their officials while the latter were travelling through Austria on the excuse of being 'in transit'.

While the Russians kept relatively quiet in their activities in Austria after that country achieved independence, they encouraged both the Hungarians and the Czechs to build up spy networks in Austria and to extend them into Italy and West Germany. Though this particular network was not outstandingly good, its disciplinary methods were as ruthless as any behind the Iron Curtain. There was the case in 1962 for example, of a young Hungarian Secret Police lieutenant who defected to Austria, bringing with him details of how his own organisation worked in Austria. To keep him safe the State Police locked him up in a police barracks in the pious hope that his enemies could not catch him. Two days later his food was poisoned and in an hour he was dead. The vengeance of Moscow had descended on him even at this distance.

Vienna is one of the Russian centres for atomic espionage, though here they concentrate mainly on commercial aspects of nuclear energy and attempts to steal the secrets of European powers engaged in nuclear research for peaceful purposes – indeed, most of the espionage carried out by the three Russian-controlled spy networks in Austria today is concerned with industrial secrets. All three networks, though working for the Russians, have been mainly filled with Czech personnel and their organisation was for this reason dealt a serious blow when the Russians sent troops into Czechoslovakia. Vladislav Bittmann, officially the press secretary of the Czechoslovak Legation in Vienna, was head of one of these networks and he quietly slipped away to a prepared refuge in Switzerland after the Russian intervention in his country. Bittmann was a charming man, very popular with Westerners in Vienna and he did, in fact, ask his wife to ring up his Western friends to apologise for his abrupt departure.

Vienna has mainly been used by the Russians as a centre for organising espionage outside Austria. In 1969 the Germans discovered that the Russians had obtained details of the radio system for rocket firing, the navigation system for Starfighter aircraft and N.A.T.O. radio codes. Evidence pointed to a spy inside the Frankfurt Battelle Institute, one of the most famous experimental laboratories in Western Germany. This led to the questioning of Josef Eitzenberger, an Austrian-born electronics expert who worked at the Institute. It was noticed that every three weeks Eitzenberger went to Vienna and further inquiries showed that he met Ivan Semjonowitch Moskalenko, counsellor at the Soviet Embassy in Vienna.

Under cross-examination Eitzenberger confessed and revealed that Moskalenko was the Soviet Secret Service controller in Vienna. Eitzenberger had provided Moskalenko with N.A.T.O. and German *Bundeswehr* secrets. Curiously enough Eitzenberger had been taken by the Russians at the end of the war and put to work in various Soviet research laboratories. He returned to Vienna in 1958 and, ironically, it was through the recommendation of the American C.I.A. that he obtained his post in Frankfurt.

Since the war the Austrian spy networks of the Soviet Union have had close links with the Italian networks, but this extends mainly to commercial espionage and not to political matters. Italy has naturally been fertile territory for Russian espionage, mainly because it has the largest Communist Party in the Western World, but also because of Italy's N.A.T.O. associations and the fact that the U.S. Sixth Fleet is based at Naples. The control centre is run from the embassy in Rome, but the most active sector is in Milan, which is more strongly Communist than most other centres.

In the opinion of Italian counter-espionage officers the quality of Russian agents in Italy has fallen off somewhat in recent years. They do not seem to have the same well-educated, professionally trained men as in the early years of the 'cold war'.

Often the Russians will pull off a coup and then ruin it by making an elementary mistake. One such was when a Soviet agent inside the Italian Foreign Office ran off extra copies of secret documents on a duplicating machine that actually recorded the amount of paper consumed. As there was supposed to be a fixed number of copies of these documents the machine quickly revealed that something was amiss.

Italy's biggest Russian spy case broke in 1967 when counter-espionage agents in Turin arrested Giorgio Rinaldi, a thirty-nine-year-old Italian parachutist and stunt man, his fifty-year-old wife, Angela Maria, and their chauffeur, Armando Girard. All three were charged with spying for the Soviet Union on N.A.T.O. bases in Italy and U.S. Air Force bases in Spain as well as gathering information of the movements of Italian and Spanish armed forces.

The spy ring in which Rinaldi operated was said to extend to Spain, France, Switzerland, Cyprus, Greece, Morocco and Scandinavia. Although Rinaldi headed the ring, his wife, who ran an antique shop and called herself Countess Zarina, was the real brains of the complex and widespread network. She was a former volunteer of Benito Mussolini's Women's Corps in World War II. In December 1967 Rinaldi was sentenced to fifteen years' imprisonment for securing and passing information. His wife received a sentence of eleven years and Girard ten years.

Rinaldi was said to have been in touch with the Russian Secret Service since 1956. He was also reported to have told investigators that three hundred people connected with N.A.T.O. were involved in his spy ring. Italian authorities described this claim as 'absolutely false', but despite all the attempts by the Western powers to hush up the case it was clear that Rinaldi's organisation was exceedingly extensive, brilliantly linked up and that he had set up spy cells at every N.A.T.O. base in Europe.

Much of the information he had amassed was never discovered so that the N.A.T.O. powers' bland assumption that the intelligence he had passed to the Russians was of 'no great strategic importance' was somewhat of a bluff. Angela Maria Rinaldi undoubtedly knew much more than she ever revealed and the discovery of the source of some of the leakages of information gave the counter-espionage agents months of work. The Italian police impounded lists of agents, communications codes and two powerful radio transmitting sets in the Rinaldi home and at the antique shop.

Soon after the Rinaldis were arrested a Russian diplomat at the Soviet Embassy in Rome, Yuri Pavlenko, was ordered to leave Italy. Pavlenko had been caught picking up papers and microfilms at a *dubok* in the countryside near Rome.

The breaking of the Rinaldi ring spelt the end of a series of triumphs for the Russians in Italy. The man mainly responsible for breaking it was Admiral Eugenio Henke, who, only a year earlier and without any previous experience of espionage, had taken over the then poorly regarded Italian counter-espionage service, S.I.F.A.R. He quickly reorganised it, weeded out the failures and within five months stamped out two other Soviet spy coups. Kir Lemzenko, a Soviet trade representative in Rome, was expelled from Italy in November 1967, after apparently bungling the task of spying on military installations in Naples with the object of penetrating N.A.T.O. headquarters in Southern Europe. Lemzenko's error was seeking secret information from a warrant officer in the Carabinieri, Italy's national police force.

In 1968 Italian counter-espionage agents unearthed another spy ring when four Italians, two of them working in the Foreign Ministry in Rome, were arrested and charged with passing information to the Soviet Union. This case resulted in the expulsion of another Russian diplomat, Ghennadi Roskoff, of the Russian Embassy's commercial office.

It was in this case that the tell-tale duplicating machine produced the vital clue that led to the arrests. It was found that the machine-operator, Ardens Polastri, was procuring secret documents dealing with Italy's economic and trade relations with other countries as well as its nuclear programmes, acquired from an archivist, Aurelio Pasquali, and then running off extra copies. These had been passed on to an Italian businessman, Lucio Quarantelli, who passed them to Roskoff. The latter was caught with Quarantelli when they kept a rendezvous near the Ponte Milvio, an ancient Roman bridge across the Tiber. A fourth man, Alfredo Catena, representing an Italian electronics firm, was also arrested and charged with having passed on technical information to Roskoff.

During these post-war years there was almost no sphere of Italian life into which Russia had not probed for secrets. Not even the Vatican was immune. In May 1952 it was announced in Rome that Father Alighieri Tondi, Professor of the Gregorian Academy at the Vatican, had been found to be a Soviet agent 'deliberately planted in the Jesuit Order'. Tondi himself touched off what became a nation-wide sensation by repudiating his faith and becoming an ardent Communist. As a youth he had been a brilliant student in engineering and architecture, then he served with Mussolini's army in Ethiopia, returning to Italy when he was twenty-eight and deciding to become a Jesuit. At what stage of his career he became a Marxist is not clear, but when he officially became a Communist in 1952 he said he had voted for the Party since 1948. He soon put the oratory he had devoted to religious work to the cause of Communist propaganda, delivering speeches at Communist political rallies and making violent attacks on the Church. He was given a job in the press office of the Italian Communist Party headquarters in Rome. In 1954 he married in a civil ceremony Signorina Zanti, who had just returned from a visit to Red China.

He was excommunicated on four counts, for renouncing his religion, abandoning the priesthood, actively furthering Communism and marrying outside the Church. And yet, in 1965, Tondi was not only readmitted to the sacraments as a lay Catholic but was given a special dispensation which allowed him to continue to live with Signorina Zanti, who refused a Church marriage and remained a Communist.

The Tondi case is exceptional; only perhaps in Italy could this happen. But, bearing in mind Stalin's eternal query – 'How many battalions has the Pope?' – the Soviet Secret Service has made a number of attempts to infiltrate the Catholic priesthood, mainly in Spain and in parts of Latin America where they actively aid revolutionary movements while remaining as priests. This is not an easy problem for the Vatican to solve: as long as such priests carry out their duties they cannot be faulted for being on the side of the poor and the oppressed. Yet without doubt infiltration of the Church and the priesthood continues and can sometimes be seen in attempts to 'liberalise' and reform the Church.

The main centre of activity of the Soviet Secret Service in the immediate post-war years was, of course, in Germany itself and in Berlin in particular. There was a running battle – often literally a running battle with guns firing at disappearing cars – as Soviet Intelligence and the C.I.A. rivalled one another in their efforts to win over or capture German scientific experts, especially those in the fields of nuclear science and rocketry.

Berlin was in effect the focal point of the spy world, with American, British, French and Russian Intelligence Services competing with one another. The M.V.D. had charge of another massive operation, that of rounding up the remnants of the German Secret Services and of deporting to Siberia and elsewhere those Russians living in areas that had been occupied by the Germans who had collaborated with them. In 1953 Lieut.-Colonel Grigori Burlitski, of the M.V.D., defected to the Americans and revealed that he had helped to organise the deportation of a million Russian subjects. They were members of the Chechen-Ingush Republic of the U.S.S.R., many of whom had collaborated with the Nazis during the German occupation. They included not only the oldest inhabitants but women and children too. The pattern for these deportations, alleged Burlitski, was always the same. A military band was sent to the main square of a city to play music and attract the crowds. Then, when it was judged that a sufficiently large number of people had gathered in the square, the band stopped playing and an M.V.D. officer would announce that they must all be transported to undefined distant destinations.

'Troops of the M.V.D. occupied these republics under the guise of resting and training. We spread friendly propaganda, familiarised ourselves with all the roads and railways, dug in firing positions and listed the name and address of every person in the area. Then, without warning, we struck,' said Lieut.-Colonel Burlitski. 'We packed the people into new lorries supplied with American aid and then into sealed cattle trucks and headed east. I would not know how many survived.'

The recruitment of spies to operate in East and West Germany and in Berlin called for a great deal of ingenuity. Risks that double-agents might be recruited had to be accepted, but each new agent in this area underwent fairly severe tests over a long period. Recruits would be used to spy on other recruits. So desperate was the need to acquire the services of more spies that kidnapping and drugging of the citizens of Berlin became a recognised mode of achieving this.

While in no way attempting to absolve the Russians from the charge of aggressive espionage directed almost entirely against their former Allies, it must also be conceded that the Soviet Union was obsessed with a desire for security and to make certain that Germany would never again be in a position to threaten and invade her. And, too often, the Americans gave the suspicious Russians cause to believe that secretly they supported the building up of West Germany as a bulwark against the Soviet Union. The C.I.A. in their own crude way were often just as ruthless, provocative and stupid as the Soviet Intelligence organisations. This was revealed in the somewhat blatant efforts of the C.I.A. to infiltrate and control anti-Russian organisations such as the N.T.S. and the various anti-Soviet underground bodies in the Balkans.

Despite the revelations of the Canadian spy trials and hints passed on by both the F.B.I. and the C.I.A. to Whitehall that there was reason to believe there were traitors in the British ranks, that trio of spies, Philby, Maclean and Burgess, was still active in the Soviet interest. Donald Maclean and Guy Burgess had both been cleared by a security probe by the Foreign Office after the war. The former, despite his disgraceful behaviour in breaking up an American girl's flat in Cairo and being arrested by the Egyptian police for being drunk while attached to the British Embassy, had been appointed head of the American Department in the Foreign Office in London, ignoring the fact that his drunken outbursts in Cairo had frequently revealed his anti-Americanism. And Guy Burgess, another man who had taken no pains to hide his own anti-American sentiments, was posted as First Secretary to Washington.

Hector McNeil, who was Secretary of State at the Foreign Office at the time, warned Guy Burgess before he set off to Washington: 'For God's sake, Guy, remember three things when you get to the States. Don't be too aggressively left-wing. Don't get involved in race relations; and above all make sure there aren't any homosexual incidents which might cause trouble.'

'I understand, Hector, that I mustn't make a pass at Paul Robeson,' grinned Burgess in reply.

Meanwhile Kim Philby had risen to great heights inside the British Secret Service. He was in the perfect position to keep his Soviet masters informed about American intentions for, as chief British adviser to the C.I.A. in Washington, he had won access to the secrets of both the U.S.A. and Britain. He was able to influence the policies of the U.S.A. and Britain and to keep Russia informed on every development.

Russia had never believed in the sincerity of the 'unconditional surrender' clause of the Allies' decision at the Casablanca Conference. Whether in retrospect it was a wise decision or not may still be in doubt. Politically, at the time, no doubt it was wise: in the long term it may have played right into the hands of Russia by prolonging the war and allowing them to occupy and dominate large areas of Europe. But Philby was quite clear in his own mind that Russia was anxious to see any attempts at a premature negotiated peace with Germany firmly frustrated. A section of the British Secret Service had been very interested in the overtures for peace hinted at by Admiral Canaris of the *Abwehr*. In the midsummer of 1943 a paper was circulated in top circles of the British Secret Service on this very subject. It was suggested that it should be generally circulated to all sections of the Service. Philby effectively blocked this proposal: the paper was seen only by a few.

The next year Otto John arrived in Lisbon as an emissary of Admiral Canaris to put forward peace feelers. Philby, then in charge of the Iberian Section of M.I.6, was again able to discredit him. Nevertheless he must have been alarmed when in 1944 John defected to the British and offered them his services. Philby more than any other man caused the British to view John with the gravest suspicion.

There was a sequel to this after the war. Otto John became head of West German counter-espionage and proved himself to be a most efficient administrator. The Russians must have been worried for he had been a member of the conspiracy to assassinate Hitler in the abortive plot of 30 July 1944. Then in 1954 John went from West Berlin to East Berlin – by his own account after being drugged by a Soviet agent, by other accounts as a defector. He escaped to the West in December 1955 and was tried and sentenced to four years' imprisonment for treasonable falsification in 1956. He was released in 1958 after the remainder of his sentence had been suspended.

Ever since then Otto John has been fighting for a retrial of his case. In his autobiography, *I Came Home Twice*, he alleged that the Soviet agents kidnapped him solely to determine whether Kim Philby was not, after all, a double-agent betraying the Russians to the British. He maintained that throughout his eighteen months behind the Iron Curtain his interrogators never asked him about his work as head of the West German counter-espionage, but that the only subject of interest to his chief interrogator was his former connection with the British Secret Service.

The truth is that the Russians believed Otto John had been an important agent of the British Secret Service and they therefore had doubts about Philby's loyalty when the latter continually denigrated John. Today, Otto John says: 'If the British had taken up the German peace feelers in 1944, then I should certainly have made the acquaintance of Philby, who was at that time the senior official in the British Secret Service dealing with Spain and Portugal. . . . I told the Russians the truth: all our peace feelers had foundered on the obstinate determination of the British to maintain their treaty obligations towards the Russians. In all my interrogations with Michailoff in which he asked for names and contacts in the British Secret Service I never mentioned Philby because I never suspected he was my anonymous adversary. Michailoff finally convinced himself that the Soviet was not being cheated by a double-crosser in the shape of Philby and that they could rely on him. In this sense Philby – I am now certain – was rehabilitated by me with the Russians without my knowing anything about it . . . without realising it I had performed the Russians an inestimable service by my statements. This is why I understand now how it came that I was no longer under Soviet supervision after the interrogations in Gagra, and why I never saw Michailoff again.'

Philby must have had many anxious moments quite apart from the Otto John affair in the post-war years. There was the case of Konstantin Volkoff, who in 1945 was the newly appointed Russian consul in Istanbul. He had called on the Acting British Consul-General in Turkey, saying he was attached to the N.K.V.D. and that he had a proposition to make. In return for payment of the equivalent of £27,500 he was prepared to give the British vital information. He gave the names and addresses of all Soviet agents in the area and then hinted that the most important part of his revelations would be the names of three Russian agents operating inside the British Diplomatic and Secret Services. The British Consul-General passed on the offer to the Secret Service and some time later Kim Philby arrived in Istanbul. The British Consul-General was somewhat disturbed at the delay by the S.I.S. in sending somebody over to see Volkoff and suggested to Philby that the dilatoriness might well have lost them the chance of obtaining important intelligence. For Volkoff could not be found.

This was not surprising for Philby had used the delay in making his visit to warn the Russians about Volkoff and to give them time to remove him. A Russian military aircraft made an unscheduled landing at Istanbul. Before the airport authorities could do anything about it a car raced down to the aircraft and put aboard a stretcher on which was the heavily bandaged figure of Volkoff. Thus Philby had been able to prevent the attempt to unmask not only himself but Maclean and Burgess as well.

Philby's next Secret Service assignment with the British was once more in Istanbul. From the viewpoint of the Russians he could hardly have been in a better place: contact with him was that much easier and he was able to mix with both sides in the espionage game without attracting too much suspicion. One subject into which he looked with especial care at the Soviet's request was that of the Albanian Legality Movement in Exile, an anti-Communist group which had and still has an American headquarters near Times Square Station in New York. Philby was in an excellent position to make such inquiries on behalf of the Russians because as early as 1946 the British had begun to infiltrate agents into Albania to set up an information-gathering and resistance network. The agents were Albanians recruited from displaced persons' camps in Greece and Italy and trained at a British establishment in Malta. Here they were taught to use parachutes, codes and radios before being parachuted into Albania, mainly into the Matia area in Central Albania where there was still a band of people loyal to the monarchy. From 1951–1953 the Americans took over the infiltrating of agents. The last operation took place shortly before Easter in 1953 when a man called Zenel Shehu, a member of the former Royal Albanian bodyguard, was parachuted into Matia with a radio operator. The militia were waiting for him at his rendezvous point – a house occupied by Albanian anti-Communists. They captured his radio and codes and forced him to broadcast an all-clear signal to his base. As a result seven more agents were parachuted in. All were arrested and shot. Within a short time the whole Albanian network was rounded up. Philby was not only completely in the picture as regards the British side of these operations, but in close touch with the American C.I.A. men who were now increasingly master-minding them. All information of forth-coming forays into Albania was passed on to the Russians well in advance.

By the beginning of 1951 evidence pointed to Maclean as the likely source of leaks of information to Russia. It was decided that he must be questioned, if only to give him an opportunity to clear himself. Philby tipped off Burgess who in turn warned Maclean that the British authorities were investigating him and the two Foreign Office men escaped from Britain in a ship from Southampton to Le Havre, taking full advantage of the British long-weekend habit to ensure there was no hue and cry until they were safely in Russian hands.

The leakages from Maclean alone were considerable. While in the U.S.A. he had had access to top secret committees and even into the Atomic Energy Commission centre, and he was also able to pass on details of uranium stockpiling from the Congo by the Western powers and of top secret material on the Korean War.

But if Maclean and Burgess were lost as agents, Philby remained for a long time afterwards. So, too, did the 'Fourth Man' spy of the Russian Secret Service in the British ranks.

Stalin's sudden death caused a silent but unmistakable panic in the Kremlin hierarchy. There was relief that the tyrant was at last dead, for the dictator had been increasingly suspicious of his own entourage in his last days and nobody felt secure. A refusal to drink too much in his presence brought instant disapproval from the Communist leader who took a fiendish delight in seeing his comrades fall drunk under his table.

But now the fear turned from the dead Stalin to the live Beria. Next to Stalin, Beria was by far the most powerful figure and he had under his control the whole Secret Service and police organisation. This fear united the remainder of the Kremlin leaders who, instead of jostling for power, secretly sought to establish a united front against Beria. Khrushchev was foremost in urging this, but it was the amiable, easy-going Georgi Malenkoff who won over the Red Army leaders to his side and finally ensured the downfall of the hated Lavrenti Beria.

Beria, strangely unaware of the moves going on behind his back, had fully intended to seize power for himself. But he made two mistakes: he failed to act quickly enough and he underestimated Malenkoff's influence with the Red Army. A month later he was arrested and executed along with Vsevolod Merkuloff, head of the Ministry of State Security, V. G. Dekansoff, head of the Foreign Department of the First Directorate, Pavel Mesnik, chief of the Department for Diversion and Terror, V. Z. Kobuloff, former general of the M.V.D., S. A. Godlidze, chief of Internal Security, and E. E. Vlodimirsky. Only Krugloff survived, primarily because he was popular with the other Communist leaders and not a self-seeker, but also because he was the only really able man left to carry on the administration of security.

Immediately after Stalin's death the M.G.B. was absorbed into the M.V.D. and Beria personally took full charge of the M.V.D. from Krugloff, no doubt something that counted in Krugloff's favour when Beria was ousted. In March 1954 there was created a new style of State Security body known as the Committee of State Security, or the K.G.B. Krugloff remained in charge of the M.V.D., while Ivan Alexsandrovich Seroff, former deputy Minister of the M.V.D., was appointed head of the K.G.B. Peter Bukhanoff became head of the First Directorate while a new figure in the Intelligence Directorate appeared in the person of Alexander Panyushkin.

Seroff was the son of a peasant, born in 1905 in the Vologda Province of Russia. At the age of eighteen he was head of his native village council and shortly afterwards joined the Red Army, rising to be chief of staff of an artillery regiment. In 1939 he was assigned to the N.K.V.D., serving as a Deputy Commissar for State Security and as such he was responsible for the mass deportations from the three Baltic states which began after their occupation by the U.S.S.R. in June 1940. He was very close to Khrushchev who was undoubtedly in part responsible for his advancement. Seroff had risen steadily in the Soviet hierarchy and in 1945, working under Marshal Zhukoff in Germany, had directed the deportation of German atomic and rocket experts to Russia. A tough, somewhat brutal-looking man with piercing grey-blue eyes, Seroff was efficient and ruthless, but on occasions charming and gifted with a macabre sense of humour laced with sarcasm. He was in charge of the security arrangements for the visit to Britain of Bulganin and Khrushchev in 1956.

The principal outcome of the reorganisation of Intelligence and the Secret Service after the deaths of Stalin and Beria was that the Communist Party established control over the security services so that, in theory at least, it should no longer be possible for one man to control them against the Party's wishes. To some extent, very slight in terms of Western freedom, but more considerable when compared with the Stalinist régime, the legal rights of the ordinary citizen in Russia were strengthened.

Not surprisingly the K.G.B. gained some ground at the expense of the M.V.D. and great pains were taken to give the K.G.B. a better image with the general public. The K.G.B. took over all responsibility for espionage and counter-espionage, controlling Soviet agents abroad and opening up a special counter-espionage service inside the Red Army. The M.V.D. had its wings severely clipped. In 1953 its Special Board was abolished and three years later its military tribunals were also discarded.

The Soviet Union needed to justify its actions after Stalin's death, particularly in relation to the execution of Beria. Curiously enough, quite unfounded rumours about Beria being pro-Western had been circulating in parts of Europe as early as 1948. A high-ranking Spanish diplomat had put about the story that Beria belied his image, that he wanted to have a secret understanding with the Western powers and to end the 'cold war'. This may well have been one of those devious ploys by Soviet Intelligence which never seem to make sense. But whatever the origins of this improbable tale a propaganda campaign against Beria was certainly launched after his death. In December 1953 it was stated, while Beria was still under arrest, that he had admitted plotting against the Soviet Government for a foreign power. The prosecutor's statement alleged that Beria's offences included joining the British counter-revolutionary movement in Baku in 1919 and for many years working 'to destroy capitalism and revive the bourgeoisie'.

There was really no need for the Russians to concoct evidence about Beria working against the Soviet Union for a foreign power. He was generally hated and after his death enough evidence of his sinister habits was provided by those who previously had been too frightened to talk. Lavrenti Beria would prowl the streets of Moscow at night in his bullet-proof Z.I.S. limousine and when he saw an attractive girl – he usually selected teenagers, but sometimes children of under ten – he would have his chauffeur pull up alongside and order the terrified girl into his car. None dared disobey him. He would then be driven to his house in the cellar of which were a number of cubicles where he incarcerated his girls. Here Beria and his deputy, Abakumoff, indulged their sadistic passions in private orgies after they had drugged their victims.

When Khrushchev succeeded Malenkoff he was able to inform

the twentieth Party Congress that 'proper control by the Party and the Government over the activity of the organs of State Security had been established'. In 1958 Seroff was dismissed from the K.G.B., thus removing the last of the Stalinist Intelligence chiefs. He was succeeded by Aleksander Mikhailovich Shelepin, a former youth leader of the Communist Party. It was now policy to give the leadership of the K.G.B. to a Party man, an administrator rather than a professional policeman or espionage agent. Shelepin is one of the Party Puritans, remorseless in his campaign against drunkenness, hooliganism and 'decadent Western pleasures'. From 1952–58 he had been First Secretary of the Komsomol, responsible for guiding the destinies of the younger generations of the U.S.S.R. As Komsomol leader he had made frequent trips abroad, taking a prominent part in international Communist Front organisations. He was one of the organisers of the Sixth World Youth Festival in Moscow in 1957.

To some extent Shelepin's function as head of the K.G.B. was to carry on with the work of improving its image. As a former youth leader he sought to publicise the K.G.B. as an honourable and patriotic service which needed recruits from the younger generation. He tried to modernise its outlook as far as was possible and his successor, Vladimir Semichastny, who took charge of the K.G.B. in 1961, had also been a director of the Party Youth Organisation. Shortly after his appointment he inspired an article in *Izvestia* which marked one of the first open attempts to glorify the K.G.B. The article included an interview with 'a senior K.G.B. officer' – Semichastny himself – who stated: 'Many young Party and Komsomol workers have joined the K.G.B. and none of the people who, during the time of the personality cult, took part in the repressions against innocent Soviet people is now in the Service.'

Semichastny not only listed the major objects of the K.G.B.'s attention – the activities of foreign intelligence services, State crimes such as treason, illegal currency operations, smuggling and the betrayal of secrets – but urged that the K.G.B. had another side to its character, 'the rehabilitation of people unjustly accused during the "personality cult". This,' added Semichastny, 'is a politically important task which our investigating units are still concerned with.'

The interview in *Izvestia* expanded on this last theme and explained how K.G.B. procedure had changed. It told of a young man serving in a Soviet mission abroad who was compromised by a foreign intelligence service. Because the young man still had 'old ideas' about the K.G.B. he was afraid to inform the Soviet authorities of what had happened and agreed to work for the foreign service. However, in due course he regretted his action and confessed it and did not lose his job. Because of such cases as those the K.G.B. had now initiated a law which allowed Soviet citizens who had been trapped into a foreign intelligence service's network to confess without being liable to punishment.

One may smile somewhat cynically at the idea of the K.G.B. retaining the services of anyone who had even temporarily served a foreign power. After all, even in the most lenient of the democracies such a lapse would hardly be pardoned. But it came as a shock to the post-Stalin régime to find that agents who had been perfectly loyal previously were defecting out of sheer fright after Beria's execution merely because they imagined that association with Beria would lead to their own arrest.

The ruthlessness is still there, but there is more evidence of the velvet glove these days and the K.G.B.'s concern to maintain and still further improve its image has continued since the late fifties. For example, for close on fifty years after the October Revolution there were no such people as 'Russian spies' in the Soviet official view. The word 'spy' applied only to other nations' spies, decadent, corrupt, working only for money and enemies of the Soviet Union. The change, and the attempt to glorify the spy, came abruptly in the early sixties. Then, suddenly, and to the surprise of the Russian people, the celebrated case of Richard Sorge was given great publicity. The decision to break an unspoken but always strictly observed taboo must have come from the very top. The Soviet spy was to be glorified. A whole spate of similar revelations followed and the Soviet press, magazines, books and television programmes revealed the names of many second-rate, small-time operatives in the Nazi-occupied territories during the war as well as those of the top spies, even delving back into the epics of Cheka spies during the Civil War.

Pride of place was to be given to such non-Russian spies as Philby and his two Foreign Office accomplices, indicating that 'these honest English Communists had worked for a better future for mankind'. The Lenin Order (Russia's highest decoration) awarded to Philby must have helped dispel the lingering ideological confusion around the task of spying for a foreign country.

The reasons for this change are multifarious. The Soviet decision to glorify some of their own star spies may have been sparked off by the publicity surrounding the case of Oleg Penkovsky, the high official executed on charges of spying for Britain and the U.S.A. in the spring of 1963. The object of the new publicity was presumably to deaden the impact of this treachery by showing that the Russians' own spies were equally efficient. Then followed a dozen or so biographies of Sorge as well as a play and a film. Next to be publicised was Colonel Rudolf Abel, of whom more later. By the time Russia's secret police celebrated their fiftieth anniversary everyone in Russia must have heard the epics of their nation's espionage game. The K.G.B.'s many failures in the field of internal security, heightened by its inability to check the mass protests that followed the Sinyavsky and Daniel trial, forced it to press on with its glorification of its own spies. One official view was that the Russian people needed to be reassured that watchful spies were actively engaged combating their enemies while they slept in their beds. Some, even higher up in the Party hierarchy, thought the publicity would be good for recruitment and stimulate patriotism. But the K.G.B. were surely being somewhat desperate when they selected non-Russians such as Philby and Blake as their K.G.B. heroes. It may even be that Philby himself persuaded them that such publicity was good for the K.G.B.'s image.

America had been so infiltrated and compromised by Soviet agents over many years and the Soviet grip was so tight that neither the F.B.I. nor the C.I.A. has ever been able to eradicate its still powerful influence and networks in the U.S.A. Indeed, the aggressive aspects of the C.I.A.'s provocative tactics in Europe, the Far East and in its approach to the Cuban problem have been a measure of the frustration felt in coping with the continued menace of the Russian Secret Service in America. Between the early thirties and the end of the forties, Russian spies had found their way into the administrative staff of the White House, the State Department, Treasury, Army, Navy, Justice, six Congressional committees, the Office of Strategic Services, the War Manpower Committee, the International Monetary Fund (where the Soviet Union has powerful influences to this day), the Government Printing Office, the Reconstruction Finance Corporation, U.S. Information Services, the North African Control Board (a World War II organisation), the United Nations, U.N.R.R.A. and many other bodies as well.

For some years Russia's principal influence in the U.S. administration was from inside the Treasury where they had suborned Harry Dexter White, assistant to the Secretary of the Treasury, Nathan Gregory Silvermaster, Harold Glasser, Solomon Adler, Sonia Gold and William Taylor. White had been able to inform the Russians of the plan envisaged by Henry Morgenthau at the U.S. Treasury for restricting German industry after the war and making Germany mainly an agricultural nation so that she could not again become a military power. In 1946 White had been appointed to an important position with the International Monetary Fund and, knowing the value of having such a key agent in this organisation, the Russians put pressure on White to initiate I.M.F. policies which coincided with Russian wishes.

Edgar Hoover, head of the F.B.I., had long suspected White and on 1 February 1946 he sent a confidential report to General Harry H. Vaughan at the White House, stating that 'information has come to the attention of this Bureau charging White as being a valuable adjunct to an underground Soviet espionage organisation operating in Washington. . . . Material which came into his possession as a result of his official capacity allegedly was made available through intermediaries to Nathan Silvermaster and William Ludwig Ullmann. Both Silvermaster and Ullmann are employees of the U.S. Treasury Department reportedly under the supervision of White. The information and documents originating in the Treasury Department were either passed on in substance or photographed by Ullmann in a well-equipped laboratory in the basement of the Silvermaster home. . . . This whole network has been under intensive investigation since November 1945, and it is the results of these efforts that I am now able to make available to you. . . . It is reported that the British and Canadian delegates to the International Monetary Fund may possibly nominate and support White for the post of President of the I.M.F.'

The F.B.I. had been incredibly lax in allowing the White affair to drag on for so long. The excuse that they wanted to catch the whole of the Soviet network is hardly valid because the urgent need was to stop the rot and check widespread infiltration. Nobody could expect in the long run to catch every agent. But the White House officials refused to heed these warnings so that White not only took up his new post but brought with him into the I.M.F. such Soviet agents as Frank Coe and Harold Glasser.

It was Whittaker Chambers who finally destroyed the major part of the network by forcing the attention of the whole nation on the hidden peril in their midst. Chambers had become a Communist back in the twenties, first working for the *Daily Worker* in America, then becoming an agent of the G.R.U. As long ago as 1932 he had been involved in the 'Ware Ring', mentioned earlier, and had been given the job of recruiting agents and informers in high places. It was Chambers who recruited White, Silvermaster, Alger Hiss, of the State Department, and many others, and also formed the pro-Communist American Writers' Syndicate. In 1938, at the time of the Stalinist purges, Chambers had a change of heart and wanted desperately to escape from the Soviet network. Yet he knew that anyone so deeply involved as he was in Soviet Secret Service ramifications, ran the almost certain risk of being liquidated if he defected. For several months he hid himself away and pondered his dilemma.

In the end Chambers compromised. He tried to buy his life by giving the Russians the impression that though he had left the network, he was keeping silent about his work for them. At the same time he managed to pass on to the U.S. authorities a few quarter-truths. His aim was for the latter to make their own inquiries and arrive at the truth without implicating him any further. But it did not work out like that. Nobody in authority paid much attention to him; Roosevelt and most of his administration were amicably disposed towards Russia and not anxious to upset their relations with the Soviet Union. It may seem strange that the Russians were so easily misled about Chambers and that they did not follow out standard practice by obliterating all trace of their man, but this was the honeymoon period of American–Soviet relations and they may well have taken the view that the goodwill of Roosevelt was worth more than the killing of Chambers.

Chambers hinted to the U.S. authorities that he had broken with the Communists and was frightened they might kill him, but he never at this stage named the vital contacts he had established for the Russians inside the U.S. administration. As the war continued he dropped a few more hints, but not even the O.S.S. took any notice. By 1948, in the atmosphere of spy hysteria in U.S.A., Chambers felt safe to tell more, concentrating mainly on Alger Hiss. Chambers was by then an editor of *Time* and Hiss had left the State Department to become president of the Carnegie Endowment for International Peace.

There were many others who deserved denunciation more than Hiss and in the early stages of this case it seemed that Chambers himself might be tried for perjury and that Hiss would be vindicated. Ultimately, after hearings before the House Committee on Un-American Activities, Hiss was indicted for perjury and sentenced to a term of imprisonment. Alger Hiss became a martyr and many people today believe he was shamefully treated. Chambers did nothing to enhance his own reputation and the Hiss affair cast a smoke-screen of confusion around the whole question of infiltration of Government services by the Soviet.

In the early fifties Russia continued to concentrate on atomic espionage in the U.S.A. as well as in Australia where the new Anglo-Australian experimental station at Woomera for testing rockets in the South Australian Desert had been set up. The N.K.V.D. had established a network in Australia during the war through Semion Makaroff and Feodor Nosoff, who was the Tass News Agency correspondent in that country. The methods adopted there were similar to those in the United States – the winning over of Russian sympathisers in the Ministries. But their efforts did not meet with the same success they did in the U.S.A. and were hindered by the poor quality of some of their chief agents. After the war Makaroff was succeeded by Valentin Sadovnikoff who was later replaced because he became altogether too friendly with Australians without producing any worthwhile results. The next man, Ivan Pakomoff, was reprimanded for indolence and Moscow became so impatient that it sent out a number of men in quick succession to speed up their work. They were Vladimir Petroff and his wife, Evdokia, who was also a N.K.V.D. agent, F. V. Kislitsyn and N. G. Kovalioff.

Petroff, who must have sensed that the other men were being sent to report back to Moscow on him, tried to safeguard himself by warning the Centre that security in Australia had been tightened up after the Canadian spy scare, that opportunities for obtaining worthwhile intelligence were limited and that the U.S.S.R. had suffered through the mediocrity of previous agents. The Centre responded by criticising Petroff for failing to give proper guidance and in the spring of 1954 ordered him back to Moscow. To return meant certain arrest and probable death, so Petroff decided to defect. Meanwhile the Russians put his wife aboard a plane for Moscow, accompanied by a bodyguard of strong-arm men from the Soviet Embassy. The plane stopped at Darwin to refuel and the Australian authorities allowed Petroff to speak to his wife by telephone. After this conversation Madame Petroff called out to Australian customs officers that she did not wish to go to Moscow. Her bodyguard promptly seized her and rushed her away towards the plane, but Australian officials intervened and she was allowed to stay.

The defection of the Petroffs caused a world-wide sensation. Russia and Australia broke off diplomatic relations and Petroff gave to the Western World detailed evidence of the extent and the methods of Russian Secret Service infiltration in the sub-continent.

Over the next few years there was an increase in the number of defecting Russian agents. Some were deliberately ordered to defect for the purposes of misleading the West. The defections revealed serious weaknesses in the Russians' methods of recruiting key personnel, but they may also have hidden a new policy by the K.G.B., a return to the *agent provocateur* tactics of the era of 'The Trust'.

There was the defection of Juri Rastoroff in Japan. Far worse was that of Captain Nicolas Khokhloff, of the Division for Terror and Diversion, as the 'Murder Squad' was now designated. Khokhloff had been selected by Colonel Studnikoff, then head of the Division, to stamp out the activities of the N.T.S. That, at least, was the ostensible purpose of the operation assigned to Khokhloff. But without in any way questioning the motives of Khokhloff himself, one may usefully ask what was the real intention of the K.G.B.

The N.T.S., sometimes known as the Society of National Unity, was founded in 1930 as the *Netsionelno-Trudovoy-Soyuz*, which, roughly translated, means the 'Producers' Party', embracing technicians, labourers, artists, farmers, engineers, professional men and producers of all kinds. It aimed to be a constructive movement to combat Communism with a definite political and social programme. The idea of the 'producer motive' was to popularise the movement within Russia by catering for the productive members of the community who would be essential to its success. The object was to improve the life of the Russian masses and to offer a worthwhile alternative to Communism.

The N.T.S. was not a Czarist movement and for that reason it was unpopular with the Czarists of the old school as with the Communists. It included among its members many who were not of Russian origin, but Letts, Lithuanians, Esthonians and Germans with Russian ancestry. For years it slumbered as an ineffective society, but the war and the creation after the war of the satellite states gave it something of an impetus. For the N.T.S. needed both funds and outside aid and during the war these came in the shape of assistance from the Nazi Intelligence. To be fair it should also be stated that at the end of the war more than two hundred members of the N.T.S., including some of its leadership, were incarcerated in Nazi concentration camps. After the war the N.T.S. was linked to the American C.I.A. through one of its members, K. Boldyreff, and, having acquired funds from American sources, proceeded to set up cells in Yugoslavia, Hungary, Rumania, Poland and Czechoslovakia.

Yet the truth is that the N.T.S. was infiltrated by the N.K.V.D. shortly after its inception and manipulated by the U.S.S.R. just as 'The Trust' had been. The Soviet Union has never made any effort to destroy this organisation and statements by Andropoff and others about its being a threat to the State can be regarded as pure propaganda. If this seems a paradoxical state of affairs, let us examine the record of Russian achievements through infiltration of the N.T.S. These have not been revealed before because the N.T.S. will never admit that it has been penetrated and the U.S.S.R. obviously has no desire to reveal the fact. Its first success was when Soviet agents inside the N.T.S. betrayed Russian monarchist organisations in Paris in the thirties, leading to the betrayal of General Kutyepoff, whose wife proved to be an N.K.V.D. agent, and the kidnapping and killing of General Miller. Towards the end of World War II the Russians obtained a great deal of intelligence about Nazi machinations by infiltrating those ranks of the N.T.S. who were actively working with the Germans.

In the early fifties the N.T.S. were busily distributing leaflets behind the Iron Curtain and in Austria and in Western Germany were led by Georgi Okolovich, whose aim was to subvert Red Army soldiers and Communist officials in East Germany. Nicolas Khokhloff, an experienced assassin, was given specific instructions to kill Okolovich. This plan was temporarily delayed by a meeting of the Foreign Ministers of Britain, France, Russia and the U.S.A., and the Russians did not wish to have a murder on their hands at such a moment. Then, in February 1954, Khokhloff went to Frankfurt and astounded Okolovich by calling at the latter's apartment, telling him he had been instructed to kill him and asking to be put in touch with the American security forces.

Now whatever Khokhloff's defection may have cost the Russians in bad publicity, they at least learned that Okolovich was in league with the C.I.A. and a great deal more about the Americans' links with the N.T.S. The Americans publicised Khokhloff's defection to the fullest extent, calling a press conference at which he described how he and two East Germans had been ordered by the K.G.B. to kill Okolovich in Frankfurt. Khokhloff gave a detailed account of the work of the 'Murder Squad'. He explained that the Ninth Section for Diversion and Terror was subordinate to the Second Department of the M.V.D. and that it was the direct successor of the Fourth General Directorate of the N.K.V.D. which, during the war, had been responsible for partisan activities in the rear of the German armies.

Great publicity was given to the weapons used by the 'Murder Squad' and these were shown to the press, photographed and widely distributed. They included dummy cigarette cases which fired silent poison bullets, powered by tiny batteries. The poison – in paste form – consisted of two-thirds potassium cyanide and one-third gum. Khokhloff revealed that the murder weapons were produced at a special laboratory at Kuchine near Moscow.

21

George Blake and Rudolf Abel

GEORGE BLAKE and Kim Philby have each in turn been designated the 'super-spy' of all foreign agents employed by the Soviet Union, although in fact neither can compare with Richard Sorge. Nevertheless, if one is to assess the two men objectively I would hazard a guess that in the long run George Blake will prove to have been the more professional.

Two recent works have been published on George Blake. One is by E. H. Cookridge, himself a wartime secret agent on the Allied side; the other is by Sean Bourke, the Irishman who helped Blake to escape from Wormwood Scrubs in 1966. Though both men knew Blake, each in his way seems baffled by him. Mr Cookridge writes: 'His life has patterns incomprehensible to the ordinary person and beyond the imagination of most of us. No work of fiction could portray his career as credible. . . . None has penetrated below the surface to give a real explanation of what made Blake the man he was, what prompted his actions.'

Yet Mr Cookridge met George Blake during World War II and worked with him both then and after the end of hostilities.

Sean Bourke has this to say: 'I first met George Blake on an educational class at Wormwood Scrubs Prison. We very soon became friends. Like everyone else at the prison . . . I was deeply impressed by Blake's charm and good manners and by his humanitarian concern for the well-being of his fellow-men. So much so, that when one day in the cell block he asked me to spring him from gaol I agreed without hesitation. But when we eventually arrived in Moscow Blake very quickly began to show himself for what he really was: a ruthless traitor.'

What each author is in effect admitting is the absolute professionalism of Blake. It is the job of the professional spy to be an enigma; for the double-agent, such as Blake, to baffle is of paramount importance.

Blake's career is in many respects a much more impressive performance than that of either Philby or Maclean. He started with all the disadvantages. Whereas Philby and Maclean were both British-born, belonging to well-known Establishment families,

Blake was only British by accident. He was the son of Albert William Behar, an Egyptian Jew married to a Dutchwoman, and was born in Rotterdam in 1922. The father acquired a British passport. During World War II, while still a boy, George Blake joined the Dutch Resistance against the Nazis, escaped to Britain and was enrolled in the Dutch and British secret organisations in London. It is possible, if not probable, that he may have met members of the Dutch Communist network inside the Resistance movement in Holland and that they may have encouraged him to remember 'the cause' when he reached Britain. In London he took the name of Blake, joined the Royal Navy as an ordinary seaman and eventually became an officer.

Because of his linguistic ability he was used on intelligence work, later became a senior agent in the British Secret Service in Germany and in 1948 was sent to Korea nominally as vice-consul, but still as a key agent.

A four-thousand word account of George Blake's career was published in two instalments in *Izvestia* in 1970, based on an interview with him. Up to the date mentioned in the last paragraph the *Izvestia* story tallies completely with the British account of Blake's early days. It does, however, give somewhat more detail of his naval service, saying that after he became an officer he was assigned to the submarine service, but in view of his perfect command of the Dutch language was transferred to the Dutch section of the S.I.S. His duty, it was alleged, was to receive coded radio messages concerning the location and time of attack on important targets in Holland which he decoded and transmitted to the R.A.F. Quoting Blake's own words, the narrative continues that after he joined the British Secret Service in Germany following the war 'then came Churchill's sadly renowned Fulton speech. It marked the beginning of the "cold war" period and the entire activity of S.I.S. made a hundred and eighty degree turn. . . . I began to fear a Nazi revival and to think that all of the sacrifices of the Soviet Union and the other socialist countries had been in vain.'

He had been ordered by the British to collect information on the Soviet occupation troops in Germany and to observe individual Soviet officers with a view to recruiting them for espionage. He was already fluent in English, Dutch, French and German: now he set about learning Russian. He decided that the Americans and British were bent on reviving German militarism and made up his mind to devote his entire efforts to frustrating Western Intelligence operations against the U.S.S.R. *Izvestia* stated 'the position of the Soviet operative Blake inside the British Intelligence Service enabled him to keep abreast of many subversive operations by S.I.S. and also by the C.I.A.'.

When the Korean war broke out Blake was taken prisoner and held in captivity by the North Koreans, suffering severe hardships. Yet throughout that time of stress, strain and brain-washing he gave no evidence of being pro-Communist to his fellow-prisoners. Commissioner Lord, of the Salvation Army, who was a fellow-prisoner, declared afterwards that 'George was a good man to be interned with. He turned his hand willingly to any kind of job, cooking, cleaning and all the other chores we had to do. He did it all with good humour, always ready to help others.'

After the 1953 armistice Blake returned to London and was given promotion in the British Secret Service, being posted to Berlin with instructions not merely to spy on the Russians but to play the rôle of a double-agent, infiltrating the Soviet espionage set-up with the full knowledge of his employers. Now if a man is asked to pose as a double-agent, any secret service takes a risk. For if such a man is to pose successfully as a double-agent he must give some information to the other side. All one can say is that the S.I.S. took a grave risk with a man who was not one hundred per cent British. The man who is used as a double-agent is a permanent security risk.

Leaving aside the question of the executive of the S.I.S. and the Foreign Office, jointly responsible for Blake's promotion, the head of the Russian section of the British Secret Service on the Continent up to about 1958 was Colonel Charles Gilson, who was stationed at Minden in West Germany. This section was later moved to Italy and Gilson, who retired shortly afterwards, blew out his brains in Rome. This is a sidelight on the Blake affair, but it is one of a number of unexplained mysteries connected with it.

Blake has since volunteered the information that one of the main functions of his British section's work in Berlin was wire-tapping the missions of Soviet bloc countries as well as the apartments of their staff. Huge sums of money were assigned to such work which, he alleges, was done sometimes in co-operation with the C.I.A. Many American as well as British secrets were passed by Blake to the Soviet.

One of the biggest of these was 'Operation Gold' in which the S.I.S. and the C.I.A. combined to build a tunnel from West Berlin to East Berlin so that Russian and East German telephones could be tapped. The decision to start this tunnel was taken in December 1953, according to Blake, who said he read the minutes of a meeting at which the decision was taken and passed the information to Moscow immediately. The tunnel was 'officially' discovered by the Russians in 1956 and they promptly turned it to propagandist advantage which greatly embarrassed the N.A.T.O. powers. The tunnel was started in a suburb of Rudow, near a cemetery, and ran for about half a mile under the barbed wire fences of the border into Alt Glienicke in East Berlin. It was at the end of the tunnel that the British-American team were able to tap the main telephone lines connecting East German Government offices, the Karlshorst K.G.B. headquarters and the Soviet Army Command with all their links to Moscow, Warsaw and elsewhere.

The Russians called a press conference in East Berlin at which Colonel Kotsuba of the K.G.B. revealed the whole story to Western newspaper correspondents and for the next few weeks more than 12,000 East Berliners were conducted on sight-seeing tours of the tunnel.

The full extent of Blake's uncovering of British and American Secret Service activities over a period of eight years is possibly still not fully appreciated. He caused the deaths and disappearance of many Western agents behind the Iron Curtain and he played such havoc with British Intelligence that their networks in East Germany, the Middle East and some Iron Curtain countries had to be rebuilt. He was also able to undermine the work of a special shop set up in West Berlin to recruit Soviet citizens as spies for the West. For all this he was awarded the Order of Lenin.

Eventually Blake was caught only because a German informant and a Polish defector gave him away. The trouble for Blake started with the arrest in Bremerhaven of Horst Heinz Ludwig, a German naval officer, who was charged with having spied for the Russians. When Ludwig made a full confession he mentioned a double-agent known by the code-name of 'Victor' who had worked for the British and passed information to the Russians. German Intelligence eventually decided that 'Victor' was Horst Eitner, an agent who had worked with Blake for the British. But by this time, in 1960, Blake had been posted to Beirut to attend a course at the British Middle-East College for Arabic Studies. By a coincidence Kim Philby was in Beirut at the same time.

Philby had had a charmed life since the flight of Burgess and Maclean to Russia. There had been hints in Parliament and in the British press that Philby was the 'Third Man' traitor who had warned the two British diplomats that M.I.5 was investigating them. But though Philby had been relieved of his key post in British Intelligence, he had been fully exonerated in 1955 from any complicity with the other British traitors. He had then become Middle-Eastern correspondent for the British newspaper, *The Observer*, based in Beirut.

In October 1960 Eitner was arrested in Berlin and charged with 'intelligence with a potential enemy'. While in prison in 1961 Eitner told the Germans that he had become a double-agent at the instigation of Blake. The Germans at first seemed to disbelieve Eitner, but they passed the information on to the British whose Foreign Office was equally incredulous. Nevertheless it was decided to make certain checks on Blake's past career.

By this time the Russians were fully aware that Blake had been 'blown' and that it was only a matter of time before he was caught. It is possible, however, that they were somewhat perturbed at the delay on the part of the British in taking action. They may even have wanted to check that this double-agent was not serving the British better than the Soviet. In such circumstances the Russians often react differently from other intelligence organisations: instead of trying to obliterate or discredit the leakage of information, they obliquely confirm it. Thus, with the Blake case, they leaked information about Blake's complicity to sources in Poland, knowing that if the Americans heard of his treachery before the British admitted it further mistrust would be created between U.S. and British security services.

The man who duly leaked this information to the Americans was Colonel Michael Goleniewski, of the Polish Intelligence Service, who defected to West Berlin on Christmas Day 1960. Flown to Washington, he gave the C.I.A. a great deal of information about Soviet espionage and included an account of how George Blake had been a Soviet spy for many years.

When the Americans passed this news on to the British it was realised in Whitehall that the Blake affair could no longer be contained by discreet inquiries. Yet astonishingly the action the British took proffered Blake at least an opportunity for escape. He was told by telegraph message to report to the Foreign Office in London for important consultations. Blake must have known by then that there was a real risk of his being unmasked, for he would have heard all about Eitner's arrest. It is possible, of course, that the Russians ordered him to return to London, that they wanted to be sure that Goleniewski's information had been passed on.

Blake said farewell to his wife, Gillian, and his two children and returned to London on 3 April 1961. He was arrested and in May 1961 sentenced to forty-two years' imprisonment for betraying secrets to the Russians.

Blake made no attempt to deny the charges: he pleaded guilty. The Attorney-General, referring to the fact that Blake had made a confession, said: ' . . . more than ten years ago his philosophical and political views underwent a change and . . . he held the strong conviction that the Communist system was the better one and deserved to triumph. It appears from his statement that for the past nine and a half years while employed in the Government service, and drawing his salary from the State, he had been working as an agent for the Russians.'

There was, however, one significant remark which the Judge made when sentencing Blake: 'I fully recognise that it is unfortunate for you that many matters urged in mitigation cannot be divulged, but I am perfectly prepared to accept that it was not for money you did this, but because of your conversion to a genuine belief in the Communist system.'

This was obviously a reference to the fact that Blake had been ordered to pose as a double-agent by the British.

It is almost impossible to list all the triumphs and failures of the Russian Secret Service in the sixties. It would be difficult to draw up a balance sheet of profit and loss. There are no Russian figures, of course, to show the numbers who have defected from them and to them. Western figures are misleading and probably suspect. The latest I have gleaned from Western Intelligence sources, when reduced to an average to allow for inaccuracies, show that in the period since 1953 some 806 have defected from the Soviet side (this figure includes East Germans, Poles, Czechs, Hungarians, etc., as well as Russians), but only 93 have gone over from the Western side to the Soviet.

There is no reason for the West to be complacent about these statistics, even assuming they are accurate, which is at least open to doubt. Under any harsh totalitarian system one must expect a large number of defectors. But for the free democracies of the West to have nearly one hundred defectors is alarming enough. It is even more alarming when one considers that many of these defectors have been men of education, enjoying social prestige and important posts. One can fairly safely assume that of the 93 who have gone over the vast majority are dedicated and fanatical supporters of the Soviet system. On the other hand, of the 806 who have defected from the Soviet side a large number have almost certainly been deliberately planted by the Russian Secret Service to mislead, sow seeds of dissension and to play the rôle of *agent provocateur* in one way or another.

Daring, ingenuity and skilful psychology were all employed in bringing off some of the Soviet's coups in the fifties and sixties. In May 1960, at the closing stages of a Security Council debate, Mr Henry Cabot Lodge, United States delegate, produced a listening device which had been introduced into America's Moscow Embassy by the Russians. It had been concealed in a carving of America's Great Seal, presented to the Embassy by the Russians. Opening the carving, Mr Lodge pointed out a compartment for the device and said that the discovery of this and well over one hundred similar devices in American buildings inside Russia and the satellite countries showed that evidence of Soviet espionage was not 'fanciful', as had been claimed. Mr Lodge revealed that 'a clandestine listening device was discovered inside this replica of the Great Seal. At the time of the discovery there was a plaster of paris ring around the edge of the Seal, which was joined at the front and the back so that it looked as though it was a solid piece of wood.

'I might add that in recent years the United States has found within its embassies, missions and residences in the Soviet Union well over one hundred such devices.'

Astute psychological understanding has been marked not only in exploiting the vices and weaknesses of persons the U.S.S.R. wished to suborn, but in playing on people's vanity. One such example is the case of Stig Wennerstroem. This Swedish Air Force colonel of middle age was angry and frustrated because he felt he had been passed over for promotion. He came of a good family with large estates to the north of Stockholm. The Russians learned of his bitterness towards the Swedish authorities and made cautious attempts to establish contact. There were invitations to parties and dinners, much sympathy tactfully expressed that he did not gain the promotion due to him, mixed with some flattery and the suggestion, casually thrown out in conversation, that if Sweden did not take him seriously the Soviet Union could use a man of his talents and would reward him with real prospects of promotion. It was one of the cleverest jobs the K.G.B. pulled off to enrol Stig Wennerstroem as an agent and he provided them with a mass of information not merely on Sweden, but on Norwegian and N.A.T.O. secrets as well. The Russians' ploy was to feed his vanity and to give him inside the Soviet Secret Service the promotion he had been refused in Sweden. Stig Wennerstroem was made a major-general in Russian Intelligence and even presented with a series of secret decorations.

In the end the Swede was caught and given a life sentence by a Swedish court. He has now served nearly nine years of his sentence, but, as a concession, has been moved from the maximum security prison at Oesteraker to an open prison at Skenaes in Northern Sweden.

Another aspect of the Russian use of psychological tactics in the espionage game is that of trapping potential agents into compromising positions and then blackmailing them into working for the Soviet Union. When new members of Embassy staffs or foreign missions arrive in Russia, or any of the satellite countries, a careful note is made of any of their weaknesses or vices. Sometimes this information is obtained from agents in territories where they have previously been posted, sometimes it results from patient shadowing of the people concerned. If a man is short of money and discontented, he is marked down as a possible new recruit. If he is carrying on an illicit affair, or has homosexual tendencies, this, too, is exploited. Sometimes the Soviet Secret Service, if they are desperately anxious for information from a foreign power, will simply trap a man by luring him to a hotel bedroom, or a private room at a restaurant, planting a female or male on him while hidden cameras record the incriminating evidence.

Typical examples of this method of recruitment of agents among foreigners are those of John Vassall and Harry Houghton. The former, son of a Church of England clergyman, was a clerk in the Admiralty who, in 1953, had been posted to the British Embassy in Moscow to work in the office of the naval attaché. It was an unwise posting in the first place for British security should have known that Vassall was a homosexual. Not only should they have known this but they should have realised that the Russians keep a dossier on such persons. The K.G.B. knew quite a lot about Vassall before he reached Moscow, just as they had acquired a dossier on Houghton before he was drafted to Warsaw. They knew, too, that Vassall loved luxury and hankered after a much higher standard of living than his job with the Admiralty could give him. So Vassall was invited to parties, lured into homosexual traps, photographed and finally confronted with the evidence. If he did not promise to spy for the Soviet Union, he would be exposed. Exposure would have been simple: a selection of compromising photographs sent anonymously to London would have been sufficient.

By 1955 Vassall was operating as a Soviet spy. He removed important documents from the naval attaché's office, handed them to a Soviet agent who photographed them and handed them back to Vassall to return to the files. Then Vassall was posted back to London to work in the Naval Intelligence Division. In October 1959 he was sent to the Fleet Section of Military Branch II, the secretariat of the Naval Staff of the Admiralty where he had access to material of considerable importance. By this time he was photographing documents himself and passing them on to the Russians. In due course Admiralty Intelligence began to realise that some of their secrets were reaching Russia. Vassall became a suspect, and was finally discovered with copies of seventeen Admiralty documents in his flat.

Harry Houghton's case was different, but there was the same technique of discovering his weaknesses and exploiting them. When Houghton, an ex-Royal Navy petty officer who had retired and become an Admiralty clerk, was posted to Warsaw, he revealed a marked tendency for heavy drinking and a love of parties. He was invited to many Polish parties and through these made the acquaintance of a member of the K.G.B. Houghton was immediately earmarked as a possible agent and when he was recalled to Britain and sent to the top secret Portland experimental establishment of the Navy was almost immediately recruited into the Soviet spy network.

When the Russians launched on their glorification of Soviet spies campaign in the mid-sixties, Colonel Rudolf Abel was the first to get this treatment while he was still alive. This occurred in the autumn of 1965 and in the following February Abel told his own story in the monthly magazine, *Young Communist*. In the same year Vadim Kozhevnikoff's novel, *Sword and Shield*, was first published in the literary monthly *Znamya*.

It is generally assumed in Russia that Colonel Abel provided the prototype for Kozhevnikoff's hero, Alexander Beloff, whose surname was a transposition of Abel in Russian. Abel himself never confirmed this, nor did the author, but when a spy film entitled *Dead Season* was released in the Soviet Union Abel appeared on the screen with some introductory remarks. The film was about a Russian spy who had operated successfully in a foreign country over many years until he was caught, tried and given a long prison sentence. Eventually he was exchanged for a foreign agent who had been apprehended in Russia. The story of the film was remarkably like the career of Abel himself.

Rudolf Ivanovitch Abel was born in Russia on 2 July 1902, some say in Moscow, but he himself says it was at St Petersburg. He came from a good family in Southern Russia and his grandfather had been a minor official under the Czars. His father travelled a great deal and took his son around with him. Abel says that his father was a member of the 'Union of Struggle for the Liberation of the Working Class' and that he helped his father distribute Bolshevik literature.

Young Abel was a talented linguist and taught English, German and Polish at a Moscow school in his early twenties. He attributed his mastery of languages to the fact that after the Revolution he was assigned to work among young political émigrés who had repatriated. In 1922 he joined the Komsomol and at the same time took up radio-telegraphy as a hobby so that when he was called up for military service he served in a radio unit. When he was demobilised he graduated as a radio engineer and then in 1927, at the age of twenty-five, joined the G.P.U. as an agent assigned to the foreign espionage branch.

That much the Russians have revealed about Abel's early days, but they say nothing about his subsequent activities prior to his arrest in the Latham Hotel, New York, on 21 June 1957. On the other hand Beloff, his prototype in *Sword and Shield*, had as a first assignment the job of getting assimilated by Baltic Germans in Riga. It is probable that Abel's first foreign assignment was the same. Abel's wartime activities were concerned mainly with Germany and he was cited in dispatches for distinguished action as an intelligence officer on the German front; by the time the war was over he was a major in the N.K.V.D. Somehow he survived even Beria's anger, for his objective reports on the German military organisation and equipment, which he compared favourably to the Russian, enraged the head of the Secret Service.

Once during the war he secured a job as chauffeur with the *Abwehr*, passing back all information he gleaned to Moscow. During the first week of the war against Russia the Germans decorated him and promoted him to lance-corporal.

Some of these known details of Abel's activities are told in *Sword and Shield*, and in that book the hero actually provided the Germans with a false map of Russian firing positions. There is no doubt that the heroism of Beloff has been gilded somewhat, yet that in no way detracts from Abel's remarkable career as a courageous agent behind the German lines.

No doubt his war-time career ensured Abel of rapid promotion in the Soviet Secret Service. He was later attached to the K.G.B. and given the rank of colonel. After the war the Russians needed to strengthen their American networks and also to replace those already unmasked. During the McCarthyite era in the U.S.A. it was difficult to infiltrate an agent as an emigrant to America and Russian practice was to take advantage of the Canadians' liberal immigration policy at a time when they were clamouring for workers willing to go to Canada. Abel was selected to go to the United States as a key agent. First he was planted in a displaced persons' camp in Germany under the name of Andrew Kayotis. He applied for entry to Canada and went there in 1947. From Canada he went to the U.S.A. and before settling in New York made himself thoroughly familiar with the whole country by travelling widely.

Abel must have arrived in New York some time in 1950. There he became the Resident Agent and controlled not only the local network but the whole of the North American, Mexican and Central American networks. He had powers never previously given exclusively to any Soviet operator in the U.S.A. and was regarded in Moscow as the best expert on America they had ever had. But Abel was much more than that: he had nerves of steel and an iron self-control and was absolutely self-sufficient and disciplined. Those years of dangerous apprenticeship in Germany had formed his character into that of very nearly the perfect agent. Yet he was never a recluse: he liked good food and wine, often cooking excellent meals himself for a few carefully chosen friends, and his favourite recreations were visiting museums and concerts.

For ten years Abel was Russia's master-spy in America and later, after he was caught, Allen Dulles, head of the C.I.A., commented with rueful admiration: 'I wish we had a couple like him in Moscow.' In effect Abel brought something of the technique of a board-room executive to bear on espionage. He was the remote, aloof controller of the networks, giving orders, receiving information, collating it and relaying it to Moscow, and he also managed the finances of the whole outfit much more efficiently than any previous spy chief. In the end he was trapped not by any mistake he had made, but because one of his agents, Reino Hayhanen, defected and gave him away.

Yet in one sense it was Abel's own request to Moscow that proved his undoing. He always insisted that he must isolate himself completely from his undercover work and as time went on and pressure of work increased he feared that absences from his normal surroundings would perhaps be noticed. He had taken the cover name of Emil Goldfus in New York and set himself up as an artist, for he could paint passably well. He found the company of unconventional, Bohemian artists a useful antidote to his serious, disciplined work as a spy-master. In the world of artists, where routine was detested and time counted for nothing, his occasional absences went unnoticed. From his artist's studio he passed his information by radio to Moscow and even as a radio-operator he had shown his caution, and indeed his genius, by devising new code forms from abstruse mathematical calculations. This enabled a mass of information to be tapped out at high speed in a much shorter time than normal messages take.

But because he wanted to conserve his time for his cover pursuits as an artist, Abel asked Moscow to provide him with an assistant director, and the Centre made a grave error in sending him a Finn named Reino Hayhanen as his assistant.

Abel at once spotted that Hayhanen was singularly unprofessional and with very little idea of what security precautions involved. When Abel paid a return visit to Moscow in 1955 he expressed his doubts about Hayhanen to the Centre. It was just as well that he did so in the light of subsequent events, but the Centre paid no attention. Abel returned to the U.S.A. in 1956 and was outraged when he learned how Hayhanen had conducted business in his absence. The Finn had continued to use one site for operating his transmitting set instead of moving it periodically; he had not even collected all the information left at various *duboks* and had closed down the shop he used as a cover without getting permission to do so.

It was soon clear that Hayhanen's trouble was that of a secret drinker. Abel undoubtedly remonstrated with him and this must have put Hayhanen on his guard, for when the assistant director was eventually recalled to Russia he defected when he reached France and asked for asylum from the Americans. Even then, despite the information which Hayhanen gave to the C.I.A. it was not easy to track down Colonel Abel. For one reason Hayhanen did not know Abel's cover name. All he knew was that Abel had a store-room somewhere in Brooklyn and that it was close to Fulton Street. However, the F.B.I. agents combed the area relentlessly and eventually found that such a store-room had been rented to a man named Emil Goldfus and that he lived in a studio.

Meanwhile Abel had been alerted by the Centre that Hayhanen had defected and told to watch his step. He immediately went down to Florida with the idea of escaping across the border to Mexico if the F.B.I. seemed to be on his trail. After a few months nothing had happened and all seemed well. But here the Centre made their second mistake: they instructed Abel to return to New York. Soon afterwards the F.B.I. traced him to his new address at the Hotel Latham where he had registered under the name of Martin Collins.

But not once did the nerveless colonel lose his head. He remained a dedicated spy to the last moment. 'Agents who remained behind [in his room] went through the wastepaper basket and found a block of wood covered with sandpaper – the block came apart, and contained a 250-page booklet with a series of numbers, all in five-digit groups, on each page. It was a cipher pad, an aid to writing coded messages. The tiny booklet . . . contained the key to Abel's personal code, printed in neat columns in black and red. . . . A stubby pencil with an eraser that concealed a cavity was also found; inside the cavity were eighteen microfilms, several of them letters from Colonel Abel's wife and daughter. One was his time schedule for broadcasts to Moscow,' wrote Sanche de Gramont in his book, *The Secret War*.

What the cool-headed Abel left in a wastepaper basket was dropped quite deliberately to mislead the F.B.I. This would be standard K.G.B. practice and if Abel had left any worthwhile evidence behind he would have paid the penalty later when he returned to Moscow.

Abel was eventually charged with conspiracy to transmit military information to the Soviet Union. On 23 October 1957 he was sentenced to thirty years' imprisonment. The capture and incarceration of Abel caused a great deal of argument and searching inquiries not only inside the K.G.B. but at a higher level. It was conceded that the Centre had made grave errors, in the appointment of Hayhanen and in ordering Abel to return to New York too soon. Not only was there realisation that Abel had been their best Resident Director, but it dawned on the Soviet hierarchy that something needed to be done to preserve morale in the Secret Service. In other words, if they possessed an exceptionally good agent he must be made to feel he had the absolute backing of the K.G.B. not only while he was on active service but when he was caught. From that day on the K.G.B. has as a matter of policy gone to every possible length to retrieve captured spies, sometimes by springing their escape, but usually by hard bargaining until they were able to exchange a Western prisoner for one of theirs. It goes without saying that to achieve such bargaining power for exchanges they have sometimes been forced to concoct or exaggerate charges against a Westerner.

Three years after Abel was sent to prison the Russians shot down the U.S. flier Gary Powers in his U-2 aircraft over Russia. As soon as Powers was convicted as a spy and sentenced to ten years' imprisonment the K.G.B. knew they had a lever for demanding the release of Abel.

The two men were eventually exchanged and the Russians were certainly the winners in this bargaining. Not only did they get back their ace agent but the release of Powers made other top Russian agents overseas feel much happier in their work. Colonel Abel was awarded the Order of Lenin in recognition of his long service in Russian Intelligence. In his last years he became well known on Russian cinema screens. He introduced a film called *The Dead Season*, a spy thriller about germ warfare experiments in the Western World. His death in Moscow was reported late in 1971.

22

Konon Molody and Yuri Andropoff

By the early nineteen-sixties Russia's State Security Committee, the body which presides over all aspects of the Secret Service, was employing more than 600,000 people inside and outside the Soviet Union. Some Western observers estimate that the total is nearer to one million, but one must allow for a certain amount of over-estimation by those who want to see their own intelligence services increased in size.

During Nikita Khrushchev's régime Party control over Intelligence became absolute. To a large extent this was achieved by increasing the number of senior posts in the M.V.D. held by Party members and cross-postings between the M.V.D. and K.G.B. There was some sensible pruning of personnel and cutting out of duplication of offices and the Secret Service probably costs less today in terms of percentage of the national budget than it did in Stalin's time. This does not mean that it is in any way less efficient.

Yet, ironically, and in a sense almost typically Russian style, it was the Soviet Committee for State Security, Khrushchev's own brain-child, which finally stabbed Khrushchev in the back and paved the way for the joint-chairmanship of Brezhnev and Kosygin. One of the main reasons for this was the failures that occurred during the period that Vladimir Semichastny, Khrushchev's choice for the post, was head of the K.G.B. Semichastny was chosen because Khrushchev wanted a trusted Party man and not a professional policeman as head of the K.G.B.

One of Semichastny's senior officers was Colonel Oleg Penkovsky, whose chief task was to collect and assess information about N.A.T.O rocketry, work for which he was admirably fitted because he had been attached to the Soviet's own rocket forces. But all the time Penkovsky had been a secret agent for both the British and Americans – a rather over-rated double-agent whose carelessness cost both the Russians and the Western World more than his information was worth. Nevertheless the Russians were slow in catching him. When they did there was considerable criticism of the K.G.B. and of Semichastny in particular. The hard-liners in the Committee for State Security decided the time had come for a return to a more aggressive attitude which would not only frighten other would-be traitors but scare away Western spies. An example of this was the K.G.B.'s handling of the affair of Greville Wynne, a British businessman who was discovered to have had contact with Penkovsky. His trial, sentence and imprisonment were somewhat of an embarrassment to Khrushchev in his attempts to have friendlier relations with the West. Then there was the Schwirkmann affair. Herr Horst Schwirkmann was on the staff of the West German Embassy in Moscow, and a few days after it had been announced that Khrushchev would visit Bonn to improve Russo-German relations, this German diplomat was seriously burned in a mustard gas attack when he visited the Zagorski Monastery. It was rumoured that the attack had been carried out by the K.G.B. to embarrass Khrushchev and to disrupt his attempts at better relations with Bonn.

There was also another reason for the attack: the K.G.B. wanted Schwirkmann out of Moscow because he had been responsible for discovering the latest listening devices the K.G.B. had installed in various embassies, including, of course, the West German. Since the Henry Cabot Lodge disclosures of the Great Seal, which the Russians had audaciously presented to the Americans as a good-will gesture, subtler 'bugging' methods had been adopted. These were often extremely tiny devices which did not require wires to external sources of power. Some transmitters were small enough to by concealed in a small knob on a desk and very often were used by the Russians in this way. After Schwirkmann's disclosures, anti-bugging techniques were established in all the major Western embassies behind the Iron Curtain.

The arrest of George Blake and the defection of Lieutenant-Colonel Yevgeny Y. Runge, who had been in charge of the First Chief Directorate of Foreign Intelligence, not to mention the final 'blowing' of Kim Philby following the disclosures of the Blake case, all created unrest in the hierarchy of the Russian Secret Service. On 23 January 1963 Philby had disappeared and, in his own terse words, 'After seven years I left Beirut and turned up in the Soviet Union. Why? It is even possible that I was just tired.'

No doubt he was tired of waiting impotently while the rival Secret Services of Britain and Russia played their own game with him. Both he and Moscow knew that though he had been officially cleared of spying against his country there were people in both M.I.6 and M.I.5 who were sure he was guilty. As a super-agent for Russia he was now a total loss. But the Russians were still far from sure what game the British were playing to allow Philby such freedom and probably still somewhat mistrustful of Philby himself. So they would not permit his return to Moscow until the last possible moment. On 3 July the same year that he escaped from Beirut Philby was made a citizen of the Soviet Union.

Finally, powerful forces in the K.G.B. turned against Khrushchev and Semichastny. When Khrushchev went off to the Black Sea coast while members of the Praesidium were plotting to overthrow him, it was the K.G.B. who gave the order for three of their senior officers to escort him back to Moscow to attend that fateful meeting when he was removed from office.

Gradually the K.G.B. began to play more of a rôle in policy-making thereafter. It was not so much a reversal to pre-Khrushchev conditions of actually having more power, but rather a compromise which blended the old methods and the new in a fine balance. In theory the K.G.B.'s powers of arrest, sentencing and banishing without judicial authority were diminished, but they still retained the power to detain and cross-examine without being questioned. The fact that Brezhnev and Kosygin now shared the responsibilities of leadership on the political plane was paralleled in the new relationship of the K.G.B. to the State Security Committee. The latter safeguarded the K.G.B. from dictatorial purges and executions such as those of the Stalinist era, while it also safeguarded the Party from attempts at political control by the K.G.B. such as might have happened under Beria after Stalin's death. The K.G.B. was more fully represented on the Party's Central Committee, thus obtaining rather greater impact politically. Indeed it is probable that today the K.G.B. has at least as much influence in the Soviet hierarchy as the leaders of the Armed Forces. From being an instrument solely of espionage and terror it has become refined into a more complex body altogether, something that has acquired a mystique of its own and which in a not easily defined way can have a political influence of its own outside of the Party's Central Committee.

The relationship of the Security Committee with the Soviet Government as such is interesting. Officially the Security Committee is a Government organisation, but the Government is always subordinate to the Communist Party itself, so that the relationship of the Security Committee to the Party is by means of the Party's Central Committee secretariat, whose chief is Mr Brezhnev. And just as Semichastny was Khrushchev's man so the present head of the K.G.B. is Brezhnev's closest political ally, Yuri Vladimirovich Andropoff.

Andropoff is a tall, neatly dressed man of fifty-seven, scholarly in appearance, with keen, darting eyes, a shrewd mind and the manner of a diplomat. He speaks English fluently and has a greater facility for accurately analysing Western policies and trends of opinion than any of his predecessors. He is an intelligence chief of the modern school and a distinct improvement on his predecessors of the past twenty years. Starting as a telegraph worker in 1930, his persistence and studies brought him by way of the Petrozavodsk River Transport Technical College and Petrozavodsk University to the C.P.S.U. Central Committee. From 1936–44 he was officially attached to the Komsomol Central Committee as First Secretary, but during the war he also helped to organise partisan detachments and was for a time stationed at Murmansk. When war ended he earned steady promotion up the Party ladder, being Second Secretary of the Petrozavodsk Party Committee and then Second Secretary to the Karelo-Finnish Central Committee.

Tactful, efficient, able to avoid being involved in Party disputes or personality clashes, Andropoff survived the Stalin era and rode the wind of change that followed it. He never allowed himself to be swayed by temporary phases in Party policy-making, sticking cautiously to the middle of the road, yet always showing sufficient imagination to anticipate what such changes would bring about. He began to get a reputation for being the man who was always right. In 1953 he was transferred to the Diplomatic Service and made Counsellor of the Soviet Embassy in Budapest, being promoted Ambassador in 1954. His advice and brilliant assessments of intelligence reports during the tense days of the Hungarian uprising and the events that followed gave him added weight in the Party. On the strength of this he was allowed to devote more of his time to liaison work between intelligence bodies and the Party, being appointed head of a special department which was set up to handle relations with Communist Parties in the Soviet-Eastern European bloc. This work further enhanced his status so that in 1962 he was made Secretary of the Central Committee, which put him on a level with Boris Ponomarev, who was responsible for relations with Communist Parties outside the Eastern bloc.

For a long time Ponomarev himself was a favourite for the office of head of the K.G.B., but it is doubtful whether now at the age of sixty-nine the scholarly Ponomarev, author of many works on the history of the Communist Party, will progress much further. Andropoff's alliance with Brezhnev gave him a distinct advantage so that it came as no surprise when he was made chief of the K.G.B. in May 1967. It is generally thought that this appointment was intended to bring the Intelligence organisation more closely under Brezhnev's control.

Andropoff has more closely co-ordinated the main Intelligence Administration of the Ministry of Defence with the K.G.B. and also, especially in his manipulation of defectors and the arrest of foreigners in the U.S.S.R., to make his influence felt in the sphere of foreign affairs. Thus in one sense he has occasionally been authoritarian in his handling of cases which are liable to affect foreign policy-making, while in another he has been at great pains to deny that the K.G.B. has any sinister rôle and to develop even further the glamorisation propaganda in favour of his organisation.

Just as the Czarist Ochrana used to publish its own *Ochrana Gazette* so, under Andropoff, the K.G.B. had its own limited circulation *Chekistsky Shornik*. The organisation is divided up into nine directorates, each of which has specified functions. The First Chief Directorate, led by Lieutenant-General Alexander Sakharovsky, collects and analyses foreign intelligence, while the Second Chief Directorate, which is much larger, employing more than 100,000 personnel, is concerned with subversive activities, economic espionage, sabotage and treason and a certain amount of routine police work such as drug trafficking and thefts of Government property. Changes in the leadership of the division are now being made. The Third Directorate is the most sinister of all and developed from the dreaded *Smersh* of World War II (an abbreviation of the Russian phrase for 'death to spies') and it is difficult to say to what extent it still indulges in liquidation, but it is certainly concerned with all aspects of counter-espionage.

There are Seventh, Eighth and Ninth Directorates, specifically so named, but there is no firm evidence of the existence of the Fourth, Fifth and Sixth Directorates, all of which previously were concerned with internal security. One must assume that rationalisation has been carried out in this sphere and that the Third Directorate has assumed most, if not all, of their activities. Major-General V. I. Aladin is the head of the Seventh Directorate which has a variety of tasks, including the recruitment of foreigners as agents, shadowing of suspects and penetration of offices. It also keeps a special watch on all embassies and missions in Moscow and is believed to employ between 3,000 and 4,000 personnel.

The Eighth Directorate, controlled by Major-General Serafim N. Lyalin, deals with code- and cipher-breaking, communications and the administration of security precautions, while the Ninth Directorate is the smallest of all and is mainly concerned with protecting leading members of the Soviet hierarchy. Its chief is Major-General V. Y. Chekaloff. The Border Guards, over whom in Beria's time the N.K.V.D. had supreme authority, now comes under a separate organisation commanded by Lieutenant-General Pavel I. Zyryanoff. This embraces customs, immigration and censorship of literature and imported printed material. The main headquarters of the administrative side of the Secret Service is in Dzerzhinsky Square in Moscow.

About the time that Andropoff took charge of the K.G.B. a Soviet spy was arrested in Johannesburg, an event which again proved shattering to some of the espionage networks. He was Yuri Nickolayevich Loginoff, who had been posing as a Canadian citizen under the name of Edmund Trinka. It was claimed that Loginoff's Canadian passport was obtained with the aid of two K.G.B. officers, named Yevgenny Mikhailovich, a Soviet consul in Canada, and 'Nick', a K.G.B. officer in Nairobi who, according to the South Africans, made use of a K.G.B. forged South African passport to obtain the Canadian document.

Loginoff, however, did not keep silent as did Abel, but talked freely to his captors. Major-General Hendrik van den Bergh, South Africa's security chief, was able to say: 'We have a fantastic amount of information and material in our possession.'

Loginoff, who was born in Moscow in 1933, had had some years of training in the Czech and English languages prior to being sent out as an agent and had even been sent on practice trips to various Western countries under false identities. From his evidence it was obvious that spy training in Russia was becoming much more thorough. He had been briefed on life in the West by Rudolf Abel, and his wife, Nira, had been recruited by the K.G.B. for an assignment to Cuba. Her mission, however, had not been entirely successful and led to a political scandal in Cuba.

Soon he gave away a vast amount of information not only on K.G.B. but on G.R.U. networks as well. It was a tremendous blow to Andropoff, coming as it did just after he had been appointed to reorganise the K.G.B. after more than a hundred Soviet agents had been exposed all over the world in the course of two years. The extent of Loginoff's missions and intelligence contacts took in Italy, Finland, Germany, Belgium, Holland, Austria, Czechoslovakia, the Lebanon, Egypt, Turkey, Iran, Australia, Switzerland, Kenya, Indonesia, France, Israel, Jordan, Libya, Ethiopia, Tanzania, the Argentine and Brazil. The agents whose names he gave to the South African authorities included Vitaly Pavloff, a key K.G.B. operator in Europe; Anatoliy Kosalapoff, director of a Baltic shipping line: Aleksy Tiblayshin, who had been working for U.N.E.S.C.O. in Paris and was later assigned to Cairo while Loginoff was there; Yuri Chekulayev, a Middle-East K.G.B. operator, and Boris Skoridoff, who had been assigned to the Soviet Embassy in London under the name of Boris Zhiltsoff. It was clear from this list that it was K.G.B. practice to put some of its operators in Soviet embassies under false names.

Loginoff had undoubtedly intended to stay in South Africa for it was disclosed that he had been negotiating with two German immigrants in Johannesburg to become a sleeping partner in their interior decorating business to obtain a cover.

Western psychological warfare specialists reluctantly admitted in September 1965 that the publication in Moscow of the autobiography of Konon Trofimovich Molody was one of the best propaganda efforts ever launched by the K.G.B.

It carried on the policy of praising Soviet spies while at the same time containing a good deal of propaganda, and again causing dissension between America and Britain. Experts in the West thought they detected the hand of Kim Philby in some of the writing, especially as it was known that he had been working for Novosti, the Moscow news agency, since he had defected to Russia.

Konon Trofimovich Molody, alias Colonel Georgi Lonoff, who was born in 1923, had his first experience of espionage at the early age of seventeen when he was parachuted behind the German lines to organise his own network at Minsk. He owed his advancement to the fact that he came to the notice of Rudolf Abel and later worked inside Germany as Abel's radio operator, thus beginning a partnership which lasted until Abel was arrested by the F.B.I. At the age of eleven Molody, bearing a Canadian passport in the name of Gordon Arnold Lonsdale, was taken to the United States by an aunt who passed herself off as his mother. The real Lonsdale had been born in Cobalt, Ontario, in 1924, so his age matched that of Molody to within a year. Young Lonsdale had been taken to Finland by his mother in 1932 and nothing had been heard of him since. Somehow the N.K.V.D. obtained Lonsdale's passport and decided to use it for an experiment in long-term espionage, for the young Molody was brought up in Berkeley, California, where he attended a private school until 1938, learning to speak English like a North American. In 1938 Molody returned to Russia, not returning to Canada and the U.S.A. until early in the nineteen-fifties when he still used the name of Lonsdale. This time he was a fully-fledged, professional agent, treading warily in view of the chain of arrests of Russian agents from Judith Koplan, Harry Gold and the Rosenbergs. Molody was, however, an apt pupil, mastering the intricacies of the *dubok* system and the blackmail tactics which Russian Intelligence uses for controlling its contacts.

Then in 1955 Colonel Abel informed Molody that his work had been duly appreciated in Moscow and that as a reward he had been given the appointment of Resident-Director in Britain. Molody wrote later: 'I could hardly believe my ears, but I was delighted at this new recognition of headquarters' faith in me.'

Molody was also delighted because he much preferred Britain to the U.S.A. and indeed once admitted that his secret ambition was 'to live like an English country gentleman'. He was the antithesis of Abel, yet complementary to him. In many respects he was more like Sidney Reilly and almost as great a womaniser, revelling in his amorous conquests, but never allowing them to interfere with his work as a spy.

Molody, under his alias of Gordon Lonsdale, went to Britain in 1955 and took rooms at the Royal Overseas League at St James's in London. Whereas Abel would probably have chosen some obscure hideout, Molody openly chose an orthodox base and from that proceeded to build himself up as an extrovert man-about-town, fond of parties, girls and concerts. He was a young man in a hurry, anxious to create the right image swiftly and to plunge into his work without delay. Molody was not one to content himself with a patient, plodding espionage game.

His tactics paid off. By the following year he had installed himself at the White House, Albany Street, near Regents Park, and became a Christmas guest of Major Raymond Shaw, U.S.A.F., at the nuclear base at Lakenham in Suffolk. Then he investigated Britain's defences while posing as a company director, selling, among other things, bubble-gum machines and juke-boxes. As a result of his discoveries Moscow obtained a great deal of information about Britain's nuclear submarine base at Holy Loch, the country's submarine and tracking system and the location of secret bases. As he later made it clear, 'my intention was to gather information on the aggressive plans of the U.S.A. and N.A.T.O. as a whole.'

Though Molody was more flamboyant than Abel he turned his flamboyance to good advantage. He knew that the go-getting, thrustful methods of an American big business man and open hospitality would enable him to forge ahead in circles where he would not be suspected. Thus he had little difficulty in establishing himself as the director of a juke-box rental business and selected for a partner a Briton named Peter Ayres, who had no idea of Molody's real rôle and was himself above suspicion. Success in business spurred Molody to greater efforts. He began to look around for other opportunities and persuaded business acquaintances to put up money for the production of a patented automobile burglar alarm. In March 1960 Molody personally entered his gadget in the Brussels International Trade Fair where it was awarded a gold medal as 'the best British entry'.

Two top Soviet agents (Morris and Lona Cohen) had escaped from the network in America after the round-up of spies in the late forties and moved to New Zealand. They adopted the names of Peter and Helen Kroger and eventually moved to Britain and came into the Molody network. In London a second-hand and rare bookshop was opened at 190 The Strand in the name of Peter J. Kroger, advertising as its speciality 'Americana from the North Pole to the South Pole'. The Krogers took a bungalow at Ruislip in Middlesex which Molody frequently visited. Afterwards Molody rather chivalrously blamed himself for involving the Krogers and repeatedly insisted that they were not active spies. It is true that he seemed genuinely grieved when the Krogers were ultimately arrested and sent to prison, but it is more than likely that he was doing some propaganda to try to ensure their early release.

As the Krogers went abroad on occasions Molody sometimes occupied their bungalow for weeks at a time. In doing this he probably took risks that Abel would never have done, though it must be admitted that he had no reason to suspect this hide-out was not absolutely safe. He had installed in the bungalow a radiogram capable of receiving from Moscow and a Ronson tablelighter which, when taken apart, was found to contain signal plans. While the Krogers were away Molody dug a cavity under the kitchen floor to conceal a small radio transmitter. This, he said afterwards, was a 'reserve transmitter', which was not even capable of reaching Moscow, though obviously it could pass information to some safe section of Russian Intelligence, possibly to the Embassy in London.

In the bathroom cabinet at the bungalow in Cranley Drive, Ruislip, was a tin of talcum powder which held a microdot reader, in a secret compartment and in the loft were hidden cameras and several thousand American dollars.

Meanwhile, Molody turned his attention to Harry Houghton, the Admiralty clerk who had been in Poland. Playing on Houghton's need for extra cash to spend on drink, Molody, posing as a U.S. naval commander named Alec Johnson, suggested to Houghton that he should work for U.S. Intelligence. Houghton was at that time working at the top-security Admiralty Underwater Weapons Establishment at Portland in Dorset and soon for sums of five and ten pounds he was passing on information from the files to Molody. The funds Houghton received swelled from tens to hundreds of pounds and then in 1958 Houghton suggested that his girl friend, Ethel Gee, who also worked at Portland, should help in supplying information, too.

It was eventually noticed that Houghton was living beyond his means as an Admiralty clerk and Scotland Yard's Special Branch kept a watch on him. Then, in January 1961, Ethel Gee and Harry Houghton were arrested in Waterloo Road, London, together with Molody, just as Gee was handing over to Molody no less than

212 pages of technical details about British warships.

For once Scotland Yard and M.I.5 made a complete job of the round-up of the network. Night searches were made at the Krogers' bungalow and they, too, were arrested. After the trial Molody was sent to prison for twenty-five years, the Krogers each got twenty years and Houghton and Gee fifteen years each.

But, as with Abel, so with Molody and the Krogers: the Russians never ceased to work day and night for their release. No doubt in the case of Molody plans were afoot for his rescue from prison. But the K.G.B. prefer to arrange these things by a direct exchange of prisoners whenever possible. Molody was eventually exchanged for Greville Wynne, a bargain that was greatly in the Russians' favour, while the Krogers were exchanged for one Briton, the lecturer, Gerald Brooke, who had merely been involved in delivering clandestine pamphlets inside Russia. Molody's trade-in for Greville Wynne three years after he was sent to prison was criticised on the grounds that the British Government had freed an ace Soviet spy for a British businessman. Whichever way one looked at it the Soviet Union had not only gained the best of two deals but had greatly boosted morale in their own spy networks. From then on Soviet spies could breathe more freely, feeling that their masters would go to extreme lengths to ensure their release. The escape of George Blake from Wormwood Scrubs was just an additional bonus in the campaign to show that Russia, unlike other powers, would not refuse to recognise her spies when they were caught, but would spare no efforts to show how highly she prized them.

Molody's morale in prison remained so high that he must have been well aware of the recent change of heart in the Soviet Union towards their chief agents when caught. He played chess and translated three books into Russian and, after he had been exchanged, asked for his translations to be sent to him in Moscow. They were all books on espionage. Molody also claimed that for a short while after World War II he had been in China and had compiled a Chinese–Russian dictionary and written a geographical book about China.

It was on 22 October 1966 that George Blake escaped from Wormwood Scrubs Prison in London. There was an immediate international search for him, ports, airports and landing strips all over the British Isles were watched. Yet all the time Blake was living quietly in an apartment only a few minutes away from the prison. A few months later he was in Moscow. Sean Bourke, the Irishman who was Blake's fellow-prisoner at Wormwood Scrubs, claims that Blake asked whether he would help him to escape and insists that the springing of the spy was not the work of foreign agents but entirely due to his own enterprise. Without in any way detracting from Bourke's part in the affair there is no doubt that the K.G.B. had planned the rescue and that they were helped by advice from Molody.

There are some grounds for believing that Molody was able to keep in touch with Moscow while still in prison. Incredibly, he and Blake were together in Wormwood Scrubs for a period so that Molody could have communicated with Blake. The facts about the imprisonment of both Molody and Blake are in themselves a damnable indictment of British security measures. During inquiries into Blake's escape some evidence suggested that Molody had helped to plan the escape at least in principle. Even when six prisoners escaped from Wormwood Scrubs and prison security was revealed to be faulty, no attempt was made to move Blake to a top security prison. Despite two pleas to this effect by the prison governor the authorities ignored his warnings. What was more, Bourke was able to smuggle miniature radio equipment to Blake in prison and carry on radio conversations with him from outside. Why were these radio talks not detected and monitored? Somebody should have picked them up.

Somehow Blake had been informed while he was in prison that all hopes of an exchange had been ruled out. Who told him? It was from this moment that he started to plan his escape. When Bourke left Wormwood Scrubs he set about making plans, keeping Blake informed by radio from a site quite close to the prison. When the moment arrived – and this was planned to the last second – Blake climbed the prison wall with a rope-ladder thrown over to him by Bourke, jumped to safety on the road below and was whirled off into the darkness of a winter night by car.

That was on a Saturday. On the Monday the Prime Minister, Harold Wilson, was personally assuring a troubled House of Commons that Blake no longer constituted a threat to Britain's security. Nevertheless the Government had to agree to set up a commission of inquiry into escapes and prison security, with special reference to the Blake case. Even with all the precautions subsequently taken George Blake actually left the country on a false passport by a sea route to the Continent. Bourke in due course followed him to Russia where he stayed for a while before returning to Eire, where he faced proceedings for extradition to Britain to be charged with aiding Blake's escape. The magistrate ordered his extradition, but when Bourke appealed he won his case and the extradition order was set aside.

Bourke said at his trial: 'I have never been a Communist . . . I don't care for politics. I sprang Blake, the Russian spy, from a slow, lingering death.' In court he stated that 'Blake was taken out of Britain in December 1966, was driven to Dover and then by ferry to Ostend. . . . Then he reached East Germany.' He did not say how Blake was taken out of the country.

Nor does Bourke's book satisfactorily resolve the mystery. He mentions two men and a woman who assisted in the escape operation, but they are shadowy figures. According to Bourke, Blake went ahead first and Bourke followed after an interval to East Germany. One thing is clear: when Bourke eventually reached Russia he found Blake increasingly hostile to him. Bourke's manuscript of the escape story was confiscated by the K.G.B. at Moscow airport. He wrote three letters asking for its return after he had gone back to Dublin, but heard nothing until in the spring of 1969 'a somewhat tattered parcel was delivered to the offices of his solicitor. It contained the original manuscript from which had been removed the entire final section which deals with Bourke's experiences in Russia. The rest of the manuscript had been heavily censored in George Blake's own hand.'

With some difficulty one can accept Bourke's story that he had not been 'hired' by the Russians and had not been in direct contact with the Soviet Embassy. The Russians, in trying to 'spring' Blake, would not have adopted such crude tactics, but there is no doubt whatever that the K.G.B. planned the whole operation and that it would not have been difficult for them to manipulate Bourke even without his being aware of just what was happening. Nobody better than the Russians could arrange for people suddenly to pop up and offer Bourke assistance in carrying out his plan. There is evidence that roundabout approaches were made to a number of Blake's fellow-prisoners who had left prison. This was all rather cleverly done, with all manner of excuses, usually on the pretence that it related to other prisoners, but each man so consulted recalled after Blake's escape that the shadowy contact men had, without exception, all inquired about Blake in a casual fashion, wanting to know whether his presence in the prison had meant special precautions being taken.

The view of the French and West German Secret Services was that Blake was definitely 'sprung' by the K.G.B. and that Bourke was manipulated as a useful decoy to draw attention away from them. The West Germans, whose Intelligence went into the whole affair in great detail, as they had a special interest in Blake in view of his machinations in their territory, were firmly convinced that Blake was not only rescued by the K.G.B. but that the British Secret Service actually connived in the deed. They are emphatic even today that Blake could not have escaped unless there was either some secret deal between the British and the K.G.B., possibly involving some complicated exchange of personnel which they did not wish to be publicised, or by somebody knowing about the rescue attempt and creating conditions under which it could be brought off. One source even suggests that Blake did not escape by the Ostend route but went over to Eire and made his getaway from there. Others, including again the West Germans, insist that somebody highly placed in the British Secret Service wanted Blake to be rescued and insists that this all points to the presence of the mysterious 'Fifth Man' Soviet agent inside Britain.

Both Molody and Blake have kept silent on really vital matters since they went to Moscow. Molody did, however, have this to say about his relationship with Blake: 'I am quite willing to state that I knew George Blake . . . I shall not say whether I knew him before my arrest. But, as the authorities are only too well aware, I certainly got to know him well afterwards when he was sent to Wormwood Scrubs to begin his sentence. I am convinced it was deliberately contrived that we should find ourselves together in gaol.'

Molody also threw some light on his exchange for Greville Wynne. 'About January 1963 I learned that British Intelligence was prepared to discuss the possibility of my exchange for a British subject held in Russia. I told the authorities I was not prepared to enter into any kind of deal over 'this. It was to be a straightforward exchange with Greville Wynne, or nothing.

'I have reason to believe the moves for our exchange were first started by our wives. First my wife, Halina, had approached the Soviet Embassy in Warsaw with the idea and had received a favourable response. Then she wrote to Mrs Greville Wynne and asked her to approach the British Government on the subject.'

This all makes sense for it exemplifies the classic pattern of K.G.B. tactics in attempting to arrange exchanges. Wives are urged to make heart-rending appeals, stories are leaked from Russia that the health of a prisoner is not good, that to save him from serious illness, perhaps even death, an exchange would be the humanitarian way out. This method was consistently used in the cat-and-mouse game which the Russians played with Gerald Brooke. When this seemed to fail they dropped hints that at the end of his sentence Brooke might be re-tried for more serious offences which had come to light since his imprisonment. The K.G.B. know full well that in a democracy pressure in the press and its influence on public opinion can sometimes force a government to agree to an exchange even when they know that the arrangement will be one-sided and a poor bargain. James B. Donovan, the American lawyer who undertook Colonel Abel's defence at his trial, revealed something of Russian methods in arranging exchanges in his book *Strangers on a Bridge*. His dealings with Russian and East German negotiators involved meeting three people masquerading as Abel's wife, daughter and cousin. The Russians sent Donovan correspondence which purported to come from Abel's wife, but which bore no resemblance in style or content to the letters which his real wife was, in fact, writing to him.

On 14 October 1970 it was announced from Moscow that Molody had died at the early age of forty-eight. The circumstances were curious, to say the least: he was said to have collapsed while picking mushrooms in a field near Moscow. One wonders whether his death announcement was a coded warning to spies all over the world. It is, perhaps, a melodramatic thought, but anything is possible in Russian espionage and the devious thought processes that lie behind it.

23

K.G.B. Tactics towards the French, Africans and Asians

BY THE end of the sixties it was easier in some respects to obtain a clearer picture of Russian espionage than had been possible in the previous decade. This was due not so much to the revelations of a few genuine defectors as to the fact that the K.G.B. were now revealing more of their triumphs.

It was no longer a question of the Russians publishing a few ancient stories of the civil wars, or Soviet-version biographies of such well-known and already unmasked spies as Molody, Abel and Philby, but what really counted was the bold, confident manner in which they lifted the curtain of secrecy on more recent coups, totally unknown to the outside world. These stories should be treated with some reserve, but nevertheless they should not be dismissed as mere propaganda.

There was the case of Afonoff (code name), who arrived in Russia with all the paraphernalia of radio equipment and codes which the K.G.B. put to use for their own ends. According to them, Afonoff's equipment was used to transmit false messages on his behalf, and replies from abroad confirmed that Afonoff was still trusted. Knowing, however, that each radio operator had his own characteristics which identify him, in much the same way as another man might be identified by his fingerprints, the K.G.B. made an excuse that further communications should be by letter only and, so they claimed, 'furnish false information to the United States Central Intelligence Agency for eight years in order to find out what the Americans were interested in and to study the various methods of communication used by U.S. Intelligence.'

The latter part of the last sentence is the real clue to K.G.B. thinking. Since the early twenties the Soviet Secret Service has been passionately obsessed with communications and this emphasis in their techniques has paid off. Despite being far behind the Western Intelligence Services in this respect in the early days, they quickly gained parity and, despite some errors in judgement in the excessive use of radio time in the early forties, they gained a substantial lead in radio techniques before the fifties had ended.

The Russians have a tremendous lead on other Secret Services in their exploitation of the defector and also of the detected spy. They will often allow the latter a freedom which other powers would never dare to give to a Soviet spy they had discovered. Certainly if they can feel sure they can pass on false information in this manner, the Russians will exploit the situation to the fullest extent – sometimes for years. They now claim that Colonel Oleg Penkovsky, who transmitted so much information to the West through Greville Wynne, was deliberately left free for a certain time.

By far the most important part of the K.G.B.'s activities is the preservation of internal security, which is tightened up or relaxed in accordance with the changes in foreign policy as much as those of domestic policy. Because of the trials of the writer-protesters, Sinyavsky and Daniel, it has been somewhat glibly assumed that Soviet policy has reverted to Stalinist principles. This is an over-simplification which the Foreign Offices of the West have been too prone to accept. The truth is that the Politburo and the K.G.B. were shocked by the crude and amateurish – perhaps over-enthusiastic would be a better description – attempts by Khrushchev to permit greater all-round freedom. Cynics in the K.G.B. compared Khrushchev with Pope John and pointed out how the latter's liberalism had thrown the Catholic Church into confusion. Then came the wave of student unrest which spread from the West to the Iron Curtain countries. This manifestation really alarmed the K.G.B. who realised that historically most Russian revolts in the past had come from students and it was this as much as any other factor which influenced the Soviet hierarchy against the 'protest-writers' and determined them to invade Czechoslovakia.

The K.G.B. has a great fear of smuggling and for this reason the task of combating smuggling is regarded as a counter-espionage responsibility in Russia, which is not, of course, the case in the West. There is one very good reason for this. During the days of the Cold War a British Secret Service unit organised the smuggling of Swiss watches into Russia where they were sold in the black market to obtain roubles. The most ironic twist to this operation was that the roubles supplied by the Russians were used to finance the work of British agents behind the Iron Curtain. More than ten million roubles were secured by these methods. It was George Blake himself who revealed this ploy to the Soviet, explaining that it was organised by an ex-Royal Marine officer who had joined M.I.6 and that one of the main links in the organisation was one Mandel Goldfinger, a prosperous and respected jeweller. Blake 'took over' the whole scheme and proceeded to work it in the Russians' interests.

Russian espionage in France in post-World War II years has been less spectacular than before that war, but there have nonetheless been successes. Immediately after the war there were Communists in high places in France: there were Communist heads of the War and Air Ministries for brief periods and for a short while the veteran Communist leader, Thorez, was Deputy Prime Minister. The Russians sent a large diplomatic mission to Paris after the war and obviously made it the spearhead of a massive espionage attack, but the Russians either did not expect Communist predominance in government to last, or mistrusted this type of intelligence, for they quickly built up independent networks. One of these, Rabcor, was based on the industrial workers' networks which had been so successful in the late twenties and early thirties.

In 1949 it was discovered that Captain René Azema, an instructor at the Pau School for Airborne Troops, had passed on secret documents relating to France's airborne divisions to the Russians. This had been blatantly done by supplying the information to a French journal, *France d'Abord*, which was run by Communists. In this instance one can only assume that the intelligence was published to embarrass the French. The editors were arrested, but by the time the case came to trial two years later interest in the proceedings had waned and the defendants were acquitted.

After the establishment of N.A.T.O. it was soon clear that many French military secrets were finding their way to the Russians and this state of affairs continued until the mid-fifties when a real attempt was made to tighten up French security. A Soviet spy ring in the Toulon naval base was rounded up and in 1954 two officials of the French Committee of National Defence, René Turpin and Roger Labrusse, were arrested on charges of treason. It was alleged that they had supplied secret military documents to a Communist agent named André Baranès. Shortly afterwards Jean Mons, the Secretary-General of the National Defence Committee, was charged with 'having endangered State security'.

With the coming to power of General de Gaulle, French counter-espionage was reorganised and strengthened and the Centre in Moscow was forced to change its whole policy of espionage inside France. One of the reasons why de Gaulle was able so smoothly to counter-attack his right-wing adversaries and the sinister O.A.S. movement in Algeria was that the K.G.B. gave instructions to all agents in France to lie low, to make no aggressive moves, and passed secret instructions to French Communists not in any way to hinder the new régime. Thus the French counter-espionage had no need to worry about Communist intrigues and could concentrate almost wholly against subversive right-wing moves.

Leonid Petrovich Kunavin, a colonel in the K.G.B., made a series of dossiers on prominent French officials known to be close to de Gaulle. His aim was to find among them one who might be manipulated. At last his search came to an end when he snapped the file shut abruptly, pointed to the name on the cover and said, 'This is our target. This is the man we can and must win over. His name is Maurice Dejean and he is the new French Ambassador to Moscow.'

Maurice Dejean had served with de Gaulle's Free French Committee in London during World War II. He had been a diplomat in New York, London and the Far East before he arrived at Moscow in December 1955. From that date Dejean was kept under constant surveillance and the dossier on him was built up. Microphones were installed in his Embassy and two K.G.B. agents, one a chauffeur and the other Madame Dejean's maid, were introduced into the Dejean ménage.

One of the virtues of the modern K.G.B. is their persistence against the odds. Kunavin had decided that Dejean was to become a Russian agent and he pursued this single aim even when all the evidence pointed to Dejean's political integrity and his loyalty to France. Hints were made to Kunavin that he was wasting the K.G.B.'s time in devoting so much attention to Dejean, but he replied that 'We do not expect Dejean to hand over to us all his files, or to give away his secrets. We don't even expect him to spy for us. No, my friend, we expect to flatter and to charm Dejean into supporting the cause of the Soviet Union. He must go back to France and influence the politicians and even the General himself in our favour.'

There followed an unsubtle, almost farcical plot to embroil not only Ambassador Dejean, but his wife as well. Two years passed and though K.G.B. agents had succeeded in enticing Madame Dejean out on picnics without her husband and introducing Dejean himself to some attractive K.G.B. female operators, no physical intimacy had been achieved. On one occasion a male K.G.B. agent who had drunk too much fell asleep when he was supposed to be flirting with Madame Dejean, a slip-up which caused him instantly to be replaced.

Finally Dejean was framed by an actress who was in the pay of the K.G.B. who 'arranged' for her husband to find the pair together. The Ambassador was beaten up by an apparently irate husband who threatened to expose the Ambassador and seek redress. Dejean immediately appealed for help to a high K.G.B. official who promised to do all he could to hush things up.

Surprisingly the K.G.B. then overstepped the mark. They tried the same tactics on a French attaché, Lieut.-Colonel Louis Guibaud. Confronting him with the evidence of his illicit liaisons in the form of a batch of photographs, the K.G.B. brutally offered him either instant publication of the details or a promise to collaborate with them. Guibaud's reply was to shoot himself, which created a panic among the K.G.B. in case he had left behind a letter at the French Embassy denouncing them. But there was no note.

Yet for all their persistent work the K.G.B. had not really succeeded in pulling off a coup. Guibaud was dead without having betrayed his country and then in 1964 Maurice Dejean returned to Paris without so far having done anything for the Soviet cause. Perhaps after the Guibaud affair the K.G.B. lost their nerve; certainly no effort was made to bargain with Dejean before he left Moscow, though doubtless the intention was to maintain contact with him after he reached Paris. But meanwhile Yuri Vasilyevich Krotkoff, the K.G.B. agent who had been used to direct the ensnaring of Dejean and Guibaud, went to London with a visiting group of Russian artists and writers. There he defected and made some remarkable disclosures to the British, including, of course, the story of Dejean and Guibaud.

The information Krotkoff gave to the British was leaked back to the Americans and the French. De Gaulle ordered an immediate inquiry into the affair, decided that Dejean had not betrayed French secrets or interests but had been indiscreet and by his behaviour threatened French security. Documentary evidence of Krotkoff's disclosures was released early in 1971 by a U.S. Senate Investigating Committee after his nine-day testimony on these matters.

A much more serious blow to French prestige was struck by the revelations made in 1968 by Philippe Thyraud de Vosjoli, formerly head of French Intelligence in Washington.

It all started with the publication by McGraw-Hill in U.S.A. of a seemingly ultra-realistic spy novel entitled *Topaz*, written by the American author Léon Uris. This told how the head of the K.G.B.'s anti-N.A.T.O. bureau defected to the Americans and revealed the existence in Paris of a Soviet spy ring code-named *Topaz*, of which the two key members were a senior French official and a close adviser – code-name *Colombine* – of the French President.

Le Canard Enchaîné, the satirical French weekly, then suggested in its columns that *Topaz* was based on fact. It went further than this by saying that *Colombine* was an accurate portrait of one of de Gaulle's most trusted Intelligence advisers. Shrewd observers of the intelligence game paid rather more attention to *Le Canard*'s allegations than did the general public. They noted that the various spy-rings organised by the Russians against N.A.T.O. were known to use the names of jewels for their code-names. The ring organised against France was actually known not as *Topaz*, but as *Sapphire*. Then it was realised that de Vosjoli had been a friend of Léon Uris.

Now while *Topaz* was undoubtedly based on truth, it was nevertheless a work of fiction in that the truth had been gilded out of all recognition except to the discerning. Indeed it was not difficult for the French to dismiss the *Topaz* legend as 'pure fiction'. For a long time they were able to suppress de Vosjoli's allegations on the same subject.

De Vosjoli had been chief liaison officer between the French Secret Service and the C.I.A. and had incurred the wrath of his French employers by being a little too enthusiastic in his collaboration with the Americans. Then he was consulted by the C.I.A. on revelations made to them by the Russian defector, Dolnytsin, and asked for an evaluation. Irritated by de Vosjoli's involvement with the C.I.A. the French ordered him to report back to Paris. De Vosjoli refused to go and resigned from the Service, alleging that the French Intelligence organisation had been infiltrated by Soviet agents.

Soon, de Vosjoli's revelations were published in U.S.A. and Britain, alleging that 200 K.G.B. operators were operating inside N.A.T.O. countries, and that there was a 'French Philby' inside de Gaulle's own entourage, a man who was privy to Cabinet secrets and an adviser to the French Secret Service.

The Americans had regarded the Russian defector's information as so important that President Kennedy sent a personal letter to de Gaulle, warning him of a Soviet spy in his entourage.

The matter was still treated as top secret in Paris, but de Gaulle ordered a searching inquiry into the existence of N.A.T.O. spy rings with the immediate result that George Paques, a French press attaché with N.A.T.O., was arrested and sentenced to imprisonment for spying.

The French official view was that the de Vosjoli affair was a C.I.A. plot aimed at embroiling de Vosjoli and exploiting anti-French sentiment in Washington, with its ultimate object being the discrediting of de Gaulle himself. Even the British correspondent of *The Guardian*, Nesta Roberts, wrote at the time that 'far from being a Soviet plot, the affair is a most competent American operation which looks like succeeding in its purpose of leaving General de Gaulle the loser if only by slight damage to his self-esteem and his public image.'

The other view was that this was a deliberate ploy by the K.G.B., that its object was to stir up anti-Americanism in Paris by involving de Vosjoli with the C.I.A. and discrediting the French in American eyes. If one compares the two viewpoints, it is surely clear that the Soviet Union stood to gain more from such a contrived plot than did the C.I.A. or the United States Government. It became equally clear that this mischievous 'revelation' came at the worst possible moment – just when Franco-American relations were improving and that it had given them a devastating setback.

It should be remembered, too, that by 1968 de Vosjoli's story was six years out of date, since he had been cut off from all French sources of information after he resigned from his post in 1962. If one bears this in mind, the whole picture becomes clearer. The K.G.B. had discovered that de Vosjoli was helping the C.I.A. more than the French, that he was a dangerous enemy with his contacts inside Cuba. No doubt the K.G.B. saw to it that Paris knew all about this collaboration. Therefore if they succeeded in indirectly engineering de Vosjoli's recall to Paris and at the same time planted on him through the Americans information which would lead him to believe that the French Secret Service was so infiltrated by the Russians that his own position inside that Service was jeopardised, the gains for the K.G.B. were formidable. De Vosjoli would have no alternative but to resign from the French Secret Service.

Yet behind the smokescreen of vague allegations there emerges one other aim of the K.G.B. at this time. This was their urgent desire to discredit one of the best brains and certainly the ablest intelligence adviser in Paris, Jacques Foccart, officially the Secretary-General for Madagascar and African Affairs, but unofficially de Gaulle's number one adviser on all intelligence matters and watch-dog on counter-espionage.

He was, in fact, the co-ordinator and supervisor of the whole range of Secret Service activities, trusted by de Gaulle more than any other man in France except perhaps for André Malraux and Etienne Burin de Roziers. Foccart was perhaps more important to the General than either of his other two confidants. Whereas de Gaulle would listen to Malraux and de Roziers, he would tell Foccart what he wanted to be done, knowing that Foccart was the one man who could carry out the most difficult assignments. Foccart was a Jew and by instinct a man of the progressive Left in a practical rather than an ideological way. De Gaulle always had a great respect for the views of patriotic, practical and intelligent Jews. More than any other man of his epoch, de Gaulle could make up his own mind about such men often against the weight of expert opinion. The attempts of the right wing to smear and denigrate Pierre Mendès-France as a secret sympathiser of the Communists, a campaign, incidentally, backed by many Americans including the C.I.A., never deterred de Gaulle from admiring and supporting Mendès-France, even when the latter was in opposition to him. When Mendès-France was Premier for a brief period not only did he consult de Gaulle, but de Gaulle supported him. It was the same with Foccart, the man whose devotion to de Gaulle and to France was fundamental.

Foccart preferred to be a power behind the scenes; otherwise he would have made an admirable Minister of the Interior. By profession he was a businessman concerned with the export of rum and sugar from Martinique, but his real genius lay in an uncanny ability to acquire information and to analyse it to perfection. Few nations in the world possessed such a mastermind of intelligence as Foccart and few, other than the Russians, realised this. Equally important in de Gaulle's opinion was the fact that Foccart had no ambitions politically. He was quite content to remain a back-room *eminence grise*.

He had always been detested by the French right wing, not only by those whose anti-semitism was a byword but by those who hated de Gaulle because he was accused of having organised and directed the de Gaulle régime's so-called 'parallel police', the organisation set up to combat the right-wing O.A.S., which came into being to fight de Gaulle's intention to give Algeria independence. It was this special force which captured all the mutinous generals, including the kidnapping of General Argoud who was brought back from Munich to Paris.

So far, it might be said, Foccart could be regarded by the Russians if not as an ally at least as a key man in backing their policy, that is to say the breaking of the right-wing in France and paving the way for Algerian independence. But by 1968 this was no longer the case. Algeria was freed, the right-wing was broken, so Foccart was no longer of any consequence, except that, from the Soviet point of view, he was de Gaulle's chief adviser on Africa. And while Foccart was a liberal in his outlook on emergent, independent Black Africa, he still put France's interests first and was not only determined that neither Russia nor China should gain more influence in that continent than France but that the extensive bloc of newly independent nations in West Africa (the former French colonies) should remain firmly allied to France. Whereas in the former British territories in West and East Africa British influence waned as Russian and Chinese influence grew, the nations of Mauritania, Senegal, the Ivory Coast, Cameroon and Gabon remained firmly linked to France in their foreign policy, and their respective financial and economic policies. For all this Foccart was largely responsible. From the Soviet point of view, Foccart had baulked the Russians and the Chinese by introducing Israeli technical and military advisers to these nations, especially to the Ivory Coast.

Matters came to a crisis when the Biafrans broke away from the Nigerian Federation and declared themselves an independent nation, thereby precipitating the Nigerian Civil War. The Russians backed the Nigerian Government, supplying them with arms, as did the British, while Foccart persuaded de Gaulle to give encouragement to the Biafrans. It was then a matter of policy that the Russians should see that Foccart was discredited. How better to do this than to win right-wing support in France by smearing Foccart as a secret agent of the K.G.B.

This is exactly what the Russians did. The man who was named by the C.I.A. as the Soviet spy at the head of French Intelligence was none other than Jacques Foccart. The planning of this inspired smear by the K.G.B. was perfectly timed. De Gaulle had long ago decided that the close relationship between the C.I.A. and the French Secret Service should be ended, complaining that the former gained information from the latter without giving anything in return and more recently he had demanded that the considerable number of C.I.A. agents in Paris should not be accredited to the French Foreign Office as diplomats but to the Ministry of the Interior simply as C.I.A. men without any special privileges. As Foccart's influence was undermined and the campaign against him waged unremittingly, so suddenly was France's policy of supporting Biafra hampered and obstructed and, more important, the small but not altogether uninfluential Biafran lobby in the U.S.A. was rendered powerless. In the end Biafra collapsed and the Nigerian Federalists won the war; the K.G.B. plot against Foccart had played a rôle in all this.

It can categorically be stated that M. Foccart is a patriotic

Frenchman and that the allegations concerning him leaked to the C.I.A. were totally false. In foolishly falling for these K.G.B.-planted stories, the C.I.A. were also damaging the long-term interests of America, while ensuring that the Russtians would gain a firmer foothold in Nigeria. It is hard to say which of the two democracies was the more foolish, the Americans in allowing themselves to believe the stories about Foccart, or the British in arming the Nigerians in the fatuous belief that this would stop the latter buying from the Russians. In the end the Russians and the British both armed the Nigerians and so Biafra was crushed.

Russia's main interest at this time was to exploit the worsening relations between the newly independent black countries in Africa and the European powers. This was achieved by backing the Frelimo terrorists in Southern Africa, supporting the Nigerians against Biafra and a big drive to ruin the remarkably good relations which, thanks largely to Foccart's wisdom, had been established between Paris and the former French colonies in Africa. The destruction of Foccart's influence was of paramount importance to the Soviet Union.

De Gaulle loyally stood by Foccart, but when he was defeated in the referendum and left the Elysée Palace, M. Poher, who became the interim President, dismissed Foccart from office. Almost immediately there was an outcry in several African countries which had formerly been French colonies against his removal. A number of African leaders went out of their way to impress on the French Foreign Office that Foccart was their own choice for Secretary-General for African Affairs. If any further proof is needed as to M. Foccart's innocence of any of the C.I.A. allegations it is surely provided by the fact that when M. Pompidou became President of France he restored M. Foccart to his post.

Meanwhile the spy networks against the N.A.T.O. powers were strengthened and reorganised between 1967 and 1970. In 1967 Vladimir Alexeyevich Gloukhoff, the manager in Holland of the Soviet airline, Aeroflot, was charged with 'an abortive attempt to obtain Dutch state secrets'. At the same time it was announced in Oslo that the Norwegian security police had uncovered a spy ring suspected of working for the Soviet Union and had arrested three of its members.

In 1969 the Belgian security police investigated reports of an anti-N.A.T.O. spy network operating in Belgium. Some time later the Brussels correspondent of Tass, Avnatoli Ogorodnikoff, was arrested on charges of 'endangering the security of the State'. He was expelled from the country. The following day the Soviet chargé d'affaires in Brussels was called to the Belgian Foreign Ministry and informed that at least one member of his Embassy staff had been involved in an elaborate spying operation.

By this time it was clear that, following the switching of N.A.T.O. headquarters to Brussels, the K.G.B. had set up a new network in the Belgian capital. An attempt had been made to steal copies of secret N.A.T.O. documents from Supreme Allied Headquarters. 'Madame X', a Belgian who had worked in the embassy of a N.A.T.O. power both in an African country and later in Brussels, was the key figure in this plot. She had been used as a source of information on the private lives of embassy officials and had accepted a salary of some £500 a year for spying. Taught to use a miniature camera and to obtain copies of documents, she applied for a post at N.A.T.O. headquarters when these were moved from Paris to Castenau near Mons. It was this move on her part which had alerted the security authorities.

At the same time the Russians suddenly extended their use of the satellite countries of Eastern Europe in the espionage game. This policy meant that the Western powers had to keep an eye on Rumanians, Czechs, Poles, Hungarians and East Germans as well as Russian spies, making counter-espionage face a formidable task. In 1970 Maximilian Kovacic, an Austrian civil servant and the editor of the Austrian Ministry of the Interior's magazine, *Öffentliche Sicherheit* (Public Safety/Security), was arrested on charges of espionage. He was found to have been in the pay of the Czechoslovak espionage service and to have passed over copies of his Ministry's documents. Kovacic used to travel to Prague from time to time to hand over these documents in person, which shows that the Russians still as a general rule keep to their policy of not making their agents report to the K.G.B. Residents in their own area. The K.G.B. had a hold over Kovacic in that they threatened to punish his numerous relatives in Czechoslovakia if he did not agree to provide them with material.

This proves that it is still criminally foolish of any nation outside the Soviet bloc to employ in a position involving national security any person who has relatives living in Communist countries. For the Austrians this must be an acute problem, for at least one Viennese in three has relatives living in one or other of the satellite nations. Yet the most alarming facet of this case is that, according to a reliable informant in the Austrian Ministry of the Interior, no civil servant in that country had reported to the security authorities any attempt to blackmail him on this basis.

During 1970 West Berlin police questioned a former British soldier about his activities. It was alleged that he had approached employees of British and U.S. installations in West Berlin as well as British and U.S. servicemen to obtain information such as the secrets of the long-range N.A.T.O. radar station in West Germany.

It transpired that this man had been living in East Germany since he left the British Army. Under interrogation he confessed to acting as a spy for the East Germans and that he had been instructed to seek out homosexuals as 'they might be vulnerable and easily exploited'.

In the autumn of 1970 Herr Schruebbers, head of West Germany's counter-espionage, stated that Communist secret services recruited on an average two new agents every day in West Germany. 'Most people became agents for money,' declared Herr Schruebbers, 'or because of blackmail, or fear of reprisals against relatives in Communist countries.' At almost the same time a N.A.T.O. spokesman confirmed that the command exercise, Vintex, planned for March 1970, had to be changed because the initial plan came into the possession of the Soviet Union. Secret N.A.T.O. documents had been put aboard both the Boeing 747 Jumbo Jet that was destroyed by Palestinian skyjackers at Cairo airport and the T.W.A. airliner blown up by guerrillas in North Jordan in September 1970.

The story of Russian attempts to steal N.A.T.O. secrets is a long, sad serial that has shown no signs of ending. Boris Savitch, a Russian engineer, was expelled from Belgium in 1970 for organising a spy ring inside N.A.T.O. headquarters. He had been arrested after trying to obtain details of French Mirage jet fighters which Belgium had been purchasing to replace obsolete American jets. The master-minding of a number of these anti-N.A.T.O. networks has latterly been carried out from Switzerland. This came to light in February 1970 after the arrest of an unnamed Swiss woman who had worked in the civil registration office in Berne. For some few years prior to this Russia had planted agents in Switzerland with identity documents provided for them by this woman. It was also discovered that another Swiss, Marcel Buttex, had been passing blank identity papers to Russian agents while he worked in the civil registration office at Lausanne.

Perhaps the most unusual case of espionage in recent times was when Otto Wiltschko was caught by the Austrian police. He looked after the airstrip at Fristadt close to the Austro–Czech border and lived in a cottage close by. His hobby was bee-keeping, the perfect cover for his activities as a spy, for he kept the transmitter which he used for sending messages to East Germany in one of his twelve beehives and a receiving set in another.

Espionage directed against the N.A.T.O. powers has become a much speeded-up rat race in the last two years. The Soviet hierarchy are much more demanding than they were five years ago. Russia's own technological advances have made them realise that in defence matters today (and with these, of course, are linked all details connected with space research and exploration) methods, devices and weapons are constantly changing.

Soviet agents are generally regarded as much more expendable than those of any other Western power. The pressure on them to produce results is much greater than it used to be: there is less willingness to wait for years to mount a coup. Perhaps the average life of a Soviet spy in one of the N.A.T.O. networks is not much more than eighteen months or two years. By that time he is either caught or moved elsewhere. An exception was the East German scientist who spent nine years spying for the Russians in West Germany's top secret biological warfare laboratory, the N.A.T.O.-affiliated Institute for Aero-Biology at Gradshaft. He was Dr Ehrenfried Petras, a brilliant young scientist who was actually given a N.A.T.O. secret security clearance by the West German Defence Ministry although he was already known to be a security risk. He used this clearance to take part in tests at France's top secret experimental rocket and space station. The extraordinary state of affairs inside N.A.T.O. revealed by the discovery of Petras' espionage made it evident that some of N.A.T.O.'s security requirements are not as stringent as those of member countries. Dr Petras was known to have relatives living in East Germany and his mother was a prominent member of the Communist Party. Incredibly, despite this, it was possible for the K.G.B. to plant him in West Germany's biological warfare laboratory with the collaboration of the East Germans. Until his escape to East Germany Petras was head of the Micro-Biological Institute in West Germany. He was recalled by the K.G.B. to East Germany only when they discovered that one of a small group of other scientist spies belonging to the Soviet had defected to the West.

Naturally, having been baulked from using Dr Petras for any further espionage, the Russians utilised him for propaganda. He was persuaded to give press conferences in East Berlin at which he claimed that 'the Bonn Government is actively preparing for biological and chemical warfare partly by the use of aerosols'. The charge was refuted by the West German Government, who claimed that their research was devoted to defence against chemical warfare.

The case of Dr Petras shows that the Russians are still employing highly-trained scientific personnel in espionage as they were in the thirties, though now, of course, there are far more of them. Dr Petras was a member of a spy ring consisting entirely of East German scientists who held various key posts all over Europe. They were placed in such centres as the International European Atomic Community of the Common Market ('Euratom') in Brussels (the Soviet spy here was the physicist, Dr Herbert Patzelt),

West Germany's Advanced Nuclear Research Centre and again in scientific circles in Vienna.

The scientist spy ring was given the code-name of 'Worried Parents' by West German counter-espionage officers because they had discovered that the telegrams sent recalling agents to East Germany all stated they must return at once because of a 'sick mother' or 'sick father'. The constant use of these phrases in telegrams was typical of the somewhat unimaginative, rule of thumb methods of the East Germans and it brought a severe rap from the K.G.B. when they learned of the misuse of this practice.

West German inquiries into this spy ring took an alarming turn when it was learned that Admiral Ludeke, a senior West German Defence Ministry official, had committed suicide after being found in possession of photographed copies of secret N.A.T.O. documents. For a while there was a real fear that the K.G.B. might have penetrated the very top of the West German Secret Service over many years. Certainly the Russians had infiltrated the West German Secret Service set up by General Reinhard Gehlen over a lengthy period. Gehlen, having become Hitler's chief of intelligence and, so it is said, infiltrated spies into Stalin's War Council, proceeded after the war to outdo the Vicar of Bray. As a prisoner-of-war in 1945, he made a deal with the Americans and so bemused that archetypal 'Cold Warrior', John Foster Dulles, that the Gehlen Organisation was financed by the C.I.A. to the tune of £200 millions.

In the fifties Gehlen was the Americans' main instrument in waging the 'Cold War'. He brought off many remarkable coups such as helping to organise the Berlin Rising in 1953 and the Hungarian revolt in 1956, as well as advising Nasser on his secret service and then infiltrating an Israeli spy into Egypt. He also infiltrated hundreds of spies into East Germany and the Soviet Union. Many of these triumphs Gehlen reveals in his own memoirs. But what is one to make of a man who first produces 'evidence' that Martin Bormann (Hitler's deputy) was killed in 1945 and then years afterwards claims he was a Soviet spy, still alive in Moscow? Gehlen does not reveal his failures in his memoirs, but the truth is that the arch-infiltrator was himself infiltrated. Over-confidence caused Gehlen to push one too many infiltrators to the other side. The Russians just let them pour in and then, as early as 1951, they quietly 'blew' the Gehlen Organisation. They took over his agents and used them against Gehlen and by this means started slowly but surely to place their key men in vital positions inside that organisation. One of the chief men they won over was Hans Joachim Geyer, who worked for the East Germans by night and for Gehlen, then West German Intelligence chief, by day. The full details of the awful truth have yet to be revealed – that by infiltrating the Gehlen Organisation the Russians were able to infiltrate the C.I.A., and the N.T.S. The man who master-minded the infiltration of first the West German and then the Americans' own network was Colonel Hans Bormann, the East Germans' counter-espionage expert. It is ironical that yet another Bormann should prove to be the undoing of Gehlen.

Any serious study of Russian espionage in relation to Asia must take into account the Soviet preoccupation with cartography. Indeed, any Russian political relationship with an Asiatic country, whether it be China, India, Pakistan or elsewhere, must to a large extent be conditioned by who draws the maps of Asia and who accepts what has been drawn. By the eighteen-eighties Czarist and Manchu expansion in Asia had divided the intermediate lands and principalities into Russian and Chinese Turkestan. The Treaty of Chuguchak in October 1864 fixed a frontier in Russia's favour and deprived China of 350,000 square miles.

China has a strong case for revision of her boundaries with Russia and possibly, though less precisely, with India, too. Certainly Russia advanced to the Pacific coast and founded Vladivostok at the expense of China. These arguments about how the maps are drawn are the crux of Sino-Soviet disagreements today. In the light of power politics it is hard to see how either side can concede territorial limitations without losing face and losing influence with respect to the rest of Asia. For this reason the K.G.B. has to a large extent controlled Russian cartography and not only insisted on the approval and censorship of maps, but even insisted on distortions of map drawing inside Soviet territory as well as along disputed borders. This policy has been developed in recent years to such an extent that it is now impossible for the Russians themselves to buy an accurate map of their country.

Each town, road, river and railway has had its position changed by a few kilometres, according to Western map specialists, and the most recent Soviet atlas, published in 1967, falsified many cartographical details previously given accurately. So marked is the censorship of Russian maps that not even university departments dealing with cartography can be sure of having access to accurate maps, which undoubtedly exist for the benefit of the military and transport organisers. The Russians have resisted all international moves among cartographic organisations to produce a world map at a scale of sixteen miles to the inch: to the K.G.B. such a scale would be far too detailed and therefore come under the category of national security.

Soviet espionage in Asia had been fairly undistinguished prior to the advent of Sorge and it remained so for many years after his execution.

The main Soviet spy centres, both for the K.G.B. and Fourth (Military) Bureau, are in Tokyo and Bangkok. There is also a strong and active espionage organisation in Rangoon, but, curiously, there appears no longer to be any serious representation in Hong Kong and Macao. Instead the Russians have built up a new headquarters in Kuala Lumpur from which espionage in Indonesia is directed. The prolonged dispute with China has naturally necessitated changes in Russian tactics in espionage. Whereas for many years immediately after the war the Chinese among the Malay population were regarded as natural allies of the Russians, the tendency in recent years has been to recruit from the Moslem Malays and to play upon their grievances against the Chinese. Certainly Kuala Lumpur has proved a better probing centre than Bangkok in the last few years.

On the Asian mainland Russia's tactics have been diversified to say the least. There is no set pattern of espionage and great pains have been taken by Moscow not to appear to be the aggressors. In other words the Soviet take far fewer risks of being discovered in the Far East than they do in the West. It is interesting that while defectors from the Soviet Union have revealed much of Russian espionage directed against the West, few if any have given any worthwhile information on espionage against China.

After the Chinese forays into Indian territory a few years ago the Russians took steps to recruit agents in the small independent states of the north of India, Bhutan, Nepal and Sikkim in particular, and one of their present ace spies operating inside China and Tibet is a Sikkimese with a Western education who has provided the Soviet with complete plans of the Lop Nor nuclear testing grounds and the equipment there.

The move to make Kuala Lumpur a major centre of espionage by the Soviet Union is, of course, linked with Russia's South-East Asian strategy. Whereas the Soviet Union has been critical of both Malaysia and Singapore in the past, now she deliberately sets out to court them. The Russians are anxious that both in Kuala Lumpur and Singapore their voice is heard at least as loudly as that of China. For this reason they have stepped up their radio *Peace and Progress* broadcasts to include a daily half-hour programme in Chinese for listeners in S.E. Asia. One of these broadcasts warned that one of Peking's aims was to turn the new Asian states against the Soviet bloc, and urged overseas Chinese to resist this campaign and 'build a progressive society'.

Russia, even in the years when she was still a close ally of Mao Tse-tung's China, has maintained underground links with the

Chinese Nationalists in Taipei. They never had any illusions about Chiang Kai-shek, but supported a somewhat optimistic belief that his son, the Moscow-trained Chiang Ching-kuo, Vice-Premier of Taiwan, might be their best long-term bet. Chiang Ching-kuo has his own lines of secret communication with the Chinese mainlanders. But it is significant that these links are with pro-Moscow Chinese who are primarily anxious to protect themselves if ever it is necessary to jump on a different band-wagon in the expected turmoil after Mao's death.

A year or two ago the Russians sent an apparently unofficial emissary of the K.G.B. to Taipei and a story was leaked that the Soviet Union might come to an understanding with Taiwan, even hinting at an exchange of envoys. The man the Russians sent to Taipei was Vitali Yevegenich Lui, better known under his Westernised name of Victor Louis. Amiable, likeable and gregarious, Lui is of French origin and was born in the Soviet Union in 1928. He was at Moscow University in 1947 when he was arrested in a Stalinist purge and charged with black market activities and alleged illegal contacts with Western embassies. Sentenced to twenty-five years' imprisonment, but released after nine years, he became correspondent of the London *Evening News* in Moscow. He is not only a competent newspaper man, but shows a distinct flair for British popular journalism and always seems to be in a position to deliver scoops – a rarity in Moscow. He indignantly refutes any connection with the K.G.B., but there seems little doubt that he has been enabled to produce newspaper exclusives from official sources. He was, for instance, first with the news of Khrushchev's sacking, of Kosygin's meeting with Chou-En-Lai, of the invasion of Czechoslovakia and of Khrushchev's death. It was Lui who provided the 'official version' of Svetlana Stalina's autobiography and arranged the first interview with Khrushchev for Western newspapers. In 1966 he arranged for the escape of Valery Tarsis with K.G.B. connivance and twelve hours before the Russians marched into Czechoslovakia he telexed a message to London that Russia was ready to depose Dubcek.

Lui has a habit of turning up in countries which are normally out of bounds to Soviet citizens. Encouraging a playboy image, he likes to spend his holidays in the West and is especially fond of Spain and Portugal. His trip to Taipei was no more remarkable than a visit to Israel to meet Mrs Golda Meir's political adviser. He lives in a luxury flat in Moscow's Leninsk-Prospekt district and has a dacha outside Moscow, with a built-in sauna bath and swimming-pool, where he gives fabulous parties with his attractive British wife, the former Jennifer Statham, who was a nanny at the British Embassy in Moscow. Some critics thought he made his presence in Taiwan too obvious and that this silenced any hope of a secret deal between Moscow and Taipei. Maybe, but he was able to keep people guessing and he paved the way for the Russians in Tokyo to take up their contacts with the Chinese Nationalists more discreetly in Japan.

Recently Russia has been aiming for better relations with Japan and instructions have been given for greater caution in espionage. But it does not seem that these have always been effectively taken. In September 1971, when Moscow called their ham radio spy in Tokyo, Xazuo Kobayashi, to give him details of his next meeting with his contact, the message was intercepted by Japanese counter-agents. The result was that the contact man walked straight into a police ambush and was revealed to be Lieut.-Colonel D. Konovoff, the Soviet assistant military and air attaché. The colonel claimed diplomatic immunity and fled from Tokyo immediately, but the harm was done. It transpired that Kobayashi had been allowed access to the American air base at Yokota, thirty miles from Tokyo, to carry on his business as a radio dealer. He had been passing documentary information about the rocket-launching equipment of Phantom jets. But worst of all the instructions to Kobayashi by ham radio was one-way only. The Japanese amateur spy could not call Moscow and was therefore unable to warn his masters that the Japanese police were already on his trail.

While Russia has to maintain a close watch on China's activities in Asia, her resources are strained by having at the same time to try to contain Chinese manoeuvres in Africa and the Middle East. In parts of Africa Russia has lost considerable ground to China – in Tanzania, Kenya and the Sudan. When the civil war between Nigeria and the rebel-held Biafra developed, Russia's offers of arms to the Nigerian Government enabled her to get a foothold in that country. And, of course, whenever Russian technicians enter any newly developed country a detachment of the K.G.B. goes discreetly with them. The Soviet Embassy in Nigeria is the third largest in the country, coming only after the United States Embassy and the British High Commission, and it has doubled in size in three years. Lagos is rapidly becoming a key centre for organising espionage in Africa. From there networks in other West African territories are directed as far south as Guinea. The size of the Lagos Embassy conceals a great deal of espionage, not directed against Nigeria, of course, but gathering reports from as far afield as the Sudan, Ghana, Sierra Leone and Senegal.

But for the time being Russia knows too well she must play a cautious game in Africa. Any espionage scandals there could ruin years of careful planning to gain a foothold economically and politically. Her main policy must be to contain the Chinese drive in Africa and, to baulk any attempts at setting up Peking spheres of influence, the Soviet Union is prepared sometimes to make some strange alliances. Having lost ground in Tanzania and Zambia, where the Chinese have gained some tactical advantage, the Russians until recently tried to counterbalance this by influencing Uganda. The manoeuvrings of Russia and China in Africa have resulted in some almost farcical groupings, especially in Uganda and the Southern Sudan, with Russians and Catholics intriguing on one side against the Chinese and the Jews on the other.

In the last few years the K.G.B. have increasingly turned their attention to the Roman Catholic Church in Africa, actually setting out to win agents among native Catholic priests and, when they cannot trap them into adherence to the Soviet scheme of things, manipulate them as protesters against imperialism and poverty. What has been a highly successful operation in parts of Latin America and the Basque country could, if unchecked, become even more dangerous in Africa. What has happened in Latin America is in itself an awful warning to the unwary and the unworldly both among the laity and the Church. The unmistakable move of the Church towards Marxism in Guatemala, for example, threatens Catholics themselves with an unexpected revolution. Half the young churchmen and even some of the Bishops are preaching the doctrine of the incompatibility of Christianity with capitalism. About fifteen per cent of the priesthood are positively Marxist and the C.O.S.D.E.G.U.A. (Confederation of Diocesan Priests of Guatemala) is Soviet-infiltrated and aimed at revolution.

Asians and Africans alike who visit Russia are pressurised to undergo training in sabotage and other subversive techniques. One Singhalese student who went home after five years at Moscow University complained that many of his colleagues had been made to attend such courses. The spokesman for a group of Kenyans who abandoned their studies at Baku University in April 1965, described it as 'more of an indoctrination camp than a university'. After the first few years of the Friendship University in Russia, in which Soviet authorities were using a number of suspect channels, such as the Communist Front organisations and 'friendship' societies, to recruit foreign students, several governments insisted that they should select the students themselves, or at least be allowed to approve them.

24

The 'Cold War' of 'Disinformation'

THOUGH THERE have been certain changes in administration and division of duties in recent years in the Russian Secret Service, the principal directorates today can be described roughly as follows:

The most important directorate (it is not actually named the First Directorate) is that which concerns scientific espionage, mainly concerned with atomic and guided missiles. This section is closely linked with another section which covers Europe and anti-N.A.T.O. espionage, the satellite countries and atomic energy for commercial purposes. Significantly, this section is also responsible for counter-espionage inside Russia.

Espionage directed against the U.S.A. and the British Commonwealth, including Britain, is also co-ordinated by another section. The main reason for this is that American secrets are frequently sought through British and Commonwealth sources and vice versa.

Curiously the Middle East and the Far East are linked together for the assessment of intelligence from these areas. This, however, makes sense when one considers Russia's interests in keeping naval forces in the Indian Ocean. Another smaller section trains agents and saboteurs to be sent abroad, sometimes to murder and kidnap leaders of anti-Soviet societies in foreign countries.

One important section spies on all the other directorates and the various Soviet Ministries, but perhaps the section which is becoming increasingly significant, especially to the Western World, is the section which maintains a constant watch on senior members of the Communist Party in Russia and is also responsible for putting out false and misleading information.

'Disinformation', as it is called in intelligence jargon, is rapidly becoming a predominant factor in all Soviet Secret Service activities. Since the advent of Yuri Andropoff great emphasis has been placed upon it. The fact that it is being consistently used as a major weapon in Soviet foreign policy has dawned belatedly on the countries of the Western World. All are now aware that it is going on, but few have yet been able to interpret it accurately. In the guessing game – and increasingly this is what intelligence is all about — Russia has established a great lead on the West.

In the past twenty years Russia has been increasingly worried about the number of defectors to the West. To counteract the information they have passed on, the Soviet Union has reacted by pumping out a mass of disinformation, sometimes by planting defectors on the West, sometimes by leaking false news through agents. Obviously the main reason is to keep the West guessing. But there is another reason which is not generally appreciated: the world as a whole is moving into a battlefield of ideas. It is a battlefield of a curious kind: it is no longer a question of an ideological contest between Communism and anti-Communism. Even the Russians are sophisticated enough today to know that this kind of contest is ineffectual, fit only for such old-fashioned Communists as one would expect to find in the British Communist Party, a body regarded by Moscow today as little more than a joke.

The battlefield of ideas is confused and confusing, no less to the Soviet Union than to the West. Now the Russians, who have to some extent been on the losing side in this battle, are developing this thesis through the medium of disinformation. They have taken a cool, hard look at the disintegration of the war between Communism and anti-Communism and sought to make this even more confusing than it is. Catholicism, long regarded as an enemy, has been infiltrated and is being used sometimes as an unsuspecting ally of Communism, while some of the other Churches have long since been acting, on occasions, parallel to Communist plans, a notable case being the support by the World Council of Churches for guerrilla activities in Southern Africa.

The Russians are, however, worried much more about the anarchichal movements in which the youth of the world plays such a rôle, the cult for Che Guevarra, the destructive philosophy of Marcuse, the L.S.D. cult of Timothy O'Leary, 'Black Power', the Minutemen, the Weathermen, the new Trotskyites and many other splinter movements. While preaching death and destruction to capitalism and the Establishment throughout the world, not one of these movements can aid Communism in the long run. Anarchism, the antithesis of Communism, can at best only be manipulated for short-term gains by the Soviet Union. The West still tends to equate these movements with Communism whereas it might more intelligently make common ground with Soviet Russia in combating them. The French students' revolt by no means helped the Soviet Union.

In examining the Russian technique for disinformation one must carefully analyse the case of Lieut.-Colonel Mikhail Goleniewski, so often cited as the most important defector to the West in recent years. As has previously been mentioned, this officer of the Polish

Intelligence Service crossed over into West Berlin on Christmas Day 1960, declared his detestation of the Communist régime and offered to supply secret information. It has been said that he had been supplying the C.I.A. with valuable information since 1958, leading to the arrest of the American diplomat, Irwin Chambers Skarbeck, who became a Soviet agent after the K.G.B. had obtained a blackmail hold on him. Before he escaped to the West Goleniewski had worked with the K.G.B. in Karlhorst.

Until he defected to the West Goleniewski's information, though useful, had been treated with a certain amount of reserve. It was only when he was brought to Washington, becoming an American citizen in 1963 and working for the C.I.A., that he was taken really seriously and, indeed, regarded as the most valuable capture in recent years. A senior C.I.A. official, Mr John Norpel, told a Congressional Committee that Goleniewski's information was 'one hundred per cent accurate'.

But was it? What really is Goleniewski's rôle? It is curious that some information known to have been provided by Goleniewski has been attributed to other defectors, to the mysterious 'Dolnytsin' and others. Was this done to shield Goleniewski, or for some other purpose, possibly to confuse the Russians?

Goleniewski has been credited with having provided the information about M. Foccart, giving the C.I.A. vital clues about Philby and Blake and with having enabled more than two hundred K.G.B. officers to be unmasked. So, too, had 'Dolnytsin' and other defectors been credited.

It is almost certain that the name Goleniewski is false. No one has established his real name. This fact alone has caused European countries to cast doubt on Goleniewski's credentials. His behaviour since defecting has been eccentric to say the least. After joining the C.I.A. he quarrelled with his new bosses and accused several C.I.A. agents of being double-agents of the K.G.B. In consequence he was dismissed by the C.I.A. who agreed, however, to pay him a 'pension' of £2,040 a year. This 'pension' has not silenced Goleniewski: he has conducted a campaign against the C.I.A., allied to critics of that organisation in Congress.

Then in 1967 Goleniewski claimed that he was the son of the last Czar of Russia, who, he alleged, did not die during the Revolution after all. He and his family escaped from the Bolsheviks and for many years lived secretly in Europe and America until the Czar's death in Poland in 1952. Goleniewski said he had been brought up by a Polish family. In June 1970 a book by Guy Richards, entitled *The Hunt for the Czar*, was published in the U.S.A. This substantiated Goleniewski's claims, asserting that he was Alexei Nicholaevich Romanoff, only son and heir of Nicholas II. The story

Richards told was a remarkable one – that the murder of the Russian Imperial family at Ekaterinburg was contrived to look like the real thing, but that the Romanoffs were spirited away, aided by an Anglo-American conspiracy.

Although Goleniewski is supposed to have made so many disclosures to the C.I.A. since 1958 it was not until four years after he defected to the West that any word about him appeared in the press and, when it did, at first both the C.I.A. and the F.B.I. issued statements aimed at disparaging the colonel's statements. It was only later that Goleniewski was hailed as the master defector of all time and the West's greatest ally behind the Iron Curtain.

Yet the truth is that the exact fate of the Czar and the Imperial Royal Family remains a mystery. No corpses were found, all evidence on the executions had been secondhand or mere hearsay. Historians and governments have blindly accepted the reports that the Romanoffs were all shot in the cellar of Ipatieff House in the Siberian town of Ekaterinburg on 16 July 1918, solely on the findings of Judge Nicholas Sokoloff who investigated the affair on behalf of the White Russians who recaptured Ekaterinburg during the Civil War. When I began to probe into this mysterious affair, which previously I had accepted as an incident proved beyond all doubt, I found not merely a lack of evidence, but indications of a conspiracy to deceive. The first investigating team sent out to examine the evidence was dismissed on the grounds of incompetence. Yet the real reason for their dismissal was that they had suggested there was no adequate proof of the executions. Judge Sokoloff's findings were based on the discovery in an old mineshaft of some of the Imperial jewels (they could have been and probably were planted there), a human finger which Sokoloff asserted belonged to the Czarina, and a mass of bones. The human finger was discovered ten months after the alleged executions, yet a photograph of it suggests it must have belonged to somebody who died days rather than weeks previously: it was also an uncared for finger, much more that of a peasant than of a member of the Royal Family. The bones, according to Professor Camps, the British forensic expert, had been chopped up and were not positively human and could even have been animal bones. In any event there were not enough of them to account for eleven corpses; nor were any skulls or remains of skulls found.

Another curious factor is that the man who was assisting Judge Sokoloff in his investigation was a member of the British Secret Service named Robert Wilton, who, as a correspondent of the London *Times*, wrote a series of articles supporting Sokoloff's deductions. Later, when challenged by French military officials, Wilton stated that 'even if the Czar and his family were not murdered, it is essential that people shall believe they are dead'.

Prominent White Russians, members of the Czarist aristocracy who are still alive, are unanimous in denying the Goleniewski allegations. Nevertheless something like a cult has grown up around Goleniewski in the U.S.A. where he lives today in semi-seclusion in the New York area, holding court among his intimates as the 'Grand Duke Aleksei', and expects to be accorded the title of 'Your Royal Highness' when addressed.

The Goleniewski stories deserve some careful analysis, for they are both confused and confusing and to this extent resemble very closely Soviet disinformation. The self-styled 'Grand Duke' identifies himself as the head of the mysterious 'Heckenschuetze', or 'Sharpshooter', the code name of an anonymous spy who had supplied the Americans with information since 1958, suggesting that he was leader of a network which in three years had passed on more than two thousand microfilms of Communist Intelligence secrets to the West. There are vague hints that this movement includes right-wing Germans as well as White Russians, that it was created by Nicholas II and directed from Poland as far back as the twenties. This part of the story serves to perpetuate the legend, long propagated by the K.G.B., that the old Czarists and the Germans worked together.

The cult which has grown round Goleniewski in his rôle of the heir to the Russian throne bears many similarities to that of 'The Trust' in the early twenties. It attracts many genuine anti-Communists and these could always be unwittingly manipulated in the interests of the K.G.B. in much the same way as were some adherents of 'The Trust'. The Soviet Secret Service has on occasions shown a remarkable degree of ambivalence towards the Czarist tradition. This is partly due to the fact that for many of the Russian peasants the Czar is still a legendary, fairytale figure much revered long after he died. It was for this reason that shortly before World War II Stalin ordered a propaganda programme, mainly manifested in films, for stressing the romantic epics of the ancient Czars and their triumphs. The idea was to stimulate national pride in the face of the Nazi threat to the Russian nation.

Nothing should ever be ruled out regarding even the most improbable of Soviet policy switches after the sensational Soviet–Nazi accord of 1939. The idea of producing a puppet Czar as a valuable propagandist for the Soviet cause has been mooted from time to time in certain Russian Intelligence circles. In recent years some documentary evidence has been circulating of an allegedly successful attempt to rescue the Romanoffs between the middle of 1918 and early 1919. This consists of a series of coded messages of an official kind suggesting Anglo-American conspiracy to bring the

Czar and his family to safety. They have the ring of authenticity, yet would seem to be highly skilled faking of top secret American diplomatic signals. U.S. authorities decline either to deny or confirm their existence. Inquiries in Moscow are met with total silence.

The building up of the legend of the Czar's son could be a devious plot not merely to create an organisation that can be infiltrated, but at the right moment to reveal that Romanoff is actually a double-agent of the K.G.B. I do not say this will happen, merely that it would fit in with K.G.B. policy if it did. But whatever the ultimate motives of the K.G.B. my own researches have convinced me that Goleniewski is being used as a deliberate plant by the K.G.B. There are many White Russians one cannot trust; either they are so out of touch with reality that they get their facts wrong, or make the wrong deductions, or they are so mistrustful (that terrible Russian vice) that they mistrust everybody, or they are either unwittingly or knowingly agents of the K.G.B. But those whose dependability to tell the truth has been proved over the years denounce the Heckenshuetze and Goleniewski as being exploited by the K.G.B., just as they regard the N.T.S. as being manipulated from within as an instrument of Soviet policy. Goleniewski's story is that he had to escape from Poland in 1960 because he had been betrayed to the K.G.B. by the wife of the Polish Minister of Foreign Affairs, who, he insisted, had infiltrated the American Embassy in Warsaw. It would seem that the aim of Goleniewski and those around him is to paint the picture of a Western world which has been almost completely infiltrated by the Soviet Union and to stir up enmities and mistrust in the American Intelligence agencies.

The late Captain Henry Kerby, British Member of Parliament, was a specialist on Russian affairs for most of his life. During World War II he worked for the British Secret Service and was imprisoned in Sweden for a period until he was exchanged for a Swedish prisoner in Allied hands. When war broke out he was serving as an honorary attaché at the British Legation in Latvia; later he was acting consul in Malmo, where his Russian contacts, and most especially his contacts with the N.K.V.D., were to come in very useful in warning the British Ambassador of Germany's intentions towards the Scandinavian countries. When he was at the War Office between 1941 and 1945 his work included liaison with the Russian Intelligence Services. Captain Kerby was at one time a Liberal and unsuccessfully contested a Parliamentary seat for this party before he eventually joined the Tories and moved further and further to the right. He was highly unpopular with the party leadership for his independent (some would say reactionary) views, but these were based largely on his wide knowledge of the world of Intelligence. A constant critic of the British Foreign Office, he made himself even more unpopular when the Tories were in office by insisting that the F.O. was covering up for traitors in their midst. Shortly before he died Captain Kerby told me that he had been warning both the British and American Intelligence that Goleniewski was a K.G.B. plant, that this information had got back to Goleniewski who had sent back reports to another Conservative M.P. that Kerby himself was a K.G.B. agent!

I quote from his last letter to me: 'I know quite a bit about the outfit, whose "chief man over here" you have seen. I am quite satisfied that they have been infiltrated for decades, serving both sides, and being subsidised by both sides, the K.G.B./C.I.A. Nor is this too surprising in that, especially since the last war, the former has completely penetrated the latter. . . .'

Captain Kerby's duel with the British Foreign Office lasted for fifteen years. He was always convinced that infiltration of the F.O. and the British Secret Service was more extensive than was ever admitted and that the mysterious 'Fifth Man' remained undetected. For my own part I believe that there are probably both a 'Fifth Man' and a 'Sixth Man' – I mean someone other than Philby, Blake, Burgess or Maclean – remaining undetected and that there is a tendency to imagine they are one and the same person. If, as certainly seems likely at least up to the late sixties, the 'Fifth Man' was still active, he could not be the same as the 'Sixth Man', who was undoubtedly the recruiter-in-chief for the N.K.V.D. in Britain during the thirties.

Jacques Bergier, a former member of the French Resistance and a member of the French 'Marco Polo' network, is an authority on many subjects from espionage and nuclear research to extra-sensory perception. Bergier seems to equate this man – 'a high British official working in M.I.5' – with 'a university professor who recruited Philby, Blake, Burgess and Maclean in the thirties'. In my opinion there are or were two separate agents.

When George Blake was 'sprung' from Wormwood Scrubs Prison, the C.I.A. were convinced he was rescued by the K.G.B. with the connivance of somebody in the British Secret Service and this information certainly did not come from Goleniewski!

Forgeries and pseudo-secret documents are increasingly being disseminated through K.G.B. sources. Not all of these are used against the West; quite often China is the target for attacks. A typical example of the latter is when in July 1969 African newspapers published photographs of Chinese postage stamps bearing the heads of African revolutionary leaders such as Oginga Odinga. In almost every case the revolutionary leader chosen was one who was either in jail or in active opposition to the government of the day. Naturally the governments concerned would have been furious with the Chinese for what they would have regarded as an unfriendly act. A certain amount of damage to Chinese interests was caused, but the Chinese were belatedly able to convince some of the governments that the stamps were a Russian forgery.

In September 1969 the West German news magazine *Der Spiegel* threw some light on the origins of top secret United States military plans which were sent in photographic copy form to various West European newspapers and magazine offices. The anonymous sender of these items claimed in a brief accompanying note that he was writing on behalf of Major-General Horst Wendland, the former deputy head of the West German Intelligence Service, who committed suicide the previous year.

The documents – code-named Plan 10-1 – apparently gave details not only of plans for the use of nuclear, chemical and biological weapons in Europe, but also of a scheme for organising guerrilla activities in Central Europe in the event of an occupation by Warsaw Pact troops. *Der Spiegel* alleged that the plan was betrayed by Robert Lee Johnson, a United States sergeant, who had already been sentenced to prison for espionage. The Soviet Government was aware by 1967 that the betrayal of the plan was known to the Americans and was therefore no longer of much use, except of course for exploitation by the K.G.B.'s Department of Disinformation. Thus copies of the plan were deliberately leaked to newspapers in the N.A.T.O. countries to spread doubt and confusion.

Sometimes the devious aims of the K.G.B. are disguised beneath a gesture of help from the so-called 'friends' of the protesting writers. It is easy to plant such concocted forgeries because the normal methods of circulation of such forbidden works in Russia today are that of *samizdat*, which means the copying out by typewriter of works of the author and surreptitiously passing on the copies to other friends. The K.G.B. can get away with such forgeries quite easily once they have obtained a *samizdat*. All they have to do is to insert one or two passages of concocted sedition into the actual works and then let it be known that the writer has not only broken the law by smuggling his book out of the country, but that he has also made a vicious attack on the Soviet State. The fact that the work is published in Britain, U.S.A. or elsewhere will be sufficient proof that it was smuggled out of the country.

Much less baffling, however, is the subtle planting of material in various parts of the world in the latter part of 1970 and the early part of 1971 to suggest that the Russians are planning to achieve dominance in the Indian Ocean. Stories have been put out that they intend to set up a base on the island of Socotra, to obtain a base in Mauritius, to acquire special facilities in Singapore and to direct certain African navies. For a long time Western Intelligence services regarded this as propaganda by right-wing, old-fashioned Imperialists, and much time was spent knocking the stories down. In fact almost every one of these rumours was planted by the K.G.B.

The Russians will still go to any lengths to rescue top agents who are in danger, or to obtain their release when they are caught. This is not only an attempt to preserve morale at the highest levels, but because the K.G.B., despite its vast numbers, still has too few really first-class operatives.

Towards the end of 1970 Russia and East Germany took the unusual step of offering the Bonn Government a major spy swap in an attempt to rescue three of their top-level agents who had been arrested in West Germany. Chief of these was Frau Liane Lindner, a qualified psychologist described by Bonn security officers as 'the biggest fish in the East–West spy net for many years'.

Frau Lindner came from East Germany to West Germany twenty-one years previously and between 1965 and 1970 she passed on to East Berlin and Moscow many of the top secrets of N.A.T.O., mainly obtained through the chief personal assistant and secretary to two successive West German Ministers of Science and Technology, Frau Irene Schulz, who was arrested in Cologne.

We have seen in the cases of Abel, Molody and Blake how quietly confident they were that the K.G.B. would sooner or later rescue them, or obtain their release. Frau Lindner was even more convinced that her masters would save her for, when interviewed by the West German security officers, she said: 'I know I shall be exchanged after serving only a short period of detention. I am prepared for the inconvenience.'

The third member of the espionage ring was a former Deputy Minister of Justice in North Rhine Westphalia, an eighty-year-old retired lawyer, Dr Heinrich Wiedemann, who was given his post in the first place by the British Military Government after the last war. Dr Wiedemann was dismissed in 1950 for 'irregularities' and it is believed that he offered his services to the Communists out of resentment at his treatment. What finally clinched his links with the other two spies was when he was seen sitting with the two women at a ballet performance in Bonn.

Exchanges of spies between East and West are now a regular feature of the espionage game in Berlin and the man who conducts these negotiations as a discreet civilian go-between is the East Berlin lawyer, Dr Wolfgang Volgel, an amiable character who has made a speciality of such work and is trusted by both sides.

The Russians started this game of swapping spies and they are not only much more adept at it than the Western powers, but they have a tremendous bargaining advantage in that they apparently have an almost inexhaustible supply of Western agents with whom to barter. (One of the aces up their sleeve in this game is a senior East German nuclear scientist, Professor Frucht, who was tried by an East German court for spying for the West Germans in 1968 and sentenced to life imprisonment.)

Frau Lindner's contributions to the Centre in Moscow include the passing on of the minutes of every West German Cabinet meeting, the blueprints of Bonn's space exploration programmes, U.S. Intelligence and Pentagon assessments of the Soviet spy-in-the-sky satellite programme, the missile systems developed by the West Germans and the joint Franco-German missile programme.

From the material obtained by the Russians it is possible to get an idea of what they are most interested in. From the details given, from queries back from Moscow, a certain picture emerges. Soviet Intelligence is obsessed with all forms of space exploration, rocket and space-ship construction, especially with details of heat-resisting metals and experiments made with them, and, above all, with espionage by space satellites. Copies of contracts made by the Bonn Government with the space and aeronautics firm of Boelkow were one of Frau Lindner's chief priorities.

The Russians went to elaborate lengths to conceal the true identity of Frau Lindner, obviously with the intention of using her elsewhere if and when she was released. She holds the rank of a Lieutenant-Colonel in the East German espionage service but in her attachment to the K.G.B. she has already been promoted to Colonel. Her forged identity documents state that she was born in the East German textile town of Chemnitz in 1927, but her real name is believed to be Ingeborg Weber and she was born in Berlin.

No power guards her space research secrets so carefully as the Soviet Union and a certain amount of disinformation on her own space achievements and aims is cunningly given out from time to time. One reason for space disinformation may be that the Russians are far more preoccupied with spy-in-the-sky espionage by satellites orbiting around the Earth and in dominating outer space in a military sense rather than putting men on to the Moon or other planets.

During 1970 Scotland Yard prepared a warning for all British Members of Parliament about a widespread K.G.B. plot to compromise and blackmail them, more especially those of known left-wing views. Unfortunately the Scotland Yard warning does not appear to have been passed on to families of British Servicemen with the N.A.T.O. troops in Germany. For in this same year a prosperous East German secret agent was arrested after having delivered a steady flow of detailed information on British troop movements along the East–West German border over a period of six years. Rolf Dreesen, of East Berlin, was living in an expensive holiday bungalow which had been built for him by the East German espionage service. He had also been running three hotels in the Harz mountains with funds provided from the same source. At one of them in the holiday and ski resort of Andreasberg the holiday guests included British Service families from the Rhine Army. Among the 'attractions' provided by Dreesen and his Berlin-born wife were pornographic films which they showed in a special cellar cinema under the hotel. Dreesen paid regular visits to West Berlin where he handed over to contact men details of all British and West German frontier force troop movements in the area adjoining the East German border, including details of missile sites and radar stations. Much of this had actually been obtained from his British guests.

When the police called at the Dreesens' villa in Westerode they found a radio transmitter, East German code books and Intelligence messages as well as a remarkably accurate 'order of battle' for British troops stationed along the East German border.

An unusual form of Soviet infiltration was uncovered early in 1971 when it was revealed that a Polish agent outwitted American counter-intelligence and penetrated Radio Free Europe, the anti-Communist radio station in Munich. During six years spent in what he termed as 'one of the main centres of ideological subversion of socialist states', Captain Andrzej Czechowicz claimed to have succeeded in tracing scores of Iron Curtain informants and to have 'blown,' several Radio Free Europe networks in Poland.

The thirty-four-year-old agent ended 'Operation Radio Free Europe' on 8 March 1971 and slipped back to Warsaw to tell his story. Usually reticent about the exploits of agents in the West, Warsaw Radio and the Polish newspapers gave Captain Czechowicz's 'revelations' the fullest publicity. He took his first step towards Radio Free Europe during a holiday in Britain in 1963, when he 'allowed the professional talent scouts of anti-communist centres to persuade him to choose freedom'. On their advice he went to West Germany and, for a while, worked for a British Service unit in Munster. Captain Czechowicz told a Warsaw press conference that he attributed his success to his ancient name, aristocratic background, and 'superb psychological preparation by the Polish Secret Service'.

The American counter-intelligence officers who did his screening, he alleged, 'fell for my political refugee bait' and in 1965 he was invited to join the radio station's East European Research and Analysis Department, the very position he most wanted. This, of course, would be an excellent post in which to spread 'disinformation'. He admitted that the screening for this post was 'tough, long and detailed', but claimed that he was able to outwit his interrogators because he had ascertained in advance the Munich chiefs' likes, dislikes and their behaviour pattern. During his work as a researcher with security clearance he managed to trace the information flowing into Radio Free Europe to their sources.

To achieve a sharing of nuclear intelligence with the West the Soviet Union is not particularly worried any longer if some of her spies are discovered. It even seems possible that the arrest of the French physicist, Dimitri Volokhoff, who disclosed many of France's nuclear secrets to the Russians, including the innermost workings of the top-secret Pierrelatte nuclear centre, in September 1971, came about through a deliberate leakage from the K.G.B.

Volokhoff was charged with espionage activity for the Russians over a period of eleven years. During much of this time he had worked for French firms engaged in top classified operations on behalf of France's civil and military nuclear programme. He had the run of all France's atomic centres. Security officials said he first started passing secrets to the Russians after a visit to the Soviet Press and Information Office in the Rue de Prony in Paris in 1960, when the Russians offered to 'exchange scientific data' with him. The son of a White Russian *émigré* and certainly no Communist, Volokhoff found his Soviet contacts changed every two or three years. Then, in 1970, Volokhoff for some unknown reason decided he wanted to 'retire' from espionage and he joined a French building firm. As a last assignment he was asked to make a complete list of all friends and business contacts whom he had met during the previous eleven years, together with a list of their weaknesses.

There is no hint that the size of the K.G.B. is decreasing. But in some of the high estimates one needs to deduct the number of Border Guards who technically come under the K.G.B., who are a cross between military patrols and customs officers, probably between 300,000 and 400,000 altogether.

Peter Deriabin, a former K.G.B. agent who defected, told a United States Committee of Inquiry in 1959 that he would say that 'the size of the foreign section of the Soviet civilian intelligence is about 3,000 officers in headquarters in Moscow and about 15,000 officers around the world'. This is a most misleading estimate. It may apply to senior officers, but it certainly does not apply to all accredited K.G.B. agents. And, as we have seen, even the K.G.B. is but the tip of the vast iceberg of Russian Intelligence.

In September 1971, following frequent warnings to the Soviet Union by the British Foreign Secretary, Sir Alec Douglas-Home, 105 Russian diplomats and officials working in London were ordered by him to return home. At that time there were only forty diplomats and thirty-eight other officials in the British Embassy in Moscow compared with more than four hundred and forty Russian diplomats and officials based in London. This was, of course, belated action by Whitehall on an espionage problem that had long concerned successive British governments: the increasing size of the Soviet diplomatic and trading missions in London. Britain's N.A.T.O. allies, and even Japan, had taken a far tougher line with the Russians on parity of representation.

Yet, cleverly and adroitly, the Russians, aided by the K.G.B.'s 'disinformation' department, turned this situation to their own advantage. A junior diplomat at the Soviet Embassy in London, Mr Vladimir Pavlinoff, gave the *Daily Express* a scoop by drawing their attention to the defection of Oleg Lyanin, a member of the Soviet Trading Delegation in Highgate, London, to the British. The object of this operation was two-fold: first to suggest that the British had been fooled by a minor defector whose chance arrest for drunken driving led to the expulsion order against the Russian diplomats; secondly, to draw attention away from the real reason for the expulsions and to suggest that the British Foreign Office had over-reacted. At the same time the Russians suggested that Oleg Lyanin had been made the excuse for an attempt by the British to sabotage any *détente* between Western and Eastern powers in Europe and to ruin the chances of four-power talks for a Berlin settlement.

Of course Oleg Lyanin had nothing at all to do with all this. He was a junior executive of no great importance, yet London newspapers embellished the story of his defection by suggesting that he had given the British 'the entire dossier on Russia's spy system', a story that must have made the K.G.B. laugh their heads off. Quite accidentally he was caught drunk in charge of a car and, not having the benefit of diplomatic immunity, was detained. Undoubtedly he gave some information to the British, but the truth is that the gay life of swinging London was what really appealed to him. A week later the story of Oleg Lyanin had become at best a poor joke, but for the whole of that time it was an embarrassment to the British Foreign Office.

The K.G.B. has over the years penetrated a number of United Nations agencies, but nowhere has this been more effective than in the Paris headquarters of U.N.E.S.C.O. (United Nations Educational, Scientific & Cultural Organisation). In December 1971 it was stated that there were seventy-two Soviet officials in the organisation, fifteen belonging to the Soviet Union's permanent delegation and the other fifty-seven on temporary posting.

Of the fifteen permanent officials at least eight are known to be K.G.B. agents, and it is highly probable that a fair percentage of the temporary staff are also engaged in some form of intelligence work. The permanent representative of the Soviet Union to U.N.E.S.C.O., Mr Kudryavtseff, is himself a senior member of the K.G.B., who has previously been found engaging in intelligence operations in other countries. Indeed, as and when the Soviet Union finds its activities curtailed in other countries, so it is likely to make increasing use of such bodies as U.N.E.S.C.O.

Reference has been made to Soviet attempts to plant information on the C.I.A. to suggest that the French Secret Service has been infiltrated by agents of Moscow. This was not merely one isolated successful ploy by the K.G.B.: it has been continuing for more than a decade. Its aim is to destroy the French *Service de Documentation Extérieure et de Contre Espionage*. As in the episode of Oleg Lyanin, the press of the Western World has done the K.G.B.'s work for it.

In November 1971 charges were made by a United States Federal Grand Jury in Newark, New Jersey, that the director of France's intelligence network in the U.S.A. was personally involved in the smuggling of five million pounds' worth of heroin into the U.S.A. earlier that year. They named a senior French intelligence officer, Colonel Paul Fournier, as having conspired with a fellow intelligence officer, M. Roger Xavier Delouette, to illegally introduce ninety-six pounds of pure heroin into the U.S.A.

Security authorities in Paris immediately suggested that this was a plot by the C.I.A. to get rid of a too efficient rival. The Americans counter-charged that if the French authorities took no action against Colonel Fournier, they would name further senior French intelligence officers alleged to be involved in drug-running.

The paths of Secret Service agents and drug traffickers frequently cross. On the American side, ironically enough, it all started when their Secret Service let loose Mafia jailbirds in 1943 to assist in the invasion of Sicily. During the Cold War in Europe it was often found among European intelligence services that in the lower echelons of espionage drug trafficking and spying were often done by the same person.

The French reacted in a remarkably cool manner. M. Debré, the Defence Minister, gave Colonel Fournier permission to make a public statement categorically refuting the massive and detailed allegations. (It should be explained that 'Fournier' is not the colonel's real name. He is known to have had a distinguished career in the Gaullist movement in World War II and has been a member of the S.D.E.C.E. for twenty-five years.)

Simultaneously with these accusations by the Americans came reports that the drug-runners in the French Secret Service had been identified with agents of the Soviet Union. As in the de Vosjoli case the hand and influence of the K.G.B. was surreptitiously present all the time, though the tangled story presented to the public would seem to be merely that of a bitter row between the C.I.A. and the S.D.E.C.E.

Bibliography

AGAR, Capt. Augustus: *Baltic Episode*, Hodder & Stoughton, London, 1963.

BILLINGTON, J. H.: *Mikhailovsky and Russian Populism*, 1958.

BOURKE, Sean: *The Springing of George Blake*, Cassell, London, 1970.

CARR, E. H.: *The Romantic Exiles*, 1933.

—— *The Bolshevik Revolution*, 1966.

CHORNOVIL, Vyacheslav: *The Chornovil Papers*, McGraw-Hill, New York, 1968.

COOKRIDGE, E. H.: *The Soviet Spy Nest*, Frederick Muller, London, 1955.

—— *George Blake, Double Agent*, Hodder Paperbacks, 1970.

CURTIN, Jeremiah: *The Mongols: A History*, Little, Brown, Boston, 1908.

DALLIN, D. J.: *The Rise of Russia in Asia*, 1950.

—— *Soviet Espionage*, Yale University Press, 1956.

DEACON, Richard: *A History of the British Secret Service*, Frederick Muller, London, 1969.

DONOVAN, James N.: *Strangers on a Bridge*, Secker & Warburg, London, 1964.

FARAGO, Ladislas: *War of Wits*, Hutchinson, London, 1956.

FLORINSKI, M. T.: *Russia, A History and An Interpretation*, 1953.

FOOTE, Alexander: *Handbook for Spies*, Museum Press, London, 1949.

GRAHAM, Stephen: *Ivan the Terrible: Life of Ivan IV of Russia*, Ernest Benn, London, 1932.

GREY, Ian: *Ivan the Terrible*, Hodder & Stoughton, London, 1964.

GREENE, F. V.: *The Russian Army and Its Campaigns in Turkey, 1877–78*, 1879.

HERZEN, Alexander: *My Past and Thoughts*, 1968.

ILCHESTER, the Earl of, and Mrs LANGFORD-BROOKE: *The Life of Sir Charles Hanbury-Williams*, Thornton Butterworth, London, 1929.

KARPOVICH, Michael: *Imperial Russia (1801–1917)*, 1932.

KENNEDY, Capt. Malcolm D.: *The Estrangement of Great Britain and Japan, 1917–35*, Manchester University Press, 1969.

KLYUCHEVSKY, V. O.: *A History of Russia: 1926–31*, 5 vols.

KROPOTKIN, P.: *Memoirs of a Revolutionist*, 1899.

LE CARON, Major Henri: *Twenty-five years in the Secret Service; The Recollections of a Spy*, Heinemann, London, 1892.

LEESON, B.: *Lost London*, Stanley Paul, London, 1934.

LOCKHART, Sir Robert Bruce: *Memories of a British Agent*, Putnam, London, 1932.

LOCKHART, Robin: *The Ace of Spies*, Hodder & Stoughton, London, 1967.

MONAS, S. L.: *The Third Section: Police and Society in Russia under Nicholas I*, Cambridge, Mass., 1961.

MOYZISCH, L. C.: *Operation Cicero*, Wingate, London, 1950.

NICOLAIEVSKY, Boris: *Azeff: The Russian Judas*, trans. by George Reavey, Hurst & Blackett, London, 1934.

OLDENBOURG, Zoë: *Catherine the Great*, trans. by Anne Carter, Heinemann, London, 1965.

ORLOV, Alexander: *The Secret History of Stalin's Crimes*.

PAGE, Bruce, and LEITCH, David, and KNIGHTLEY, Philip: *The Philby Conspiracy*, revised and updated edition, Signet Books, New York, 1969.

PARES, B.: *My Russian Memoirs*, 1931.

PHILBY, Kim: *My Silent War*, Grove Press, New York, 1968.

POKROVSKY, Professor M. N.: *History of Russia: From the Earliest Times to the Rise of Commercial Capitalism*, Martin Lawrence, London, 1932.

PLATONOV, Professor S. F.: *A History of Russia*, New York, 1925.

PORETSKY, Elisabeth K.: *Our Own People: A Memoir of Ignace Reiss and His Friends*, Oxford University Press, London, 1969.

PRATT, Fletcher: *Secret and Urgent: The Story of Codes and Ciphers*, Robert Hale, London, 1939.

REED, J.: *Ten Days That Shook the World*, 1962.

RICHARD, Guy: *The Hunt for the Czar*, Peter Davies, London, 1971.

ROWAN, Richard Wilmer, and DEINDORFER, R. G.: *Thirty-three Centuries of Espionage*, Hawthorn Books, New York, 1967.

SETH, Ronald: *Forty Years of Soviet Spying*, Cassell, London, 1965.

SMITH, Edward Ellis: *The Young Stalin: The Early Years of an Elusive Revolutionary*, Cassell, London.

STEPHENSON, Graham: *History of Russia: 1812–1945*, Macmillan, London, 1969.

STEPHYAK, S.: *Underground Russia*, 1883.

SUMNER, B. H.: *Russia and the Balkans 1870–1880*, 1962.

TARLE, E. V.: *Napoleon's Invasion of Russia*, 1942.

THOMSON, H. W., and PADOVER, S. E.: *Secret Diplomacy: A Record of Espionage and Double Dealing: 1500–1815*, Jarrolds, London, 1937.

TROTSKY, L.: *The History of the Russian Revolution*, 1965.

— — *My Life*, 1930.

VASSILYEV, A. T.: *The Ochrana: The Russian Secret Police*, George G. Harrap, London, 1930.

WHITE, John Baker: *The Soviet Spy System*, The Falcon Press, London, 1948.

WILLOUGHBY, Major-General Chas A.: *Shanghai Conspiracy: The Sorge Spy Ring*, E. P. Dutton, New York, 1952.

WILSON, Sir Robert: *The Invasion of Russia*, 1960.

ZEMAN and SCHARLAU: *The Merchant of Revolution: The Life of Alexander Israel Helphant (Parvus) 1867–1924*, 1965.

ZETLIN, M.: *The Decembrists*, 1958.